2000

TCHAIKOVSKY:
THE EARLY YEARS
1840–1874

TCHAIKOVSKY:

THE EARLY YEARS
1840–1874

by

DAVID BROWN

NEW YORK
W · W · NORTON & COMPANY · INC
1978

ISBN 0-393-07535-2
LC 78-61150

Printed in Great Britain at
The Camelot Press Ltd, Southampton

To Elizabeth

CONTENTS

ILLUSTRATIONS

following page 192

PREFACE

As a student shortly after the Second World War I could scarcely have believed that twenty-five years later I would embark on a large study of Tchaikovsky. His music, of course, appealed to me then, but I suspect I was a little ashamed of the strength of my response, regarding it as a youthful foible that I would outgrow with adult maturity. Time has proved me wrong. True, my values have shifted, and some of the passages that would once have moistened the tear ducts now sound merely overblown or even tawdry. Yet no longer is he (as, again, I probably suspected) a sort of inspired idiot to whom tunes happened, a man devoid of any real musical intellect, who possessed simply a limited armoury of compositional weapons which he had learned to train with devastating effect upon the more sensitive nerve ends of adolescent susceptibilities such as mine. Instead the intervening years have disclosed qualities in him that I had never suspected, and with which I believe he is still far too rarely credited.

Part of the reason for this is that we in the West are familiar with but a relatively small portion of his work. The most gaping void in our knowledge is the operas. Only two of the nine have ever established themselves in the Western repertoire, and while it must be confessed that there is some dreadfully dull stuff in the neglected seven, there is also some of the very best music Tchaikovsky ever wrote. The circumstances of our operatic life are such that I fear we are likely to continue living in this ignorance: yet do we give him proper credit for those pieces that we can frequently hear in our concert halls, or on our radios and record players? And what of the man himself? Was he just a neurotic homosexual, retreating into himself and releasing all his self-pity in an uncontrollable deluge through his music? Perhaps nowadays we are scarcely so simplistic, yet this image is not completely dead. In fact, the real Tchaikovsky was a person who seems to have aroused universal affection, a man who was devoted to his family and his real friends, possessing a notable fund of common sense, a marked understanding of some aspects of human nature, by no means unsociable with those he really liked and trusted, with a sense of fun and an open-handed generosity that endeared him to all who came to know him properly, and who could not only pour out some of the most deeply lacerated music ever written, but also produce musical inventions as fresh and open-hearted as anything any of his contemporaries could write.

My aim in this study is twofold. First, I have tried to draw as rounded a portrait of the man as is possible from the surviving evidence. I have not attempted any deep elucidation of his personality, for I am not a medical psychologist, nor do I wish to add to the quantity of half-baked commentary and even mischievous rubbish masquerading as penetrating psychological insight that has been written on some other composers in recent years. I think, even without such illuminations, that enough emerges from the abundant and sometimes eloquent documentary evidence to reveal a good deal about the many sides to the personality of this fascinating man. I have examined his childhood, student and early professional years in especial detail because I believe these yield uniquely valuable information about his character, throwing light upon the origins and development of certain of the dominant personality traits of his mature years, revealing other facets that the circumstances of his later life tended to smother, and showing, too, the musical environments in which his talents were fostered, and the nature of the teaching and guidance to which he submitted his musical gifts in his search for a technique and style. While I hope that enough precise biographical data from his adult years is given to enable all but the most specialist scholar to cull the facts that he is likely to require, the crucial, and by far the most revealing events of his maturity are his compositions themselves. This brings me to my second aim (though really it is my *prime* one): I hope, through examining his music in as much detail as space permits, to define some of its main characteristics, demonstrate its variety, and show something of the constant freshness with which Tchaikovsky approached major compositional problems. I have no wish to claim for him a place among the very greatest composers, but I do hope to substantiate that his continuing right to a significant position in our musical experience is based not merely upon his ability to provide us with an easy emotional release, but upon his stature as a creator in the whole context of Western musical culture, a stature which grows from his sheer musical inventiveness, his notable compositional resourcefulness, his masterly technique, and from a musical intelligence at times fertilised by insights that amount to genius.

The main source for any study of Tchaikovsky's music must be the complete edition of his work issued by the Russian state publishing house between 1940 and 1971. The level of accuracy of such Soviet editions is rarely high, but these volumes have made available not only many of Tchaikovsky's works that have long been difficult to obtain in

the West, but also a fair number of pieces – student exercises, the opera
The Voyevoda, and the first version of *Romeo and Juliet*, for example –
which have never before been printed. Needless to say, his church music
has been primly ignored. Soviet editions are normally issued in such
limited quantities that they rapidly become unavailable, but Edwin
Kalmus has reprinted all these volumes, excising the editorial prefaces
and commentaries but incorporating the church music from another
source. Regrettably the quality of some of these reprintings is
abominable. The complete edition is also incorporating Tchaikovsky's
literary works and letters, some of which have likewise been unknown
until now. Numerous other documentary volumes exist, for the Soviet
authorities have always been very generous in their output of such
books, and since these are normally provided with a very thorough
editorial apparatus, they make admirable sources for the Western
scholar, even though the not infrequent variations of text between
different editions do raise some problems. The Soviet authorities guard
their Tchaikovsky archives very closely, and the Western scholar is
compelled to rely almost exclusively on secondary sources. I have
examined as wide a range of these as possible to resolve as best I can the
differences between them. The multiple references in footnotes record
the range of sources used, and should provide a variety of convenient
references to Russian-language readers. I have noted variants only
where these involve conflicts on matters of substance or fact.

The main sources for the biographical material in this study are listed
on p. 16. As for the examination of the music, there is, frankly, little that
has been of service. Most Soviet writing is too heavily conditioned by
political considerations and the pressure to 'propagandise' for it to be of
much use to the Western scholar, although there are occasional studies
in depth that are invaluable, such as Boris Yarustovsky's investigation
of Tchaikovsky's operatic dramaturgy. Nor do Western sources contain
a great deal that is significant. Here my greatest debt has been to Gerald
Abraham, and above all to his masterly study of the operas, still to my
mind the best bit of writing on Tchaikovsky in English. Recently there
have appeared two useful shorter studies of the composer: Edward
Garden's efficient contribution to the Master Musicians series, and John
Warrack's admirable study, which is especially fascinating for its lavish
pictorial illustrations of Tchaikovsky, his family, friends and colleagues,
and of the places associated with him. I have not attempted to provide so
liberal a fund of illustrations, and my reader will consult Mr Warrack's
book with profit. He will find supplementary value, too, in Vladimir
Volkoff's examination of the composer's personality, about which the
author is concerned to debunk a good many popular misconceptions; if

Mr Volkoff is not always convincing, his book remains invaluable for making us pause before accepting too readily the image of the composer that tradition has conjured. The reader will also find useful the copious and generally reliable translations of source material by Barbara von Meck in *Beloved Friend*, which deals with the relationship between the composer and his wealthy patroness, Nadezhda von Meck. He is unlikely to be deceived, however, by the lurid historical novel that Catherine Drinker Bowen wove around this invaluable documentary evidence. Finally he may very profitably consult the English version of Tchaikovsky's diaries, though Wladimir Lakond's translation is not impeccable.

My publishers have been more than generous in the space they have made available to me in these three volumes, and I have felt a corresponding duty to use it responsibly. I have thus restricted myself very much to the man and his music, resisting temptations to incorporate more background information than seemed absolutely necessary, and only examining in any detail those persons who were close to Tchaikovsky and of fundamental importance to his life and music. The one matter on which I have been deliberately expansive is the opera plots. There is little chance that the scores of the majority of these works will ever be published with an English translation, and my very detailed accounts of their plots will, I hope, make the operas significantly easier for the English listener to follow.

In transliterating Russian names I have, for the sake of consistency, resisted the temptation to use a Western equivalent (Peter for Pyotr, for instance – though I have retained the familiar 'Peter the Great' and 'Catherine the Great'); only when the name is not really Russian at all have I reverted to the Western form (thus Jurgenson instead of Yurgenson). Though all Russian first names are followed by a patronymic – that is, the name of the father with the suffix '-ovich' or '-evich' for boys, and '-ovna' or '-evna' for girls – in general patronymics are omitted from the text of this book, but are given in the index, together with the dates of birth and death where known. Many Russian surnames have a different ending when used for a woman (thus Alexandra Tchaikovskaya, Nadezhda Rimskaya-Korsakova). I have preserved this distinction.

Titles and texts of works in Western languages have been retained in the original, but all Russian titles and texts have been translated into English, except for those of folksongs. Many first lines of these are colloquial and make very unconvincing titles, while a number defy translation. In musical illustrations the Russian text has been transliterated, and where it has any meaning of substance, a rough, sometimes summary translation has been placed beneath.

During Tchaikovsky's lifetime the Russian calendar was twelve days behind the Western. All dates have been converted to conform to the latter. In quotations, less precise chronological references have been adjusted to a Western equivalent (e.g., 'at the end of January' has been changed to 'at the beginning of February', 'in the middle of September' to 'at the end of September', and so on).

In musical examples from orchestral scores, all woodwind and brass instruments play at the written pitch.

In the writing of this study I am indebted for help with books and scores to Dr Anthea Baird, Music Librarian of London University, and Mr A. Helliwell of the library of the School of Slavonic and East European Studies of London University. For practical assistance I am especially grateful to Mrs Miriam Phillips, my splendidly efficient typist, and to my wife, who gave invaluable aid in checking, and to whom this work is dedicated.

UNIVERSITY OF SOUTHAMPTON DAVID BROWN
AUGUST 1977

Main Literary Sources for Volume I
with abbreviations

TLP 1– TCHAIKOVSKY (P.), *Polnoye sobraniye sochineny: literaturnïye proizvedeniya i perepiska* [Complete edition: literary works and correspondence] In progress (Moscow, 1953–)

TD TCHAIKOVSKY (P.), *Dnevniki* [Diaries] (Moscow/Petrograd, 1923)

TMKS TCHAIKOVSKY (P.), *Muzïkalno-kriticheskiye stati* [Critical articles on music] (Moscow, 1953)

TPB TCHAIKOVSKY (P.), *Pisma k blizkim* [Letters to his family] (Moscow, 1955)

TPJ 1–2 TCHAIKOVSKY (P.), *Perepiska s P. I. Jurgensonom* [Correspondence with Jurgenson], 2 vols. (Moscow, 1938–52)

TPM 1–3 TCHAIKOVSKY (P.), *Perepiska s N. F. von Meck* [Correspondence with Nadezhda von Meck], 3 vols. (Moscow/Leningrad, 1934–6)

BVP BALAKIREV (M.), *Perepiska s P. I. Chaykovskim* [Correspondence with Tchaikovsky], reprinted in FRID (E.) [ed.], *M. A. Balakirev: vospominaniya i pisma* [Balakirev: Recollections and letters] (Leningrad, 1962)

DTC DOMBAYEV (G.), *Tvorchestvo P. I. Chaykovskovo* [Tchaikovsky's works] (Moscow, 1958)

KVC KASHKIN (N.), *Vospominaniya o P. I. Chaykovskom* [Reminiscences of Tchaikovsky] (Moscow, 1896)

PVC PROTOPOPOV (V.) [ed.], *Vospominaniya o P. I. Chaykovskom* [Reminiscences of Tchaikovsky] (Moscow, 1962)

TZC 1–3 TCHAIKOVSKY (M.), *Zhizn P. I. Chaykovskovo* [Tchaikovsky's life], 3 vols. (Moscow, 1900–2)

YDGC YAKOVLEV (V.) [ed.], *Dni i godï P. I. Chaykovskovo* [The days and years of Tchaikovsky] (Moscow/Leningrad, 1940)

One musical source is also abbreviated in references:

T50RF TCHAIKOVSKY (P.), *50 Russian Folksongs*, arranged for piano duet by Tchaikovsky (Moscow, 1869)

I

ANTECEDENTS AND CHILDHOOD I:

VOTKINSK

————————————————

EARLY IN MAY 1830 a young dilettante composer left Russia for Italy. Mikhail Glinka was twenty-five. For the past seven years he had lived a largely idle life in St Petersburg, indulging his passion for music, adorning the city's salons as a singer and pianist, purveying mostly limp drawing-room romances and sets of sparkling, vapid piano variations, yet undertaking nothing that could in any way pass for a systematic musical education. His passion for Italian opera had been growing; now, with his fertile hypochondria inventing a convenient excuse for seeking a warmer climate, he was embarking upon a three-year expedition to indulge his latest enthusiasm in its native land. The result, so different from what he had expected, was to be of profound importance not only to Glinka himself, but to the future of Russian music. Familiarity with Italian opera bred in him an increasing aversion; it brought him to realise that the lightness and warmth of Mediterranean music did not offer him a congenial idiom for his own creative efforts. As he himself wrote in his *Memoirs* some twenty years later: 'All the pieces I composed to please the inhabitants of Milan . . . only served to convince me that I was not following my own path, and that I could not sincerely be an Italian. A longing for my own country led me gradually to the idea of writing in a Russian manner.'[1]

Prompted by this self-discovery, Glinka delayed his return to Russia to undertake some five months of systematic study in Berlin with Siegfried Dehn, a pedagogue who fortified Glinka's technique with exercises in fugue and with chorale harmonisations. While in Italy, Glinka had determined to compose an opera that would be truly Russian both in subject and musical character, and soon after his return to Russia in 1834 his attention was drawn to the tale of Ivan Susanin, the peasant who in 1612 or 1613 had, at the cost of his own life, saved the

[1] *M. I. Glinka: Literaturnïye proizvedeniya i perepiska*, ed. A. S. Lyapunova, vol. 1 (Moscow, 1973), p. 260.

first of the Romanov tsars from marauding Polish troops. Glinka's imagination was immediately fired; for some two years he worked on the opera, and in December 1836 *A Life for the Tsar* was performed with spectacular success in St Petersburg. Russia had been given its first large composition of substantial worth.

After the triumph of *A Life for the Tsar* Glinka was quick to project a second opera. His choice for subject ultimately fell upon Pushkin's fairy-tale poem *Ruslan and Lyudmila*, and during the next five and a half years the piece was composed in a manner so spasmodic and unsystematic as to ensure a disorderly result. It is not surprising, therefore, that when *Ruslan and Lyudmila* was first heard in 1842, six years to the day after *A Life for the Tsar*, it was a comparative failure. Yet musically Glinka's second opera was far richer than its predecessor. Besides consolidating the synthesis, already begun in *A Life for the Tsar*, of Russian melodic characteristics with Western styles and techniques, it provided the next generation of Russian composers with idioms, procedures and structures which they avidly made their own. From it they gained an heroic manner, a 'magic' idiom, oriental stylisation, the changing background technique, vivid suggestions for musical caricature, and advanced harmonic procedures that included the use of the whole-tone scale. Indeed, no other work has ever had such a seminal importance in the annals of Russian music.

By happy historical coincidence, the very years which saw the creation of Glinka's two operas also witnessed the birth of most of the major figures of the next generation of Russian composers. The eldest of these was Alexandr Borodin (b. 1833), who was also to become a scientist of international repute. Then followed Mily Balakirev (b. 1837), who studied mathematics at Kazan University, but abandoned this to settle in St Petersburg and become the despotic mentor and guide of a self-consciously nationalist group of composers. One of this group was Borodin; of the others the most important were Modest Musorgsky (b. 1839) and Nikolay Rimsky-Korsakov (b. 1844), the former an ex-army officer and minor civil servant, the latter a naval officer by profession. César Cui (b. 1835), an authority on military fortifications, was of more limited talent and made a deeper mark as a musical journalist than as a composer.

All these men were musical amateurs who, like their idol, Glinka, acquired their musical educations haphazardly as best they could. By contrast the remaining major Russian composer born during these years received a fully professional grounding in composition. This not only provided him with a technical equipment that was more broadly based and systematic than that of any of his nationalist contemporaries;

it also inculcated in him a degree of Western influence that they would have found inimical. Yet to say that Pyotr Ilich Tchaikovsky was a cosmopolitan in opposition to the nationalist circle around Balakirev is an oversimplification. Indeed, at two periods of his life Tchaikovsky came under the direct influence of Balakirev, on both occasions with impressive results. Let it be said at the very outset of this book that Tchaikovsky was really as Russian as any, though the form of his Russianness was distinct from that of Balakirev's group. We may gain a clue to this difference from their diverging attitudes to Glinka's two operas, for whereas it was *Ruslan and Lyudmila* that dominated the interest of the Balakirev circle, Tchaikovsky was more attracted to *A Life for the Tsar*. It is easy to see why. Glinka's second opera was the more radical musically, displaying an abundance of attitudes and techniques that differed sharply from those of Western practice; it thus offered a splendid range of suggestions to any who sought alternatives to the styles and methods of Western composers. His first opera, on the other hand, was more rooted in Western musical techniques – yet both its subject and its basic musical material were more overtly Russian. Thus it was likely to have the greater appeal to a composer who valued and commanded these basic techniques of Western music, yet who equally wished his music to reflect the character of the race to which he belonged.

At the very outset of his monumental biography of his composer brother, Modest Tchaikovsky was at pains to emphasise how aware Pyotr Ilich was of his Russian nationality – and also how scornful he was of any delusions of dynastic grandeur, in this case the pretensions of some members of his family to aristocratic connections:

> Though indifferent to any eminence among his ancestors, he was not indifferent to their nationality. The aristocratic pretensions of some of his relatives elicited from him the mockery of incredulity, but any suggestion that they were Polish in origin irritated and angered him. Love for Russia and all things Russian was so deep-rooted in him that it did in fact break down his complete indifference in all other respects to questions of birth, and he was very pleased that a distant ancestor on his father's side was an Orthodox member of the gentry from the Kremenchug region.[2]

This ancestor was Tchaikovsky's great-grandfather, Fyodor, who had fought under Peter the Great at the battle of Poltava in 1709. Before the composer's birth there had been in fact a notable tradition of military service in the Tchaikovsky family. Tchaikovsky's own father, one of a

[2] *TZC*1, p. 10.

family of twenty children, had four brothers who survived to adult years, of whom one, Ivan, was killed in Paris in 1814 during the Napoleonic campaigns, while another, Pyotr, participated in no less than fifty-two battles against either the French or the Turks, was severely wounded several times, and was, like his brother Ivan, decorated with the order of St George (fourth class) for his bravery. Despite such hazards, Pyotr lived to a ripe old age, and before his death in 1871 he was to play a small role in the life of his composer nephew. Both of Tchaikovsky's remaining uncles on his father's side also served for some time in the army.

On the other side of the family, Tchaikovsky's maternal grandfather, Andrey Assier, was a Catholic of French extraction whose father had emigrated to Prussia. Andrey moved further east, took Russian nationality, and carved a successful career for himself as a Russian customs official. His first wife (the composer's grandmother) was the daughter of a deacon of the Orthodox Church. Andrey was subject to a nervous disorder resembling epilepsy, a complaint which was evidently hereditary, for his eldest son likewise suffered from it, and though Tchaikovsky's mother seems to have escaped the ailment, Tchaikovsky himself was said to have been prone to it in his early years. Andrey's eldest son was a moderately competent amateur musician, as were also two of his daughters, Ekaterina and Alexandra, the composer's mother. Yet these three appear to be the only earlier members of Tchaikovsky's family to have had any real ability or interest in music, and Modest commented that, of the eighty or so members of the family living at the very end of the nineteenth century, only about ten had any kind of musical endowment. 'The great majority of our remaining relatives are distinguished by a kind of exceptional indifference to music bordering almost on aversion,' he noted, a trifle acidly.[3]

Modest Tchaikovsky, who is the source for the foregoing details of ancestors on his father's side, was able to draw upon the family memoirs which his own father had started to write in 1873 at Pyotr Ilich's request. Unfortunately, however, Ilya Tchaikovsky was always reluctant to talk about his own past and, in consequence, broke off his written reminiscences as soon as they required him to give some account of himself. This reserve about himself was balanced by a complete openness to all about him:

> He was, according to all who knew him, an unusually likeable, cheer-ful and straightforward man. Kindness – or, more accurately, an abundance of love – was one of the chief traits of his character. In his youth, his years of maturity, and in his old age he trusted people

[3] *TZC*1, p. 13.

implicitly, and loved them. Neither the difficult school of life, nor bitter disappointments, nor grey hairs ever killed in him the capacity to see each man with whom he had dealings as the embodiment of all merits and virtues. His trustfulness knew no bounds, and even the loss of all the fortune that he had built up with great labour, and lost because of this trustfulness, did nothing to make him more realistic. To the end of his life everyone he knew was an 'excellent, honourable, good fellow'.[4]

This little character sketch does much to explain Ilya's variable fortunes. He had been born on 1 August 1795 and, unlike his four brothers, had no military training. Instead he was sent to the School of Mining Engineers from which he graduated with a silver medal in 1817. To judge from his subsequent career (and Modest's testimony), he was a thoroughly capable, if not outstanding mining engineer. His level of intelligence was only average, and in the theatre and music he had no more than a dilettante interest. As a young man he had taken up the flute, evidently without much success, and had given it up before his second marriage. The theatre was a far more durable attraction, and even as an old man he normally paid a weekly visit to a play or opera, usually giving way to tears even when the piece being performed contained nothing that might be expected to prompt such a reaction. In view of this strong if indiscriminate response to drama, it may seem less surprising to us that Ilya should show understanding of his son's mature decision to devote himself professionally to the art of music.

On 23 September 1827 Ilya had married Mariya Keiser, and a daughter, Zinaida, was born in 1829. Soon after this his wife died, and on 13 October 1833 he remarried. His second bride, Alexandra Assier, was eighteen years his junior. In 1816 her mother had died, and in 1819, at the age of six, she had been placed in a school for orphan girls in St Petersburg where she received an admirable education. When she left in 1829 her attainments included a high proficiency in French and German, enough skill as a pianist to play dances, and an ability to sing pleasantly. 'From the testimony of people who knew her,' wrote Modest, 'she was a tall stately woman, not particularly beautiful, but with an enchanting expression in her eyes, and looks that involuntarily drew one's attention. Certainly all who saw her unanimously affirm that there was something exceptionally attractive about her appearance.'[5] Pyotr Ilich, again according to Modest, remembered her as 'a tall, rather ample lady with a wonderful look, and hands which, though not small, were unusually beautiful'.[6] Unlike her husband she kept her personal

[4] *TZC*1, pp. 14–15.   [5] *TZC*1, pp. 16–17.   [6] *TZC*1, p. 17.

feelings very much to herself and was very sparing in her expressions of endearment, preferring to show her kindness in deeds rather than words. At home Ilya was content to let her take command. The picture Modest paints is of a stable, contented home in which two people, very different in age and temperament, had achieved a thoroughly satisfactory living and working arrangement.

The first child of the marriage, a daughter named Ekaterina, died in infancy, and before the next was born the couple had left St Petersburg for Votkinsk, where Ilya had been appointed manager of the state-run iron works. There, on 21 May 1838, a son, Nikolay, was born to them, and on 7 May 1840, a second son, Pyotr, the future composer.

Votkinsk is situated some 600 miles east of Moscow. It had long been important for its metal works, founded in 1759, and in 1870 it was to boast the very first open-hearth furnace in the whole of Russia. Inevitably life in a town closer to Siberia than to Moscow must have been very provincial, but Ilya's prestigious appointment, with its more than adequate salary and wide powers which included the command of a hundred Cossacks (in addition he actually owned some ten serfs), ensured that the Tchaikovskys' spacious house became the centre of an active social life of the sort that Ilya's hospitable disposition found so congenial. In addition to a very well-educated English family, Votkinsk had a considerable number of young people who had come from St Petersburg to work there, and this ensured that a breeze from the wider world ventilated the musty parochialism of the town. Ilya was happy and prosperous, and had therefore no material worries when his wife bore him a daughter, Alexandra, on 9 January 1842, and a third son, Ippolit, on 22 April 1843.

The growth of her family responsibilities compelled Alexandra to enlist help with the education of her eldest charges, and when in August 1844 she set out for St Petersburg to visit her own relatives and her stepdaughter, Zinaida, who was at school there, she had the added intention of seeking out a governess for her eldest child, Nikolay, and her niece, Lidiya Tchaikovskaya, who was one of her husband's family dependants. It was during the time of this visit that there came Tchaikovsky's first juvenile effort at composition, an event recorded by Ilya in a letter to his wife: 'Sasha [Alexandra] and Petya have composed a song, "Our mama in St Petersburg".'[7]

The governess engaged by Alexandra was a Frenchwoman, Fanny Dürbach, a twenty-two-year-old experienced teacher who, according to Modest, 'knew both French and German equally well, and whose morals were strictly Protestant'.[8] Fanny accompanied Alexandra on her return

⁷ YDGC, p. 13.   ⁸ TZC1, p. 19.

to Votkinsk in November to begin what she herself later described as 'the happiest time of my life'.[9] In her recollections of the four years she spent with the Tchaikovskys, Fanny recounted this journey:

> Mrs Tchaikovskaya, Nikolay and I took about three weeks from St Petersburg to Votkinsk, and during the journey we became so closely acquainted that when we reached the factory we were on thoroughly intimate terms. The kindness and courtesy of Mrs Tchaikovskaya, the good looks, even handsomeness of Nikolay, disposed me towards my companions, while the meticulous good manners of the latter [Nikolay] was an assurance that the task before me would not be difficult. Yet, all the same, I was very uneasy. All would be well if, on my arrival, I had to deal only with Mrs Tchaikovskaya and her son – but before me lay acquaintance with people and a way of life that were completely unknown. And so the closer we got to the end of our journey, the more my concern and uneasiness grew. But when at length we arrived at the house, one moment sufficed to show that all my fears were groundless. A host of people ran out to meet us, there began rapturous embracing and kissing, and it was impossible to distinguish the family from the servants in the crowd. All were made equal by an undivided, living joy; everyone greeted the return of the mistress of the house with equal warmth and affection. Mr Tchaikovsky came up to me and, without a word, embraced and kissed me like a daughter. This simplicity and the patriarchal character of his action at once set the stamp of approval upon me, and sealed me almost as a member of the family. I had not just arrived; rather, like Mrs Tchaikovskaya and her son, I also had 'returned home'. Next morning I set about my work without the slightest agitation or fear for the future.[10]

Fanny Dürbach's recollections of Tchaikovsky and his family were recorded by Modest in 1894 after the composer's death. Living as she had been for the last forty years in provincial France at Montbéliard, near Belfort, she was probably less conditioned than was Modest by a realisation of her former charge's international eminence. Though the passage of time had lent a certain aura to memories of fifty years before, there is no reason to doubt the essential reliability of her record, and it provides the only eyewitness account from the first eight years of the composer's life. Fanny appears to have been an admirable governess, and to have elicited the same degree of affection from the Tchaikovsky family as she had conceived for them. The four-and-a-half-year-old

[9] *TZC*1, p. 21.   [10] *TZC*1, p. 21; *PVC*, pp. 389–90.

Pyotr immediately fell under her spell and clamoured tearfully to be allowed to attend the lessons, outstripping his fellow pupils so that by the age of six he could read French and German with complete ease. At times the image of the young Pyotr conjured up by Modest with the aid of Fanny's memories might suggest a candidate for instant canonisation on the grounds of intellectual prowess and moral virtue, but on the debit side it was conceded that Pyotr could not match the good looks of Nikolay, nor the latter's customary tidy and well-groomed appearance. Indeed, Pyotr was 'eternally shock-headed, carelessly dressed',[11] and seemed to have an urchin's capacity for getting dirty without trying. Yet, despite these less admirable features, there can be no doubt that the young Tchaikovsky had a markedly attractive personality, and Fanny certainly developed an especially strong attachment to her youngest pupil. She responded to the sensitivity and tenderness in his nature, and remarked the contrast in character between him and his brother:

> Once, in connection with some assignment that both brothers had done badly, I reproached them and, amongst other things, said that I pitied their father who worked to earn money for his children's education while they were so ungrateful that they did not value this, and were careless in their work and duties. Nikolay listened to this and ran out to play as happily as ever. . . . But Pierre [Pyotr] remained pensive all day, and going to bed that evening (when I myself had quite forgotten the reproof I had administered that morning), suddenly dissolved in tears and began talking about his love for his father, and making excuses for the ingratitude towards his father that was unjustly imputed to him. I tell you, you couldn't help loving him, because he loved everybody. There was no more ardent protector of everything that was weak or unhappy. Once he heard that someone was going to drown a kitten. Having discovered the identity of this monster of cruelty who was contemplating such a terrible villainy, he begged for mercy. Then he rushed home, ran into the study where his father was sitting with some business colleagues and, thinking that there could be no other talk in the house than about the cat, triumphantly set their minds at rest with the joyful news of the 'deliverance'.[12]

This tender nature, which seems to have made him, of all the Tchaikovsky children, the favourite with everyone who knew them, was joined to a hypersensitivity which foretells the later composer. 'His sensitivity was extreme, and so one had to deal with him very carefully. Any trifle could upset or wound him. He was a child "of glass". As for

[11] *TZC*1, p. 24.   [12] *TZC*1, p. 26; *PVC*, p. 392.

reproofs and admonitions (for there was no question of punishment where he was concerned), what would have been water off a duck's back to other children affected him deeply, and if the degree of severity were slightly increased, it would upset him to an alarming extent.'[13]

Our gratitude is also due to Fanny for a simple but touching record of Tchaikovsky's early love of his country, as well as of the ingenuous tact with which he avoided giving offence to his French governess:

> Once, during a break for recreation, he sat down before an atlas and examined it. Coming to a map of Europe, he suddenly began to cover Russia with kisses, and then made as if to spit on all the remaining portion of the world. I stopped him and began explaining to him that it was shameful to behave thus to beings who, like himself, addressed God as 'Our Father', that it was bad to hate fellow men because they weren't Russians, and that it meant he was spitting on me also, because I wasn't Russian. 'You don't need to scold me,' replied Pierre. 'Didn't you notice that I had covered France with my hand?'[14]

With Fanny's advent, Nikolay, Lidiya – and Pyotr – passed very much into her charge. 'We lived quite apart from the adults,' she recalled:

> We joined them only at mealtime. We were left to ourselves not only in our work but also in our amusements. The evenings before a Holy day [i.e. mostly Saturday evenings] we spent upstairs in our own quarters reading and talking. In the summer a carriage was put at our disposal and we took rides through Votkinsk's delightful surroundings. On week-days, from six in the morning, all the time was strictly allocated, and the day's programme was carried through punctually. Because the free hours during which the children might do what they wanted were very restricted, I insisted that they should devote them to physical exercise, and on this matter I always had to wrangle with Pierre, who invariably wanted to go to the piano after a lesson. However, he always obeyed readily enough, and ran around, playing happily with the others. Nevertheless, he constantly had to be directed to do this. Left to himself, he most readily turned to music, reading, or writing verses.[15]

To the end of her life Fanny kept the exercise books and papers containing some of these juvenile verses, and even in 1894 she refused to

---

[13] *TZC*1, p. 26; *PVC*, pp. 391–2.
[14] *TZC*1, p. 28 (in third person singular); *PVC*, p. 392.
[15] *PVC*, pp. 390–1; *TZC*1, p. 28.

part with them to Modest, only permitting him to copy out their contents for his biography. Besides such things as a translation into Russian from a French schoolbook, *L'Éducation maternelle*, random historical notes on Napoleon, Peter the Great, Louis XIV, XVII and XVIII, and birthday greetings in verse to Fanny and Zinaida, there is a celebration in French of Joan of Arc who, many years later, was to be the subject of one of Tchaikovsky's operas. He had read her story in Michel Masson's *Les Enfants célèbres*, which had been a favourite book with all the Tchaikovsky children at Fanny's Saturday evening reading sessions. The seven-year-old Pyotr celebrated his French heroine in a thirteen-line poem and a prose introduction to a full transcription of Casimir Delavigne's poem, *Mort de Jeanne d'Arc*. Also preserved were several patriotic pieces and a number of little lyrics consisting of prayers, religious narrations, and sentimental effusions such as might be expected from a child subjected to the sternly moral and pious instruction of a God-fearing governess of the 1840s. All but one are in French and show a competence in the language very creditable in a child only seven or eight years old. They include such pieces as 'L'enfant parle à son ange gardien' (dated 1847), 'Prière d'une petite fille tout-à-fait orpheline', and – with all the world-weary wisdom of an eight-year-old – 'La vieillesse d'un homme qui parle en songe à l'âge de 60 ans'. 'Mort d'un oiseau', mistakes and all, will serve as a sample of Pyotr's style and competence:

> Elle dort dans une place, sans tombeau
> Elle n'est point comme un homme dans la terre endormie
> Cependant elle n'est point du tout rien du tout pour Dieu
> Elle lui est quelque chose, sa vie n'est pas perdus.
> Pauvre petit, n'aie pas peur
> Les enfant te mettrons dans la terre froide
> Ils t'orneront de fleurs
> Ils te feront un tombeau
> Oh! le bon Dieu ne l'a point oublié
> Oh! toi petit oiseau tu ne peux pas te souvenir de lieu[16]

Such creations prompted Fanny to dub Pyotr 'le petit Pouchkine'.[17] All his subsequent letters to her were written in French.

Fanny's reign as governess to the Tchaikovsky children ended in 1848. On 18 February Ilya retired with the civil rank of major-general and a pension. He had already opened negotiations for another position, and this finally necessitated a removal to Moscow. Thus on 8 October the

---

[16] *TZC*1, p. 41.   [17] *TZC*1, p. 44.

whole family quit Votkinsk. Since the intention now was that Nikolay, Lidiya and Pyotr should be sent to school, Fanny declined to go with the family, finding instead an excellent position in another household. To lessen the agony of parting for the children, it was arranged that she should slip away while they were still asleep early on the morning of the very day they planned to leave for Moscow. Despite the hope that preparations for their own departure would distract the children, Pyotr was badly upset, and at their first overnight stop 'didn't know what to do with himself, kept asking everybody for pen and paper so that he could write [to Fanny], but couldn't finish a single letter. He was nearly in tears and said he simply couldn't send anything: on the best of the letters he'd made five blots.'[18] Nearly a year later the same correspondent, Pyotr's cousin, could write again to Fanny: 'When we received your letter, dear Fanny, Petenka read it aloud and cried a lot. He loves you very much.'[19]

Tchaikovsky owed a vast debt to Fanny. She had laid the foundations of an excellent education, had stood guard over his moral welfare, and her care and attentions had provided some substitute for the warm expressions of affection of which his own mother seems to have been incapable. Yet there was one crucial debt he did not owe Fanny: she was no lover of music and when, about a year after she had been installed with the Tchaikovsky children, a liberated serf, Mariya Palchikova, began giving Pyotr piano lessons, Fanny was unenthusiastic. She had more sympathy for his literary exertions. Pyotr's earliest musical experiences had come from the orchestrion which his father had bought soon after they had settled in Votkinsk. This species of barrel organ, which was nevertheless capable of imitating quite elaborate orchestral effects, enchanted Pyotr. 'He couldn't hear enough of it,' wrote Modest:

He was particularly captivated by the pieces of Mozart that it played. The composer himself [Tchaikovsky] asserted repeatedly that his passionate worship of that genius had its beginning in that unspoken delight, that 'holy rapture' which he experienced during his early childhood on hearing the orchestrion play Zerlina's aria, 'Vedrai carino', and other extracts from *Don Giovanni*. In addition this same orchestrion acquainted him with the music of Rossini, Bellini, Donizetti, and it was probably from this that there stemmed his love of Italian music that remained with him all his life, even when the persecution of it was in full swing in serious musical circles during the '60s and '70s.[20]

---

[18] Letter of 18 Oct. 1848 from A. V. Popova to Fanny Dürbach. Quoted in *TZC*1, p. 45; *YDGC*, p. 16.

[19] *PVC*, pp. 393–4.   [20] *TZC*1, pp. 42–3; *YDGC*, pp. 13–14 (partial).

Even before the arrival of Mariya Palchikova, Pyotr had picked out tunes from the orchestrion's repertoire on the piano, and when forbidden the instrument he had sometimes continued fingering the tunes on whatever surface came to hand. An over-vigorous exercise of this practice on a window led to a broken pane and a badly cut hand, and Modest asserted it was this incident that persuaded his parents to take his brother's musical inclinations seriously and summon Mariya. She was a quiet, modest girl, evidently reasonably competent, though her knowledge of the repertoire was very restricted, and within three years her pupil could read music as well as she. Pyotr must have liked her, for some thirty-five years later, in 1883, when she suddenly wrote to him revealing that she was in difficulties, he instructed his publisher, Jurgenson, to send some money to this woman to whom 'I am very, very indebted'.[21] The other person to whom he was musically beholden in Votkinsk was a Pole called Maszewski, whose skill in performing Chopin mazurkas was outstanding in a town which Modest admitted was devoid of any musical life outside domestic circles. Impressed by Maszewski's performance, Pyotr himself prepared two mazurkas by Chopin for one of the Pole's visits, winning such approval that Maszewski bestowed a kiss upon the delighted boy. 'Never have I seen Pierre so happy and contented as on that day,' recorded Fanny.[22]

If we discount 'Our mama in St Petersburg', it appears that Tchaikovsky, like Glinka before him, made his earliest attempts at composition in piano improvisation. Again it is Fanny who provides not only the basic evidence but also vivid witness to the effect of music upon the boy:

After work or long periods of letting his imagination loose at the piano he was always nervy and on edge. Once the Tchaikovskys had guests, and the whole evening was spent in musical entertainments. Because it was a holiday the children joined the adults. Pierre was initially very lively and happy, but towards the end of the evening became so tired that he went upstairs earlier than usual. When I went to the nursery some time later he was not yet asleep. Instead, his eyes glistening, he was weeping agitatedly. When I asked what was the matter with him, he replied: 'Oh, it's the music, the music!' But there was no music to be heard at that moment. 'Get rid of it for me! It's here, here,' said the boy, weeping and pointing to his head. 'It won't give me any peace!'[23]

[21] *TZC*1, p. 44; *TLP*12, p. 24.
[22] *TZC*1, p. 45; *YDGC*, p. 16.
[23] *TZC*1, p. 44; *PVC*, p. 391; *YDGC*, p. 16 (partial).

Except for a trip to Sergiyevsk with his mother in the summer of 1845 to visit the mineral springs, Pyotr had never made any extensive journey outside Votkinsk. When Zinaida was brought home in December 1846 on completing her schooling in St Petersburg, this half-sister, whom he had never before seen, brought into the household a breath of a wider, more glamorous world – or so it seemed to the young Pyotr, to whom she appeared a fairy-like being, who talked of the capital's gossip, its delights and manners, of its theatres and fashionable dances, some of which she taught the other children. Now, with the translation of the whole family to Moscow, Pyotr had a chance of experiencing a little of this sort of world for himself.

2

CHILDHOOD II:

ALAPAYEVSK AND ST PETERSBURG

ON 21 OCTOBER 1848 the Tchaikovsky family arrived in Moscow, only to encounter two misfortunes. First, the post upon which Ilya had set such store did not materialise, for he had indiscreetly revealed his expectations to another who had then used the information to obtain the position for himself. Next, the nurse engaged for the younger children fell a victim to the cholera epidemic that was raging in Moscow, and nearly died. Ilya hurried off to St Petersburg in an attempt to settle his affairs, leaving his wife in sole charge of the family. Finding it difficult to manage all the children herself, she entrusted some of their supervision to Zinaida, who was neither by temperament nor experience competent to handle such responsibility. In any case, Zinaida favoured Nikolay to Pyotr, and Modest believed that the latter's subsequent coldness towards his half-sister sprang from the treatment she accorded him at this time. Bowed down, too, by the misery of parting from the friends and familiar places of Votkinsk, Pyotr unburdened himself in a letter to Fanny: 'We've already been more than three weeks in Moscow, and every day all our family remembers you. We're so sad. . . . When I recall it [our life in Votkinsk], I want to have a good cry. For the moment Zina is teaching us.'[1]

In the middle of November the whole family joined Ilya in St Petersburg. The tribulations of Moscow were behind them, but for Pyotr another trial began when, very soon after their arrival, he and Nikolay were enrolled as day pupils in the fashionable Schmelling School. After the intimacy and sympathy of Fanny's regime, the boys were precipitated into the impersonal world of a large school in midterm, with much work to catch up. They left home at eight in the morning, returned at five, and sometimes had to labour over their homework until midnight. The strain quickly began to tell upon Pyotr, whose attendance became erratic. Then in December both boys contracted measles. The debilitating effect of this illness probably

[1] *TLP*5, p. 5; *TZC*1, p. 46.

exacerbated their dispirited condition. 'The children are not what they were in Votkinsk,' wrote Alexandra. 'Their freshness and gaiety have disappeared. Nikolay is always pale and thin – Pierre also.'[2] And to the beloved governess she further confided: 'Pierre wept for joy when he got your letter, dear, good Fanny. Each day the children recall you. Pierre says that he wants to convince himself that his stay in St Petersburg is a dream – that he wants to wake up in Votkinsk, near his own, dear Fanny. Then he would be the happiest of mortals.'[3]

In fact for Pyotr the strains of the Schmelling School were almost over, for while Nikolay made a good recovery from the measles, Pyotr did not, and in February 1849 he succumbed to what the doctors diagnosed as an ailment of the spinal cord, though we may well imagine the root of the trouble was psychological, not physical. All activities were unconditionally banned for an indefinite period. It was nearly June before he was fully active again, and by this time the family was no longer in St Petersburg, for in the spring Ilya had been appointed manager of the privately owned works at Alapayevsk. Thus in early May the family moved yet again.

While in St Petersburg the short-lived tribulations of school had been balanced for Pyotr by musical compensations. He had started piano lessons with a certain Filippov who seems to have been an admirable teacher, if we may judge from the boy's rapid progress. In addition he had frequently been taken to the opera or ballet, which must have impressed him profoundly. Now, however, he was back in the impoverished cultural life of the Russian provinces. Alapayevsk, his new home, was situated in the Urals, some 300 miles further east than Votkinsk. As a mining centre it was even older (its first factory was founded in 1702), and the social and cultural life a good deal sleepier. Modest described it as 'a village by comparison with Votkinsk',[4] and Ilya's position was far less prestigious, though the house provided for the family proved to be comfortable enough. It is no cause for wonder that the family upheaval aggravated Pyotr's unsettled state, and he had to submit again to the supervision and tuition of Zinaida, though this time without the company of Nikolay, who had remained in St Petersburg at the School of Mining Engineers, which their father had once attended. Yet any benefit Pyotr may have gained from being spared constant demonstrations of special favour towards his elder brother were offset by the reports of Nikolay's successes contained in letters home. In any case, he longed for Nikolay's companionship. His character had been affected by his illness earlier in the year, so much so that his mother had been driven to tears by the change in him.

[2] *TZC*1, p. 48.   [3] *TZC*1, p. 48.   [4] *TZC*1, p. 49.

As his health improved he regained something of his old amiability, and early in June Lidiya could inform Fanny that 'we pass the time without being bored. In the morning until midday we have lessons with Zina; then we work, read in the evenings, and sometimes we dance with one another or sing to Petya's accompaniment. He plays very nicely; you might believe he was a grown man. There's no comparison between his present performance and his playing in Votkinsk.'[5] Yet, for all this, he was still not fully himself. The clearest evidence comes from a letter one of Fanny's friends wrote her at this time:

> What I know of Pierre Tchaikovsky grieves me very much, and I can judge how much this change would sadden you. For me this child was always the best of the bunch, and I cannot conceive how his character, which gave promise of so many noble feelings, could change. I can imagine how much his parents must regret that you are no longer with their children. In particular Pierre, poor little thing, has lost a lot in this respect, and I am not at all surprised that he is doing less well, for no one has managed to keep up the education that he received from you.[6]

His indolence even caused him to neglect writing to Fanny, and when her reply to his long-overdue letter was read out to him, it drove him to tears, evidently because of its reproaches. Despite Lidiya's testimony, his interest in music seems to have receded for the moment, and the only pleasure he could find (so he told Fanny) was in reading. He had devoured Gogol's *Christmas Eve*, upon which he was later to compose one of his best operas, and now he asked Fanny's advice about whether he would be able to manage Fénelon's *Télémaque*, and also *Lettres de Mme de Sévigné*. He had dipped into Chateaubriand's *Le Génie du christianisme*, without being able to understand it. By August, however, he was getting less fretful, and when a new governess, Anastasiya Petrova, arrived on 6 December to take over the education of the Tchaikovsky children, he seemed once again to be completely himself. The advent of his cousin, Amaliya Schobert, helped to fill the gap left by Nikolay. Pyotr no longer felt so solitary and, as the eldest of the children, took the lead in organising their games, an activity in which he showed such inventiveness that when he left Alapayevsk he was required to write out sets of 'Rules of the game' which the other children might follow in his absence.

The new governess was an orphan straight from school, and only eighteen or nineteen years old. As with Fanny, her apprehensions on

[5] *TZC*1, p. 50.　　[6] *TZC*1, p. 51.

becoming a member of the Tchaikovsky household disappeared on meeting the family. In everything except languages she was probably better equipped than Fanny to undertake their education, and within less than six months she had well prepared Pyotr for entrance to (as it turned out) the School of Jurisprudence. Like Fanny, she had no interest in music, though she was to give her name to Tchaikovsky's first written-down composition. Anastasiya was a sympathetic person who might have been expected to maintain her initial personal success with Pyotr. However, the change in his character that had accompanied the earlier upsets and upheavals of the year was not simply a temporary response to the problems and tensions that beset him then. It was more fundamental, and within a couple of months the tears and touchiness had returned. Alexandra was again in despair, and Fanny became the recipient of a mother's anxieties:

> Dear and good Fanny! . . . Though I must say frankly that I am satisfied with my present [governess] – yet all the same it is not my good, dear Fanny, nor are the children the same as when they were with you, especially Pierre, whose character is very changed. He has become impatient, and at every word spoken to him that is not to his liking, there are tears in his eyes and a ready retort. And what's the reason for this? Of course, there is the youth of a governess who is not able to understand his character and inclinations so as to make him more amenable and sensible. All the same, I hope that, once he's gone to the school where Nikolay now is, he will have to break himself of these little whims. But I beg you, dear Fanny, not to mention this in your letter if you are going to write to him.[7]

The fact is that Pyotr was going through one of those difficult stages of growing up that afflict most children. We may sense it in another way in the changed tone of his letters to Fanny. His earlier ones had been direct and open, with the ingenuous frankness of the true child, eager to share the little events of its life. But now there creep into them traces of a stiffer, more self-conscious tone which betokens a first awareness of those formalities that regulate the modes of adult intercourse. It is impossible, too, not to believe that the impending break with his everyday family life had a good deal to do with his overwrought emotional state, for memories of the Schmelling School cannot have increased his relish for returning to a similar institution in St Petersburg. He was again finding pleasure – and emotional release – in his music. 'I'm always at the piano, which greatly cheers me when I'm

[7] *TZC*1, pp. 54–5.

sad,' he informed Fanny early in March 1850.[8] Unfortunately there was no one in Alapayevsk who could help him in this quarter. In May, Mariya Palchikova arrived to teach Sasha, but she could offer Pyotr nothing now. In any case, she could have spent little time with him, for on about 11 August Alexandra left for St Petersburg with Zinaida, Pyotr and Sasha, leaving Ippolit and her new twins, Anatoly and Modest, born three months before on 13 May, in Alapayevsk.

One of the main aims of this mission was to arrange for Pyotr's further education. The intention, as Alexandra told Fanny, had been that Pyotr should join Nikolay at the School of Mining Engineers, but for some reason the School of Jurisprudence was ultimately selected. Alexandra would certainly not have changed her mind lightly, and her husband kept up a barrage of advice and exhortation in his letters from Alapayevsk. For Pyotr's needs there was a special requirement: 'Don't, of course, forget about his music either. It would be wrong to abandon a good thing already begun,' he counselled,[9] providing added evidence of that unobtrusive but positive approval that he gave Pyotr in the latter's favourite recreation. Meanwhile on 3 September,[10] immediately after arriving in St Petersburg, his mother had taken him to see Glinka's *A Life for the Tsar*. The performance was quite certainly a travesty, for the sets and costumes made for the première nearly fourteen years earlier were still in use. Two years later Glinka himself was to visit the production and, appalled by the staging, the orchestral sound and the perverse tempi of the conductor, to flee before the end of the evening. There is no record of the impact the opera made on the young Tchaikovsky, but a year later the impression was still vivid enough for him to remember that it was the first anniversary of the event.

As he was two years too young to enter the School of Jurisprudence itself, Pyotr was enrolled in late September[11] in the preparatory class, having successfully passed the entrance examination. Nikolay's welfare was already being supervised by Modest Vakar, an old friend of Ilya Tchaikovsky, and it was arranged that he should perform the same service for Pyotr. Alexandra stayed until the beginning of October to allow her second son to settle into his new school, and then prepared to return to Alapayevsk. Her husband had foreseen how terrible this parting would be for Pyotr. 'Dear Petya is accustomed to the caresses of a father and mother; now he is going to be deprived of this happiness for

[8] *TLP5*, p. 10; *TZC1*, p. 56; *YDGC*, p. 20.

[9] *TLP5*, p. 14; *YDGC*, p. 20.

[10] *YDGC*, however, gives the date of the Tchaikovskys' arrival in St Petersburg as three or four days after this event.

[11] Modest says early September.

a long period – and when our sensitive child finds the parting difficult, you will naturally impress upon him the need for courage.'[12] When it finally happened it could not have been worse. According to Modest, Pyotr recalled it as 'one of the most terrible days' of his life:

The incident took place at the Central Turnpike where it was usual to go at that time to see off those who were taking the Moscow road. Besides the two boys, Zinaida Ilinishna's uncle, Ilya Karlovich Keiser, went along. He was to return to St Petersburg with the children. On the way there Petya shed a few tears, but the end of the journey seemed a long way off and, cherishing every second that he could look at his mother, he appeared comparatively calm. But with actual arrival at the place of parting, he lost all self-control. Pressing himself against his mother, he could not bear to let her go. Neither caresses, consolings, nor promises of a quick return had any effect. He heard and saw nothing, and seemed almost to become one with the beloved being. They had to resort to force to tear the poor boy away from Alexandra Andreyevna. Still he clung to her with all his might, not wishing to let her go. At last their efforts succeeded. She took her seat in the carriage with her daughters. The horses started to move – and then, summoning up his last strength, the boy broke loose from Keiser's hand, and rushed after the carriage with a cry of mad despair, trying to grab hold of the footboard, the splashboard, whatever came to hand, in a vain hope of stopping her. . . .

Never in his life could Pyotr Ilich speak of that moment without a shudder of horror. The impression of that first intense grief only paled in comparison with one yet more intense – the death of his mother.[13]

Scarcely had he suffered this blow than his misery was exacerbated by a particularly cruel tragedy of which he was the unwitting but blameless cause. Immediately after his mother's departure scarlet fever broke out at the school, and the boys were either sent home or told they would have to remain incarcerated throughout the period of quarantine. Modest Vakar had pity on Pyotr and took him into his own home. Pyotr himself escaped the disease, but it appears that he was a carrier of it, for Nikolay, the elder of Vakar's sons, contracted it. Despite their anxiety the parents did all they could to hide the serious nature of their son's illness from Pyotr, and to reassure him that no blame attached to him when, on 6 December, Nikolay died. There is no direct record of the effect upon Pyotr, but Modest was doubtless correct when he said it was devastating.

[12] *TLP*5, p. 14.   [13] *TZC*1, p. 61.

These two dreadful incidents marked the beginning of two years of great personal unhappiness for Pyotr. Not that there was any lack of sympathy and kindness from those around him. Despite the loss of their son, the Vakar family continued to look after his welfare and to welcome him and his brother Nikolay to their home on Sundays. Their constant kindness is amply documented in Pyotr's letters home. When the Vakars moved from St Petersburg in April 1851, another of Ilya's friends, Ivan Weitz, briefly replaced Modest Vakar as supervisor of the boys' welfare, and from May the task was undertaken by Platon Vakar, Modest's brother, who during the summer holidays of 1851 arranged for the two boys to spend six weeks at the country house of relatives, an interlude which Pyotr's deep and abiding love of the countryside made the more enjoyable. He could, of course, see Nikolay on most Sundays, and there were other relations, too, who could provide company and comfort. He was fully aware of the sympathy he met from all sides, and he quickly gained sufficient hold upon himself to be able to settle into work at school. Some of the teachers also showed marked kindness to him. In particular Joseph Berrard, a teacher of French and the master in charge of Pyotr's class during his first years, understood something of the feelings that were agitating the boy, and gave him special attention. At the end of April 1851 Berrard took him to a children's court ball, and afforded him his first glimpse of the Tsar, 'as close as the divan is to the writing desk in Papa's study,' as he wrote home.[14]

Yet despite such diversions (rare as they seem to have been) and personal kindnesses, the agony of separation continued unabated. In a life so dominated by study there was little news to convey to the family; instead his letters home become vessels into which he can pour all his distraught feelings. They overflow with expressions of affection for all the family. His parents are addressed with every form of loving diminutive; they are 'wonderful', 'dear', 'beautiful angels', 'beautiful ones'. Constantly there well up precious memories of events and incidents from his past life, especially when anniversaries arrive. 'Last week Advent began, and you, my angels, are faithfully fasting, because in those happy times when I was with you, you always did this. And now I remember how joyfully we received the Christmas tree from you. But I shan't be able to join in with Sasha, Polya, Malya, Katya and Mina. But at least I shall remember it.'[15] Christmas, birthdays and namedays all prompt tender and often tearful memories: 'On Wednesday, 7 May [1851], I celebrated my birthday and cried a lot when I remembered the

[14] TLP5, p. 26; TZC1, p. 67.
[15] TLP5, p. 16; TZC1, p. 64. Polya was brother Ippolit; Malya, Katya and Mina were cousins, daughters of his mother's sister, Elizaveta Schobert.

happy time I spent last year in Alapayevsk.'[16] Any news of illness at home, especially when his mother is sick, causes him terrible anxiety. Above all he longs for his parents to come to St Petersburg. Constantly they raised his hopes and then disappointed them. His father was to have arrived in February 1851, and wishful thinking that his mother might come too is balanced by a sense of shame at wanting so much to see her. 'Forgive me, dear Mama, for expecting you as well by February, but I have a sort of premonition that I shall see and kiss you. I can see that Kolya [Nikolay] has a much stronger character than I because he has not been so lonely.'[17] Up to the last minute he believes that his father will come, but unfortunately Ilya was not granted leave of absence, and a visit from both parents was put off until June. Pyotr's hopes – and anxieties – rise again: so does his insistence. 'But if, my beautiful angels, you do not come, then we shall be very lonely. I think your dear hearts will take pity on us, and that you'll come. But in any case you must come for many reasons. And so we shall expect you in June without fail!'[18] By May his worries as to whether they will come are greater still. In the event his fears were well founded and his reproaches were bitter: 'You said [we'll come] *in June, with everybody, for always!'*[19]

Finally on 12 September his father arrived in St Petersburg, and took Pyotr to live with him for the two or three weeks of his stay. The outcome of his father's main purpose for this visit at least brought the prospect of deliverance from the loneliness Pyotr had endured during the last year. Partly because he had to make provision for the education of Sasha and Ippolit, but even more, perhaps, because he was in conflict with the management of the Alapayevsk works, Ilya had determined to resign and bring the whole family to St Petersburg. During this visit he made his final break with the Alapayevsk authorities and told his wife to prepare for the move to St Petersburg.

As for Pyotr's schoolwork, he was delighted to be third in the examinations in February 1851, and to get good marks for conduct. But in March he lost a Sunday outing through laziness. 'I ask your forgiveness,' he wrote home contritely. 'I shall try to learn better so as not to distress you. I know I shall cause you tears because of this. I cried too, but my tears don't help my charming angels [i.e. his parents].'[20] He then launches into a verse about prayer which has little reference to his present regret, but is a symptom of his reawakened interest in literary composition. The day before, he confides, he had written a full account of his life since his mother's departure. The school examinations took place early in June, and again he did extremely well in everything except

[16] *TLP*5, p. 27; *TZC*1, p. 68; *YDGC*, p. 22 (partial).   [17] *TLP*5, p. 17; *TZC*1, p. 64.
[18] *TLP*5, p. 25.   [19] *TLP*5, p. 33.   [20] *TLP*5, p. 22.

Latin and religious studies. The mental development of the child is clearly evidenced in his letters. On 23 June, having arrived at the Vakar country house outside St Petersburg to spend six weeks of his summer holiday, he clearly describes his surroundings (still in less than perfect French), and in early November he again waxes poetical, perhaps revealing something of his happier frame of mind now that he knows the family will soon be reunited in St Petersburg:

> Mes chers et bon anges
> Papa et Maman!
> Déjà les derniers jours du mois d'Oktobre, déjà l'hiver s'achemine à grands pas pour remplacer l'autômne, il n'ya plus ni de feuilles vertes, ni de gazon, le soleil en se fachant ne brille et ne rechauffe plus, on n'entend plus le beau ramage des hirondelles, on ne voit plus le ciel d'azur, et toute la nature semble s'atrister.
> De quoi donc? est-elle fachee, se fache t'elle? de ce que l'autômne est trop lente? Oui! c'est la cause de sa tristesse: elle veut que le mois de *Janvier* arrive plus vite, elle veut que le mois de *Juin* arrive plus vite, elle veut que toute la creation devienne de nouveau heureuse: oui! c'est ce que je veux aussi . . . moi . . . je veux revoir un melange de vert avec toutes les couleurs imaginables, mais ce que je veux les plus, je veux revoir mes anges![21]

Again at the end, the letter has twisted round to his longing for his parents. With the news that they would soon join him in St Petersburg, his impatience appears to increase rather than decrease. The constantly disappointed hopes of the past year seem to have made his trust in the future so insecure that his letters sometimes sound confused about his expectations of their arrival. The news that they would not after all be coming in December was a cruel blow. Finally it was to be the following May. We may sense the boy's growing joy in his last letter home before his parents finally joined him. At last St Petersburg would really become his home:

> Today is Good Friday. . . . I am spending the time very happily. Of course you're not here, but on the other hand the kindness of Platon Alexeyevich [Vakar] and Mariya Petrovna [his wife] and everyone passes description. Spring is already beginning, the Neva is rapidly thawing, and already we're forbidden to go on it. When you receive my letter your beautiful Neiva, which differs from our river only in its 'i', will certainly be thawing. See how I have already become

[21] *TLP*5, p. 39; *TZC*1, p. 71 (partial).

accustomed to living in St Petersburg, so that I can even talk of 'our Neva', 'our home'; in a word, I am completely like an inhabitant of St. Petersburg.

But *soon, soon* I shall not be writing you letters, but I shall talk with my angels in person. Ah! How lovely it will be for the first time in my life to arrive home from the School, to see you, kiss you. I think this will be the greatest happiness that has ever happened to me.[22]

The early summer of 1852 was joyful for another reason as well. Despite fierce competition, his own earlier uncertainties, and his comparative youth, Pyotr passed the examination admitting him to the School of Jurisprudence[23] which he entered as a fee-paying student.

Pyotr's musical life during these past two years had been severely restricted by the demands of his schoolwork. He does not appear to have been taken often to the opera or ballet, and the only pieces we know he saw were the ballets *Giselle* by Adam and *The Naiad and the Fisherman* by Pugni, and Weber's opera, *Der Freischütz*. As for his own musical activities, these seem to have been confined to a not very systematic playing of the piano. Twice in his letters he mentions such occasions. One was when he played a piece called 'The Nightingale'[24] which, being his mother's favourite, brought back a flood of nostalgic memories. The other was an incident in November 1851 which brought him into trouble with M. Berrard:

I was playing the piano when some pupils passed the room. I was playing a polka, and several of them began dancing. Then some more came and did the same. M. Berrard, who was downstairs, heard the noise going on overhead. He hurried up to stop it. When my comrades heard the door opening, they rushed off in a flash. I was left alone, and M. Berrard asked me who the dancers were. There were so many of them that in my confusion I had forgotten who they were. Then the duty-pupil came along and told him who had been dancing. At that, M. Berrard looked at me with displeasure, and said I had lied.

'I needn't tell you the other details because you'll know everything when you come to St Petersburg,' he concluded apprehensively.[25] Despite Pyotr's obvious embarrassment at being apprehended in a mildly illicit,

[22] *TLP5*, p. 52; *TZC1*, p. 73.
[23] His marks, out of a possible 12 for each subject, were: religious studies, 11; Russian language, 12; arithmetic, 10; history, 9; French, 11; Latin, 11; German, 10; geography, 10.
[24] Presumably the very popular piece by Alyabyev.
[25] *TLP5*, p. 41.

though harmless frolic, it is possible that he was upset only by the reproach of having lied. If his lifelong delight in practical jokes is any pointer, he probably savoured the mischievous aspect of the incident. Modest, who bluntly disapproved of such pranks, asserted that his brother's taste for them was exceeded only by his relish in recounting them after the event. During the summer of 1852 the reunited Tchaikovsky family spent some time at a dacha on the Black River, just outside St Petersburg, and Modest related two escapades, in one of which Pyotr engineered the drenching with cold water of his brother Nikolay and a cousin, who had perched themselves on a ladder beneath a balcony to eavesdrop on Zinaida, Lidiya and a female cousin while they were confiding to one another their affairs of the heart. The high spirits of this little incident probably reflect Pyotr's blissfully happy frame of mind now that he was with his family again – and especially with his mother. When he entered the School of Jurisprudence in the autumn, he was immeasurably proud on the occasions when she visited his school, and when she called upon her sister who lived opposite, he delighted in blowing kisses to her from a dormitory window. At weekends his great joy was to share with her the news of the past week.

As for his progress at school, it was now to become a steady decline into competent mediocrity. The School of Jurisprudence, founded by Prince Pyotr Oldenburg, was already a distinguished institution with a high reputation. Though other subjects were taught, its real function was to provide a vocational training in law, and those who successfully passed its final examination received official preference in the civil service to graduates from the University. The School's pupils were mainly upper-middle class, with a smattering of high aristocratic names which gave it a special prestige. The principal, a certain Yazïkov, had been chief of police in Riga, and had been appointed in 1849 more for his gifts as a disciplinarian than as a lawyer. The School had been infected by some of the liberal ideas that swept Europe in the late 1840s, and Yazïkov imposed a regimented control upon the place. Though this had been relaxed by the time of Pyotr's enrolment, he found himself in a society of strict order. He was fortunate in being assigned for his first three years to Ivan Alopeus as tutor. This former artillery captain was one of the best-liked and most committed teachers of the whole staff, and Pyotr was to retain affectionate memories of him all his life, as also of Alopeus's successor, Baron Edouard-Prosper[26] de Baccarat, an amiable Frenchman but incompetent French teacher, with a passion for Racine and Molière. Pyotr's recollections of the priest, Mikhail Bogoslovsky, were equally vivid, though they had little of affection in them. What

[26] Possibly Edgar-Prosper.

made a profound impression upon him was Bogoslovsky's learning and strict principles, and Modest asserted that the priest's influence accounted not only for Tchaikovsky's lifelong practice of attending mass on feast days whenever he could, but also his subsequent active concern as a composer for the state of Orthodox church music. Indeed, from Modest's account, Bogoslovsky's was the only lasting influence that Pyotr carried away from the School of Jurisprudence. The picture he paints of the other teachers is of men with variable competence applying it without much enthusiasm to whatever subject they had to teach. As for Pyotr himself, he was average in all things except mathematics, for which he had no ability. Like most of his teachers, he seems to have been conscientious without being enthusiastic, and his interest in the law diminished when he reached the senior classes whose teachers, though sometimes knowledgeable, were dull. Modest summarised it thus: the School 'prepared an ungifted but conscientious toiler for a profession alien to his nature – that of, as Pyotr Ilich himself later put it, "a bad civil servant" – and nothing more.'[27] Tchaikovsky's brief career in legal service was a living testimony to this.

Of the pupils in Pyotr's class by far the most brilliant was Alexey Apukhtin, who was to become a popular poet in St Petersburg society, with a paunch as famed as his verses. Later Tchaikovsky was to set a number of Apukhtin's texts. Apukhtin's prodigious gifts were already recognised at school, and the adulation he received, coupled with his difficult character, ensured that he had few friends. Pyotr was one of this small circle. Another who, like Apukhtin, was to be a colleague of Tchaikovsky in his later employment at the Ministry of Justice, was Vladimir Gerard, the future founder of a society for the prevention of cruelty to children. Pyotr fired Gerard with a love of opera by taking him to a performance of Rossini's *Guillaume Tell*, and subsequently the two friends often attended the opera together, as well as French plays. They also shared in their social life. 'I remember,' wrote Gerard, 'how, thanks to a meeting with the pretty sister of one of the law students, we both got an invitation to a ball at the Zalivkina boarding school, and that we both danced assiduously.'[28] Evidently at this time Pyotr still experienced a normal attraction to the opposite sex. To Fyodor Maslov, another classmate and Ministry colleague, we are indebted for some of the most valuable personal reminiscences of Tchaikovsky during his time at the School of Jurisprudence. Apukhtin, Gerard and Maslov, together with Tchaikovsky, were responsible for a journal, *The School Messenger*, to which Pyotr is known to have contributed 'A History of Literature in our Class', written, according to Maslov, very wittily. Yet

[27] *TZC*1, p. 95.   [28] *TZC*1, p. 104.

perhaps the most enduring relationship from his schooldays was to be with Vladimir Adamov, whom Modest characterised as 'a rare combination of a most diligent, committed student (and subsequently also an equally diligent and committed civil servant) and a nature filled with aesthetic yearnings and sympathies'.[29] Adamov's legal career was to be as successful as Tchaikovsky's was disastrous. Nevertheless as individuals they had a natural compatibility which was sealed further by Adamov's great love of music and the countryside. Together they paid frequent visits to the Italian opera, and dreamed of walking holidays through Switzerland and Italy. Adamov's death in 1877 was to be a severe blow to Tchaikovsky.

All accounts suggest that Pyotr was well liked, both by the staff and his fellow pupils, and that his relations with everyone were uniformly cordial. There is equal unanimity about his carelessness, even slovenliness of appearance, and about his disorganised mode of existence. His trustfulness was boundless. During his last years at the School he kept a diary which, as its title *Everything* suggests, was a record of all his innermost secrets: yet he habitually left it in his desk, despite the open invitation this offered his schoolfellows to pry into its contents. The generosity with which he distributed his father's books among his friends was matched by his own casualness in returning volumes lent to him. Several such law books, Maslov discovered, were still in Tchaikovsky's possession in 1869. Maslov also recalled how he and Pyotr had revised for their last examinations in the Summer Garden. 'So that we shouldn't have to lug around our notes and textbooks, we concealed them in the hollow of one of the old linden trees, protected from the rain by boards. At the end of each examination, I removed my papers, but Tchaikovsky constantly forgot to do this, and his study materials are perhaps still decomposing in one of the trees in the Summer Garden.'[30] His forgetfulness was notorious, and some found such traits infuriating. As one school friend later expressed it: 'it needed all the exceptional, ineffable charm of his personality to make you forget Tchaikovsky's absent-mindedness, carelessness and slovenliness.'[31] His one real vice that would have brought severe retribution upon him, if it had been discovered, was smoking. Most of his friends came from among the 'quiet ones' who conformed with the rules, but this practice earned him the respect of the 'dare-devils' too, and increased the circle of his acquaintances. One cannot believe, however, that his motives were simply bravado or a seeking after popularity or notoriety, but rather that his highly strung organism very early found relief in 'the bliss' (as he himself later put it) of inhaling tobacco smoke. His craving

[29] *TZC*1, p. 99.   [30] *TZC*1, p. 98.   [31] *TZC*1, p. 98.

for tobacco was finally to become so absolute that he himself admitted it
was no longer a pleasant amusement but an addiction.

The School of Jurisprudence was the centre and the one constant
factor in Pyotr's life for the next seven years. On the musical front he
seems to have gained very little from it, certainly nothing that could
credibly count as the first stage of a professional musical education.
There were two members of staff who successively gave instrumental
lessons during Pyotr's years at the School, but only from the second, a
certain Franz Becker, who was a member of a firm of piano
manufacturers, did he have any tuition, and the fruits of this were
negligible. But with the teacher of singing, Gavriil Lomakin, it was a
somewhat different matter. Lomakin had already had a distinguished
career as a voice trainer before ever Tchaikovsky came under his
tutelage. During the 1850s he was one of the most sought-after teachers
in St Petersburg, and instructed the Tsar's Imperial Chapel Choir. In
1862 he was to be the co-founder with Balakirev of the Free Music
School, acting as its director for the first five years of its life, with special
responsibility for the choral side of its activities. At the School of
Jurisprudence Lomakin's responsibilities were purely choral. Pyotr was
an excellent treble, and during the summer of 1852 his aunt, Ekaterina
Alexeyeva, who was his one family ally in musical activities, taught him
the soprano part of a coloratura duet from Rossini's *Semiramide* which he
is reported to have sung well, taking particular pride in his ability to trill.
Lomakin spotted his vocal talents very early and recruited him to bear a
part in the trio to be sung at the St Catherine's Day service conducted by
the bishop. More than a quarter of a century later Tchaikovsky could
still recall the thrill of this event:

> From the very beginning of our academic course we prepared our-
> selves for this solemn day. During my time the choristers were good.
> When I was a boy I had a splendid treble voice, and for several years in
> succession I took the top part in the trio which three boys sang at the
> altar at the beginning and end of the bishop's service. The liturgy,
> especially at the bishop's service, produced the deepest poetical
> impression on me then (and it sometimes does even now). . . . How
> proud I was that I was participating in the service with my
> singing! . . . Afterwards we remembered that wonderful day for all the
> rest of the year and longed for it to come again as quickly as
> possible.[32]

Lomakin was also quick to perceive how useful Pyotr's musical

[32] *TLP*8, p. 434; *TZC*1, pp. 120–1; *TPM*2, p. 262.

competence would be in choral activities. 'From the day of his entry [to the School], he was a chorister, and for the first three years was among the second trebles, of whom he was the leader. This was necessary because that was where they put the trebles who had poor voices and ears. The proximity of these "false" comrades caused him suffering,' Maslov recalled.[33] When he was nearing the end of his course at the School, Pyotr had a brief experience of directing music. It was evidently the School's practice to entrust the direction of the vocal trios to a senior boy, and in 1858 this responsibility was given to Pyotr. But in this capacity he was a failure, as Maslov recorded: 'He didn't remain director for long, not more than two months, because he showed neither the ability nor the desire to command.'[34] Later it was to cost Tchaikovsky infinite suffering before he could gain assurance as a conductor.

In addition to such serious musical activities he entertained his friends in school with various musical tricks, such as playing the piano with a towel covering the keyboard. He was far less willing to oblige with a demonstration of anything that might involve public confession of his personal inner feelings. He normally became irritated when asked to exhibit his considerable facility for playing by ear, and his improvisations remained essentially private affairs.

In fact, it was outside the School that the most significant part of Pyotr's musical life was to be found. His aunt Ekaterina performed a far more valuable service than just teaching him his part in the duet from *Semiramide*: she took him through the whole of Mozart's *Don Giovanni* at the piano, thus opening up to him this opera's full riches of which he had glimpsed only a part from the orchestrion in Votkinsk. Twenty-six years later, in 1878, he recalled the crucial importance for him of this overwhelming revelation of Mozart's genius. 'The music of *Don Giovanni* was the first to make a tremendous impression upon me. . . . Through it I penetrated into that world of artistic beauty in which soar only the greatest geniuses. . . . I am indebted to Mozart for the fact that I have dedicated my life to music. He gave the first jog to my musical powers; he made me love music above all things in this world.'[35] From two years later, 1854, dates the first composition that he seems to have committed to paper. This was a piece composed in August and dedicated to the family governess, Anastasiya Petrova; it was called appropriately *Anastasie Valse*, and is the first of his compositions to survive. A little later that year Pyotr showed the first positive signs of an ambition to be a composer of something more than trifles such as this. Back in July he had requested a libretto for an opera from Viktor Olkhovsky, whose

[33] *PVC*, p. 395.   [34] *PVC*, p. 395.
[35] *TZC*1, p. 82; *TLP*7, p. 181; *TPM*1, p. 264.

brother, Evgeny, had married Zinaida in January. Pyotr was fired by Olkhovsky's work (a one-act piece called *Hyperbole*) when he received it in the autumn; nevertheless, despite his general approval of it, the fourteen-year-old composer did not find it faultless: 'It corresponds entirely with my wishes: just one thing – there are too many arias and recitatives, and very few duets, trios and such like.'[36] Not surprisingly nothing came of this project. His next known creative effort, a romance, 'My genius, my angel, my friend', composed, it seems, in 1857 or 1858, has survived. As might be expected, it is a child of the Russian drawing room, not the Italian opera house. Though unremarkable as music, its sustained melancholy does credit to a composer still so young and relatively untutored.

In 1856 Pyotr had begun a friendship with the Italian singing teacher, Luigi Piccioli, a Neapolitan who had settled in Russia in the 1840s, and whose wife was a friend of one of Pyotr's relatives. Later Piccioli was to be a teacher at the St Petersburg Conservatoire. He was of indeterminate age, though probably older than the fifty years to which he confessed. Terrified by any idea of old age or death, he sought to preserve the illusion of youth not only by cosmetics but even, some said, by a device (situated, so Modest and Anatoly decided, beneath his neckerchief) which stretched his skin and thus obliterated his facial wrinkles. Yet there seems to have been more to Piccioli than this bizarre portrait would suggest, for he was a sharp-witted, passionate, life-loving man. His musical tastes were rigorously exclusive. He poured scorn on the Beethoven symphonies, the Bach B minor mass, Russian church music, gipsy music and *A Life for the Tsar*; for him the only music was Italian opera, and his passionate partiality for Rossini, Bellini, Donizetti and Verdi not surprisingly inflamed Pyotr's attraction to the genre.

By this time Pyotr's thoughts were already fastening, albeit only tentatively, upon a career in music. In 1855 he had started lessons with Rudolf Kündinger, a twenty-three-year-old German pianist and pedagogue who had arrived in Russia five years earlier and who, like Piccioli, was to become a professor at the St Petersburg Conservatoire. Kündinger was another of Tchaikovsky's earlier contacts from whom Modest extracted recollections after the composer's death, and his account provides the clearest surviving assessment of Pyotr's musical abilities during his teens. 'From 1855 to 1858,' Kündinger remembered,

our work was interrupted only in the summer months. During this time my pupil had his successes, though these were not such as to arouse in me any particular hopes on his account. To Ilya Petrovich's

[36] *TLP5*, pp. 54–5; *YDGC*, p. 24 (partial).

question whether it was worth his son dedicating himself ultimately
to a career in music, I replied in the negative, in the first place because
I did not see in Pyotr Ilich the genius that subsequently manifested
itself, and secondly because I had myself experienced how hard was
the lot of a professional musician in Russia at that time. . . . If I could
have foreseen who was to grow out of the lawyer of those days I would
have kept a diary of the course of our lessons. But I must say that
unfortunately it didn't occur to me with what sort of a musician I was
dealing, and so the details of how my pupil developed musically are
very unclearly preserved in my memory. Certainly his abilities were
notable: a strikingly fine ear, [a good] memory, an outstanding hand,
but all this gave no cause to foresee in him even a brilliant performer,
let alone a composer. There was nothing surprising in this: before
and since Tchaikovsky I have had occasion to meet not infrequently
young people with such gifts. The one thing that did to a certain
extent arrest my attention was his improvisations. In them could
certainly be vaguely sensed something not quite ordinary. In addition
his harmonic flair sometimes struck me. At that time he scarcely knew
anything of musical theory, but when it chanced that I showed him my
compositions, he several times gave me advice about the harmonic
aspect – advice which, for the most part, was sensible.

On my recommendation my pupil for some time took lessons in
the theory of music with my brother, Auguste, now deceased. How
long this went on I cannot say, but in any case it was for not more than
one season. Nor do I remember why these studies were discontinued.

I gave lessons once a week on Sundays. With regard to technique
the fruits of my labours during these three years were not especially
significant, probably because Tchaikovsky did not have time for the
necessary practice. Very often we finished the lesson by playing duets.
Afterwards I stopped to lunch with the Tchaikovsky family (I
remember there was a large number of young ladies), and then we
went together to the University concerts, which at that time were the
only refuge for music lovers. How low the level of musical
requirement then was is apparent from the fact that these, the best
symphony concerts, were given *without rehearsal*.[37]

Yet the really critical event of Pyotr's years at the School of
Jurisprudence had nothing to do with his studies or the friends he made
there, nor even with the activities of the Kündinger brothers, important
as these certainly were, but with his home life. It was the Tchaikovskys'
normal practice to spend the summer outside St Petersburg, and that of

[37] *PVC*, pp. 397–8; *TZC*1, pp. 122–3 (partial, with text re-ordered).

1853 was to prove the last which Pyotr was to enjoy in the company of his beloved mother, for in June 1854 she contracted cholera. A numbed silence seems to surround the ensuing train of events until 1856, when Pyotr at last brought himself to communicate the news to Fanny Dürbach:

Finally I have to tell you of a horrible misfortune which befell us two and a half years ago. Four months after Zina's departure, Mama suddenly fell sick with cholera, and though she was dangerously ill, she recovered her health, thanks to the redoubled efforts of the doctors. But this was only temporary, for after three or four days of convalescence, she died without having time to say farewell to all those around her. Although she didn't have the strength to utter a word distinctly, it was nevertheless understood that she wanted to take final communion, and the priest arrived in time with the blessed sacraments, for after taking communion she rendered up her soul to God. On the day of Mama's funeral Papa in his turn fell ill with cholera so that his death was expected imminently. But thanks to God, in a week he recovered.[38]

Alexandra Tchaikovskaya died on 25 June 1854. As a last resort she had been immersed in a hot bath to counteract her extreme cold, but to no avail. Modest noted that the case history of her illness was to be almost exactly repeated thirty-nine years later when Pyotr died of the same disease. Ippolit's fragmented memories of that final day are also preserved. 'When Mama had declined into a dangerous condition, all the children without exception were transferred to Aunt Liza's house. . . . When Mama's death was felt to be imminent, I can't remember who, but someone who had come from Salt Street [where the Tchaikovskys lived] – Aunt Liza, I believe – discussed which of the children should be taken to receive Mother's blessing. I remember they took Sasha and Petya. . . . [Later] I rushed off . . . to Salt Street. . . . I ran up to the doors of our house just as Petya and then Sasha came out, who told me "It's all over".'[39]

We can only speculate on the precise effect of his mother's death upon Pyotr, but it was certainly shattering. Yet, just as he had somehow forced himself to adjust outwardly to his circumstances when his mother had returned to Alapayevsk in 1850, so now he settled back into his daily routine. Ilya convalesced with his children at Oranienbaum (Lomonosov) on the Gulf of Finland that summer, perhaps with a special awareness that his family was breaking up around him. In January Zinaida had

[38] TLP5, pp. 56–7; TZC1, p. 79 (partial).   [39] TLP5, p. 58.

married Evgeny Olkhovsky, and had gone to live in the Urals. Lidiya, Ilya's dependant, had become engaged to Evgeny's elder brother, Nikolay, and was to marry in the autumn. Feeling unable to cope with all the children himself, he arranged for Ippolit to enter the Naval Academy that autumn, and enrolled Sasha in the fashionable girls' school at the Smolny Institute. At the same time he arranged that his favourite brother, Pyotr, should come with his wife and children to share quarters with him in St Petersburg. Thus, towards the end of 1854, Ilya's son Pyotr found himself a member of a new and much enlarged household.

Uncle Pyotr was a remarkable character. In his youth he had been a fanatical adherent of the Orthodox Church, so much so that he might have been expected to become a monk. Instead he went into the army, survived fifty-two battles, and then embarked on the campaign of matrimony with a Lutheran wife. By this time he was middle-aged, and, having fathered a succession of three sons and five lively, life-loving daughters whom he had quite failed to subordinate to the strict code of conduct he had built for himself upon his Orthodox beliefs, he retired to his study where he busied himself with writing endless tracts on mystical subjects, emerging only to eat, to read the popular paper *The Northern Bee* with brother Ilya, and to take a daily walk. Yet he was not altogether a joyless person, for before each constitutional he spent some time with his wife wrapping up sweets and gingerbread in small packages which he stuffed into his pockets. Then he set out on his walk and, recorded Modest, 'on each encounter with a child, he took out one of the packets and, letting it fall, said: "A parcel from heaven!", then, without more words, proceeded on his way, pretending he wasn't there.'[40] By contrast his wife, Elizaveta, had no compunction about enjoying life's blessings. Her religious persuasions told her such things came from God, and she saw to it that her daughters enjoyed the best of literature, music, drawing and the theatre, and led a healthy social life. Thus their home became a natural meeting place for young people, and Pyotr participated actively in this society and its various amusements, deriving great benefit from such relationships and activities – until at midnight Uncle Pyotr emerged from his study and started silently extinguishing the lights as a sign to all that it was time to go home or to bed.

This congenial family life lasted three years. Then, in the autumn of 1857, the brothers decided to disentangle their families and live separately once again. Sasha, now fifteen years old, had just left school, and Ilya put her in charge of his household and the twins, a duty she seems to have discharged admirably. It was as well that there was now a

[40] *TZC*1, pp. 107–8.

person to whom Ilya could delegate his domestic affairs, for in the spring of 1858 financial ruin befell him. The previous year he had unwisely entrusted his money to a certain Natalya Yachmeneva, the widow of an engineer, who had now lost it all, along with her own money, to a retired cavalry officer and landowner called Bekleshev. Natalya Yachmeneva immediately joined with Bekleshev in a legal battle which was waged for over four years before the case was finally decided against her. During all this period Ilya never ceased to hope that his money would be regained; nevertheless, he had to face the fact that currently he had no income. He was forced to move his quarters and, now nearly sixty-three, to look for paid work again. For Pyotr this disaster meant the end of piano lessons with Kündinger. Fortunately, through the agency of an influential friend, Ilya secured the directorship of the Technological Institute. Thus his financial position was restored and the family moved into the comfortable flat that went with the post. They were joined by their relatives, the Schoberts (who had taken in Ilya and his children during their recent misfortune), and his new affluence enabled him and his augmented household to resume something of their active social life.

On 25 May 1859 Pyotr graduated from the School of Jurisprudence, thirteenth in his class, with the rank of titular counsellor which put him on the very lowest rung of the civil service ladder. His childhood was over. Despite some painful experiences and unsettled periods, it had been, outwardly at least, happy enough. His family life had been stable, and had provided a range of pleasures and opportunities favourable to the proper development of his personality and gifts. In addition to the secure relationship with his parents, there had been no lack of other children with whom he could share his games and activities. By the standards of his own day he had been exceedingly lucky in his education, and though the fostering of his musical skills and perceptions had been hopelessly inadequate as a preparation for the profession itself, there is no sign that Pyotr had felt seriously deprived, for as yet he sensed no very strong urge to make music the centre of his life. Of course there had been the misery of the two-year separation from his family, but he seems finally to have coped with this; with reunion, this desperate loneliness became an unhappy memory, nothing more. What went on in the recesses of his mind in his moments of solitude we do not know. Nevertheless, there are no signs of any yearning to draw away from his fellow beings into the world of a recluse, where morbid brooding might ferment unnatural thoughts and practices. Indeed, Pyotr seems to have been not only a sociable child, but a positive leader in matters of pleasure and fun. Yet the sources of his later suffering seem to have been in him from the very beginning, and his problems would perhaps still have been unavoidable even if the circumstances of his early life had been quite different. Fanny Dürbach early recognised his hyper-sensitivity, and it is perhaps above all through his passionate relationship with his mother that we may perceive the seeds from which sprang those growths of psychological abnormality which insidiously bound themselves round him, constricting, distorting and unbalancing his emotional life until, unable to channel itself into the closest of personal relationships, that life burst out importunately, and with blazing force, through his music. This metaphor may itself seem inflamed, but the account of Tchaikovsky's life that will be unfolded in the following pages cannot but expose the extremity of his case.

As all now know, the main root of Tchaikovsky's personal problems was his homosexuality. Nineteenth-century Russian society would allow nothing of the tolerance and understanding shown in present-day attitudes. Tchaikovsky's torment was twofold. Firstly, he knew that he would suffer a large measure of social rejection if any homosexual activity of his became public knowledge. Secondly – and this must surely have had the deeper significance to this hypersensitive and gentle man – he felt tainted within himself, defiled by something from which he finally realised he could never escape. The consequence was that this lovable, outwardly fun-loving child was to develop in time into a neurotic adult whose biography is a case history of psychological and emotional problems as acute as any among creative artists. Yet these more extreme problems were still some years away in the future. Just how acute his homosexual tendencies were at this time we do not know; nor do we know whether he had engaged in active homosexual practices at the School of Jurisprudence. After graduation, Pyotr and some school friends departed on a walking tour through the Sergiyevskaya heath near St Petersburg. The impression made upon him by the events and experiences of this trip, insignificant though many of them must have been in reality, was enormous. It was the same the next year when he visited Imatra with its famous waterfall just over the Finnish border. Modest disclosed that his brother could recall every detail of these little expeditions, and twenty years after this walking tour he still kept on his writing desk stones which had been inscribed by his companions. Perhaps it is a measure of the oppressive drudgery and boredom of the legal career upon which he was about to embark that these brief breaks from the routine of office work should have afforded such vivid and long-cherished memories.

3

CIVIL SERVANT AND

MUSIC STUDENT

ON 15 JUNE 1859 Tchaikovsky received an appointment in the Ministry of Justice. Six months later, on 22 December, he was made a junior assistant to the head of his administrative department; exactly two months after this he became a senior assistant – and there he remained for the next three years until his final abandonment of the civil service for music. As Modest succinctly put it: 'his career was uncomplicated'.[1] Precisely what his duties were is not known, but they can have been of little moment, for when Tchaikovsky himself was questioned not so long afterwards about them, he had to confess that he could not remember what they had entailed, though he always insisted that he had been a conscientious worker. Yet Modest suspected that his superiors had to suffer a good deal. It was even alleged that on one occasion Tchaikovsky, while carrying a document signed by his chief, stopped to talk to someone, and that during the conversation he absent-mindedly tore pieces off the paper and ate them, so that the whole had to be copied afresh. Modest himself doubted the authenticity of this tale, but admitted that it was thoroughly consistent with his brother's lifelong habit of devouring pieces of theatre programmes in this way.

Again, as at school, it was not the work but the people he mixed with that remained in Tchaikovsky's memory. In fact, he later admitted that in his social life at that time he had positive ambitions to enter higher society, and that the frustration of these pretensions caused him bitter disappointment. Modest even asserted that in his pursuit of pleasure his brother sought only the company of people of his own age, and that his relationships with both the younger and older members of his family, and even with his father, became quite distant. Yet, despite this and Tchaikovsky's own confession of social aspirations, it is possible that the image Modest projected of his civil servant brother as no more than a pleasure-seeking, empty-headed social butterfly was exaggerated. Because Modest, now approaching his teens and soon himself to enter

[1] *TZC*1, p. 113.

the School of Jurisprudence, was amongst those excluded from Pyotr's closest circle, he probably felt a resentment that inflated into something enormous those activities which drew his brother away from the family. Nor is there any real evidence for the insinuations of some writers that Tchaikovsky was at this time indulging in dark and covert personal practices. Outwardly he retained the normal appearance of a heterosexual, attending dances and engaging in light amours. Significantly, perhaps, there is no sign of passionate response on his side to any young lady who evinced interest in him; rather he was flattered by the proof such incidents afforded that some women found him attractive. As he reported of one conquest: 'Sophie Adamova told me that last year both Varenka girls were seriously in love with me. . . . My self-esteem was greatly flattered by this tale.'[2] Nevertheless, while there can be no doubt about the vanity and even foppishness of Tchaikovsky at this time, nor about his vigorous pursuit of a lively and vapid social existence, it is probable that such things were important to him more as an escape from the boredom and sterility of his professional employment than because he found them wholly satisfying in themselves.

During the summer months Ilya Tchaikovsky moved outside St Petersburg to where the Technological Institute had a villa reserved especially for students unable to afford the journey home for the summer vacation. With these fifty or so extra residents the Tchaikovsky/Schobert ménage was able to enjoy a rich fund of diversions including home-made fireworks and theatrical entertainments. Tchaikovsky's purely social circle continued to widen. His facility for improvising polkas, waltzes and the like, and his readiness to play for dancing made him popular at parties. At the same time, however, his more fruitful friendships with Apukhtin and Piccioli continued to develop. At one stage he was meeting Apukhtin every day to read and discuss poetry. But it was the ballet, the Italian opera and French plays that attracted him more than anything. Of ballets only those with a fantastic or magic element really appealed to him, and *Giselle* was his favourite. As for opera, the Italian company was by far the most proficient of all the musical ensembles in St Petersburg at that time and, with Piccioli to fan the flames of his enthusiasm, Tchaikovsky deepened his passion for *Don Giovanni*, broadened and consolidated his knowledge of Rossini, Bellini, Donizetti and Verdi, and also made further acquaintance with operas by other composers like Weber and Meyerbeer. The former's *Der Freischütz* he already knew, and the latter's *Les Huguenots* was to have a considerable direct influence upon his own

[2] *TLP*5, pp. 63–4.

later music. Of all Western nations it was the French whose culture had the strongest attraction for him, and to the end of his life he retained his love of the minor dramatist, Octave Feuillet, whose *Le Roman d'un jeune homme pauvre* he saw so many times at the French theatre in the early 1860s that he knew it virtually by heart. Tchaikovsky himself sometimes took part in amateur theatricals. He possessed some limited acting talent and a gift for comic mimicry that seems to have been enjoyed in domestic circles, especially when it had been lubricated by a glass of wine. However, he was inclined to overact greatly, until on one occasion a sharp reproof hissed by a fellow performer during one of his more gross exhibitions so covered him with shame and confusion that he abandoned such performances for a long time. Even in a trivial domestic milieu like this it seems that his artistic conscience could be prodded into wakefulness.

Within the family circle the most important event of Tchaikovsky's first two years of civil service employment was the wedding of his sister Sasha to Lev Davïdov on 18 November 1860, and her subsequent removal from St Petersburg to the Ukraine. Tchaikovsky and his sister had been quite close; there is no doubt that her departure left a very real gap in his present life, and he was to maintain as close a relationship as distance permitted, both with her and her husband. Later their home at Kamenka, near Kiev, was to become a refuge in some of his times of greatest trouble, and their children, especially his nephew, Vladimir, were to provide him with pleasure and companionship in later years. Very soon after Sasha's marriage there began a correspondence between brother and sister which is a valuable source of information on Tchaikovsky's inner life. His letter to Sasha of 22 March 1861 is the first personal document to have survived from his hand since 1856, and its opening reveals the capacity for sympathy, tempered with brotherly firmness, of this now full-grown man:

I have just read, Sasha, your letters to Papa and Malya. Such sadness, such a muted but gloomy hopelessness is apparent in them that they made me both wretched and irritated. Aren't you ashamed to be in such a state of mind? Forget the past, banish dear memories – look to the future boldly: you will see how many quiet joys, how much good fortune it will bestow upon you. By August you will already be a mother:[3] at the same time Aunt Liza and Malya will appear before you. With fussing over your child a year will pass unnoticed – then a trip, albeit brief, to St Petersburg: meetings with friends, relatives – yes indeed, I should like to be in your position! And a husband whom

[3] Sasha's first child was a daughter, Tatyana.

you love? No, cheer up, try only to be well and, most of all, don't look back at the past. Train yourself to do this, and you'll find that you'll stop being melancholy.[4]

The decree abolishing serfdom had just been promulgated, and the previous Sunday, so Tchaikovsky informed his sister, he had gone to church to see what effect it would have upon the serfs when it was read out. Doubtless Sasha and her husband, who had been entrusted with the management of his brothers' estates at Kamenka, were very much preoccupied with the consequences of this event, far more than Tchaikovsky. For us the greatest interest of this letter lies elsewhere, where Tchaikovsky recounts part of the previous evening's events:

At supper my musical talent was discussed. Papa assures me that it isn't too late for me to become a professional musician. It would be splendid if that were so – but the point is this: if there is talent in me, it is still most likely that it's impossible to develop it by now. They've made a civil servant out of me – and a bad one at that. I try to improve as best I can, to do my job more seriously – and suddenly, at the same time, I am studying thorough-bass. . . .[5]

Here at last is the first really clear evidence that Tchaikovsky, now nearly twenty-one, was seriously thinking of abandoning the profession for which he had been trained, and of embarking instead upon the basic preparation needed for a career in music. As yet nothing is decided, and he himself has doubts about its feasibility. The rest of the letter contains much gossip and trivia about his social engagements, but in fact the period of his life during which the pursuit of social pleasures and diversions reigned supreme was drawing to a close. There is no point in particularising such events. The period of Lent saw the closing of the theatres and the curtailment of other amusements, and during February and March 1861 Tchaikovsky had whiled away part of this closed season by visiting his cousin, Alexandra Kartsova, at her home in Medved, near Novgorod. Soon after returning to St Petersburg he was offered the opportunity of travelling farther afield. A certain Vasily Pisarev, an engineering friend of his father, required an interpreter for a journey to Western Europe, and Tchaikovsky was invited to go in this capacity. He accepted with alacrity, was granted leave of absence from the Ministry, and towards the middle of July left for the border. This was a great event for him. 'Crossing the frontier was a solemn and poetic moment,' he

[4] *TLP*5, p. 60; *TZC*1, pp. 132–3; *TPB*, p. 3.
[5] *TLP*5, p. 61; *TZC*1, pp. 133–4; *TPB*, p. 4; *YDGC*, p. 29.

wrote home to his father. 'Everyone crossed themselves, and the last Russian sentry shouted to us "God be with you", solemnly waving his hand.'[6] On 18 July he and Pisarev arrived in Berlin.

Tchaikovsky's letters home reveal his excitement at being abroad for the first time, and his lively response to the places he visited. They also confirm the new and very close relationship he had just begun with his twin brothers, for every letter has some solicitous thought or enquiry about them, or some snippet of advice for their welfare. Berlin, where he spent four days, was not much to his taste, and his view of the German capital was to remain ambivalent all his life. It reminded him of St Petersburg, but was dowdier and more oppressive. He thought German food funny, but approved of the large helpings he received. German dancing he considered even more hilarious; German women he found repugnant. His severest strictures were reserved for his first impressions of Berlin's music; he saw Offenbach's *Orphée aux enfers*, and pronounced the performance beneath criticism. Hamburg was a very different matter. He and Pisarev arrived there on 22 July, before going on to Antwerp, via Cologne. 'Hamburg is incomparably better than Berlin. . . . In general the week there flew by; there were a great number of amusements. We spent each evening very pleasantly, sometimes taking a walk, sometimes going to a dance with women of doubtful morals (this town abounds in them), sometimes visiting places where the inferior part of the population enjoys itself. It's all extremely jolly and varied.'[7] Clearly Tchaikovsky wanted his father to know that he was now a mature young man who was discovering what life was really about. He was not much enamoured with either Antwerp or Brussels, in which he spent some boring days while Pisarev was engaged on business. But Ostend delighted him. He spent three days there. 'I love the sea terribly, especially when it roars. . . . I have bathed very industriously. Men and women bathe together in the open sea,' he added, providing further evidence for his father that his education in the ways of the world was being successfully pursued.[8]

London was the next stop. He arrived there by 8 August, and stayed about a week, visiting Westminster Abbey, the Houses of Parliament, and paying two visits to the Crystal Palace ('the building is certainly magnificent, but the interior is somehow too motley').[9] On one of these visits he heard Handel's Hallelujah Chorus performed by a choir of 'several thousand voices', and was overwhelmed by the effect. He was equally in danger of being overcome by the stuffiness of the Thames tunnel, but was enthralled by the Cremorne Gardens ('I've never seen

[6] *TLP5*, p. 64; *TZC1*, p. 141; *TPB*, p. 5.   [7] *TLP5*, p. 66; *TPB*, p. 7 (partial).
[8] *TLP5*, p. 67; *TPB*, p. 8.   [9] *TLP5*, p. 67; *TPB*, p. 8.

anything like it. When you go in it's like something enchanted').[10] He was less impressed by Patti when he attended one of her concerts, though later he was to be among her most fervent admirers. 'London is very interesting,' he concluded, 'but it makes a certain gloomy impression on my soul. The sun is never seen; it rains all the time. The *food* is very much to my taste. It's simple, even unsubtle, but liberal in quantity, and tasty.'[11]

It was to Paris, however, that he looked forward most eagerly, and when he arrived there on 14 August he was not disappointed. Although Pisarev was paying Tchaikovsky's expenses, his father had also contributed some pocket money, and he was therefore anxious that Ilya should know that this trip abroad was providing some gain in professional matters as well as in pleasure:

> In general life in Paris is extremely pleasant. There you may do everything you like: the only thing that's impossible is to be bored. Get up and out on to the boulevards – and already you're gay. . . . When at home we play on a very tolerable piano. . . . We provide ourselves with many generally inexpensive pleasures, but we do not forget to visit also the places of the law. I'll tell you the details by word of mouth. We go to the theatre almost every day, and we've been to the opera twice (*Trovatore* and *Les Huguenots*). Of course both the performances and the theatres themselves are much inferior to those in St Petersburg, but the production is markedly good and [so are] many of the ensembles. . . . In a week I shall go and stop with Lidiya Olkhovskaya [who was staying at a resort in Normandy], and when there I'll go bathing. I don't know what will happen after this: in any case, I shall be back at the beginning of October.[12]

What exactly happened during the latter half of this excursion to the West remains a mystery. Two things are certain, however: first, that Tchaikovsky had contracted a debt of about 300 roubles to Pisarev, and second, that this adventure upon which he had embarked with such excitement, ended disastrously. His relationship with Pisarev had quickly become uneasy, and finally they had quarrelled and parted. Why is not known, but since his account to Sasha of the breach is as secretive as it is outraged, one can only wonder whether Pisarev had made some homosexual advances to Tchaikovsky which had repelled the latter. If so, it lends some support to the view that Tchaikovsky's homosexuality

[10] *TLP*5, p. 68; *TPB*, p. 8.
[11] *TLP*5, p. 68; *TZC*1, p. 142 (partial); *TPB*, p. 8.
[12] *TLP*5, pp. 68–9; *TZC*1, p. 142 (partial); *TPB*, p. 9.

was not yet very positive. Certainly when he returned to Russia at the beginning of October he was alone, and thoroughly disenchanted with the expedition, as his letter of 4 November to Sasha makes amply clear. The whole document is a graphic revelation of his state of mind:

What is there to tell you about my journey abroad? It's better not to talk about it. If ever I committed any colossal folly in my life then this journey is it. You remember Pisarev? Imagine that beneath that mask of *bonhomie*, from which I took him to be an unpolished but worthy gentleman, there are hidden the most vile qualities of mind. Up till then I had not suspected that such incredibly base persons existed on this earth. Now you will have no difficulty in appreciating what it was like for me to spend three months[13] tied inseparably to such a pleasant associate. Add to this that I spent more money than I ought, that I got nothing useful out of the journey – and you'll agree that I am a fool. . . . Don't conclude from this that it's bad abroad, or that a journey is a bore. Quite the opposite – but it needs complete freedom of action, sufficient money, and some reasonable cause for going. . . . You won't believe how profoundly happy I was when I arrived back in St Petersburg. I admit I feel a great weakness for the Russian capital. What can I do about it? I have become too inured to it. Everything that's dear to my heart is in St Petersburg, and outside it life is simply impossible for me. Moreover, when my pocket isn't too empty, my morale is high: and at first after my return I had roubles at my disposal. You know my weakness? When I have money in my pocket I sacrifice it all to pleasure. I know it's shameful, it's foolish. Strictly speaking I cannot have any money for pleasure; there are exorbitant debts that demand repayment, there is need of the most basic essentials – but I (again through weakness) take account of none of these, and enjoy myself. Such is my character. How shall I end up? What does the future promise for me? It's terrible to think of it. I know that sooner or later (but, more likely, sooner) I shan't have the strength to cope with the hard side of life, and I shall be broken into smithereens. But until that happens I am enjoying life as best I can, and sacrificing all to pleasure. On the other hand, the last two weeks have been unpleasant in every way. At work it's gone extremely badly, my roubles have long since evaporated – unhappiness *in love*. But all this is nonsense: the time will come when things will be cheerful again. Sometimes I even weep, and afterwards I walk along the Nevsky [Prospect], return home on foot – and already I've been

[13] This is not strictly true, since Tchaikovsky and Pisarev parted well before the end of the trip.

diverted. . . . I have begun studying thorough-bass, and it's going extremely well. Who knows, perhaps in three years you'll be hearing my operas and singing my arias.[14]

Immediately on his return Tchaikovsky had at last set about laying the foundations of a technique in composition. Six weeks later he confided in Sasha again:

I wrote to you, I believe, that I'd begun studying musical theory – and very successfully. You'll agree that, with my tolerable talent (I hope you won't take this as boasting), I should be ill-advised not to try my luck in this field. The only thing I fear is lack of will power: perhaps laziness will claim her own, and I shan't hold out. However, if the opposite happens, then I promise I'll become *something*. You know that I have the strength and the ability – but I'm afflicted with that illness called 'Oblomovism',[15] and if I don't conquer it, then of course I could easily go under. Fortunately time has not yet run out.[16]

On his return from Paris Tchaikovsky had resumed work at the Ministry, and was soon applying himself with notable zeal, for he had his eye on a position he knew would become vacant, and was hoping that promotion and thus an increase in salary – and more free time – would come his way. His social round had also been renewed (Modest especially recalled him performing in domestic theatricals at this period), but he was now curtailing some of his former activities for, as he further confided to Sasha, his life was acquiring a new sense of purpose: 'I don't go to the theatre as often as before. Two evenings a week I'm occupied with lessons; on Fridays I go alternately to Piccioli's and [Mariya] Bonnet's. On Sundays I'm at home; on Mondays I almost always play piano, eight hands, at someone's house.'[17] It is probable that this last activity was providing a very necessary ingredient of his musical education, for not only did he need to develop a proper compositional technique; he also had to make up his lamentably deficient knowledge of certain basic areas of musical literature. He was well acquainted with the current operatic repertoire, but of symphonic music he was virtually ignorant. Modest stated that at this time he knew absolutely no Schumann, and couldn't even number the Beethoven

---

[14] *TLP*5, pp. 69–70; *TZC*1, pp. 144–5; *TPB*, pp. 10–11.
[15] Oblomov, the central character of Goncharov's novel of the same name, epitomised the negative side of the Russian character, its indolence and ineffectiveness.
[16] *TLP*5, pp. 71–2; *TZC*1, p. 147; *TPB*, p. 12.
[17] *TLP*5, p. 72; *TPB*, p. 12.

symphonies correctly. The monopoly which the Imperial Theatres and the Philharmonic Society held of the capital's musical life ensured that, except for the Sunday concerts at the University, purely orchestral concerts, until the founding of the Russian Musical Society, were confined almost exclusively to four weeks within the period of Lent. In consequence Tchaikovsky, like most musicians of his time, made his first acquaintance with many of the masterpieces of the orchestral repertoire through piano arrangements for one or more performers. Modest confirmed this, adding his own personal recollections of the change wrought in his brother's behaviour by his new, serious preoccupation with music:

> I can attribute to this period two striking discoveries: first, that brother Pyotr and work were two compatible concepts, and second, that besides pleasant and interesting music, there existed also an uncommonly unpleasant and boring kind which was much more important than the former. I remember perfectly my brother's relentless playing for several hours on end, not of operas and the melodious pieces I liked so much, but of certain abominable preludes and fugues which were beyond my comprehension. His persistence in this matter plunged me into as much perplexity, and caused me as much disappointment as his sweating over manuscript paper for long hours which, as I then thought, could have been spent much more pleasantly in chatting or going for a walk. My surprise was boundless when he explained to me that he was 'solving problems'. It seemed strangely absurd to me that such a nice entertainment as music had something in common with hateful mathematics. At the same time I learned that Beethoven was not at all such a bore as I had thought, because his symphonies, which Pyotr began to perform as piano duets with various companions from the courses at the Mikhailovsky Palace, not only pleased me, but one of them, the fifth, straightway delighted me. A change also began to make itself felt in Pyotr Ilich's way of life. Of his social acquaintances he remained staunch only to his old friends, Apukhtin and Adamov. For the rest, he began visiting only those who had some care for music.[18]

The centre of Tchaikovsky's new musical activities was the course organised by the Russian Musical Society (RMS) which had been founded two years earlier. The driving force and provider was the Tsar's German-born aunt, the Grand Duchess Elena; the musical leadership was given by Anton Rubinstein, whose brilliant international career as a

[18] *TZC*1, p. 148.

pianist and distinguished record as a composer ensured that his prodigious musical gifts enjoyed a prestige uncommon at that time for any native-born musician in Russia. Till now the country had had no music school that provided a basic professional training in music, and the new RMS, as well as promoting concerts, aimed to organise classes that would do something to remedy this lack of musical instruction. The Tsar was persuaded to bestow his patronage on the venture, and in November 1859 the inaugural concert was given, with Rubinstein playing one of his own piano concertos. The Society's new classes were held at the Grand Duchess's home, the Mikhailovsky Palace, and the teacher of musical theory was Nikolay Zaremba. It was to this man's guidance that Tchaikovsky had now submitted his talents.

Much odium has attached itself to Zaremba's reputation, especially in consequence of Balakirev's bitter opposition to the musical attitudes he represented, and to Musorgsky's merciless lampooning of him in his song, 'The Peepshow'. Zaremba was a man of sterling, if limited, virtues and glaring deficiencies. Like Tchaikovsky, he had been trained for the law. His personal sympathies were thoroughly Teutonic, and these were consolidated by a course of study in Berlin with Adolph Marx. Zaremba was a fluent teacher, thorough and devoted, and was far from being simply the dry, shrivelled musical intellect and enemy of art that the Russian nationalists represented him to be. He revered Beethoven, especially the last works, but his sympathies had progressed no further than Mendelssohn. Of Berlioz, Schumann – and Glinka – he would admit to knowing nothing. His greatest defect seems to have been a complete lack of any sort of imagination or real musical inventiveness. His composition bible was the textbook of his teacher, Marx, after which he would set his students to study strict counterpoint and the church modes as expounded by Bellermann. Tchaikovsky was driven through these disciplines successively in his first two years with Zaremba. Having no inventiveness, Zaremba was incapable of taking a student's exercise and improving it except by imposing the tramline rules of composition which he seems to have learned to command so thoroughly himself. This inability to work outside set procedures inevitably turned Zaremba into a pedant who subjected his pupils to a severely conservative and rigid course in musical technique. But while it was true that his teachings had little practical relevance to live compositional practice in the 1860s, it is probable that his exacting instruction in certain basic mechanisms of composition was precisely what Tchaikovsky needed at this stage. Later the composer was to rebel against the musical attitudes and practices that Zaremba represented, though he continued to respect him as a man. Yet in one thing he always admitted his debt to this teacher. When he had started at the RMS's classes, he had still to learn a rigorous professional discipline, and Zaremba, quickly spotting his easygoing approach to work, admonished him to apply himself more seriously, the more so since he had undoubted talent. The advice was remarkably fruitful, for it was to this single reproof that Tchaikovsky himself attributed the sedulity and energy which subsequently characterised the way he tackled a major composition.[19]

For the moment the zeal with which he worked Zaremba's exercises was actually exceeded by the diligence he showed at the Ministry. In the urgency of his ambitions for promotion he circumscribed further his personal recreations, even bringing work home in the evenings. It was all in vain. The next vacancy was offered to another, and Modest believed that this was his brother's Rubicon as far as the Ministry was concerned, for after this his energies were directed with increasing resolution into his musical studies, while his application to his official duties became perfunctory. With Nikolay now in the provinces, Ippolit in the navy, and with the departure of the Schobert contingent in 1862, Tchaikovsky was left with only his father and adored twin brothers. Home must have seemed a very quiet place, and the absence of social distractions within the family itself favoured an even more single-minded pursuit of his musical studies. Now that the constriction of the family circle had drawn Tchaikovsky and his father even closer together, Ilya's moral support was probably all the more keenly felt. One thing is certain: the process whereby the civil servant was being transformed into the musician continued quietly but inexorably.

Tchaikovsky's next step towards the musical profession is documented in a letter to Sasha of 22 September 1862. There is no doubt from the tone of the letter, especially when it is compared with the one he had written to her a year before, that he has found a new and unprecedented degree of inner contentment. He is happy in his home life, is discovering afresh the joy of family relationships, writes nothing at all of social trivia and gossip, and reveals a more mature, but by no means ponderous seriousness:

> I now live alone with Papa and, just imagine, I simply don't find this in the least boring. . . . I dine at home every day. . . . In the evening we quite often go to the theatre (the Russian one), or play cards. . . . I make arrangements for dinner, and generally serve as an intermediary between Emilya Konstantinovna [the cook] and Papa, of whom for some reason she is terribly afraid. Recently there has been

[19] According to Kashkin, Rubinstein was responsible for this reproof.

a great number of holidays so that Anatoly, Modest and Alyosha[20] have been at home very often. . . . Tolya [Anatoly] often recalls Kamenka and tells us a lot about you all. According to him everyone has fallen in love with Tanya. I've stolen from Alyosha the picture of you with Tanya, and I very often admire it. Papa was very disturbed when he heard from you that you'd stopped breast-feeding your daughter. . . . I have entered the newly opened Conservatoire, and the course there starts in a day or two. Last year, as you know, I spent a great deal of time on musical theory, and now I am firmly convinced that, sooner or later, I shall exchange my work for music. Don't think that I imagine I'll become a great artist. It's simply that I want to do that to which my calling draws me. Whether I shall be a famous composer or an impoverished teacher, my conscience will be easy – and I shall have no painful right to grumble at fate or people. Of course I shall not finally give up work until I am finally sure that I am an artist and not a civil servant. . . .

This morning I got up unusually early. I was wakened by Tolya and Modya going off to school. Apropos of which, I may say here that my affection for these two beings, and (this is confidential) especially for the former, becomes greater and greater every day. Inwardly I cherish and am terribly proud of this, the best feeling of my heart. In sorrowful moments I have only to think of them, and life becomes dear to me. I shall try my best to replace with my own love their mother's caresses and attentions which they, unfortunately, can neither receive nor remember – and it seems that I am succeeding.[21]

The St Petersburg Conservatoire had been opened on 20 September, only two days before Tchaikovsky wrote to Sasha. It had developed out of the success during the previous two and a half years of the RMS's classes. It was housed in a well-appointed building alongside the river Neva, and the director was Anton Rubinstein. Its staff boasted such eminent performers as the violinist, Henryk Wieniawski, and the pianist, Theodor Leschetizky, the latter to become one of the most famous of all late-nineteenth-century piano teachers, processing a whole generation of performers who achieved international status. The new institution was, indeed, exceedingly well endowed. Zaremba was responsible for composition and Tchaikovsky enrolled at once in his class, placing himself under Cesare Ciardi for flute,[22] and Anton Herke for piano. At

[20] A younger brother of Lev Davïdov, Tchaikovsky's brother-in-law.
[21] *TLP5*, pp. 73–5; *TPB*, pp. 13–14; *TZC1*, pp. 149–50 (the penultimate paragraph only).
[22] Rubinstein had made provision out of his own pocket for twenty students to learn

some time he also briefly studied the organ with the German organist, Heinrich Stiehl. Tchaikovsky was deeply impressed by the instrument in the Petropavlovsky Lutheran church where he had his lessons, and through it he became acquainted with Bach's organ works. Strangely, it never induced him to write a single piece himself for organ.

At the Conservatoire that autumn Tchaikovsky encountered two other young men who were to figure prominently in his future life as a composer. One was a nineteen-year-old violinist, Vasily Bessel, who in 1869 founded a publishing firm which was to print a good many of Tchaikovsky's earlier compositions. Unfortunately the cordiality between the two men was later impaired. The other, whose friendship was to be far more enduring and important, was Herman Laroche. He was five years younger than Tchaikovsky, and for the first fifteen years of his life had remained inseparably tied to his mother who had undertaken virtually his entire education. He was a weakly child, very unsure of himself socially because of his unnaturally restricted upbringing, but of remarkable intellectual endowment. He had a phenomenal memory, and could speak German, French and English. He was composing by the time he was ten, but though he had voraciously devoured Adolph Marx's teachings on composition, he had no formal guidance until 1860, when he began studying with Alexandre Dubuque in Moscow. Through Dubuque he became acquainted with the music of Bach, Haydn and Mozart, using their works as models for his exercises. He then tried his hand at quartet composition. The resulting work was heard by a colleague of Anton Rubinstein, and on the strength of this Laroche was invited to enrol as a student at the St Petersburg Conservatoire.

Tchaikovsky's attraction to this pallid, overprotected youth was immediate and lifelong. Laroche's far wider familiarity with musical literature was of immense value to Tchaikovsky in the broadening of his own base of knowledge, and Laroche became a companion of his leisure hours; above all, he proved to be a most valued supporter and critic (though a very erratic one) of Tchaikovsky's own music. During their student days the two friends met one evening a week to play major works in duet versions illicitly loaned to them by a kindly assistant in a local music shop. In this fashion during their first year of friendship they came to know Beethoven's Ninth Symphony and the whole of

wind instruments so that he could start a students' orchestra. Tchaikovsky studied the flute for two years, making sufficient progress to play in Haydn symphonies, and even to participate in a quartet of four flutes at a soirée attended by Clara Schumann. Rubinstein also provided out of his own pocket the funds necessary to ensure the organ lessons given by Heinrich Stiehl.

Schumann's opera, *Genoveva*, and *Das Paradies und die Peri*, as well as his Third Symphony. It was the last work, together with Rubinstein's Ocean Symphony, that impressed Tchaikovsky most: by contrast *Lohengrin* had no appeal for him, and he judged Wagner's talents much inferior to those of the Russian composer, Alexandr Serov, whose opera, *Judith*, had just received its sensationally successful première in St Petersburg. The benefactor who made these musical riches available to them was Osip Jurgenson, whose brother, Pyotr, was to become the principal publisher of Tchaikovsky's music, and one of his foremost friends.

Enrolment in the Conservatoire marked a further consolidation of the musical element in Tchaikovsky's life, and a corresponding step towards his resignation from government service. The final decision was not taken hastily, or without the knowledge of other close members of the family. His father's unequivocal acceptance of his decision was touchingly documented by Tchaikovsky sixteen years later:

> I cannot recall without tender emotion how my father treated my flight from the Ministry of Justice to the St Petersburg Conservatoire. . . . Although it pained him that I had not fulfilled those hopes which he had placed upon my career in the service, although he could not but grieve, seeing that I was voluntarily impoverishing myself in order to become a musician, yet never in a single word did he make me feel that he was dissatisfied with me. He inquired about my intentions and plans with nothing but the warmest interest, and in every way gave his approval. I am very, very indebted to him.[23]

Brother Nikolay, on the other hand, was firmly against it, telling Tchaikovsky bluntly that there wasn't a hope that he had in him the talent of a Glinka. Tchaikovsky's response was equally firm: 'Perhaps I shall not be compared to Glinka – but you'll see: you'll be proud of your relationship to me.'[24] Nikolay never forgot his brother's look, nor the tone of voice in which these words were uttered. Sasha, too, was apprehensive, and on 27 April 1863 Tchaikovsky wrote to her, again providing eloquent testimony of his resolution:

> I see that you are taking a lively interest in my position, and look with misgiving upon the decisive step I have taken on my life's journey. And so I, too, want to explain to you in detail what I intend to do, and what I hope for. You won't, of course, deny my abilities in music,

[23] *TLP*7, pp. 161–2; *TZC*1, p. 150; *TPM*1, pp. 245–6.
[24] *TZC*1, p. 129; *YDGC*, p. 32.

nor that it's the only thing at which I'm any good. If that is so, then it is clear that I must sacrifice everything to setting in order and developing that which God gave me at birth. To this end I began studying musical theory seriously. So long as this hasn't hindered me from doing my work also, I have remained at the Ministry, but because my [musical] studies are becoming more serious and exacting, I must of course choose one or the other. It's impossible to work conscientiously along with my musical studies. I cannot all my life receive a salary for nothing, nor is this allowed. In consequence there remains only one possibility: to resign from service (the more so, since I can always go back to it). In a word, after long reflection I have decided to put myself on the reserve list, giving up my staff position and its salary. Don't conclude from this that I intend to run up debts or, in order to replace my salary, to solicit money from Papa, whose position now is far from brilliant. Of course, I have little behind me materially – but, firstly, I hope in the coming season to be given a post at the Conservatoire (as an assistant to a professor); secondly, I have already got some teaching for myself next year; and thirdly – and this is the most important – because I have completely renounced social pleasures, elegant attire and suchlike, my expenses have been reduced to an exceedingly small scale. After all this, of course, you'll ask: what shall I be at the end when I've finished learning? I am certain only of one thing: that I shall become a good musician, and that I'll never be without my daily bread. All the professors at the Conservatoire are satisfied with me and say that, with diligence, much may come of me. I do not write all the above boastfully (I don't think this is in my character), but I speak to you openly and without any false modesty. I dream of coming to you for a whole year when I have finished my Conservatoire course to write something big amid the peace and quiet – and then I shall go out to face the trials of the world.[25]

Tchaikovsky's decision was made the more difficult and hazardous by his father's changed circumstances. Because Ilya was finding that his directorial duties at the Technological Institute were becoming too onerous for him as a result of disagreements with the authorities, he resigned during the spring of 1863. Despite the fact that he could now hope for even less financial support from his father, who had only his pension and could offer him no more than bed and board, Tchaikovsky's resolution held, and on 13 May his own resignation took

[25] *TLP*5, p. 77; *TPB*, pp. 14–15; *TZC*1, pp. 156–7.

effect.[26] He was now at last a full-time student of music, poor but contented. 'In a small narrow room . . . having space for only a bed and a writing table, he joyfully began his new, arduous life, and sitting through the night over his musical tasks, was completely happy and serene, being assured that he was now set upon his true course.'[27] Modest was always in danger of romanticising the image of his brother as an artist, but the essential truthfulness of this portrait is beyond doubt.

Having resigned, Ilya took the twins to spend the summer with Sasha at Kamenka. This was a useful way of economising on his household expenses while he paid his debts, and it says much for the unity of the Tchaikovsky family that Zinaida was prepared in the same way to receive him in the spring of 1865, and to keep him a whole year in order to ease his predicament. Left alone in St Petersburg for the summer of 1863, Tchaikovsky accepted Apukhtin's invitation to stay with him and his family at Pavlodar, near Kaluga. Apukhtin, however, became bored with his home life and took himself off to visit friends, leaving his guest to endure as patiently as he could the tedium of the parents' household. Back in St Petersburg in the autumn, Tchaikovsky had the pleasure of becoming acquainted with the mother and sisters of Lev Davïdov, Sasha's husband. The family had come to live in St Petersburg, and Tchaikovsky was enthralled by the old lady, Alexandra, and her memories of Pushkin's visits to the Kamenka estate long before Tchaikovsky's birth. It was said that Pushkin not only wrote his poem, *The Prisoner of the Caucasus*, at Kamenka; on one of his visits, in 1820, the greatest of Russian poets had become involved with the conspirators who, five years later, precipitated the Decembrist uprising. Alexandra's husband had been condemned to penal servitude for his part in the revolt, and she had followed him to Siberia where he served his sentence. On this same visit Pushkin had engaged in an affair with Alexandra's sister-in-law, upon whose young daughter, Adèle, he wrote a poem which later inspired one of Glinka's loveliest songs. Although she was already in her sixties when Tchaikovsky first knew her, Alexandra Davïdova outlived him by two years. He also quickly became acquainted with Elizaveta, the eldest daughter (who had known Gogol as well as Pushkin), and Vera, the youngest. Some members of the family were to entertain hopes during the next two or three years that Tchaikovsky

[26] In fact Tchaikovsky requested what was in effect a transfer to the reserve list, thus shedding all duties and receiving no salary, while leaving the way open for a return to work. In consequence he still had to make formal application each summer for leave to be away from St Petersburg. It was not until the autumn of 1867 that he finally submitted his full resignation.

[27] *TZC*1, p. 159.

would make a match with Vera, who was a particularly committed amateur pianist and singer. Vera also shared these hopes, and her emotional involvement with Tchaikovsky was to cause him a great deal of embarrassment and distress, as we shall see.

Back at the Conservatoire in September 1863, Tchaikovsky enrolled in Zaremba's class on form and Rubinstein's on instrumentation. His studies were already focusing more exclusively on composition, for in January he had been allowed to withdraw from the obligatory piano class.[28] Now that his father had also returned to St Petersburg from Kamenka he was able to take up residence again with him and the twins. Ilya could still only afford to feed him; otherwise Tchaikovsky had to fend for himself, and he did this by giving lessons, partly on musical theory and partly on the piano, a time-consuming occupation since it involved trudging round to the homes of his pupils. It is some sign of Rubinstein's confidence in Tchaikovsky that he helped him to find pupils. The gain from this activity was small – never more than fifty roubles a month, Modest estimated. He had already managed to find some engagements as an accompanist, sharing concerts with, among others, his flute teacher, Ciardi, including one at a soirée of the Grand Duchess Elena. During Lent 1863 he had even accompanied at concerts in the Maryinsky and Bolshoy theatres.

It is not surprising that his personal appearance reflected his changed material circumstances. Gone was the elegant youth of the previous two or three years. His hair was now long, and his clothes the worn-out relics of his life as a dapper young man-about-town. He continued to go to the theatre when he could, but his only regular social outing was on Mondays when he joined a group of artists and men of letters at a friend's home. Here he would sometimes entertain the company by playing Mozart, Beethoven, Schumann and Mendelssohn – but never any of his own works. As yet he had no confidence in the quality of his own creations, and kept them to himself. Indeed, Modest stated that his whole life at the St Petersburg Conservatoire was something on which his brother could never be drawn, though he was always willing enough to talk about his childhood, his days at the School of

---

[28] This class met twice a week at eight o'clock in the morning. Tchaikovsky was already a very accomplished pianist, capable of tackling such a piece as Liszt's paraphrase of the sextet from Donizetti's *Lucia di Lammermoor* 'cleanly, clearly and confidently, although somewhat crudely and coldly', according to Laroche (*TZC*1, p. 165). Laroche added that this was the very opposite of what one might have expected from Tchaikovsky, but attributed this restraint to the composer's dislike of sentimentality. The present author once heard the late Helen Henschel vouch for the coldness of Tchaikovsky's piano playing. Laroche also recorded that Tchaikovsky had a very pleasant baritone voice, singing with marked cleanness and accuracy of intonation.

Jurisprudence, or his later life at the Moscow Conservatoire. The process of becoming a composer was to him a private affair.

Thus for information about Tchaikovsky's studies and activities at the St Petersburg Conservatoire, we have to rely upon the witness of those who knew him, upon what is known of the musical course, and upon those of his works that have survived from this period. According to Adelaida Spasskaya, one of Tchaikovsky's fellow students, he was immensely active out of official classes, aiding Rubinstein in organising musical events, accompanying the choir, and helping with the orchestra, both as a conductor during rehearsals and as timpanist and flautist. Though Tchaikovsky later frequently conducted at concerts, his earliest experiences on the rostrum were a terrible strain, so much so that he felt his head would roll off his shoulders. To forestall this catastrophe, for some years whenever he was conducting he would clutch his chin with his left hand to hold his head in place, while directing with his right. According to Bessel he was always to be found at free moments poring over scores in the stuffy Conservatoire library, thus supplementing the growing knowledge he was able to gain of the operatic and orchestral repertoire from the privilege that Conservatoire students enjoyed of attending opera rehearsals in the Imperial Theatres, and also the Sunday morning rehearsals for the RMS's series of orchestral concerts.

He was singularly fortunate in his principal teacher. As a pianist Anton Rubinstein's reputation was second only to that of Liszt. Only eleven years older than Tchaikovsky, he had received help from the great Hungarian virtuoso during an early tour as an infant prodigy. In 1845 Rubinstein had gone to Berlin for guidance in composition from Siegfried Dehn, the scholar and pedagogue to whom Glinka had turned for similar help twelve years earlier. But whereas Glinka had used his studies with Dehn simply to develop greater reserves of compositional skill which he might then apply independently to opening up a whole new territory of Russian music, Rubinstein was content to exercise his far more limited creative talent within the German styles implicit in Dehn's teachings. Of contemporary composers, Schumann and Mendelssohn were the most potent influences upon his music, which he wrote with a remarkable and often fatal facility. Today, from his numerous operas, oratorios, chamber works, six symphonies, five piano concertos, and mound of songs and piano pieces, only the notorious *Melody in F* keeps his memory alive, at least among young pianists.

In 1848 there began Rubinstein's association with the Grand Duchess Elena which led ultimately to the founding of the St Petersburg Conservatoire. His reputation has been much tarnished by his position at the head of the Russian musical establishment which Balakirev so vigorously opposed, and also by his lack of sympathy with nearly all Tchaikovsky's mature work – a lack of sympathy that contrasts so strongly with his brother Nikolay's moral and practical support of the composer. Yet Anton had great positive qualities. His musical sympathies and interests were enormous. He revered Bach, and was one of the first to include music by the English virginalists in his recitals. He was adamant, too, that his pupils should play from editions that faithfully represented the composer's own intentions. And, however deficient his own music may have been in personality and inventiveness, there is no denying its technical competence. As a teacher he was not only inspiring and exacting, but also a man who could be unstintingly generous with his time and energies in helping others. After occupying himself with his own affairs all day, he would devote from six to nine in the evening to teaching. According to Alexandr Rubets, another of Tchaikovsky's fellow students, Rubinstein would sometimes start a class in composition by reading some verses, and would then forthwith require sketches for a musical setting either for solo voice or chorus, according to the student's preference. The next day the finished composition was to be presented. At other times he would require a student to improvise a rondo, a polonaise, a minuet, or some other form:

> Over and over again he repeated how harmful timidity was, advised that one should not stop over a difficult place, but leave it and press on, accustoming oneself to write in sketches with indications of this or that form – and to avoid resorting to a piano. I remember that on one occasion he came into Zaremba's class, beaming all over, and, taking Zaremba's arm, said: 'Come into my room. I'll acquaint you with one of Tchaikovsky's essays in composition.' Zaremba was on the point of resisting, saying that he'd have to break off his own explanations when he'd only just begun. 'No matter, I'll let you return straight away. Just listen to Tchaikovsky's assignment.' We, fifteen people in all, entered the hall in a merry crowd, where we found only two people, Tchaikovsky and Kross. . . .[29] Tchaikovsky had been told to write music to Zhukovsky's 'Midnight review'. I couldn't bear the thought of this, and observed that Glinka had already written a romance on this. Rubinstein shrugged his shoulders and replied: 'So what? Glinka wrote his own music – and Tchaikovsky his own.' . . . Tchaikovsky's piece turned out to be not a romance but an entire complex picture having nothing in common with Glinka's

---

[29] Gustav Kross, later a professor at the St Petersburg Conservatoire, was the first pianist to perform Tchaikovsky's Piano Concerto No. 1 in Russia.

composition. The accompaniment to each verse was varied and intricate. . . . Tchaikovsky had written the piece quickly in two days.[30]

This evidence is enough to show Rubinstein's enlightened approach to the teaching of composition, and his insistence that the realisation of a musical conception must not be frustrated and allowed to die simply on some small but intractable technical obstacle. It was an approach calculated to foster a full development of the imagination. So, too, this evidence shows how quick he was to perceive and publicly encourage Tchaikovsky's talents – and also to stretch them with hard work, the strain of which, nevertheless, Tchaikovsky's physique seems to have been able to stand. Laroche, too, vouched for the veneration in which Rubinstein was held, and his selfless, if somewhat fearsome relationship with his students. He was the very opposite of Zaremba. Where the latter was eloquent, Rubinstein had mastered none of his many languages; where Zaremba had each word of a lecture carefully prepared and each class systematised, Rubinstein – so Laroche believed – five minutes before each lecture had no idea what he was actually going to say, relying instead on the inspiration of the moment. This lack of preparation, coupled to his unresolved problems with the Russian language, made his presentation disorderly, but his teaching was remarkably stimulating, and he seems to have had a knack for devising ways of reviving flagging interest. Tchaikovsky certainly revered Rubinstein, while remaining alive to his shortcomings, including his severe limitations as a composer and the triviality of many of his compositions. He quickly discovered one of Rubinstein's blind spots in the instrumentation class, for Rubinstein would admit no orchestral complement other than one used by Beethoven, Mendelssohn or Schumann (though he did allow trumpets and horns with valves). His students, on the other hand, had had opportunities to familiarise themselves with the orchestras of Berlioz, Meyerbeer and Liszt. In 1863 Wagner himself had conducted a series of concerts in St Petersburg, including excerpts from his as yet unperformed *Der Ring des Nibelungen*. Tchaikovsky does not appear to have been any more enthusiastic about Wagner's actual music in 1863 than he was thirteen years later when he went to Bayreuth as a music critic to cover the first cycle of Wagner's tetralogy. But Wagner's orchestration was a very different matter, and provided a rich field for dissension with Rubinstein, who dealt conscientiously with the new resources in his lectures, and then expected his students to have nothing to do with them.

So much for Tchaikovsky's principal teachers: what of his musical

[30] *PVC*, p. 412.

tastes? As might be expected, these were idiosyncratic, though they did not exclude some ability, as certain of his later critical writings show, for making perceptive judgements about some types of music. In any case, at this early stage in his career, when his serious preoccupation with his subject had been of only short duration, his musical preferences and antipathies were bound not to have crystallised or stabilised. Certain works – *A Life for the Tsar*, *Don Giovanni*, *Der Freischütz*, Schumann's *Das Paradies und die Peri*, and the great C major Symphony of Schubert – remained lifelong favourites, but other pieces, like Beethoven's Eighth Symphony, were subject to wide fluctuations in his favours. His most violent dislikes at this period were not for particular composers but for certain textures. Laroche heard him declare many times that he would never write a work for piano and orchestra, for piano in combination with stringed instruments (this was his pet hate), or for string quartet or quintet because he could not bear the sound of these media. He even once swore that he would never compose romances or small piano pieces. Yet at the same time he could enthuse about the beauty of the actual music of some piano concerto, or revel in the songs of Schubert, Schumann or Glinka. It was, as Modest neatly put it, a 'platonic' hatred. Besides *A Life for the Tsar*, Tchaikovsky had a passionate admiration for Glinka's incidental music to the drama, *Prince Kholmsky*, and he was delighted with *Ruslan and Lyudmila* when the revival of this opera in 1864 at last afforded him the opportunity (of which he availed himself repeatedly) of judging it properly. Yet his veneration for Glinka did not prevent him later from developing reservations about *Ruslan*.

A year earlier, in 1863, he was able to attend the rehearsals of Serov's new opera, *Judith*, and his admiration for this work was immediate and enduring, more so than his enthusiasm for Serov's next opera, *Rogneda*. Like Tchaikovsky after him, Serov had attended the School of Jurisprudence and then entered the civil service. Fortified by the persuasions of his fellow student and best friend (and, later, worst enemy), Vladimir Stasov, he composed in a dilettante fashion, adoring Beethoven and Meyerbeer, and for a time admiring Glinka. After an unremarkable career that included little that could pass for a serious study of music, he established himself in the 1850s as the first Russian music critic of significance. Hearing *Tannhäuser* in 1858 turned him into a fervent Wagnerian, thus putting him into opposition not only to Stasov (and also the ideals that Balakirev and his group were later to represent) but also to the rival Conservatoire party led by Rubinstein, whose musical sympathies stopped with Mendelssohn and Schumann, and who would have nothing to do with the 'new music' of which Wagner's works were representative. With so few friends the auspices for success were not good for the new opera which Serov now planned to compose for St Petersburg. In the event expectations were confounded, for *Judith* had an immediate triumph, not least with the young Tchaikovsky (his unfavourable comparison of Wagner with Serov has already been noted). It says much for Tchaikovsky's personal impartiality that his musical approval of *Judith* was not shaken by Serov's outspoken hostility to the Conservatoire, to Rubinstein and, by this time, to Glinka, whom Serov now judged far inferior to Verstovsky; nor was he prejudiced by his recognition of Serov's personal foibles and vanity when he met him in person.[31] Whatever the limitations of Serov as a composer, he was for most Russians of the middle and late 1860s the greatest of active native composers (with Rubinstein, of course). Serov, like Rubinstein, had too little individuality to have more than a marginal influence upon Tchaikovsky's own music, though the success of *Rogneda* in St Petersburg was to have a coincidental, but absolutely crucial consequence for Tchaikovsky's own career. Serov was also to be the unwitting posthumous cause of one of Tchaikovsky's finest works.

Other composers who roused Tchaikovsky's interest at this time had far more effect upon him. One such was Berlioz, another Meyerbeer: of the latter's operas, *Le Prophète* above all, though *Les Huguenots*, *Robert le diable* and *Dinorah* also enjoyed Tchaikovsky's favour. Yet the most surprising, and initially the most momentous of his admirations was for the overtures which Henry Litolff had written for two operas by the German composer, Griepenkerl. According to Laroche, these two overtures, *Robespierre* and *Die Girondisten* (especially the latter), together with Meyerbeer's to his brother's play, *Struensee*, were the main agents for arousing Tchaikovsky's lifelong interest in programme music. The influence of Litolff, added Laroche, was far stronger in Tchaikovsky's early overtures (including *Romeo and Juliet*) than that of Liszt, whose *Orfeo* was the only one of his symphonic poems to stir Tchaikovsky's enthusiasm in his Conservatoire years. Laroche rightly considered Liszt's influence upon Tchaikovsky to have been marginal and ephemeral. Only later did Tchaikovsky come to like the Faust Symphony. Nor was he much impressed at this time by Gounod's opera, *Faust*, judging it inferior to Pugni's work on the same subject. Later, however, he pronounced Gounod's work to be a masterpiece.

Three songs appear to be all that has survived from Tchaikovsky's compositions of his pre-Conservatoire period. It is known that at some time during the last four months of 1862 he composed a musical joke for

---

[31] On this occasion at Serov's Dostoyevsky was present, and 'talked a great deal of nonsense about music, like a true author with neither education in music, nor a natural ear for it' (*TZC*1, p. 181).

piano, dedicating it to his new friend, Laroche. The inspiration for this was a choral fantasia by Konstantin Lyadov on the Russian folksong 'Vozle rechki, vozle mostu', which Tchaikovsky also used as the basis of his own piece. This seems to have vanished. Of the songs, 'My genius, my angel, my friend' has already been mentioned. One of the remaining two is 'Zemfira's Song' from Pushkin's poem, *The Gipsies*, a vigorous setting in which Tchaikovsky already displays some capacity for simple but effective tonal colouring. Kündinger had spotted his harmonic flair; certainly the harmonic enterprise shown in the latter half of its first two verses is the most striking feature of 'Zemfira's Song'. The other song was composed on an anonymous Italian verse, 'Mezza notte'. With its lilting $\frac{6}{8}$ pulse it has a direct affinity with Glinka's 'Venetian night' of some thirty years earlier. Though pleasant enough in its commonplace way, there is absolutely nothing in it to mark it down as the work of Tchaikovsky – or, indeed, of any composer in particular. Nevertheless, Tchaikovsky was sufficiently proud of it to make it his first published composition.

From his first year at the Conservatoire there exists a handful of exercises, some for string ensembles, though mostly involving other instruments also. All are equally anonymous in style, and have little or no musical value. Some are crude and clumsy, while others try to do too much within their small dimensions so that the sequence of ideas and the transitions are gauche. Yet some of these student exercises do prophetically reveal a commendable facility for devising neat little decorative counterpoints, especially short running semiquaver passages. Above all, a few confirm Tchaikovsky's considerable harmonic resourcefulness, not only in their liberal use of various seventh chords, but also in their enrichment of the contrapuntal flow with dissonant decoration. Melodically, however, these student exercises are remarkably disappointing, uninventive, and sometimes downright feeble, giving scarcely a hint of the abundant store of splendid, characteristic melody that Tchaikovsky was so soon to command.

Six other compositions are known from this first year of study. Three – an unnamed oratorio, an orchestral piece, *The Romans at the Coliseum*, and some music for the fountain scene in Pushkin's *Boris Godunov* – are lost. The fourth is an incomplete Allegro in F minor for piano from which, in 1867, Tchaikovsky derived *Scherzo* in his Three Piano Pieces (*Souvenir de Hapsal*), Op. 2, and the fifth is a set of nine variations for piano on an indifferent theme in A minor. In this last work it is again Tchaikovsky's harmonic inventiveness that produces the best music, notably in the adagio eighth variation (Ex. 1). The remaining piece is a setting for unaccompanied chorus of an evening prayer, 'At bedtime',

Ex. 1

by Nikolay Ogaryov, whose tastefully sentimental verse stirred Tchaikovsky to a succession of short-breathed phrases, some quite haunting, which accumulate into a composition of genuine appeal. Tchaikovsky himself thought well enough of it to arrange it soon after for chorus and orchestra.

No one examining these early compositions and exercises would suspect for one moment that their creator was anything other than a talented young man who might ultimately turn into a competent musical artisan, nothing more, Then suddenly, without the slightest warning, during the summer vacation of 1864, Tchaikovsky emerged as a real composer, not yet completely assured, of course, nor commanding that full range of technical resource which was to turn him into the most accomplished of nineteenth-century Russian composers, yet already prodigiously endowed, and speaking with a voice unmistakably his own. To call the overture, *The Storm*, his first masterpiece would be an overstatement, but it showed a fabulous talent at which his earlier music had not even hinted. Not until his First Symphony, begun two years later, did he match the quality of this work.

4

STUDENT AND TEACHER:

THE STORM AND FIRST SYMPHONY

ALEXANDR OSTROVSKY WAS the dominating Russian playwright of the second half of the nineteenth century, and *The Storm* (1860), best known in the West through *Kat'a Kabanová*, the opera Janáček based upon it, is reckoned by many to be his masterpiece. The play concerns Katerina, married to a pallid young man dominated by his mother, Marfa Kabanová. Katerina is oppressed by this regime and has fallen secretly in love with another man. When her husband, despite her desperate pleading, goes on a journey to Moscow without her, she succumbs to her passion. After her husband's return a great storm breaks, and her terror of being struck dead drives her to confess her guilt. Hounded by her mother-in-law, she drowns herself in the Volga.

Tchaikovsky quickly fell under the spell of this highly charged drama, and for some time wished to make an opera out of it. By the spring of 1864, however, he had modified his intention,[1] and cast the subject as a brief programme for a concert overture, scribbling it out on a piece of manuscript paper on which he had done an orchestration of two of Schumann's *Symphonic Studies*:

> Introduction: adagio (Katerina's childhood and her whole life up to her marriage), allegro (intimations of the storm); her yearnings for true happiness and love. Allegro appassionato (her spiritual struggle). Sudden change to evening on the bank of the Volga: again a struggle, but coloured by a certain feverish happiness. A foreshadowing of the storm (repetition of the motif after the adagio, and its further development). The storm; a climax of desperate struggle and death.[2]

It had been Tchaikovsky's hope to spend the summer of 1864 with Sasha at Kamenka, but his financial resources would not permit this. In

[1] Modest's statement that his brother's change of plan was due to Kashperov having written an opera on the subject is questionable, since Kashperov's opera was not produced until 1867.

[2] *TZC*1, p. 192; *TLP*5, p. 81; *DTC*, p. 325; *YDGC*, p. 34.

the event he had no reason to complain about the alternative, which was an invitation to the estate of a friend, Prince Alexey Golitsïn, at Trostinets, near Kharkov. Golitsïn provided Tchaikovsky with an enchanting holiday, including a splendid entertainment for his name day on 11 July. In these favourable circumstances, with an abundance of free time, Tchaikovsky was able to press ahead with the large orchestral piece that Rubinstein had prescribed as his vacation exercise, and which Tchaikovsky optimistically hoped would find a place in one of the programmes of the RMS. Thinking that he might satisfy the Conservatoire's requirements and his own wishes at the same time, he decided to make the programme he had drawn from *The Storm* the basis of his piece for Rubinstein. On 5 September, the day before he was due to leave for St Petersburg, Tchaikovsky was struck down with a fever. Being thus forced to delay his return, he sent the completed work to Laroche for conveyance to Rubinstein.

The latter's displeasure might easily have been predicted. A glance at the score, with such illicit things as its cor anglais and harp, would have been enough to rouse Rubinstein's fears, but the offence did not end there, for the composition itself was filled with musical inventions which Rubinstein would never have countenanced in his own work – nor, thus, in that of one of his students. The luckless Laroche vividly recounted the outburst that ensued when, having delivered his friend's piece, he returned a few days later to hear the verdict:

> Never in my life had I received such a dressing-down for my own misdemeanours as this time (I remember it was a beautiful Sunday morning) I had occasion to hear for the sin of another. With unconscious humour Rubinstein posed the question thus: 'If you had dared to bring me such a piece of your own work . . .' – and then proceeded to reprimand *me*, as they say, with all guns blazing! Having completely exhausted all his reserves of anger, the Conservatoire's quick-tempered director saved nothing for the real culprit, so that when Pyotr Ilich arrived several days later and went along in his turn to hear the verdict, he had an exceedingly sweet reception and, for his part, received only a few brief reproofs.[3]

It is possible, of course, that Rubinstein perused the score again, recognised that it had qualities, albeit unpalatable ones, and decided that immoderate censure of the hypersensitive Tchaikovsky might inhibit that development of the imagination upon which he, Rubinstein, set such store.

<hr>

[3] *TZC*1, p. 171.

In the end, though Tchaikovsky contrived to retain clear vestiges of his original programme, he cast *The Storm* as a sonata structure. The folksong, 'Iskhodila mladentsa',[4] which is heard in the introduction, doubtless relates to Katerina, though it scarcely conveys the happy childhood she recalls in Act 1 of Ostrovsky's play. Rather this whole introduction suggests a scene and a person set for tragedy. Marfa Kabanová, the evil genius of the tale, intrudes peremptorily,[5] her music (allegro) centring upon the supertonic seventh chord in its first inversion – a chord for which Tchaikovsky had already shown a strong liking in some of his Conservatoire exercises. The exposition foretells the storm in its first subject, and Katerina's longings form the second, a section composed of two distinct elements as in Tchaikovsky's next orchestral piece on tragic love, *Romeo and Juliet*. In the development her spiritual struggle is depicted in a fugato based on a derivative of the opening phrase of the exposition; this fugato flanks a section in which elements of the storm music are counterpointed to her second-subject material. The evening scene by the Volga is painted in a brief interlude (moderato) before the recapitulation, at the end of which the sudden intrusion of Marfa Kabanová's music ushers in the final tempest and catastrophe.

Tchaikovsky's decision to adjust his original conception to sonata principles, rather than to follow Liszt's practice of allowing the programme to condition the musical structure, supports Modest's and Laroche's belief that the Hungarian's influence was not particularly strong in Tchaikovsky's work. In fact, of all major composers, it is perhaps to Berlioz that Tchaikovsky is most indebted in *The Storm*. Certainly the immensely resourceful variety of colour in the scoring and the judicious use of doublings disclose the French master as Tchaikovsky's mentor far more than Liszt. The creator of *Harold en Italie*, who had introduced his solo-viola hero with the lightest of orchestral supports, would have looked approvingly at the equally delicate accompaniment Tchaikovsky accords his folktune when he plays it for the second time in the introduction. Yet, despite some passages very redolent of Berlioz (and Glinka, too, should perhaps be given some credit for Tchaikovsky's textural clarity), much of *The Storm* has the familiar and individual sound of Tchaikovsky's own mature orchestration. Already he is showing that natural facility, also possessed by Berlioz, of conceiving his ideas directly in terms of orchestral textures

---

[4] Later used by Tchaikovsky as No. 1 of *T50RF*. Musorgsky also employed it as the basis of Marfa's solo near the beginning of Act 3 of *Khovanshchina*.

[5] Allegro, bar 46. Though not in the original programme, Tchaikovsky informed Modest that this passage depicted Marfa Kabanová.

and colours. Liszt, by contrast, had to learn his orchestration with much labour and, to the last, tended to conceive initially in pianistic terms. There was, however, another side to the coin: Tchaikovsky, like Berlioz, had no natural ability to think in piano textures.

To the assured orchestration of *The Storm* is added auxiliary colour from its tonal proclivities. Though the second subject in the exposition reaches the expected dominant, it is recapitulated in the submediant, and the great majority of the other tonal shifts are to the mediant or submediant areas. Even the concluding cadence (G sharp major–E major) is an ultimate assertion of this relationship. This basic feature of the broader tonal strategy is reinforced at a more local level, never more clearly than at the beginning of the wholly admirable second subject (Ex. 2). The string line that from the second bar counterpoints the flute/oboe

Ex. 2

theme already shows Tchaikovsky's gift for creating pathos through poignant, uncloying chromaticism. This passage is better known from its later use, in a less effective string presentation, at the opening and close of the slow movement in Tchaikovsky's First Symphony. So, too, the second limb of the subject, while scarcely exuding the full-breasted languor of love of the corresponding section of *Romeo and Juliet*, nevertheless breathes a tremulous longing.

The Storm is an inconsistent work. The fugato (one place which suggests Liszt's influence) is moderately effective but short-winded, and the whole development lacks the cogency of the same section in *Romeo and Juliet*. On the credit side no passage is better than the first subject (Ex. 3), which employs a variety of harmonic/melodic tensions and

resolutions within each of its diminutive phrases, thus ensuring a restless ebb and flow that vitalises its rigid two-bar symmetries without impairing the urgent momentum. Indeed, the entire exposition, the dark opening which ushers in the piece, and the little interlude by the Volga are beautifully characteristic conceptions, skilfully realised, while the whole work is lucidly designed and free from overstatement and structural prolixity. Yet Tchaikovsky chose never to publish *The Storm*, even in a revised form, nor even to perform it later when he might so easily have done so. His rejection was hardly kind to this, the first and by no means the least attractive of his true musical children.

Tchaikovsky's next session at the Conservatoire passed uneventfully. He was now giving some instruction in the obligatory harmony class, and this helped his financial position. His private teaching and accompanying continued, of course. For the summer of 1865 Rubinstein obtained a commission for him to translate into Russian Gevaert's recent *Traité général d'instrumentation*, which Jurgenson intended to publish. This time Tchaikovsky was able to spend the vacation at Kamenka. The estate had seen hard times and provided few of the luxuries he had enjoyed the previous summer at Trostinets, but it had beautiful surroundings in which he could stroll, and there was an excellent library belonging to Lev's elder brother, Nikolay, the head of the estate (and, Modest asserted, a conservative who was responsible for luring Tchaikovsky away from his mild liberalism – not that the composer was ever very politically minded). Above all there was Sasha, her family, and his twin brothers who had come from St Petersburg with him. In these congenial surroundings he sketched an Overture in C minor, though he did not complete the instrumentation of this until the following January. Before the end of the autumn he had also completed the Overture in F for small orchestra and the String Quartet Movement in B flat which incorporated a folktune he had noted down from the gardeners at Kamenka that summer, and which he subsequently re-used in his *Scherzo à la russe* for piano, written in 1867 and published as his Op. 1, No. 1. One of the tasks that Tchaikovsky had set for himself at Kamenka had been to collect Ukrainian folksongs which he hoped he might use in future compositions, but he was sadly disenchanted by those he heard, for he felt they were artificial and inferior to White Russian melodies. Only this one tune did he feel was worth using.

The Quartet Movement is a pleasant piece, giving impressive evidence of the skill Tchaikovsky was fast acquiring in handling conventional musical mechanisms and building from them a fluent structure. It is generally a better piece than the four-movement Piano Sonata in C sharp minor which also dates from some time in 1865. The linear thought favoured by the quartet texture came naturally to Tchaikovsky, for it encouraged flexibility of phrase and rhythm within a flowing continuum of sound. But as soon as he had to write an extended piece for solo piano, the shade of Schumann at his chunkiest and squarest all too often reared itself, conditioning his thoughts towards inflexible phrases balancing one another in monotonous regularity. Yet, this much said, it must be conceded that the first movement's mechanical phrase symmetries by no means stifle Tchaikovsky's melodic gift. His own personality, if not yet fully formed, may be discerned in the restless and varied ebb and flow as one lyrical phrase succeeds another in the second subject, while the seventy-five or so bars of this section show a formidable ability to organise melody on a large scale. Already the exposition's closing theme, with its long initial note released into a group of lower-pitched crotchets, exemplifies a melodic opening which Tchaikovsky was to use a number of times in the following years (Ex. 4).

Ex. 4

The slow movement is less admirable: it has a certain pallid appeal, though there are some faceless phrases, and a good deal of infelicity in the piano writing. The finale replaces melodic substance with lumpy rhetorical gesture, and the second subject, in its determination not to be imprisoned in four-square periods, veers to the opposite extreme and finally slips into an ambiguity of phrase structure which comes dangerously close to incoherence. Tchaikovsky thought sufficiently well of the scherzo to revive it later as the basis of the third movement in his First Symphony.

The summer finished less pleasantly than it had begun. The journey back to St Petersburg was slow, hair-raising because of unskilled drivers, and hungry. While at Kamenka Tchaikovsky had experienced some eye trouble and this continued when he arrived back in the Russian capital in early September, making it impossible for him to work in the evenings. In addition he was suffering from haemorrhoids. To add to these discomforts there were new financial worries; his father had just left for an extended stay with Zinaida in the Urals, and in consequence Tchaikovsky found himself without a home. In fact, Ilya had just married his third wife, Elizaveta Alexandrova, a widow who had been on the fringe of the Tchaikovsky family since 1862, and with whom the composer was on very good terms. Zinaida, however, had not taken kindly to her new stepmother, and the latter did not accompany her husband on this visit, instead spending the remainder of the year apart from him with her own brother in St Petersburg. Despite his liking for his stepmother, Tchaikovsky had no wish to lodge with her; thus he sought accommodation for himself. His first furnished room proved uncongenial, and after a month he moved in with his aunt, Elizaveta Schobert. Here he encountered two problems: noise which obstructed work, and damp which made him fearful of bringing over his piano, and which brought on all sorts of uncomfortable ailments. Fortunately Apukhtin was vacating his own flat for the last six or seven weeks of the year, and offered it to Tchaikovsky. Among others to whom he had cause to be grateful were Piccioli and his father's new wife, both of whom often invited him to dinner. To his stepmother he was constantly indebted: 'I don't know what I'd have done without her,' he told Sasha.[6] Certainly but for her he would have been in dire trouble when his tailor threatened him with legal action if a bill was not settled.

For a moment the certainty of receiving a monthly salary made Tchaikovsky's former government service seem attractive to him, and one friend seriously offered to obtain for him a vacant inspectorship of fresh foodstuffs. 'To the great good fortune of the consumers of these foodstuffs – and of the composer himself – the matter got no further than being talked about,' commented Modest drily.[7] His stepmother made arrangements that satisfied the importunate creditor, and Tchaikovsky's prospects for the future were shortly to be brightened by the offer of a post which he might take up when his Conservatoire course was finished at the end of the year. Nikolay Rubinstein, Anton's brother, invited him to become the teacher of musical theory in the classes run by the Moscow branch of the RMS, of which Nikolay was director. Though the remuneration was pitiful – only fifty roubles a month – Tchaikovsky decided to accept the appointment. This offer provided great moral encouragement. So, too, did Anton's general approval of his translation

[6] *TLP5*, p. 86; *TPB*, p. 19.   [7] *TZC*1, p. 199.

of Gevaert (into which Tchaikovsky had quietly slipped some examples of Glinka's scoring). Above all Tchaikovsky was delighted to hear that the first-ever public performance of one of his own works had been conducted by none other than Johann Strauss the younger, the 'waltz king' himself, at a concert in the Pavlovsk Park. The work was Tchaikovsky's *Characteristic Dances*, which had been completed by the preceding spring. Later he used them as the *Dances of the Hay Maidens* in his opera, *The Voyevoda*. It seems very strange that Tchaikovsky should have been ignorant of this impending première, but he saw the advertisement of the concert (which took place on 11 September) too late to be able to attend. Laroche was there, however, and reported favourably.

Other performances of Tchaikovsky's works occurred before the year was out, and it was these events above all which compensated for the problems and uncertainties in his daily life, and provided some assurance that there was a future for him in music. On 12 November his String Quartet Movement[8] in B flat was played by a quartet of his fellow students (the violist was Bessel), and exactly a fortnight later he himself directed his Overture in F at another Conservatoire concert. This was the first time he had appeared before any sort of audience as a conductor, and the nervous suffering he endured has already been recorded.

Meanwhile, on 24 October, he had been set the task of writing a cantata on Schiller's 'An die Freude' as his graduation exercise. With the finale of Beethoven's Ninth Symphony before him, Tchaikovsky must have felt, to say the least, uneasy; in any case, it was a formidable task to complete in little more than two months, and November and December had to be largely devoted to this. The public examination, which incorporated a performance of the cantata, took place on 10 January 1866. Unable to face the ordeal of public scrutiny, Tchaikovsky absented himself, to the intense and reasonable annoyance of Rubinstein, who seriously considered withholding the diploma until Tchaikovsky had fulfilled what the regulations required. However, the director relented, the cantata was performed in the composer's absence, and the truant received his diploma together with a silver medal. The final report on his abilities and achievements described him as excellent in the theory of composition and instrumentation, good at orchestration, extremely good as a pianist, and satisfactory as a conductor.

Of the four substantial pieces Tchaikovsky composed during his last

---

[8] There is no evidence of the existence of other movements, though it is possible the work was a complete quartet of which three movements were subsequently lost or destroyed.

six months at the Conservatoire, the graduation cantata was the most ambitious. No work of his excited more extremes of critical opinion than this piece, though it should be added that Laroche's overwhelming endorsement of it was the *only* positive approval it gained from anyone. '*This cantata is the greatest musical event in Russia since* Judith [by Serov]. It is immeasurably higher, both in inspiration and craftsmanship, than *Rogneda*,' he cried. '. . . *You are the greatest musical talent in present-day Russia*. More powerful and original than Balakirev, more lofty and creative than Serov, immeasurably more cultured than Rimsky-Korsakov, *I see in you the greatest – or, rather, the only hope for our musical future*.'[9] To set against this effusion were dislike from Rubinstein, disappointment from Serov, and a blistering verdict which was to come from César Cui, the spokesman of the Balakirev group:

> The Conservatoire composer, Mr Tchaikovsky, is utterly feeble. It's true that his composition, a cantata, was written under the most unfavourable circumstances: to order, to a deadline, on a given subject, and with adherence to well-known forms. But all the same, if he had any gift, then at least somewhere or other it would have broken through the fetters of the Conservatoire. To avoid saying much about Mr Tchaikovsky, I will say only that Messrs Reinthaler and Volkmann would rejoice unutterably at his cantata, and would exclaim ecstatically: 'Our numbers have been increased!'[10]

To be fair to Laroche, his enthusing over Tchaikovsky's cantata was occasioned more by the promise it held for its composer's future than by its intrinsic merits. Nor was Cui the most balanced or open-minded of critics. Yet for once his merciless arrow had flown close to the mark. Tchaikovsky planned his cantata in six movements, with a careful tonal balance in the whole conception, and an exploitation of some striking key changes between movements. Within movements there are frequent abrupt tonal shifts which are one of the main agents (but sometimes, alas, the only one) for giving the music some forward movement. Though there is nothing in the opening prelude that would immediately suggest Tchaikovsky as the composer, it starts not unpromisingly; but as the volume of sound is made to grow, the poverty of the noble vein Tchaikovsky proposes to mine swiftly becomes all too apparent. Trite harmonies, loudly delivered as support to platitudinous melodic phrases, debase the epic into bombast, and this degeneration is confirmed by the interminable first chorus which, devoid of any melodic

---

[9] *TZC*1, p. 205; *DTC*, pp. 277–8.
[10] *TZC*1, p. 204; *DTC*, p. 278 (partial).

interest or rhythmic variety, hymns 'joy' in singularly dispiriting terms. When treating solo voices Tchaikovsky, like Glinka, could readily assume a watery Italianate manner and engage in note-spinning to order – an ability which is paraded in the ensuing quartet. The chorus and bass solo of the fifth movement, with its exploitation of a more dissonant harmonic resource, is on a slightly higher level, but the only passage of real interest in the whole cantata is the unaccompanied choral conclusion to the quartet (No. 3), where the lines

> If any has not known these blessings,
> Let him silently slip away from us, weeping

prompted Tchaikovsky to shed the stock gesture and exploit a textural variety and plangent harmonic manner which show that a real composer is lurking within this otherwise dreary musical verbiage (Ex. 5). But this is merely a brief respite, and the last movement, with its passages of obligatory fugal texture, finally routs any attempt by the truly creative Tchaikovsky to replace the aspiring diplomate, intent upon displaying the attitudes and techniques that will gain the approval of those who have his final award in their gift.

Ex. 5

[If any has not known these blessings, let him silently slip away from us, weeping.]

If the Overture in F is not a strong work, at least it may be relieved of the charge of pretentiousness. It won sufficient approval from Anton Rubinstein to gain a performance by the Conservatoire orchestra on 26 November 1865. It fared better than its companion in C minor upon which Tchaikovsky had worked at Kamenka and which he scored during the month after his graduation. Despite the failure of *The Storm* with Rubinstein (and with Laroche, who called it 'a museum of anti-musical curiosities'[11]), Tchaikovsky was not going to waste this earlier piece entirely, and rescored (and partially rewrote) the introduction, leaving it in the same key but prefacing it with twenty-seven new bars based upon the same material and starting in C minor. The following allegro vivo was completely new. The completed overture found favour with no one except Laroche, being rejected by Nikolay Rubinstein, by his brother Anton, and by Konstantin Lyadov, director of the Imperial Russian Opera in St Petersburg. While this overture, deployed as a conventional sonata structure, lacks that individuality and distinctiveness of invention which the inspiration of Ostrovsky's play had drawn from Tchaikovsky in *The Storm*, this unanimous verdict was less than just. Tchaikovsky's abundant, if scarcely first-rate invention keeps the piece moving admirably, the themes of the second subject do have some very real character, and the development opens excellently, even though later it has some stretches of mechanical contrapuntalism. Even so, it is a great improvement on that of the Piano Sonata. Later Tchaikovsky wrote across the title-page of his manuscript: 'Overture, written in Moscow in January 1866, and performed nowhere (a strange abomination).' The concluding ejaculation plainly referred not to the overture's failure to gain performance, but to its quality. It is too harsh a judgement. In any case, Tchaikovsky demonstrated that he did not despise it completely, for he freely plundered it for material to go into his opera, *The Voyevoda*. At the end there occurs a cadential tonic/flattened submediant phrase over a four-note whole-tone bass (Ex. 6) which was transplanted essentially unchanged into the finale of the Second Symphony.

Ex. 6

Nikolay Rubinstein looked more favourably upon the Overture in F, however, and agreed to conduct it at a concert of the Moscow branch of the RMS on 16 March 1866. Nevertheless, he saw some of the work's

---

[11] *TZC*1, p. 205. Laroche had little liking for anything that savoured of programme music.

more blatant shortcomings, and insisted on the composer rewriting it for this performance. Tchaikovsky revised the scoring throughout, making it more effective by ironing out some of the practical problems, and increasing its weight by thickening out the sound (his original orchestra had been a small one, incorporating only one trumpet and one horn; now he used two trumpets, four horns and three trombones). Far more important, however, was his decision to rewrite completely some of the weaker passages, and to make the whole overture a far more substantial piece. Thus he blew up the introduction to four times its original size, replaced the transition and codetta of the exposition, vastly expanded and rewrote the climax of the development, and interjected a brief recollection of the introduction before passing to the recapitulation. The latter acquired an expanded transition, and the whole piece was given a huge and completely new coda, introduced by a fugato. There is no doubt that the second version of the overture is better and more effective than the first, and it scored a great success, eliciting warm and unanimous applause. 'Even more flattering to my self-esteem,' Tchaikovsky wrote to his brother, Anatoly, two days after the performance,

> was the ovation accorded me at the supper which Rubinstein gave after the concert. I was the last to arrive, and when I entered the room exceedingly long applause rang out, during which I bowed very clumsily in all directions, and blushed. At supper, after the toast to Rubinstein, he himself proposed a toast to me – again there was an ovation. I am writing all this to you in such detail because this was virtually my first public success, and therefore very agreeable to me (one more detail: at the rehearsal the players applauded me). I will not conceal that this circumstance has greatly increased the charm of Moscow in my eyes.[12]

Considering that Tchaikovsky was a very new composer just out of the Conservatoire, the success of this work is not surprising, nor undeserved. Yet, even in its revised version, it is an inferior piece to the Overture in C minor, far weaker in its thematic material and hollower in development. Good craftsmanship is simply not enough, and the Overture in F remains, like all Tchaikovsky's other compositions written so far – except, of course, for *The Storm* – of little more than documentary interest.

The Moscow branch of the RMS, within which Tchaikovsky was now to teach, had been founded in 1860 by Nikolay Rubinstein. Like its

---

[12] *TLP*5, p. 104; *TZC*1, p. 237; *DTC*, pp. 327–8; *TPB*, p. 30.

model in St Petersburg, it prospered, and in 1866 became a fully fledged conservatoire of music. Tchaikovsky had not been Nikolay's first choice as teacher of musical theory: that had been the far more illustrious Serov. However, the overwhelming success of *Rogneda* in November 1865[13] had made Serov decide to withdraw his acceptance of the post, for he could see better reasons for remaining in St Petersburg. Nikolay then asked his brother to suggest an alternative candidate from among his own students, and Anton had proposed Tchaikovsky. In addition, the critic Nikolay Kashkin, one of Nikolay's Moscow colleagues, had heard a good deal about Tchaikovsky from Laroche and had suggested the former to his director. Thus the offer had been made and accepted. Having finished his course in St Petersburg and received his award, Tchaikovsky wasted no time in setting out for Moscow, where he arrived on 18 January. Before leaving he endeavoured to persuade Anton Rubinstein to include his graduation cantata in one of the concerts of the RMS in St Petersburg, but his former teacher refused unless radical revisions were made. Persuaded by Laroche (in the letter which included the flattering assessment, already quoted, of the work's significance), Tchaikovsky decided not to concur with Rubinstein's demands, and the cantata was never heard again.

Tchaikovsky began 1866 in a very unsettled emotional state. The labour of completing his graduation cantata, and the unavoidable strain associated with the final examination, had taken a terrible toll of his nerves. Not only depression, but 'hatred of the human race' afflicted him, so he told Sasha,[14] and the move to Moscow was beneficial to his mental condition. Yet separation from his friends and family, especially the twins, was a severe wrench. Not surprisingly, as during the painful two years in the preparatory class at the School of Jurisprudence, letters started flowing from his pen. Partly they chronicle the details and personalities of his new existence, but they are also expressions of longing and love for those from whom he is separated. He is as concerned as ever over the twins' welfare, exhorting Modest to work harder (counsel that was to be constantly reiterated during the next few years), and dispensing at length simple, but very sound advice to Anatoly, who worked hard but was having an adolescent's self-doubts about his own significance and usefulness. When he asks for something like a diary of their school life, one suspects it is to provide a means of keeping an eye on them as much as a medium through which he can share vicariously in their daily lives.

[13] Modest stated that the invitation to his brother had come in September. In this he was clearly mistaken, for he also says that it was the success of *Rogneda* that made Serov withdraw and thus open the way for Tchaikovsky.

[14] *TLP*5, p. 93; *TPB*, p. 24.

The swiftness of the change to Moscow made it all at first a little unreal. 'It still seems that I have landed here somehow by accident,' he wrote to his stepmother nine days after his arrival.[15] If he still felt that his integration into the new environment had scarcely begun, this was no fault of Nikolay Rubinstein, who had immediately taken his new colleague under his wing, and within twenty-four hours installed him in his own home. 'I'm living at Rubinstein's,' Tchaikovsky informed the twins after four days in Moscow:

He's a very kind and sympathetic man, without any of that certain inaccessibility of his brother – but then, on the other hand, he cannot match him as an artist. I occupy a small room alongside his bedroom and, to tell the truth, in the evenings when we go to bed at the same time (which, however, it seems will happen very rarely), I feel inhibited: I'm afraid that the scratching of my pen will hinder him from sleeping (we are separated by a thin partition) – and, meanwhile, I'm frightfully busy. I scarcely go out, and Rubinstein, who lives a rather disorderly life, cannot stop wondering at my diligence. . . . So far I've hardly got to know anyone, but I've already become quite intimate with a certain Kashkin, a friend of Laroche, and a very good musician. One evening Rubinstein dragged me almost by force to some people called Tarnovsky [Konstantin and Elizaveta] who, however, were very nice. . . . I have some very, very melancholy moments, but generally I feel an irresistible thirst for work, and this is a great comfort. I have almost orchestrated the larger part of my summer overture [in C minor], and to my horror it's come out a lot longer than I had ever anticipated.[16]

Rubinstein had already taken Tchaikovsky to the theatre, where the level of performance roused him to enthusiasm, and to the opera which he judged to be 'very bad'. He had also heard a concert conducted by Rubinstein himself. The orchestra he considered good, the choir magnificent, but he was not much impressed by his new director's gifts as a conductor, and even less by the concert Rubinstein conducted a week later: 'bad' was Tchaikovsky's blunt verdict to Modest. 'In general he's an amazingly nice man – only I don't understand how he's come to earn his great authority as a musician here. As a musician he's very ordinary; he can't be compared with his brother.'[17] Nor in general was Tchaikovsky much impressed by his new colleagues in Moscow, rating them (with a few exceptions) lower than their counterparts at the St

[15] *TLP*5, p. 95; *TPB*, p. 23.   [16] *TZC*1, p. 222; *TLP*5, p. 91; *TPB*, pp. 21–2.
[17] *TZC*1, p. 231; *TLP*5, p. 97; *TPB*, p. 25.

Petersburg Conservatoire. Later, however, he was to revise radically his unfavourable impression of Rubinstein.

Tchaikovsky delivered his first lecture on 25 January ('I was terribly flustered, but it went off all right,' he informed Anatoly).[18] His regular classes were to be held twice a week, on Tuesdays and Fridays at eleven o'clock. First he had to assess the musical abilities of those who wanted to enrol, many of whom turned out to be young ladies. Yet he seems quickly to have mastered his nerves, and to have achieved an easy relationship with his fair pupils, despite his belief that Muscovites were uncertain of temper. 'My classes are going very successfully,' he could report a fortnight later, 'and already I'm enjoying an unusually sympathetic relationship with the Moscow ladies whom I teach, and who are in general distinguished by being passionate and excitable. . . . Little by little my shyness has passed completely.'[19] Though as yet he had not acquired many friends, those people he had met had for the most part proved amiable. He had discovered Dickens, too, for Rubinstein had gained him access to the Commercial Club which had an excellent library. 'I am laughing wholeheartedly over Dickens's *Pickwick Papers*. There's no one to observe me, and sometimes the thought that no one hears me laughing makes me enjoy myself all the more. I advise you to read this book,' he counselled the twins. 'If you find satisfaction in reading fiction, then at least you should choose such writers as Dickens. He has much in common with Gogol – the same directness and truthfulness in his humour, the same ability to depict a whole character through a couple of its tiniest traits – although he hasn't Gogol's depth.'[20] His relaxed delight in the world of Dickens suggests that his frame of mind was now more equable than it had been a few weeks earlier.

January 1866 was a crucial month in Tchaikovsky's life, not only because it saw the beginning of his career as a professional musician, but because during these four weeks he met for the first time four men who were to become lifelong friends, and of profound importance in his professional life. Although all four were already leading figures in Moscow's musical life, none was more than five years older than Tchaikovsky. The one with whom he most swiftly achieved a close relationship was the 'certain Kashkin'. Nikolay Kashkin, the son of a Voronezh bookseller, was a self-taught musician who had been giving piano lessons himself by the time he was thirteen. In 1860 he had come to Moscow and studied the piano with Dubuque. At this time he had met

[18] *TZC*1, p. 228; *TLP*5, p. 92; *TPB*, p. 22.
[19] *TZC*1, p. 232; *TLP*5, p. 98; *TPB*, pp. 26–7.
[20] *TZC*1, pp. 231–2; *TLP*5, p. 98; *TPB*, p. 26.

the fifteen-year-old Laroche, and it was largely due to Kashkin that Laroche had built up that broad knowledge of the musical repertoire which was so valuable to Tchaikovsky after they had met in St Petersburg two years later. Kashkin taught both the piano and musical theory for the Moscow classes of the RMS, and was subsequently a professor at the Conservatoire for thirty years. Yet he is best remembered today as a music critic. His first article was published in 1862, his last in 1918, two years before his death. Kashkin was a remarkably kind and sympathetic man, and the friendship between him and Tchaikovsky was instantaneous. The St Petersburg expatriate had cause to be grateful for the hospitality quickly offered by Kashkin and his new wife, and for the wise advice in all matters, musical and non-musical, for which the critic was noted. Kashkin's recollections of Tchaikovsky, published three years after the composer's death, are very valuable, though his memory was not infallible.

In his role as critic Kashkin was to do valuable service for Tchaikovsky's cause, but this by no means matched that afforded by Nikolay Rubinstein who, both as a musician and, even more, as a friend, had an influence upon Tchaikovsky's career as great as that of any man. Though some said that his natural talent for music was greater than that of his brother Anton, Nikolay had turned away from his earlier musical studies to become a student in the Law Faculty of Moscow University. His brief career in the office of the Moscow Governor-General seems to have been no more distinguished than that of Tchaikovsky in the St Petersburg Ministry of Justice. In fact Nikolay never actually resigned his civil service rank, though his period of active service was very short. So, too, was his marriage; wed in 1855, he and his wife endured no more than two years of each other's company. Piano pupils provided his main source of income, and his reputation as a teacher in Moscow quickly assured him a very comfortable existence. An inveterate gambler, and devoted to nocturnal carousings, it was only after the founding of the Moscow branch of the RMS in 1860 that the twenty-five-year-old youth began to display his full gifts. He proved himself efficient and energetic, now revealing great talents as a conductor, as well as blossoming more fully as a pianist. Yet somehow he managed to find time to sustain his endlessly active social life (his wide connections in all sections of Moscow society were immensely beneficial to his new undertaking), and also to indulge his passion for gambling at the English Club, and for drinking. Despite his social success and his taste for the less lofty pleasures of this world, he remained in musical matters an uncompromising idealist, unsparing of his own time and resources in helping other musicians and fostering the concert life of Moscow. No one had more cause to be grateful for this than Tchaikovsky.

Rubinstein's 'right hand', as Laroche called him, was Konstantin Albrecht,[21] whose father had conducted the first performance of *Ruslan and Lyudmila* in 1842. Of German extraction, Albrecht was the very opposite of Rubinstein. A man of retiring personality, he was equally indefatigable in his administrative work for the Conservatoire, but kept his services to it very much to himself, and in his private life had few friends. However, besides being an excellent cellist, he was a much sought-after chorus master in Moscow's diverse educational circles. His talents for composition were greatly admired by Tchaikovsky, though the potential of these was never fully realised, partly because of his endless work for the Conservatoire but also because of an evident incapacity (shared, alas, by a number of far more gifted Russian composers) to apply himself to the prolonged labour of writing a large-scale piece. Albrecht's tastes were individual, to say the least. He had a childlike enthusiasm for things mechanical, and a talent for inventing devices of absolutely no practical use. His other two passions were geology and entomology. Each summer he collected butterflies, and had built up quite an impressive collection. In political matters his opinions were ultra-conservative; in musical matters he was as radical as anyone in Moscow, and was devoted to Wagner. Yet even here he was inconsistent, for later he was to complain that the new Russian school of composers had 'gone too far'. Tchaikovsky became one of Albrecht's small circle of friends, being attracted to him both by his kindness and devotion to those who got to know him and also by his particular brand of linguistic humour, which often arose involuntarily from his inability, despite having lived in Russia almost all his life, to master Russian verbs. When short of funds, it was to Albrecht that Tchaikovsky frequently turned for a loan.

Finally there was Pyotr Jurgenson, for whom Tchaikovsky had already made his translation of Gevaert, and who was the younger brother of the St Petersburg Jurgenson who had supplied copies of piano duets to Tchaikovsky and Laroche. In 1861 Pyotr Jurgenson, despite very limited financial resources, had started his own music publishing firm in Moscow. With constant help from Nikolay Rubinstein, he had by 1866 set the enterprise on a secure foundation, and was, in the early days of the Conservatoire, able in his turn to aid Rubinstein with his business expertise. Something of an idealist as well as a businessman, Jurgenson declined to publish light music, aiming to make available to Russians the finest of the Western classics in reasonably priced editions. He was to nineteenth-century Russia what Alfred Novello was to England. He was also anxious to promote the

---

[21] Originally called Karl, he changed his name to Konstantin when he embraced Orthodoxy.

compositions of the best young Russian composers, among whom he quickly placed Tchaikovsky. Jurgenson was to be his main publisher (and Tchaikovsky Jurgenson's main composer), a firm friend, and a practical counsellor in his private affairs.

All four of these men will figure prominently in the following pages. Of the others whom Tchaikovsky met at this time in Moscow, the one whom he must have been especially delighted to know was Alexandr Ostrovsky. In 1865 Ostrovsky and Nikolay Rubinstein, together with Prince Vladimir Odoyevsky, an older man of wide cultural interests and skills who had played a significant role in Glinka's creative life, had founded an Artistic Club which became the central meeting place for all types of people active or interested in the arts. Tchaikovsky's introduction to Ostrovsky was accomplished at one of the two meetings of the Club he attended during January. Ostrovsky was soon to become one of his most tireless companions at evening card parties. Tchaikovsky's favourite at this time was eralash, a game similar to whist, in which he could prove an infuriating partner through his inability to concentrate.

Having quickly installed Tchaikovsky under his own roof, Rubinstein set about processing him for his new role in Moscow's life. He introduced him to as many people as he could persuade Tchaikovsky to meet, dragged him off to masquerades (which he hated) and to the theatre. Rubinstein was concerned, too, for Tchaikovsky's personal appearance, for the latter had made his entrance to Moscow dressed in a very aged coonskin coat given him by Apukhtin, who had used it for country outings, and which set the standard for the rest of Tchaikovsky's attire. 'All my first month's salary will go on new clothes. Rubinstein requires me to buy these, saying that my present ones are not decent enough for a professor of musical theory,' the composer lamented to Anatoly.[22] He 'looks after me like a nurse,' Tchaikovsky wrote to the twins nine days later. '. . . Today he insisted on giving me six brand-new shirts (don't tell the Davïdovs or anyone about this), and tomorrow he wants to cart me off by force to his own tailor to order some clothes.'[23] While the director of the RMS had a strong sense of the standard of dress to be expected of his staff, he must also have realised that the impecunious Tchaikovsky, who had already lamented to his family the high cost of living in Moscow, could not yet be expected to buy such things for himself. His wardrobe was completed by a frock-coat that Wieniawski had left behind a year earlier when visiting Rubinstein. Unfortunately the Polish violinist was both taller and stouter than

[22] *TZC*1, p. 228; *TLP*5, p. 92; *TPB*, p. 22.
[23] *TZC*1, pp. 230–1; *TLP*5, p. 97; *TPB*, p. 25.

Tchaikovsky, but this did not diminish the latter's pride in wearing this stylish, if ill-fitting garb.

One suspects, too, that Rubinstein made some attempt to direct Tchaikovsky's creative plans. Now that Nikolay had refused to perform the Overture in C minor, Tchaikovsky turned his thoughts elsewhere. 'I am beginning to think about an opera,' he reported to St Petersburg. 'All the libretti that Rubinstein has given me have proved to be extremely bad. I have alighted upon another subject, and want to write the words myself. It will be a simple rehash of a tragedy. The poet Pleshcheyev is here, however, and has agreed to help me in this.'[24] What the play was is not known, and no more was heard of this project, for Tchaikovsky's attention was quickly engrossed during February by the revision of the Overture in F. Meanwhile his confidence as a teacher was growing: 'my shyness has vanished without trace, and I'm beginning to assume little by little the physiognomy of a professor,' he told Sasha.[25] Though Moscow still seemed like a foreign city, he was getting used to it, his depression had dispersed, and he was (or so he confided to Modest) becoming interested in one of Konstantin Tarnovsky's nieces, 'who is so lovely that I've never seen anything like her. I confess I'm very much occupied with her.'[26] Within a week or two, however, he had decided he was not in love with her, and soon after this she married an officer.

A further stage in his acclimatisation to Russia's second city was reached on 16 March with the highly successful performance of the Overture in F under Rubinstein. The composer was looking forward to an Easter break in St Petersburg, and to spending the summer again with Sasha and the twins. There is just one small mischievous request to Sasha: 'I would hope that you won't by that time be in "an interesting condition", and I request Lev to be careful about this.'[27] It was as well that his morale was now in good condition, and that the success of his overture had afforded him audible proof from so many people of their favourable opinion of his talents as a composer, for his sensitive personality had now to withstand the savage blow of Cui's review of his graduation cantata in the *St Petersburg Gazette*. This appeared nearly three months after the event, on 5 April, while Tchaikovsky was in St Petersburg. The mother of one of Tchaikovsky's pupils recorded the composer's own account of the effect of Cui's review upon him. 'When I read that frightful judgement, I don't know what I did with myself. My vision grew dark, my head span, and I ran out of the café like a madman.

[24] *TZC*1, pp. 232–3; *TLP*5, p. 99; *TPB*, p. 27; *YDGC*, pp. 42–4.
[25] *TZC*1, p. 234; *TLP*5, p. 101; *TPB*, p. 29; *YDGC*, p. 44.
[26] *TZC*1, p. 235; *TLP*5, p. 102.
[27] *TLP*5, p. 102.

I didn't realise what I was doing, nor where I was. All day I wandered aimlessly through the city, repeating "I'm sterile, insignificant, nothing will come out of me, I'm ungifted". . . .'[28] Cui's article was hardly encouraging to a young composer who was just embarking on his first symphony.

Tchaikovsky started work on his Symphony in G minor in March 1866 and for the rest of the year the composition of this piece was to be the most important single factor in his life. His daily routine had now established itself, and he outlined it in a letter to Anatoly in early May:

> I get up between nine and ten. While lazing around in bed I talk with Rubinstein, and then drink tea with him. At eleven I either give a lesson lasting till one, or get down to my symphony (which, by the way, is going sluggishly), and thus occupied, I stay in my own room until half past two. During this time Kashkin or Valzek (a professor of singing who has become a new friend of mine) usually drop in on me. At half past two I go to Ulitin's bookshop on Theatre Square, where each day I read through all the newspapers. From there I sometimes take a walk to the Kuznetsky bridge. At four I dine, mostly at the Tarnovskys', sometimes at the Niluses' (in all I've been there three times in three weeks), or at an inn. After dinner I either go for another walk or stay in my room. In the evening I almost always drink tea at the Tarnovskys', though sometimes I go to clubs (I've been to the Artistic Club three times, twice to the Merchants', and once to the English), where I read journals. At midnight I always return home. I write letters or [work on] the symphony, and read in bed for a long time.[29]

If Rubinstein had made any attempt (and it is impossible to believe that he had not) to make Tchaikovsky a boon companion of his own pastimes, it seems that the latter had successfully eluded him and established his own way of life, though he continued to reside with Rubinstein, and to share on occasion in his drinking bouts. During the year Tchaikovsky's circle of friends further widened. In addition to Berthe Valzek, there was the splendid actor Prov Sadovsky, who became very close to him. Much later, in November, he at last met Prince Odoyevsky, and was deeply impressed by his nobility of character, his intellect, and his deep knowledge of, amongst other things, music. Yet far more important for his future life was one consequence of getting to know Konstantin de Lazari, a baritone at the Bolshoy Theatre. This acquaintance had begun in the spring, and it was de Lazari who

[28] DTC, p. 278.   [29] TLP5, p. 108; TZC1, p. 240 (partial); TPB, pp. 32–3.

introduced him to Vladimir Begichev, the head of repertoire (later Intendant) of the Moscow Imperial Theatres, whose wife was an amateur singer and composer. Both the Begichevs were talented, both had led irregular lives which lent them a romantic aura, and both were exceedingly popular. By her first marriage Mariya Begicheva had two sons, Konstantin and Vladimir Shilovsky, both of whom were to play an important part in Tchaikovsky's later life. Konstantin collaborated on the libretto of *Eugene Onegin*, and it was on his estate at Glebovo, near Moscow, that Tchaikovsky composed most of this opera. Later he was able to repay something of this personal debt to Konstantin when the latter, through mismanagement of his own affairs, fell on hard times; Tchaikovsky arranged for a royalty on each performance of *Eugene Onegin* to be paid to him for his share in the libretto. The friendship with the younger brother, Vladimir, was more important still. Already at fourteen something of an infant prodigy, this sickly but handsome child became Tchaikovsky's pupil, and later his host on his estate at Usovo (near Tambov), and a frequent companion of his travels. Tchaikovsky even permitted Vladimir to compose the entr'acte to the second act of his opera, *The Oprichnik*.

Apart from events connected with his own compositions, two incidents probably remained most clearly in Tchaikovsky's memory from the last nine months of 1866. One was the inauguration of the new Conservatoire, the other a most uncomfortable occurrence at the Bolshoy Theatre on 17 April, the day after his return from spending Easter in St Petersburg. His arrival had coincided with an attempt on the life of the Tsar, Alexandr II. Russia reacted with a violent outburst of patriotism; according to Kashkin, Nikolay Rubinstein led a party of students and others round Moscow, singing the Russian national anthem at strategic places. It was rumoured that the would-be assassin, an unbalanced young man called Karakozov, was a Pole, and when Glinka's *A Life for the Tsar*, an opera concerned with the deliverance of the first of the Romanov tsars from Polish soldiers, was performed at the Bolshoy the next day, it turned into a highly emotional demonstration of loyalty. Tchaikovsky, whose patriotism possessed none of Rubinstein's fervour, was present but, according to Kashkin, remained unaware of what was going on around him. Instead, being intent on studying Glinka's orchestration, he sat with his nose in the score,

not noticing the indignant looks nor subsequently the mutterings of his neighbours, nor connecting these mutterings with himself. Meanwhile his neighbours were becoming really enraged by the fact that some insignificant being was 'at such a time' interested in the music, and was poring over his score. Finally there was heard a threatening demand that he should leave forthwith, and only then did the unfortunate musician notice that he was the centre of general attention from all around. He was terribly embarrassed, took fright, and rushed off to save his skin while there was yet time.[30]

In the letters he wrote to Sasha and the twins within a few days of the performance, Tchaikovsky made no mention of his unfortunate role in the evening. It is, of course, unlikely that he would do so, and he even summarises events as though he had been there to the very end of the performance. Nevertheless, whatever the reliability of Kashkin's memory, Tchaikovsky deplored the way in which patriotic passion had wrecked the performance, and he described the final débâcle, providing a bizarre example of that entanglement of art with socio-political matters to which the Russian race is so prone:

> In the last scene of Act 4, when the Poles have to kill Susanin, the singer performing this role began scuffling with the chorus which represented the Poles, and being a very strong man, he toppled a lot of them – and the rest, seeing that the audience approved of art, truth and decency being made laughing-stocks, fell down – and the triumphant Susanin left the stage unharmed, waving his arms menacingly to the deafening applause of the Muscovites.[31]

The opening of the new Conservatoire took place on 13 September. By now Tchaikovsky was becoming accustomed to living in Moscow, and the miserable pittance of his initial salary which had made the last eight months so difficult was replaced by one somewhat more than twice as large. Thus the inauguration of the new institution was for him a special pleasure. To make sure that Glinka's music should be the first to be heard in it, he played from memory the overture to *Ruslan and Lyudmila* on the piano after the inaugural dinner. He had been called upon to make a speech earlier in the evening, and one supposes that this must have been a nerve-racking event for him. However, he seems to have managed such occasions surprisingly well. His task had been to propose the health of his former teacher, Anton Rubinstein, and in 'warm, unusually eloquent words' (as one journal put it)[32] he was able

---

[30] *KVC*, pp. 21–2; *YDGC*, p. 45.

[31] *TLP*5, pp. 106–7; *TZC*1, p. 238; *TPB*, p. 32. At the next performance the singer who was sharing the part of Susanin endeavoured to maintain this innovation. This time, however, the chorus were less submissive, and the curtain had to be brought down on a free-for-all.

[32] *YDGC*, p. 46.

to pay public tribute to the man to whom he felt he owed so much.

Yet, despite such memorable events, 1866 was dominated by toil over his First Symphony. Modest asserted that none of his brother's works ever caused him more labour and suffering than this one. Nothing is known of the early stages of composition, except that by the beginning of May, as recorded earlier, it was going 'sluggishly'. Already the strain was affecting the composer's health: he was sleeping badly, his 'apoplectic strokes', as he called them, had started again and were worse than ever before. 'My nerves are again as upset as they could be. This is for the following reasons: 1, my lack of success in composing the symphony; 2, Rubinstein and Tarnovsky who, noticing that I'm edgy, spend all day frightening me by the most varied means; 3, the ever-present thought that I shall soon die and won't even complete the symphony successfully.'[33] That hatred of the human race, which he had experienced a few months earlier in St Petersburg, was returning. A week later the weather had improved, and with it his morale. In addition, on 13 May his Overture in F had been successfully performed in St Petersburg under Anton Rubinstein. The press had ignored the event completely, but Apukhtin had reported the audience's enthusiasm, and it is more than probable that the success of this performance, the first occasion upon which any work of his had been heard in the Russian capital at a fully public concert before a genuinely musical audience, raised his spirits. Delighted as he was by the encouragement he received in Moscow, this was still to him a provincial city. What he longed for most of all was the approbation of St Petersburg – of Anton Rubinstein, Zaremba, and of the Russian capital's musicians and audience. Thus this successful public début must have stimulated his creative faculties, and less than six weeks later, on 19 June, he could report that he had begun scoring the symphony, and that his health was satisfactory, though he had lost a whole night's sleep a few days earlier through working too long, with the consequence that his 'strokes' had returned.

Three weeks previously, on 27 May, he had gone to St Petersburg to see his father, who was to return within a fortnight from his protracted stay with Zinaida, and to resolve with the twins the question of where they were to spend the summer vacation. His own intention had been to go to Kamenka, but in the end financial problems made it impossible for the twins to go too. He himself had also taken fright at alarming reports of road conditions between Moscow and Kiev, and had decided that he would not venture to Kamenka by that route. In any case he was almost penniless; indeed, his finances were so straitened that he spent the first

[33] *TLP*5, p. 109; *TZC*1, p. 241.

night in St Petersburg on the streets for lack of funds for lodging. Finally Ilya provided enough money for Anatoly to go to Kamenka, while Tchaikovsky and Modest accepted an invitation from the Davïdovs to spend the summer with them at a place just outside St Petersburg on the way to Peterhof. In early June they installed themselves in their dacha which had many attractions: it was close to the dacha in which they had spent such pleasant summers when Ilya Tchaikovsky had been director of the Technological Institute, it was not far from the Sergiyevskaya heath where Tchaikovsky had spent several glorious days with some friends after leaving the School of Jurisprudence, and it was only ten minutes' walk from where his father was also passing the summer with his new wife and her family. Thus they could meet daily.

During his stay with the Davïdovs Tchaikovsky took a short break from work to visit with Apukhtin the island of Valaam in Lake Ladoga, and was enchanted by all he saw there. Meanwhile at the dacha he enjoyed daily walks, now taking them more often by himself (much to Modest's disappointment), and giving his company to the family only in the evenings. When these were devoted to music, the works he played were invariably Mendelssohn's Italian Symphony, the First or Third Symphonies of Schumann, or the latter's *Das Paradies und die Peri*, the first part of which especially delighted him. In these pleasant circumstances he laboured over the next two months with his symphony, but soon he was again falling victim to his nervous attacks, brought on by struggling with his composition not only during the day but also into the night. By the beginning of August these had become so alarming that a doctor was summoned, who declared him to be 'one step away from insanity',[34] and who for a time even despaired of curing him. The numbness of his bodily extremities and the hallucinations he suffered were so frightening that he never again engaged in nocturnal composition.

At the end of August Tchaikovsky returned to St Petersburg with the symphony still unfinished. Despite this he was anxious to hear the verdict of his former teachers, Rubinstein and Zaremba, on what he had so far completed. There was no comfort to be found in this quarter, for they damned the piece and refused even to consider it for the performance Tchaikovsky had hoped it would receive at a concert of the RMS. Zaremba disapproved, amongst other things, of the first movement's second subject, a section of which Tchaikovsky was especially proud (later Tchaikovsky concurred with Zaremba and in 1874 substituted a completely new second subject).

On 3 September Tchaikovsky arrived back in Moscow, and it is

[34] *TZC*1, p. 248; *DTC*, p. 329.

probable that he laid aside the symphony for a while since, with the opening of the Conservatoire and the resumption of his teaching commitments, there had come a commission from Nikolay Rubinstein for a Festival Overture on the Danish national anthem, to be played during the visit to Moscow of the Tsarevich and his Danish bride. The Conservatoire had been opened in new accommodation, and Rubinstein took up residence in part of the building, Tchaikovsky moving in with him. The two men took their meals at the Albrechts', an arrangement that was maintained for many years. Tchaikovsky's relationship with the couple had now become very close, and he was delighted that they had already singled him out to be a godfather to their third child, whose birth was imminent. Since Tchaikovsky's teaching load was not more than twenty or so hours a week, there was a certain amount of time for composition; the problem was that a home so close to the Conservatoire became a natural meeting place for the staff and other visitors, and even in his own room Tchaikovsky could find neither the peace nor the privacy in which he could compose. Thus he was forced to find an alternative working place, and one of his favourite refuges became the inn, the Great Britain, whose spacious rooms were relatively empty by day, and therefore quiet.

Despite the difficulties, the overture was finished by 24 November, and Tchaikovsky was again taking up the symphony to revise it. For a second time he submitted it to the judgement of the two St Petersburg pundits, probably during the short visit he paid to the Russian capital during the Christmas break. This time the Adagio and scherzo passed muster, though the symphony as a whole was still found unworthy of performance. Modest believed that this second rejection aroused such bitterness in his brother that he ceased from that moment to care what St Petersburg thought of his work, pinning all his hopes upon Moscow. In fact, the first movement to be heard anywhere was the scherzo, which Nikolay Rubinstein performed at an RMS concert on 22 December in Moscow, though without any success, according to Modest. It was Nikolay, too, who was entrusted with introducing the Adagio and scherzo to St Petersburg at an RMS concert on 23 February 1867. Tchaikovsky was unable to be present, but Anatoly could report some success this time. 'The applause was satisfactory, though there were no calls for the composer,' he wrote to his brother in Moscow.[35] Tchaikovsky had won for himself at least one firm admirer in the St Petersburg press – a certain A.D., who expressed surprise that the symphony's reception had not been warmer; it had 'undoubted merits. It is melodious to the highest degree, and excellently scored.'[36] A whole

[35] *YDGC*, p. 48.   [36] *TZC*1, p. 263; *YDGC*, p. 48.

year went by before the work was at last heard in its entirety. The performance under Nikolay Rubinstein at an RMS concert in Moscow on 15 February 1868 was a reward for Tchaikovsky's long labour and patience. This time it was his turn to report on the work's fortunes to Anatoly: 'My symphony scored a great success, particularly the Adagio.'[37] Yet despite this enthusiastic reception, over fifteen years passed before it was heard again.

To the end of his life Tchaikovsky retained an affection for his First Symphony, and when in 1883 he wrote to Nadezhda von Meck that 'although it is in many ways very immature, yet fundamentally it has more substance and is better than many of my other more mature works,'[38] he was speaking nothing other than the truth. Neither the title, *Winter Daydreams*, given to the whole symphony, nor the specific headings above the first two movements offer much insight into what follows. They probably betray the example of Mendelssohn, whose Italian Symphony was occupying Tchaikovsky's attention while he was in the throes of composing this symphony. For Mendelssohn, the neo-classicist whose music is normally so little marked by the emotions or sensations produced by external events or objects, the inspiration of sunny Italy or dour Scotland could have a pronounced effect on the character of his musical invention. But Tchaikovsky was just about incapable of producing a work which did not incorporate something of his own experience, and nothing in the symphony as a whole is really illumined specifically by these titles; in the last two movements he gave up all pretence of evocative intent. Certainly the listener who doesn't know that the first movement is 'Daydreams of a winter journey' and the second 'Land of gloom, land of mists' is unlikely to be handicapped by his ignorance.

The earliest movement in origin was the scherzo, which Tchaikovsky salvaged from his C sharp minor Piano Sonata of the previous year, transposing it down a semitone for its new context. Apart from the four bars of introduction and a couple of bars inserted before the tonic return of the main theme, Tchaikovsky left the scherzo as it was, though he made one or two other minor adjustments. Transference to the orchestra meant that some thematic detail with which two hands could not cope might now be fully realised. The watery trio was scrapped altogether, and replaced by what was to be the first of a whole line of orchestral waltzes from Tchaikovsky's pen. If Mendelssohn must be given some credit for the scherzo (though it lacks the urbane fleetness of that composer's delicate conceptions, and the end has a positively

[37] *TLP*5, p. 133; *DTC*, p. 330; *YDGC*, p. 53; *TPB*, p. 39.
[38] *TLP*12, p. 279; *TPM*3, p. 235.

Russian robustness), Tchaikovsky is completely himself in the waltz. The little wind counterpoints that are incorporated when the waltz theme returns to its beginning (Ex. 7a) have their precedents in Glinka – as, for instance, when Glinka brings back the beginning of *his* 'waltz' theme at bar 74 of the entr'acte to Act 3 in his *Prince Kholmsky* music (Ex. 7b).

The relevance of the title Tchaikovsky gave to his second movement is badly compromised by the very first eight bars, for they had already done service to open the second subject of *The Storm*, where they had embodied Katerina's 'yearnings for true happiness and love' (see Ex. 2) – though it must be conceded that their character is considerably changed by now being scored for strings alone, and played adagio instead of allegro. The main body of the movement is a store of full-hearted, lyrical melody, very much Tchaikovsky's own, beautifully scored, and exhibiting already many of those characteristics which were later to find their most natural habitat in his ballet scores. Likewise the bassoon obbligato (for it is much more than a mere bass) and the little darting flute phrases which periodically counterpoint the oboe's long-breathed melody are already unmistakably his (though, again, the suggestions for these latter were probably provided by Glinka). Nor does the tune (Ex. 8a) leave any doubt about its creator's nationality. In particular, the third phrase, with its latent plagalism and especially its end (x), is Russian to the core, and the octave rise (y) which concludes the next is one of the clearest fingerprints of Russian folksong. The fifth and sixth phrases are essentially reflections of phrase three, and substantiate the Russianness of this melody not merely by reflecting the same characteristics as that phrase, but also by the very fact of being variants of a shape already heard. In addition – and this is very important for another reason altogether – this process of phrase repetition, so characteristic a feature of many Russian melodies, is applied on a much broader scale between different sections of this movement. Thus the theme of the first episode (pochissimo più mosso [Ex. 8b]) takes its departure from phrase four of the original tune, while an important thematic ingredient of the section before the restoration of the tonic (a section too slight to be termed a development) is a conflation of this same phrase with the first (Ex. 8c). These relationships do much to create the impression of a movement which is essentially monothematic, and which is sustained throughout its considerable length primarily by melodic means. To do this successfully would be no mean achievement, and it says much for Tchaikovsky's powers of melodic inventiveness and organisation that he is able to support this melodic span and give the movement an expressive weight befitting its symphonic function.

Yet melodic resourcefulness is not the whole story of Tchaikovsky's

Ex. 7

a.

Ex. 8

success. On the face of it, a species of simple rondo (here ABA [x] BA. x is the quasi-developmental section before the tonic's return) seems an inept structural choice if the intention is to build the movement as a single melodic span. By means of the melodic relationships already charted Tchaikovsky has broken down the boundaries between the compartments of a normal rondo, and he has fostered continuity by ending each section in a key different from that in which it started, thus providing a tonal dynamism which propels it towards the next.[39] Yet a fundamental problem remained – that the central ritornello of a simple rondo habitually returned to the tonic, and was therefore a point of relative relaxation. Expressed through the metaphor of a bridge, the central ritornello was a middle pier, whereas Tchaikovsky's intention was to create a single arch. To achieve this he scrapped the tonal principle of the simple rondo, and devised instead a gigantic ternary key scheme (Ex. 9) which maintains the tonal tension throughout the central ritornello. As used in this movement it is a simple solution to a simple problem, and in itself would warrant little comment. Nevertheless, this process of tonal adjustment had deeper implications, for it could radically redefine the traditional role played by each component part of a movement. Later such tonal reinterpretation of a familiar structural pattern was to be far more significantly exploited by Tchaikovsky, notably in the Fourth Symphony and the Piano Trio.

The remaining two movements are both sonata structures, though of markedly different achievement. The finale, in the tonic major, has some

---

[39] One wonders whether Tchaikovsky's decision to enlist music from *The Storm* was a late one, prompted by the need to provide a tonic conclusion to a movement whose main section, like all the others, finished out of key. Because of this, something had to be added to provide a conclusion in the tonic.

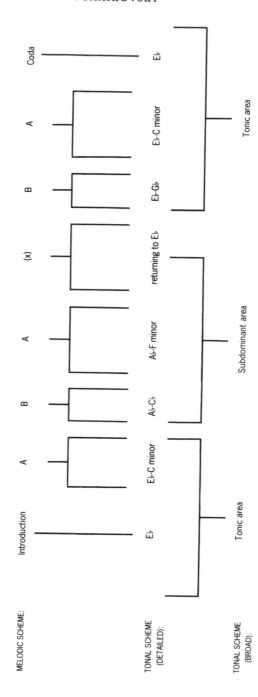

Ex. 9

attractive material, a folksong, 'Raspashu li ya mlada, mladeshenka',[40] serving as the basis both of the introduction and of the swaggering second subject, and also playing some part, it seems, in begetting the first subject, a good vigorous theme into which the introduction is skilfully led. Departures from conventional precedent are the setting of the second subject in the mediant minor, and the incorporation of part of the slow introduction into the recapitulation, between the two subjects. This occasions the most striking passage in the whole movement, the lead to the second subject, constructed from out-of-step slow scales in contrary motion set against sustained horn notes so as to produce some dissonances which even today sound moderately astringent, and which must have affronted Rubinstein and Zaremba (Ex. 10 contains less than one-fifth of this extraordinary passage, probably

Ex. 10

[40] Kashkin provided some interesting information about Tchaikovsky's view of this folksong: 'Unfortunately this song had suffered badly from becoming one of the town songs with the widest currency. In particular its ending, which is manifestly not from folksong, very much troubled Pyotr Ilich, who turned to various connoisseurs of Russian folksong such as Prov Sadovsky and Ostrovsky who knew a great number of folksongs by heart. But no one knew anything but this current town version, in which form it was left in the symphony.' (*KVC*, p. 29; *TZC*1, p. 272.) A variant of this same tune also appears as No. 39 of Prokunin's collection of folksongs arranged by Tchaikovsky in 1872–3. This version sounds no more uncorrupted than that used in the First Symphony finale.

modelled in part upon the lead to the recapitulation in the first movement). The more puzzling, in view of this, is the studied display of conservatoire contrapuntal skills so prominent elsewhere in the movement. Like many Russians, Tchaikovsky had a considerable facility for decorative counterpoint, whether inventing an attractive line to set against another tune, or devising neat combinations of existing ideas (the latter was to be a point of departure for many of his developments); like most Russians he had no aptitude for organic counterpoint of the sort from which a whole movement might naturally grow. On the other hand, he knew perfectly well that if his trim little contrapuntal syntheses were pushed sequentially, perhaps with modifications of detail, through a variety of keys, or if a new synthesis entered abruptly in a new key, it was possible to give an illusion of organic growth. Thus in this movement Tchaikovsky parades his contrapuntal skill in the modulatory sections – the transitions and the development: the latter is largely a fugato (or, rather, a series of imitative entries in different keys) on a fragment of the first subject. Setting aside the merits or otherwise of such sections, the fact is that they faced Tchaikovsky with some huge intractable lumps of music which he had no hope of digesting into an organic symphonic structure. All he might do was take them as they were, and assemble his other sections around them, smoothing the joins as best he could. To be fair, these contrapuntal passages are expertly manufactured, and they have no shortage of energy; indeed, vigour is well sustained throughout the whole movement, and the proportions are generally satisfactory. Yet the result could not be other than a cobbled movement which the badly overblown coda does nothing to improve.

The substantial patches of first-rate music in this finale make the fundamental flaws of the movement the more regrettable; it is sadder still when the symphony had begun so well. The opening stretch of the first movement is enough to scotch the hoary legend that Tchaikovsky was completely devoid of any real symphonic aptitude. His natural ability to think in terms of organic symphonic procedures was certainly limited, and his compositional equipment reveals glaring deficiencies when compared with that of the greatest classical masters. Tchaikovsky himself, one of the most touchingly honest of composers where his own limitations were concerned, was fully aware of his symphonic problems, but his frank confessions of his own difficulties have too often been accepted at their face value as a final judgement upon his whole work. As a symphonist he did himself less than justice, for a composer who could show so much resourcefulness in modifying sonata structure so as to make it more compatible with the type of music nature had decreed he should write was no helpless bungler. Nevertheless his victories were sometimes hard won, never more so than in the creation of this symphony, as we have seen. Till now he had been content to become a competent craftsman shaping movements as best he could according to received practice; now he realised that if (to shift the metaphor) his symphonic flora were not to remain merely artificial, he had to put down his own roots. In the first movement of this symphony he began this operation in earnest.

To grasp the extent of his achievement we must be clear about the issues involved. The classical composer had built his sonata structures in two fundamental ways. One was by thematic argument, the other by tonal organisation, and of the two the latter was the more important and the more problematic. Contrary to often-held opinion, the greatest difficulty did not lie in the development, despite its multiplicity of key shifts, but in the exposition, where the composer had to time a single fundamental move from the opening tonic to a different, usually closely related key. What we experience in the finest classical expositions is not just a modulation but a process of controlled tonal dynamism. Such a command of tonal growth was utterly beyond Tchaikovsky, and this alone would have denied him the symphonic mastery of a Beethoven. The tonal planning of the first movement of this First Symphony is an admission of this – and, at the same time, a perfectly reasonable way of circumventing, if not surmounting this deficiency. But before examining this aspect of the symphony, we must return to the matter of thematic argument. Just as any competent student can learn to handle the mechanisms of modulation, so he can acquire a serviceable technique for infiltrating a texture with constant repetitions of a single motif, thus creating the illusion that it is from this thematic nucleus that the whole tissue is growing. Yet to make such a motif a genuine agent in the generation of a movement requires something more than this, as Tchaikovsky realised, and it was one of the problems he now tackled. He could never solve it completely, for it could never be natural for a composer whose fundamental gift was so thoroughly lyrical to build an entire movement in this way. Yet he was not without a certain measure of the true symphonist's gift for organic thematic growth, as the opening of this first movement brilliantly demonstrates.

Let us look in more detail at what happens. The first thing to observe is that the harmonic element is fined down to a minimum. There is virtually no harmonic movement, and the purely harmonic filling is normally supplied by only two notes at any one time. These are rarely more than a third apart, thus leaving vast vistas above and below in which the thematic material which is the life force of this first subject may manœuvre freely. Against the two-note accompaniment in the violins the first theme (*A*) enters on flute and bassoon two octaves apart (Ex. 11b). This is a fresh, airy tune, especially Russian in its high content of fourths and its repetitive behaviour, plastic in phrasing, and with a melodic contour that centres firmly upon G. At bar 20 the theme begins again on the violas, but this time a little chromatic motif on the flutes fills the gap between the first two phrases (Ex. 11a): a new musical idea (*B*) is

Ex. 11

being born. The first theme (*A*) follows a new course, hints at a tonal excursion, imposes itself briefly upon the new flute line – and then, via a neapolitan sixth, is swiftly pulled back into a chord of G minor – and for the third time it all begins again. Only one phrase of the first theme is heard, however, for where the flutes had before merely stuttered a tiny motif, an articulate, fully formed *B* now takes over the field (Ex. 11c).

It is perhaps fair to say that *B* is less a theme with fixed contours – though a fundamental phrase is embedded in it (see *a* in Ex. 11c) of which much is made in the coda (see the bass of Ex. 13) – than a chromatic principle, metred primarily through the influence of the symphony's very first phrase, yet free to turn upwards or downwards at will. (It recurs in another guise to conclude both the exposition and recapitulation; in the latter [Ex. 11f] it very naturally prompts a resurgence of its earlier incarnation [*a* in Ex. 11c] as the basis upon which to launch the coda [see Ex. 13].) As an idea to complement, yet contrast with *A*, it is admirable, but it has wider ramifications. Being

Ex. 11

chromatic, it has, of course, particular potential both for tonal manœuvring and for harmonic colouring; and in music in which so much of the purely harmonic element consists of only two notes, the complete pitch freedom of a chromatic line enables *B* to enjoy a maximum range of options as the third note of the triad – that is, as the determinant of the harmony. From bar 40 Tchaikovsky is quick to exploit this, producing an arresting harmonic incident by thrusting two emphatic E naturals against the constant B flat and G in the violins (see bars 6 and 9 of Ex. 11c), and, in so doing, to offer a hint of challenge to the tonic. From bar 49 this whole incident is repeated with different scoring. By bar 58, however, the tonic has still proved unassailable, and *B* prepares a new strategy (Ex. 11d). It can do little against the dominant seventh implicit in the held D and C in the horns, but when the upper horn rises to E flat, the way is open for it to loosen the key, determine the harmony and finally the tonal direction, for the horns' minor third can be made to fit into a number of different chords and key contexts. So *B* takes its chance, twists itself in tight little formations that begin to confuse the tonal issue, three times declares a four-quaver descending motif which interprets the horn notes as part of a diminished seventh, and then, abetted by flutes and clarinets suddenly flickering upwards on a dominant seventh of B flat, it drops its F sharp to F natural and supports a perfect cadence in B flat, in which new key the first theme re-enters radiantly.

This is a masterly symphonic opening by any standards. The material

is fresh and is applied to excellent effect, the texture is of exemplary clarity, the scoring is clear and contrasted. Above all, the music has grown, it seems, not through artifice but as living tissue, and it continues to do so as the first subject, again through the operations of *B*, is moved first to C flat (written B) and then back towards the tonic. Tchaikovsky's symphonic application of melodic elements is nowhere better illustrated than in what follows, for *B* suddenly reverses its role, yielding up its chromaticism to co-operate diatonically in preparing the return of that very tonic which it has done so much to dislodge (Ex. 11e). Finally, with G minor reinstated, this potent little agent, whose machinations have done most to determine the course of the first subject, is content to transform itself into a simple chromatic bass supporting a forthright reassertion of the opening material (Ex. 11e: bars 9 ff.). And this brings us back to the matter of broader tonal organisation. By its conclusion this whole first subject has spread itself over some 130 bars, and has ended exactly where it began, in the tonic. This is something no classical symphonist would have done at this stage of the exposition, especially after the tonal excursions which had already taken place. Being entirely devoid of ability to devise a planned tonal growth embracing a large span of music, Tchaikovsky has swung to the opposite extreme, rigidly segregating his two subjects by constructing the first as a huge, tonally closed paragraph built upon the interaction and alternation of two

Ex. 11

themes, the one repetitive and static, the other chromatically emancipated and tonally subversive. The second subject, in the dominant, is correspondingly large-scale, is equally rich tonally, and equally key-enclosed. With two such massive but self-contained chunks as these two subjects, what was to be done about the transition? Tchaikovsky's solution was as bold, in its own way, as it was basic: to reduce it to the simplest possible terms, short of abandoning it altogether. Though Tchaikovsky was to lament with some truth that his seams always showed, it is difficult to believe that a more extensive link could have improved upon the mere half-dozen bars of dominant preparation for the new key which he placed between the two subjects.

The version of the symphony we hear today was made in 1874 when the work was about to be published. In fact, Tchaikovsky changed little when making this revision, leaving the scherzo untouched, introducing only a few very tiny cuts into the slow movement and finale, and

simplifying rhythmically the lead to the recapitulation in the latter (Ex.
10 is from the revised version). The one piece of really drastic surgery
was in the first movement, where he excised the first part of the second
subject, replacing it by a brand-new section (bars 137–89 of the published score; the last nine bars of this were made to slide into the
material of the concluding bars of the section they replaced). The new
material certainly displayed a more generous lyricism and richer tonal
colouring, but something was sacrificed, for the supporting bass of the
rejected material had incorporated the thematic derivative from the first
subject (see the bass in Ex. 12); indeed, this derivative had ultimately

Ex. 12   Allegro tranquillo

turned into an explicit quotation of the first-subject fragment in the last
two bars of Ex. 11e. Eight years later, however, Tchaikovsky must have
decided that this inter-subject relationship was unprofitable, and
abandoned it.

   The development opens well, initially taking the concluding motif of
the exposition and transforming it on four horns into a phrase which
anticipates by more than twenty years the *Valse des fleurs* from the
Nutcracker ballet. Most of what follows is made up by combining or
contrapuntally working pieces of material extracted or derived from the

exposition, and building these little syntheses into blocks of up to six bars long which are then sequentially repeated. In the middle, where contrapuntal imitation assumes control, it might look as though the movement will fall into that contrived bustle which does service in so much of the finale, but the pitfall is swiftly avoided, and the lead back to the recapitulation is one of the most arresting moments in the whole symphony. The coda, too, is admirable. During the revision of 1874 the first part had to be redesigned. There had been no need to change the development, for it had not used any material from that portion of the second subject which had been changed. In the recapitulation the first part of the second subject had, of course, to be revised (bars 522–46 of the second version were new), and the coda had opened (Ex. 13a) by

Ex. 13   [1866]

placing some of the now discarded material above repetitions of the phrase *a* of Ex. 11c. Tchaikovsky's solution was as economical as it was deftly done: to leave the bass unchanged, but adapt some of his new second-subject material to fit above it, supplying some chromatic filling that might have come straight from Glinka (Ex. 13b). The coda closes as

Ex. 13   [1874]

adroitly as it had opened, reversing the process of thematic growth of the movement's opening as *a* disintegrates in the bass. It is an end that perfectly combines symphonic function with expressive intent, and worthily rounds off Tchaikovsky's finest symphonic movement to date.

5

FIRST OPERA:

ENTER BALAKIREV

TCHAIKOVSKY ALWAYS RETAINED some pride in his Festival Overture on the Danish national anthem. During the very last year of his life, when Jurgenson was about to publish the work, he could still write that 'it is very effective, I remember, and far better as music than *1812*'.[1] The overture, begun soon after his return to St Petersburg in September 1866 and completed on 24 November, had, as recorded earlier, been commissioned to grace the celebrations attending the Moscow visit of the Tsarevich and Princess Dagmar, his new Danish wife. Tchaikovsky's pride in his tribute was not misplaced, for the overture is forthright, effective music, scored in bold colours, and making its points with a directness appropriate in such a public offering. The union of the two realms is musically symbolised by the incorporation also of the Russian national anthem. Phrases from the Danish tune are heard in the solemn introduction, mingling freely with material of Tchaikovsky's own devising. The Russian national anthem makes its entry in a modified form towards the end of this introduction, where it is accompanied by a figure extracted from the first line of the Danish tune – a musical courtship to be consummated only much later. Though the allegro vivo first subject opens with the last phrase of the Danish anthem, the exposition material is free, except that this same imported phrase does influence the F sharp minor melody in the centre of the second subject. The development deals consecutively with material from each anthem, presaging the full union of their opening phrases which is finally effected in the dominant preparation for the coda (Ex. 14). It only remained for Tchaikovsky to compliment the future Empress of Russia by a full statement of her national hymn.

The royal couple's visit had been scheduled for the end of the year, but it was postponed until the following April, by which time the expected performance of the piece had been cancelled because (as the journal, *The Voice*, put it) 'the talented young composer for some reason

---

[1] *TZC*1, p. 260; *DTC*, p. 332; *TPJ*2, p. 244.

Ex. 14   Allegro vivo

[Danish Anthem]

[Russian Anthem]

took it into his head to set forth our Russian national anthem in the minor key, which completely transforms the character of this well-known melody.'[2] It must have been the unsuitability of such treatment for an official occasion that had decided Rubinstein upon a performance at a charity concert earlier in the year, on 10 February. Nevertheless, though the Tsarevich did not hear the overture, he expressed royal gratitude by a gift of gold cuff-links with turquoises, which Tchaikovsky promptly sold to Dubuque.

With the overture finished, Tchaikovsky spent the next weeks revising his First Symphony. Yet even while engaged on this, he was fastening his thoughts upon an opera. The first news of this is given in a letter to Anatoly of 20 November 1866: 'Now I shall be taken up by the revision of the symphony, and then perhaps I shall gently set about an opera. There is hope that Ostrovsky himself will write a libretto for me on his *The Voyevoda* [The Provincial Governor].'[3] Very soon after this Tchaikovsky provided an Introduction and Mazurka for Ostrovsky's dramatic chronicle, *Dmitry the Pretender and Vasily Shuisky*. These were probably composed very quickly, for the brief Introduction is little more than an arrangement of extracts from the theme and first variation of his A minor piano variations of 1863–4, and the Mazurka is simply good functional dance music, though Tchaikovsky did consider the main theme worth using again three years later in his *Mazurka de salon*, Op. 9, No. 3, for piano. He completed the two pieces by 11 February 1867, and it may have been gratitude aroused by them that persuaded the major Russian playwright to undertake the task of providing a libretto for this young and far from established composer. Ostrovsky wasted no time; on 17 March the first act was in Tchaikovsky's hands, and three days later he started composition.

On that very day he received a request from Nikolay Rubinstein for a piano piece which the virtuoso might perform in a forthcoming RMS concert, and the result was the *Scherzo à la russe*, based upon the same

[2] *TLP5*, p. 114; *DTC*, p. 333.
[3] *TLP5*, pp. 113–14; *TZC1*, p. 261; *YDGC*, p. 47; *DTC*, p. 15; *TPB*, p. 33.

Ukrainian folksong that Tchaikovsky had already used in his student Quartet Movement in B flat. So far he had published only one piece, the song 'Mezza notte', which by now he would doubtless have disowned. The new scherzo was to become the first work in which, as a fully professional composer, he felt sufficient confidence to commit it to a wider and permanent existence, and later in the year Jurgenson printed it as Tchaikovsky's Op. 1, No. 1. Its companion, the *Impromptu*, published as Op. 1, No. 2, found its way into print by accident. In fact it was a much earlier piece from Tchaikovsky's student years, and had been written down in a manuscript book in which there were still some unused pages. It was on these spare sheets that Tchaikovsky wrote out the new *Scherzo à la russe*. When Rubinstein passed the manuscript book to Jurgenson so that the scherzo might be engraved, the latter did not realise that the impromptu was not intended for publication. It was only when Tchaikovsky received proofs of both pieces that the mistake emerged. Initially displeased, he subsequently relented and allowed both pieces to be issued.

As Modest observed, his brother's progress on his new opera was slow, at least when compared with the speed at which he was to write such works after he had acquired some experience of operatic composition. Nor did he help himself when he lost Ostrovsky's libretto for the first act, and was forced shamefacedly to ask the playwright to start once again from the beginning. It seems improbable that Tchaikovsky was able to do any work on the opera during May, for Ostrovsky did not start rewriting the libretto until 16 June. By this time Tchaikovsky had left Moscow for St Petersburg, and was lamenting that he had no text to work on. 'At the beginning of June, before leaving Moscow, I called on you,' he wrote to Ostrovsky,

> but you were already in the country. It was very sad for me to go off for the summer without a single line of libretto, but now I am even a bit glad of this circumstance for, on the assumption that you have not yet started on the second act, may I dare to submit to your sympathetic consideration the following new plan for Act 2. . . . I ask you not to hurry. I shall devote this summer to completing and orchestrating the first act. Then during the following winter and summer I hope to compose the remaining three.[4]

This letter was written on 22 June, and exactly a week later Ostrovsky dispatched to him an instalment of the libretto, probably the rewritten first act. Beyond this he was to contribute very little to *The Voyevoda*.

[4] *TLP*5, pp. 118–19.

Perhaps Tchaikovsky's letter gives one clue to why Ostrovsky cooled towards this collaboration. He was Russia's most popular playwright and a very busy man, as he pointed out in his reply – though he did promise to go on. He can hardly have been pleased at having to write out the first act again, and now this young composer was proposing to tell him how the dramatic plan should be organised. Even if he agreed that Tchaikovsky's suggestions were improvements, such revisions were bound to prolong the task and hinder Ostrovsky's other commitments. The changes Tchaikovsky suggested were not incorporated into the libretto, and by the end of the summer, having now completed and scored the first act, he was becoming exasperated by the playwright's lack of productivity. 'I've just returned from Ostrovsky's,' he wrote to Anatoly on 12 September, soon after his return to Moscow. '. . . [He] continues to cheat me. I read in the papers in St Petersburg that he'd finished my libretto, but this has proved to be utterly false intelligence. I have only with difficulty extracted from him a half of the old act [in fact, the first scene of Act 2].'[5] On 2 October he tried another direct approach, this time by letter: 'I know you're busy, I know your brother composer bothers you – but all the same, I've decided to disturb you with my request. For the sake of all that's holy – find a free minute for me and finish what you've promised. I shall pine away if I don't get the scenes I lack from Act 2.'[6] It was of no avail, and eight days later he had to report to Anatoly: 'Ostrovsky's gone to St Petersburg for a while. When he returns, I'll saddle him up.'[7] In fact, except for supplying the words of Mariya's Song, which Tchaikovsky based upon a folktune, 'Kosa li moya ti, kosïnka', noted down from the singing of a peasant woman during a day's outing to Kuntsevo, a beauty spot near Moscow, in the early autumn, Ostrovsky contributed no more, and Tchaikovsky was left to complete the dramatic plan and the text by himself.

Now realising that the partnership was at an end, he set about the work with vigour. Within less than two months he could write cheerfully to Modest not only that he had finished the third act, but that an impending performance would give Moscow a foretaste of the new work: 'The opera's dances, which I orchestrated at Hapsal, are going to be performed at the next [RMS] concert.'[8] These dances were a revision of the *Characteristic Dances* he had composed in 1865 while in St Petersburg, and which Johann Strauss had conducted at Pavlovsk that same year.

[5] *TLP5*, p. 121; *TZC1*, p. 278; *TPB*, p. 35; *YDGC*, p. 50; *DTC*, p. 16.

[6] *TLP5*, p. 122; *YDGC*, p. 50 (partial); *DTC*, p. 16 (partial).

[7] *TLP5*, p. 123; *TZC1*, p. 279; *TPB*, p. 36.

[8] *TLP5*, p. 128; *TZC1*, p. 280; *TPB*, p. 37; *DTC*, p. 16. It is not certain whether Tchaikovsky's statement that he had finished Act 3 signifies that the whole opera was complete, or whether, at this stage, the opera was still in four acts.

The performance of this revised version (*Dances of the Hay Maidens*), which Nikolay Rubinstein conducted on 14 December, was such a success that Jurgenson immediately proposed to publish it in a piano duet arrangement. Even more satisfying, perhaps, was a verbal request for these dances from St Petersburg. This was a complete reversal of the roles which Tchaikovsky and the capital's musical establishment had been playing less than a year before over his First Symphony, and he was determined to ensure that the new status he had suddenly achieved before their eyes should be reflected in their future relationship. 'I've written to say that I'll only hand them over when I've received an official letter signed by all the directors,' he told Anatoly with relish. 'Zaremba has informed me via [Nikolay] Rubinstein that I shall receive such a letter. If that's so, then you'll hear them. These rascals treat me too offhandedly; they must be spat upon so that they may appreciate my value.'[9]

By now Tchaikovsky was thoroughly settled in Moscow. Since the beginning of the year he had once again enjoyed the company of Laroche, who had joined the staff of the Moscow Conservatoire on finishing his course in St Petersburg. At Laroche's he met the mathematician, Nikolay Bugayev, who had talked deep into the night about the latest discoveries in astronomy. The depth and range of Bugayev's learning brought home to Tchaikovsky the limitations of the formal education he had received at the School of Jurisprudence. Just as a year before he had delighted in the *Pickwick Papers*, so now he ended May Day by reading Turgenev's new story, *Smoke*, judging the loss of an evening of communal festivities to have been a sacrifice worth making for this pleasure. Tchaikovsky was always a voracious and very rapid reader. According to Kashkin, it was Gogol, Pushkin, Ostrovsky and Tolstoy whom he loved most, though he also devoured Dostoyevsky. Of foreign writers besides Dickens, he read Thackeray in translation. Before leaving Moscow for the summer, he orchestrated a Festival March by a Czech musician resident in Moscow, a certain K. I. Kral, which was to be performed at a reception at Moscow University for guests attending an Ethnographic Exhibition. Kashkin, who cited it as an example of the speed at which Tchaikovsky could work, stated that this scoring was completed in some forty-five minutes. This was not the only service Tchaikovsky performed to another composer's music during 1867, for he also made a piano transcription of Dargomïzhsky's Ukrainian dance fantasia for orchestra, *Kazachok*.

It had been Tchaikovsky's intention to spend the summer of 1867 in Finland with Anatoly. Kamenka was out of the question, but he thought

---

[9] *TLP*5, p. 129; *TZC*1, p. 282 (partial); *TPB*, p. 38; *DTC*, p. 16 (partial).

he could find a cheap refuge in the Finnish backwoods with one of his brothers, and this year it was to be Anatoly's turn. Modest was to go with the Davïdovs to Hapsal (Haapsalu) on the Estonian coast. In the middle of June Tchaikovsky and Anatoly took the steamer to Vyborg, and from there paid a visit to Imatra, whose beauties Tchaikovsky had first admired seven years before. It was at this point that his improvidence in deciding that a hundred roubles could suffice Anatoly and himself for the whole summer became apparent. Indeed, his funds had already been so drained that scarcely enough remained for their return fare to St Petersburg. Taking the first steamer back home, their despair was increased when they found that their father had gone to Zinaida in the Urals, and that the rest of their family and friends were also out of the capital. There was no financial help or refuge to be found there, and all that remained possible was to travel third class by steamer to join Modest and the Davïdovs. This meant travelling on deck, and at night they nearly froze to death. By 22 June they had arrived in Hapsal.

But for a loan from Sasha and a sum received from Moscow, Tchaikovsky's position would have been desperate. As it was, when he had installed himself in cheap lodgings with his brothers, their financial predicament permitted them to order meals for only two, and the third had to share these. It was a hungry summer, though the Davïdovs did as much as they tactfully could to relieve the brothers' pangs. Tchaikovsky had arrived in Hapsal feeling ill-disposed towards the place, but he soon found it tolerable and, despite his material privations, settled down to enjoy the company of his brothers and the Davïdovs. In the evening he and the twins sometimes read plays together, especially enjoying de Musset's *On ne badine pas avec l'amour*, *Les caprices de Marianne* and *Le Chandelier*. He had intended to avoid involvement in the wider society of Hapsal, but ended up 'getting acquainted with everyone'.[10] He noted with some pride how his brothers, now seventeen, were acquiring social graces, though this evidence of approaching adulthood was not to inhibit the constant salvoes of advice, exhortation and reproof contained in his letters to them. His main preoccupation was with *The Voyevoda*. 'My opera is progressing very fairly,' he wrote to Sasha on 1 August, 'and on that score I'm completely satisfied with myself. But what's bad is this: constantly in Hapsal I have occasion to be convinced that there nestles within me an illness called *misanthropy*. I am having frightful attacks here of hatred towards people.'[11]

This aversion was not new. Previously it had arisen when he had been under severe strain from work, and it had provided the first really

[10] *TLP*5, p. 121; *TZC*1, p. 272.
[11] *TLP*5, pp. 119–20; *TZC*1, p. 271; *YDGC*, p. 50 (partial).

positive sign of some psychological condition lying outside the circle of those reactions that normal balanced mortals may experience under circumstances of prolonged stress. Yet on this occasion it does not appear to have been caused by overwork. Rather it may have been the consequence of another type of stress which Tchaikovsky certainly experienced that summer at Hapsal, and which Modest very significantly ignores. When chronicling the social life of Tchaikovsky's earlier years, Modest had been ready enough to record any little incident that might signify the stirrings of an attraction towards a member of the opposite sex, and to substantiate such incidents with excerpts from his brother's letters. But it was during this summer at Hapsal that, for the first time, Tchaikovsky had to cope with an emotional entanglement which was serious to a degree that he could not ignore, and which must have been an open challenge to his sexual nature. Vera Davïdova had fallen in love with him – or so she believed. Her feelings were far from new, as Tchaikovsky was quite certainly aware, and they had reached Sasha's ears; now daily contact with the object of her affections made concealment impossible. Sasha had become disturbed by what common sense told her was a dangerous emotional situation, and had reproached her brother for going to Hapsal at all. On 20 August he replied, providing the clearest evidence that survives of the situation and of his own feelings regarding it:

You ask why I decided to go to Hapsal, knowing that a person was living there for whom my presence was not without its dangers. In the first place, because there was nowhere else to go; secondly, I wanted to spend the summer with them all; and thirdly, because it seemed to me that, if what you suggest is really the case, then my absence would be more harmful to her than my presence. When I'm not there my person can, very likely, be imagined as worth loving. But when a woman who loves me has daily contact with my far from poetic qualities, such as slovenliness, irritability, cowardice, triviality, self-esteem, secretiveness, and so on – then, believe me, the halo that surrounds me when I'm afar will evaporate very quickly. Perhaps I'm blind and stupid, but I swear to you that I have noticed in her nothing except the most ordinary, friendly liking for me. And so, don't be angry with me, and for God's sake don't think that I'm deliberately inflaming a tender heart through some Pechorin-like[12] pride or malice, so that later I may strike at it with even colder indifference. I am quite incapable of such gross baseness, the more so since there are

[12] Pechorin was the heartless hero of Lermontov's novel, *A Hero of Our Time.*

no limits to the love and esteem which I entertain towards the whole of that family.[13]

These are the stiff, correct sentiments of an honourable man determined to do the honourable thing. Even more, they are the words of a man who himself feels no response but remains detached and, one suspects, uncomprehending. Faced, however, with this challenge to his emotions, he must have suspected at the very least that his own impassivity reflected not so much a simple lack of response to this particular woman as a fundamental incapacity to respond to any overture from any woman. Realisation of this would be torment enough, and even if he managed to smother his awareness of it during this summer, Vera was to provide him with more cause for agonising self-knowledge during the coming two or three years.

When Tchaikovsky left Hapsal for St Petersburg on 26 August, he took with him not only the fruits of his work on the opera, but also three piano pieces which were to be issued as his Op. 2 under the title *Souvenir de Hapsal*, with a dedication to Vera Davïdova. The second of these, *Scherzo*, was a reworking of a student piece, the other two were new. The last of the set, *Chant sans paroles*, was to become one of Tchaikovsky's most famed compositions, and an obligatory choice for any anthology of his piano music. Yet none of these three pieces adds anything to his stature as a composer.

In early September he arrived in Moscow to resume his Conservatoire duties and proceed with the opera as best he could. He continued to visit the English Club, and regretted that he could not become a full member because he could not afford the subscription. His lack of money was a continual aggravation, and there can be no doubt that he carried out his intention of extracting some from his father when the latter passed through Moscow in mid-October on the way home from his summer with Zinaida. Shortage of funds did not, however, prevent Tchaikovsky enjoying an excellent performance of Molière's *Tartuffe*, and on 11 November he attended the première of Kashperov's opera, *The Storm*. 'Since they started writing operas there's never been such an abomination,' was his verdict.[14] However just this judgement may have been, it could hardly be expected that a composer who had already enshrined his own vision of Ostrovsky's play in a splendid overture would be receptive to another's musical conception of the same subject.

Among his various social engagements was a party at Dubuque's, the first occasion on which Tchaikovsky confessed to having got 'a little

[13] *TLP*5, p. 120.
[14] *TLP*5, p. 127; *TPB*, p. 36; *YDGC*, p. 52.

drunk'.[15] There is no doubt that, with his wide and firmly established social life, he was currently living a well-lubricated existence. 'However hard I try to live quietly, it's impossible to get by in Moscow without hard drinking and good food,' he informed Anatoly. 'By way of example I will tell you that on each of the last five days I've returned home late at night with my stomach stuffed full. However, don't think that I'm doing nothing,' he added hastily. 'From morning until dinner time I am continuously busy.'[16] There is no reason to doubt the truth of this; Kashkin vouched for the diligence, orderliness and assiduity that already characterised Tchaikovsky's creative labours, and for his habit of devoting the morning, when he could, to composition. Among his new social activities were two contributions to domestic entertainments at his friends, the Lopukhins. For one he composed some couplets for Pavel Fyodorov's *The Tangle*, and in another, apparently for the first time since his civil service days in St Petersburg, he acted a part (that of a doctor) in a little play. To do this meant exposing to the spectators a side of himself, even if under the mask of the character he was personifying, and this trivial occasion is perhaps the most cogent proof of how much Tchaikovsky now felt himself to be a real member, accepted and secure, of that Moscow society he had entered barely two years before.

Such exhibitions of himself were rare, however, and his diffidence to any parading of his musical accomplishments remained extreme. With Kashkin and Laroche he was always happy to spend an evening of music-making, playing through instrumental pieces (he was to develop an enviable skill at sight reading both piano and orchestral scores) and singing romances by obscure composers, of which he possessed an enormous pile. Never would he perform his own compositions, however, nor would he sing willingly if Rubinstein was within earshot. Another of this small circle of friends in whose company he felt secure enough to risk baring a little of his real self was Ivan Klimenko. Klimenko was an architect by training who had once taken harmony lessons with Laroche in St Petersburg. There, possibly at Serov's house, he had met Tchaikovsky. Now that Klimenko had moved to Moscow to take up an appointment with a railway construction company, the friendship was renewed and developed.

A far more portentous encounter of this period (though one that was never to lead to the kind of intimate relationship Tchaikovsky enjoyed with Klimenko) was with Vladimir Stasov. This was Tchaikovsky's first direct contact with a member of Balakirev's circle, and the meeting took place during the events which attended the second visit to Russia of

[15] *TLP*5, p. 121.
[16] *TLP*5, p. 127; *TZC*1, p. 280; *TPB*, p. 36.

Berlioz, now an aged and ailing man. Though the formal invitation to the French composer had come from the Grand Duchess Elena, it was Balakirev who was the true instigator of this visit. Between concerts in St Petersburg, Berlioz travelled to Moscow, where he twice appeared very successfully as a conductor,[17] once for the RMS, the other time at the vast riding school before an audience of over twelve thousand. On both occasions the programmes were largely devoted to Berlioz's own works. At the Conservatoire a dinner was given in his honour, on which occasion Tchaikovsky paid a handsome tribute in French to the distinguished visitor. Though he always retained a profound admiration for Berlioz's orchestration, Tchaikovsky held some strong reservations about his actual music. Nevertheless, the spectacle of this 'helpless, bent figure', as Kashkin remembered him,[18] deeply moved Tchaikovsky. Moreover this Frenchman symbolised the invincible artist; he was the embodiment 'of disinterested toil, of blazing love for art, a spokesman for vigorous, noble endeavours in the battle against obscurantism, stupidity, routine, intrigue and illiteracy',[19] as Tchaikovsky himself expressed it. Such a man could not but rouse Tchaikovsky's veneration, and the memories of this brief encounter with Berlioz, the first really great composer he had met face to face, remained with him the rest of his life.

Of Tchaikovsky's reactions when he was first confronted by Balakirev nothing is known. Nevertheless, when the latter arrived in Moscow hard on Berlioz's heels in mid-January, it is certain that he and Tchaikovsky did meet. So far the most influential men in Tchaikovsky's musical life had been the Rubinstein brothers; now, to this duo, was being added a third figure who was to leave a personal mark upon Tchaikovsky's creative career as deep as that of any man. This former mathematics student from Kazan University had enjoyed the patronage and encouragement of the distinguished amateur writer on music, Alexandr Ulïbïshev, in his native Nizhni-Novgorod, and it was Ulïbïshev who took the eighteen-year-old youth to St Petersburg in 1855, where he met and deeply impressed Glinka. 'Never have I met a man in whom I found views so close to my own on everything concerning music,' the doyen of Russian music had informed his sister, Lyudmila Shestakova. '. . . He will in time become a second Glinka.'[20] Less than two years later Glinka

---

[17] On 8 and 11 Jan. 1868.

[18] *KVC*, p. 43; *TZC*1, p. 284.

[19] *TZC*1, p. 284. Modest's source for this was a notice his brother wrote in 1873 on Berlioz's overture, *Les Francs-Juges* (see *TMKS*, p. 132).

[20] From Lyudmila Shestakova's recollections of her brother, quoted in *Glinka v vospominaniyakh sovremennikov* (Glinka as remembered by his contemporaries), ed. A. Orlova (Moscow, 1955), p. 291.

was dead, and the leadership of that national tradition of Russian music which Glinka had roused to life now devolved primarily upon Balakirev. He entered into his inheritance with vigour, energetically championing the cause of Glinka's music, and gathering round himself a group of composers – Cui, Musorgsky, Rimsky-Korsakov and Borodin – whose destinies he moulded. He found valuable allies, too, in the Stasov brothers, Vladimir and Dmitri, whose views on music coincided closely with his own. Dmitri was a lawyer and one of the founders of the RMS, while Vladimir was a true polymath, a passionate nationalist and a prodigiously prolific writer, one of the most distinguished Russian scholars and writers on fine art, who was also the author of the first biography of Glinka, and who subsequently employed his pen as a propagandist for the cause of Balakirev and his fellow nationalists. Yet it was less as a writer than as a source of ideas for subjects upon which they might compose operas or orchestral pieces that Vladimir performed his greatest service to Balakirev's group – and, in the case of his plans for a fantasy overture on Shakespeare's *The Tempest* and a symphony on Byron's *Manfred*, to Tchaikovsky.

It would be fascinating to know how Tchaikovsky had viewed Balakirev during his student years at the St Petersburg Conservatoire, for by that time Balakirev, though only three years Tchaikovsky's senior, was the very active centre of a musical party which was stoutly opposing the ideals represented by Anton Rubinstein and the brand of musical education which he fostered, and to which Tchaikovsky was already submitting himself. In 1862 Lomakin (Tchaikovsky's old vocal teacher at the School of Jurisprudence), with Balakirev as his assistant, had opened the Free Music School which aimed to provide musical instruction purged of the reactionary and anti-national tendencies which Balakirev saw embodied in Rubinstein and his Westernising party. To offset the prestige conferred upon the classes of the RMS by the Grand Duchess Elena, the Free Music School obtained royal patronage in the person of the Tsarevich Nikolay.[21] Besides free classes, the School promoted concerts, and during the next five years Balakirev and Lomakin conducted these, furthering the cause in Russia of Berlioz, Schumann and Liszt, paying active homage to Glinka and Dargo-mïzhsky, and introducing the first works of the younger Russian composers, Musorgsky, Cui and Rimsky-Korsakov, as well as of Balakirev himself. What Tchaikovsky, the most talented student of Rubinstein's Conservatoire, thought of such enterprises, and how much

[21] Nikolay died in 1865. The new heir to the throne was his brother Alexandr, honoured (with his wife) by Tchaikovsky in the Festival Overture on the Danish national anthem.

contact, if any, he had with them is unknown; from the evidence of his biography Balakirev and the Free Music School simply did not exist during those three and a half years before he left for Moscow to join the Conservatoire staff in 1866 – though he did hear Rimsky-Korsakov's First Symphony when it was performed just before Tchaikovsky's own graduation.

Then, in 1867, the musical scene in St Petersburg saw some abrupt changes. Anton Rubinstein relinquished the conductorship of the RMS concerts, and the man appointed to replace him was, of all people, Balakirev. The resources of the RMS permitted it to promote far more concerts than ever the Free Music School had been able to mount, and Balakirev suddenly found himself the most powerful individual in the capital's concert life. Rubinstein's influence had already waned when, earlier in the same year, he had handed over the directorship of the Conservatoire to Zaremba; Balakirev's power correspondingly waxed greater when, in February 1868, after Lomakin's resignation as director of the Free Music School, he was appointed Lomakin's successor. The Balakirev whom Tchaikovsky first met at the beginning of 1868 was therefore a far more powerful figure than the one upon whom he must have gazed a few years earlier from behind the walls of the St Petersburg Conservatoire. And it was, of course, this same Balakirev who would be conducting his *Dances of the Hay Maidens* in St Petersburg – always assuming, that is, that the directors sent the signed application which Tchaikovsky had stipulated as a condition for releasing this composition to them. It seems possible that Tchaikovsky, confronted by Balakirev himself, relented, contenting himself with a personal request from Balakirev to which he acceded in a letter of 2 February 1868. The impression made upon him by Balakirev, and the sudden high opinion he had formed of this great new power in St Petersburg's musical world, is amply attested by the concluding sentence:

> In accordance with our agreement, I am sending you the score of my *Dances*. If it's possible to perform them in some concert you are conducting, then I shall be extremely obliged to you. If, however, this is impossible, be so kind as to return them to me when an opportunity arises – and at the same time send me a word of encouragement if you can. I should find it pleasant in the highest degree to receive such a thing from you.[22]

It is possible that Tchaikovsky, mindful of the scathing opinion of his talents expressed two years earlier by Cui in his review of the graduation

[22] *TLP*5, p. 131; *BVP*, p. 118.

cantata, wanted to hear from the leader of the nationalists himself some favourable verdict on his work which might counter Cui's pronouncement. Tchaikovsky's letter is formal, even starchy, but also reveals a deference that comes from genuine respect. As for Balakirev, his reply foretells that authoritative, paternalistic role he was proposing to assume in Tchaikovsky's creative life. Circumstances prevented him from performing Tchaikovsky's dances, though Konstantin Lyadov did conduct them at one of the Lent concerts promoted by the Imperial Theatres on 29 March. The request for some encouragement is neatly sidestepped by a compliment to Tchaikovsky's musical stature. In any case, Balakirev preferred to give his opinions in person and at length so that (though he does not admit this to Tchaikovsky) he might press his views more forcefully, and with more certainty of being able to impose them:

> Regarding the word 'encouragement', this, as far as you are concerned, I consider not only inappropriate but also dishonest. Encouragements are only for the little children of art, but from your score I see you are, both in orchestration and technique, a fully fledged artist to whom only *strict criticism* and not encouragement is to be applied. When we meet in person I shall be very pleased to give you my opinion. . . . It will be far better when we're [both] in Moscow to play through the piece at the piano and examine it bar by bar. Let us not substitute criticism for lively argument!
>
> You would give me great pleasure by sending me [a copy of] your translation of the textbook on orchestration.[23]

These first letters exchanged with Balakirev set the tone of this new and crucial relationship for Tchaikovsky. During the next two years Balakirev's despotic influence was to grow until it became, albeit briefly, the most powerful agent in Tchaikovsky's creative life. For the moment, however, his relations with Balakirev and his circle were cautious, and musically 1868 was largely occupied with the completion of work on *The Voyevoda* and preparations for its production. The year started with a mixture of discomforts and pleasures. Laroche was ill, and had moved into Tchaikovsky's own room adjoining the Conservatoire so that he could be sure of being able to continue his teaching. Tchaikovsky's devotion to Laroche – and his ready willingness to suffer discomfort for the sake of a friend – is underlined by this sacrifice of his own quarters. He felt concern for Laroche's welfare in another respect, too, for the latter had become engaged to 'a very nice Conservatoire student – very

[23] *BVP*, p. 118.

poor, however, yet (surprisingly) actually in love with him. All the same, it's great foolishness on his part,' he declared to Anatoly.[24]

On 15 February 1868 his First Symphony was at last heard in its entirety. Its substantial success evidently caught Tchaikovsky somewhat unprepared. 'There were many calls for the composer,' one eyewitness recalled, 'and he appeared, casually dressed, to bow very uncomfortably and inelegantly, nervously crumpling his hat in his hands.'[25] Awkward he may have felt, but otherwise the success of his symphony was unalloyed pleasure, more than can be said of the concert at the Bolshoy Theatre sixteen days later at which his *Dances of the Hay Maidens* was played. It was gratifying to have a work performed twice in one season, but this time Tchaikovsky had been requested to conduct the piece himself. Since it was a charity concert at which many other artists were also giving their services, he could hardly refuse, though he was desperately apprehensive. He himself left no record of the occasion, but Kashkin did:

I went behind the scenes where the débutant-conductor was, and approached him. He told me that, to his own surprise, he wasn't feeling in the least scared. We talked a little, after which, before his piece, I went off to my seat in the stalls. Soon after this Pyotr Ilich appeared, and my first glance told me that he had gone completely to pieces. The orchestral players were already arranged on stage, and he walked between their desks bending forward just as though he wanted to hide himself. When he finally reached the rostrum, he had the appearance of a man finding himself in a desperate situation. He completely forgot his own piece, saw nothing that was in the score, and failed to give the players their cues in those places where it was really necessary. Fortunately the orchestra knew the piece so well that the players paid no attention to his wrong directions, and played the *Dances* quite satisfactorily, simply grinning when they looked towards the composer.[26]

Despite this unhappy exhibition, the dances were well received. Afterwards Tchaikovsky confided to Kashkin that he had again been afflicted with the sensation that his head would keep falling to one side if he had not made constant and strenuous efforts to keep it upright. It was nine years before he again ventured on to the rostrum.

March 1868 saw Tchaikovsky's début in another capacity: as music

[24] *TLP*5, p. 132; *TPB*, p. 39.
[25] The Countess Kapnist, quoted in *TZC*1, p. 285, and *YDGC*, p. 53 (partial).
[26] *KVC*, p. 42; *TZC*1, p. 286; *YDGC*, pp. 53–4 (partial); *DTC*, pp. 16–17.

critic. In later years he was to find this a useful, if uncongenial, way of augmenting his income, and though, as might be expected, his views and judgements frequently suffer from imbalance and idiosyncrasy, he also showed on occasion considerable acumen. The subject of his first notice, printed in *The Contemporary Chronicle* on 22 March, was Rimsky-Korsakov's *Fantasia on Serbian Themes*, which had first been performed in Moscow the preceding December, and which was repeated in the same concert as Tchaikovsky's *Dances of the Hay Maidens*. Tchaikovsky's tone is approving and encouraging, though with reservations. As criticism the notice aims to be balanced; it is also precisely what might be expected of a composer who wished to find favour with the Balakirev circle, but who wished it to be clear that he was no uncritical neophyte, let alone a sycophant. After pondering briefly the fallibility of audiences (and of the Moscow public in particular), lamenting the dearth of informed criticism, and taking to task the anonymous reviewer who had condemned this newest work 'of this young, talented musician upon whom so many brilliant hopes are set by all who love our art',[27] Tchaikovsky briefly reviews Rimsky-Korsakov's First Symphony, which had first been heard in St Petersburg on 31 December 1865, ten days before the one and only performance of his own graduation cantata. In Tchaikovsky's opinion, the symphony's

> first and last movements – conspicuous neither for originality in melodic invention, nor for beauty in that contrapuntal exploitation of themes which is carried to such striking perfection in the great school of German music, nor for integrity of structure, nor for brilliance of scoring – were the weakest parts of this first essay in the field of symphonic music. But in the Adagio and scherzo a strong talent proclaimed itself. In particular the Adagio, founded upon a folksong about a Tartar captive, struck everyone by its rhythmic originality (it is in $\frac{7}{4}$), its charming orchestration, which is not, however, either precious or effect-seeking, by its structural novelty, and most of all by the freshness of its purely Russian harmonic turns, and immediately showed Mr Rimsky-Korsakov to be a remarkable symphonic talent.[28]

Tchaikovsky admits he has heard none of Rimsky-Korsakov's subsequent works except for this new fantasy, of which he gives some

[27] *TMKS*, p. 26. Tchaikovsky's reproach is the more notable, considering that this same article had included some very favourable comments on Tchaikovsky's own *Dances*.

[28] *TMKS*, p. 26.

account before concluding with a paragraph which qualifies his rapturous description of the fantasy's actual train of events, and sounds a note that is markedly avuncular, considering that his subject is only four years younger than Tchaikovsky himself:

> One may say with confidence that our young composer has advanced significantly in all respects during the two years between the appearance of his symphony and the Moscow performance of the *Fantasia on Serbian Themes*. But we do not want to contend that Mr Rimsky-Korsakov is yet advancing along his own road with the firm tread of a talent that is fully matured. His style is not yet defined. The influence of Glinka and Dargomïzhsky, and imitation of Mr Balakirev's methods declare themselves at every step.
>
> Let us remember that Mr Rimsky-Korsakov is still a young man, that his whole future is before him – and there is no doubt that this remarkably gifted being is destined to become one of the best ornaments of our art.[29]

Modest drew attention to the ambivalence of his brother's attitude towards the 'mighty handful' (or 'Kuchka', as they became known in Russia). Tchaikovsky recognised the sincerity of these men and the great talent that some at least of them possessed, even though he was often not attracted to the creations in which these talents were embodied; his well-schooled technique, for instance, could not accept what he saw as the rough empiricism of Musorgsky's style. It seems that he could be more open in his association with the Kuchka when he was well away from them in Moscow. There, free from their direct pressures to convert his creativity to their creeds, he could cultivate his association with them entirely on his own terms, especially by becoming, as Modest described it, their 'delegate' in Moscow, acting as an intermediary between them and the RMS or Jurgenson, and looking after their interests generally. His later notices were to include critical comment on works of the St Petersburg group, and these show him openly appreciative of their work, especially of that of Balakirev and Rimsky-Korsakov. Yet, as Modest admirably summarised it, 'he did not wish to become one with it [the Kuchka], he refused to take up the symbol of its faith, but he considered it both desirable and worthy of his calling to gain recognition from it without making concessions, to take up its challenges (both *Romeo* and *The Tempest* were composed on suggestions from Balakirev and Stasov) and to emerge triumphant with a solution to the suggested task, but to reveal his solidarity with them only when the

[29] *TMKS*, p. 27.

artistic requirements were worthy.'[30] These attitudes were reciprocated by the Kuchka in their own way.

There is some cause to regret that the two clear parties in late-nineteenth-century Russian music ever acquired the labels 'nationalist' and 'Western' (though, for convenience, this book will continue to use them). After all, even Anton Rubinstein was to become self-consciously national in some of his later works, while Balakirev, like Tchaikovsky, all his life freely employed the contrapuntal techniques of Western music, even opening his piano sonata with a fugal exposition. Borodin actually wrote string quartets – much to the disgust of Musorgsky, who was the one member of the Kuchka to turn his back resolutely on all aspects of Western style which could be excluded from his own work. More accurate, though less than ideal descriptions of these two parties, certainly during the 1860s and '70s, might have been 'radical' and 'traditional', the adherents of the latter being suspicious or hostile to the new trends in music, wishing instead to preserve in their own works what they saw as the best in the Western tradition of the immediate past, while the former were eager to explore further the new musical territories being opened up by contemporary innovators, and to incorporate into their new revelations a full exploitation of their national musical resources, not as incidental embellishment but as a formative factor in their style and technique. Tchaikovsky, educated in the traditionalist camp, had had ample opportunity to discover what was best in the music and the values that Rubinstein and Zaremba cherished, and he was far too balanced ever to reject these completely. Then came the move to Moscow, the migration into a freer musical environment led by a man far more open-minded and musically less prim than his brother, and peopled with young fellow musicians no longer disposed to accept inherited authority as their own unquestioned creed. Tchaikovsky had already shown in *The Storm* some violent intimations of his own musical independence; now, as a rapidly maturing composer, he needed the nourishment of new attitudes and styles so that his musical frame might achieve its full unstunted stature. Thus he was bound to be attracted by the exciting new explorations of the Kuchka. He needed, too, to redeem in their eyes the terrible judgement that one of their number had pronounced at his first encounter with any of Tchaikovsky's works. Yet, while seeking their society, he feared being engulfed by them, and the moment he sensed that Balakirev's catalytic power might swamp him, he was to draw back.

His first acquaintance with other members of Balakirev's group occurred very soon after this article on Rimsky-Korsakov had been

[30] *TZC*1, p. 290.

printed. It found favour with them all, and when he visited St Petersburg during April, they greeted him warmly. The Kuchka's preferred meeting place was currently at Dargomïzhsky's, where the dying, house-bound composer was struggling to finish his opera, *The Stone Guest* (Tchaikovsky had already met Dargomïzhsky in Moscow). Balakirev also invited Tchaikovsky to his own home. It proved to be a hectic and taxing Easter break, and when the composer arrived back in Moscow towards the end of the month, the longing for solitude flooded in upon him.

Perhaps he had had a surfeit of human company; certainly Vera had been affording him more torment. His letter to Sasha of 28 April reveals all too clearly that he had thoughtlessly given Vera some cause to believe that he might intend to share her future. 'Perhaps Vera has told you how in Hapsal we often jokingly talked together of some future farmhouses of our own, where we might quietly live out our days.'[31] One wonders whether Vera had really taken it all so lightly, or whether the 'farmhouses' had really been in the plural. As for Tchaikovsky himself, he avers that what he wants is solitude, and that marriage has no part in this. He takes it for granted that Sasha will provide all the services of a wife: 'Do not doubt that sooner or later you will have to assign a part of your maternal care to your ageing and weary brother. Perhaps you think that such a condition of the spirit will lead a man to want to marry. No, my dear, future companion. Besides, because of my lassitude I am too lazy to establish any new conjugal relationship, too lazy to take my place at the head of a family, too lazy to take upon myself responsibility for the fate of a wife and children. In a word, marriage is for me unthinkable.'[32] And then, following this world-weary romancing, the true reason for this vision of escape tumbles out. After the airy ease of his dreams in the first part of this letter, the scarcely lucid prose of the next paragraph exposes the anguish that Tchaikovsky is suffering:

The one thing that torments and frightens me is Vera. Tell me: what should I do, and how should I act in regard to her? I well understand how all this ought to finish – but what will you tell me to do if I feel that I would conceive a hatred for her if the question of fulfilling our relationship in marriage should become serious? I know that she from pride, and others from ignorance or for external considerations, expend a good deal of imagination on this. But I know also that, whatever the obstacles, it is I who would have to take the initiative in this matter [of making a proposal of marriage], and would have to consider her favourable decision the greatest happiness for myself, for there are no beings as wonderful as she is. But I am so

[31] *TLP5*, p. 136; *TZC1*, p. 274.   [32] *TLP5*, p. 136; *TZC1*, p. 274.

base and ungrateful that I cannot act as I should, and I am terribly tormented. Help me set my mind at rest – and for God's sake, tear up this letter.[33]

Beset by such emotional strains, Tchaikovsky must have welcomed the chance of escaping that summer to a place away from Russia where there was no risk of an extended confrontation with Vera. Thus when Vladimir Shilovsky invited him to be his guest on a tour abroad in return for music lessons, he accepted with alacrity. The party was completed by Shilovsky's stepfather, Vladimir Begichev, and the baritone, de Lazari. On 7 June the four men left for Berlin, where they spent a week. Their intention had been to visit some of the picturesque spots in Europe, but Shilovsky, who was already showing signs of tuberculosis, became ill, and they headed for Paris where the invalid wished to consult a particular specialist. By 1 August, when Tchaikovsky wrote to Sasha, they had been five weeks in the French capital. Having on his previous visit seen most of the interesting sights of the city, Tchaikovsky had relinquished the role of a tourist in favour of a simple and settled routine. 'I get up quite late, go to breakfast, and read the papers. Returning home at about midday, I undress completely (the heat is indescribable) and keep myself busy [with *The Voyevoda*] right up to dinner time. At six I dine with my companions or alone. I spend the evening at the theatre.'[34] What again particularly impressed him about both the theatre and the opera companies in Paris was the absence of star performers and the splendid efficiency of the ensembles. Everything was thoroughly studied and prepared, and attention was paid to the minutest details. 'At home we have no conception of performance such as this,' he lamented to Sasha.[35]

A week later Tchaikovsky left Paris, spent several days at Sillameg, near Narva, where the Davïdovs were staying, and then travelled with them to St Petersburg. At the beginning of September he was back in Moscow. Though his teaching load at the Conservatoire had been increased, so had his salary, and this prompted the thought that he might now be able to escape from living with Rubinstein. However, he quickly had to admit to himself that this was still impracticable. Term began on 14 September, and Tchaikovsky found he had so lost the habit of teaching that he was overcome by nerves and had to withdraw from his first class for ten minutes to avoid fainting. That evening he ran into Apukhtin at the theatre. For some reason Tchaikovsky had offended

[33] *TLP*5, pp. 136–7; *YDGC*, p. 54 (partial).
[34] *TLP*5, p. 138; *TZC*1, p. 293; *TPB*, p. 40.
[35] *TLP*5, p. 138; *TZC*1, p. 294; *TPB*, p. 41.

Apukhtin, and the latter tried to avoid him. However, Tchaikovsky insisted upon talking with him, offered explanations that soothed his wounded friend, and subsequently enjoyed with him several pleasant social evenings which helped soften the blow of having to return to his professorial duties. More prolonged strains and excitements came from finding himself precipitated into the preparations for the production of *The Voyevoda*. He had devoted what time he could the previous winter to composing the opera, and before the end of February he had set about scoring the third act. 'I want to finish the opera by the summer,' he had written to Anatoly. 'I already have another libretto in mind.'[36] What this was is not known. Tchaikovsky's hopes of having *The Voyevoda* completed by the summer were not fulfilled, and the orchestration was only at last finished during his stay in Paris.

On his return to Moscow, Tchaikovsky had immediately placed his new work in the hands of Stepan Gedeonov, the director of the Imperial Theatres. Gedeonov wasted no time, and distributed the parts among the chosen performers, intending to mount the opera in October. Tchaikovsky did not take this too seriously; the time for rehearsal seemed impossibly short and, in addition, an Italian opera company was installed in the Bolshoy Theatre and was absorbing the services of both the resident orchestra and chorus. Thus he thought that December would be the earliest at which the opera could be produced. He had not reckoned with Gedeonov's determination, however, for on 25 September he informed Modest with some alarm:

The day before yesterday, I received unexpectedly a summons to present myself at the theatre. How surprised I was when I discovered that there had already been two chorus rehearsals of my opera, and that the first one for the soloists had been fixed for the next day. I attended this and accompanied the singers. Just imagine, Gedeonov wants to have the opera ready by 23 October, and now everyone here is going mad so that His Excellency's wish shall be fulfilled. I have strong doubts that it will be possible to learn such a difficult piece in one month, and I am already appalled at the thought of the running about and fuss that I shall have to face. There will be rehearsals every day. The singers are very satisfied with my opera.[37]

Gedeonov's precipitate preparations had taken Tchaikovsky aback, but the latter quickly grasped the lunacy of attempting to introduce a new work by a native composer while a visiting Italian company was

---

[36] *TLP5*, p. 133; *TPB*, p. 39.
[37] *TLP5*, p. 141; *TPB*, pp. 42–3; *TZC1*, pp. 298–9 (partial); *DTL*, pp. 18–19 (partial).

engrossing the attention of Moscow audiences, and within a fortnight of his letter to Modest he had written to Gedeonov, telling him that he would withhold the full score of his opera, and thus force the production to be postponed until December. Gedeonov was compelled to capitulate, and the rehearsals were discontinued until January. In the meantime Ostrovsky, who must have been impressed by Tchaikovsky's achievement, had put forward a scheme for a second opera:

> The other day I was dining at Ostrovsky's, and he himself suggested that he should write a magnificent new libretto for me. The subject had been in his mind for twenty years. Up to now he had remained undecided to whom he should offer it – and he has finally chosen me. The action takes place in Babylon and Greece in the time of Alexander the Great, who himself participates actively in the opera. In it representatives from two nations of classical times, the Hebrews and the Greeks, are in conflict. The hero is a young Jew who is disappointed in his love for a young Jewess who, for reasons of ambition, prefers Alexander. In the end he [the young Jew] becomes a prophet. You cannot conceive how magnificent the plot is.[38]

Tchaikovsky's enthusiasm was short-lived, however, for nothing more was ever heard of this subject.

Further stimulus to public interest in the forthcoming production of *The Voyevoda* was given by a very successful performance under Nikolay Rubinstein of the *Dances of the Hay Maidens* at a charity concert on 20 December, and Tchaikovsky (using the pseudonym 'Cramer') concocted a potpourri from the opera for Jurgenson to publish: the dances had, of course, already appeared in an arrangement for piano duet. When rehearsals resumed in the New Year, Tchaikovsky was again most gratified by the zeal with which the singers were preparing the piece, and this reassured him that, despite problems during rehearsals, all would be in reasonable order by the première. His morale must have been raised by news of a second performance in St Petersburg of his dances, again conducted by Nikolay Rubinstein, on 6 February 1869. This performance occasioned a review by Borodin in which he rated the scoring far higher than the musical content of the dances.

The Voyevoda was at last heard on 11 February 1869 at the Bolshoy Theatre as a benefit performance for Alexandra Menshikova, who created the part of Mariya. Two days later Tchaikovsky was able to write happily to Modest: 'My opera went very well. Despite the very banal libretto, it had a brilliant success. I took fifteen curtain calls, and was

[38] *TLP5*, p. 144; *TZC1*, pp. 299–300; *TPB*, pp. 43–4.

presented with a laurel wreath. The performance was pretty good.'[39] He was flattered also by some complimentary letters he had received. Yet the opera could not have been all that successful, for it survived only four further performances, the last being on 14 March.[40] It was never again heard during Tchaikovsky's lifetime, and subsequently he destroyed the score, though for reasons Gerald Abraham has proposed (see footnote on p. 153), he may not have done this until many years later. Fortunately the orchestral material, except for the harp part, survived, as well as a number of other separate sources from which it has been possible to restore nearly all the vocal parts. The opera was revived in Leningrad in 1949.

If it is difficult to reconcile Tchaikovsky's own account of a great success with the complete failure of the work to hold the public's interest, Kashkin's recollections may help to clarify the situation. 'The staging of the opera was incredibly impoverished,' he remembered. 'The whole was done with odds and ends of scenery and any old costumes.'[41] Kashkin's accusations of bad staging are supported by other eyewitnesses. There were severe shortcomings in the performing forces, too. The orchestra was good, but the chorus was indifferent. Despite adequate resources for mounting operas, there was neither the ability nor the will to use them to best advantage. The chief conductor, Ivan Schramek, had plenty of experience, but was lazy and untalented – and did not like Russian music anyway. His deputy, Eduard Merten, who conducted *The Voyevoda*, was talented and energetic, but too young to have much authority. As for the singers, they were willing enough, but their musical skills were too limited to cope with anything outside their normal experience, and Tchaikovsky's parts presented them with certain new problems they could not properly surmount. Nor was Tchaikovsky the man to help in such circumstances. 'Those who knew Tchaikovsky at a later time,' Kashkin added,

know how modest he was in his demands upon those who were performing his works, how easily he was satisfied, and how difficult he found it to make any observation to a singer, male or female, even when they themselves asked him for it. In this matter Pyotr Ilich's reserve knew no bounds. He was, in a way, quite ashamed to bother artists with the performance of his works, but at the same time he was still not satisfied with everything – and during the staging of his first opera he was quite incapable of making any serious observation,

[39] *TLP*5, p. 155; *TPB*, pp. 49–50; *DTC*, p. 21.
[40] The second act alone was given in an evening of miscellaneous items on 9 March.
[41] *KVC*, p. 57; *TZC*1, p. 312; *DTC*, p. 20.

of making any demands. He simply suffered, and only longed for the end of his torture.[42]

Under such circumstances it is impossible to believe that the performance could have been very satisfactory, or have had any chance of making a forceful impact upon the audience. In this work Tchaikovsky enjoyed no more than a *succès d'estime*.

What press reaction there was to the opera was at best respectful. There was certainly no enthusiasm. By far the most significant notice was that penned by Laroche, who started with a complimentary preamble on Tchaikovsky as a composer in general (though he was careful to establish his impartiality by pointing to a few of his subject's shortcomings), and then proceeded to review the opera, commending what he heard as its best bits, but being quite unsparing in setting out its weaknesses. Most significant were what he saw as the stylistic sources of *The Voyevoda*. He accused Tchaikovsky of relying too heavily upon German models:

> In his style there can clearly be heard his affinity with the most recent imitators of Schumann. . . . Mr Tchaikovsky's music wavers between German (the predominant) and Italian styles. . . . But from time to time in *The Voyevoda* there appear Russian folktunes which the composer takes as themes for extensive development, and which he treats with indubitable taste and refinement. It is these songs more than anything that expose the non-Russian character of all the remaining numbers. . . . Mr Tchaikovsky shares with the most recent German composers a predilection for the orchestra and indifference to the human voice. . . . Very often the sonorous, beautiful scoring completely drowns the performers' voices, and the spectator on such occasions can only look in his libretto and simply guess what they are singing about.[43]

However strong his personal reservations about his friend's opera, Laroche was tactless in the extreme to have proclaimed them so publicly. Tchaikovsky read the article and was terribly upset by it. The next day, when he met Laroche, he expressed his bitterness very bluntly. The result was a rift between the two men, and only after two years were they properly reconciled. The point which gave Tchaikovsky greatest offence – Laroche's accusation of a basic non-Russianness in the music – was a thoroughly unjust criticism, for *The Voyevoda* is in fact filled with

[42] *KVC*, pp. 55–6; *TZC*1, p. 311; *DTC*, p. 20.
[43] *TZC*1, pp. 316–17; *DTC*, pp. 24–5.

invention which has affinities with the native music of Russia itself. Prince Odoyevsky was far nearer the mark in a brief note he made in his diary after attending the dress rehearsal of the opera. 'The Russian musical character predominates, but the gifted Tchaikovsky has also not resisted a desire to gratify the public with various Italianisms.'[44] Had he, in addition, recognised the strong infusion of French and German ingredients, Odoyevsky's private judgement would have been incontrovertible.

Ostrovsky's *The Voyevoda* was first performed in 1865. It had originally been intended that the opera should be in four acts, but after Ostrovsky had ceased to be a partner in the project, Tchaikovsky took the decision to cut it down to three. Modest was highly critical of the content of his brother's final libretto:

> Everything that comprises the main charm and enchantment of the comedy – that is, all the real-life and fantastic part of it – was ruthlessly omitted, and only the pallid and empty story of the unsuccessful amorous adventure of a lascivious and cruel old man was preserved. There is no trace in the opera of the lively and colourful folk scenes, nor of the detailed delineation, so vivid and striking, of less important characters such as Nedviga and Nastasya Dyuzhaya, et. al.; there is no trace in the opera of the Domovoy, of the gloomy figure of Mizgir, of the stately, blessed hermit, of the pilgrimage procession, nor, finally (and most important of all), of the Voyevoda's dreams. And the guilty one in all this is, it seems, Pyotr Ilich himself and not Ostrovsky.[45]

This may be true enough, but Tchaikovsky was wise in recognising that the sort of incidental decoration which may be excellent in a play could very well, if there was a lot of it, be damaging in a libretto – at least, if he was the man who had to set it. Had he been Musorgsky who, at the very time when Tchaikovsky's opera was being produced, was immersed in composing his own *Boris Godunov*, he might have risen magnificently to the opportunities for crowd scenes, local colour, and for the vivid realisation of character detail which makes that masterpiece of Russian opera such a marvellous panorama of living and breathing human beings. But Tchaikovsky was no Musorgsky. He had little real dramatic ability except in so far as his personal identification with a character might permit him to project something of himself into that character's music. He lacked completely that particular brand of originality which enabled Musorgsky to splinter the formal patterns and materials of Western opera and reshape them to articulate so clearly the traits,

---

[44] *DTC*, p. 19.   [45] *TZC*1, pp. 295–6; *DTC*, p. 18.

behaviour and emotions of real, ordinary Russian individuals and groups. What Tchaikovsky needed was an economical and clear plot which did not require a response that went outside established operatic precedents, and which could accommodate lengthy and static set-pieces without blowing the whole up to Wagnerian proportions. This is precisely what the final libretto of *The Voyevoda* provided.

The real problem is that the story is a contrived melodrama with stock situations and characters who are types, not individuals. The tale is set in a large town on the Volga in the middle of the seventeenth century, and runs as follows:

ACT 1. *The garden of Dyuzhoy, a wealthy merchant.*
An offstage women's chorus begins a folksong (No. 1), and then enters, followed by Mariya and her sister, Praskovya (Dyuzhoy's daughters), and a nurse, Nedviga. Mariya is bored. Enjoined by the nurse, the chorus sings the second verse of their song (bar 58). Mariya silences it, and the conversation touches briefly and dispiritedly on the forthcoming marriage of Praskovya to the Voyevoda, Shalïgin. Nedviga bluntly denounces the match as unsuitable (bar 74): 'A fine bridegroom! . . . He's an evil old man. You'll shed many tears with him!' Mariya, who longs to be married herself, changes the subject, and sings (No. 2) the beginning of a song about a beauty who has been imprisoned in a high tower. She breaks off because she does not know how the story continues. However, she mischievously invents her own end (in $\frac{5}{4}/\frac{6}{4}$), telling how the beauty's parents and the guards fall asleep so that her lover can reach her. After the women have teased Nedviga, who refuses to tell the real end of the tale, the nurse upbraids them for their frivolity (bar 155), but Mariya takes their part (bar 174): 'If there is no love in our own lives to give us delight, we shall be glad to rejoice in it even if it's only in a fairy tale.' Slowly the stage empties, and the voices fade.

Bastryukov, in love with Mariya, enters with Rezvy and other servants (No. 3). The thought of a splendid banquet in reward fortifies the servants' resolve to keep watch and, if necessary, rescue Bastryukov if he should be intercepted when he tries to see Mariya. After opening up a way through the fence, the servants withdraw and, left alone, Bastryukov serenades Mariya, calling her to him (No. 4). She enters (No. 5), and after agitated greetings, she declares her intention of marrying him ultimately, though he can foresee an obstacle to this in the imminent marriage of the Voyevoda, who is his enemy, to her sister. In the ensuing duet (andante non troppo) she counsels patience, but promises that if any attempt is made to force her to marry someone else, then she will come to him. Bastryukov endeavours to persuade her to leave with him forthwith, but she persists in her resolve, calms him when he desperately declares that they will never see each other again (allegro vivo), reaffirms her constancy (allegro vivace), and they finally part. As she leaves, Rezvy rushes in (No. 6) to say that the Voyevoda has come. Bastryukov hides. Shalïgin, Dyuzhoy and his wife, and the Jester enter (No. 7). Dyuzhoy invites the Voyevoda to drink with him, while Nastasya, his wife, nags at him, and the Jester makes sardonic comments.

Nastasya will not drink, saying that it will make her incoherent (bar 56), while the Jester, being cross at not being offered a glass, leaves (bar 74). Shaligin now demands to see his future bride (bar 90). Dyuzhoy and Nastasya plead (tranquillo) that he has seen her once, and that he is not now supposed to meet her again until the wedding. Suddenly the Jester's cry is heard from the bushes (allegro), and Mariya rushes in (bar 126), pursued by him. The Voyevoda is immediately smitten by her (bar 162), and declares that he wants her, not Praskovya (bar 213). Dyuzhoy straightway agrees to his new demand (bar 221), despite Nastasya's protests. The Voyevoda pays court to Mariya (No. 8), who is so appalled at the prospect that she longs to throw herself in the Volga. After an extensive ensemble they all go into the house.

Bastryukov and Rezvy emerge agitatedly from the bushes (allegro semplice). The Jester observes what is going on (bar 69) and rushes off to tell the Voyevoda. Mariya appears in the porch (allegro agitato) and declares that she will now come with Bastryukov. His servants break down the fence, but before they can all leave, Shaligin and the Dyuzhoys return, also with servants (bar 93). The Voyevoda signals for Bastryukov to be taken, but the latter's servants protect him. Mariya falls into her mother's arms. Bastryukov despairingly bids farewell to Mariya (bar 101), who vows that she will still be his alone, while the Voyevoda fumes because his servants are not apprehending Bastryukov. This stalemate continues into the first part of the finale (No. 9). Mariya and Bastryukov reaffirm their love (bar 57). Bastryukov prepares with his servants to leave by boat (bar 89): 'We will wash away our grief on mother Volga,' he sings (adagio). Shaligin again tries to have him taken, and the act ends with further affirmations from all of their individual intentions and wishes, the Voyevoda swearing vengeance for the insult he has suffered.

ACT 2, SCENE 1. *An entrance hall in Bastryukov's house.*
A group of Bastryukov's servants, with lanterns and torches, are awaiting his return from hunting (No. 1). Bastryukov, Rezvy and some other servants enter (No. 2). Bastryukov is still sorrowful: 'Has my former happiness gone for ever?' he asks, as he begins his aria (bar 20), and longs for death (meno mosso), but his servants plead with him. As he finishes this lament for his lost Mariya, Rezvy tells him (bar 99) that Dubrovin, a fugitive from the Voyevoda, wishes to see him. Bastryukov agrees, reflecting (bar 122) that Dubrovin may be able to bring him comfort. Dubrovin enters (No. 3), and tells (bar 16) how two years earlier Shaligin had abducted his wife by force and ruined him so that he had to become a fugitive (bar 36). Bastryukov asks (bar 53) Dubrovin to help him rescue Mariya, and Dubrovin reveals (bar 59) that the Voyevoda is leaving the next day on a pilgrimage, and that it has been arranged that Olyona, his wife, and Mariya will be in the garden that night awaiting deliverance. They agree on joint action.

ACT 2, SCENE 2. *[In the Voyevoda's home.]*
Veiled hay maidens dance (No. 4) around Mariya, who is silent and dejected. Nedviga comments upon Mariya's changed disposition (No. 5), and asks (bar 15) whether she would prefer to be left alone. After all have departed (bar 19), Mariya sings (cantabile) the tale of an imprisoned maiden and a nightingale, and of the joy of freedom. As she finishes, Olyona rushes in (No. 6) as though to

report a disaster which happened when she was doing the washing by the river; when she sees no one else is present, she tells Mariya (bar 11) that while she was washing a dress, a woman had approached and delivered a secret message from Bastryukov that Mariya should be in the garden the next night; it will be safe because the guards will have been made drunk. Mariya asks (bar 29) how Olyona herself came to be imprisoned, and she tells of how the Voyevoda had stolen her from her husband whom he had imprisoned and would have killed, had God permitted it. For the last two years he has been wandering, she knows not where. She plans (bar 88) to be in the garden with Mariya. She explains that in order to have an excuse for speaking to Mariya she has said that she had dropped one of Mariya's veils into the river while washing; it was then only natural, of course, that she would have to come and ask forgiveness. The two women sing (No. 7) of their desires and impending happiness, and their excitement increases (No. 8). Nedviga and the other women enter (No. 9), and Olyona again pretends to be a distressed servant confessing to the accident of the lost veil. Mariya feigns anger, and says she will make Olyona work harder to atone for her fault, keeping Olyona always with her – and then turns to Nedviga: 'And for her misdemeanour she is to eat from the boyars' table.' The bewildered Nedviga tells the chorus (bar 50) to sing and dance, and the scene ends with a khorovod (bar 69).

ACT 3. *A courtyard, with a tower and staircase on one side.*
Bastryukov and Dubrovin enter. Dubrovin reveals (No. 1) that he has made the guards drunk, and that the ladies will soon come down the staircase. The restless Bastryukov walks to the back of the stage (bar 31), leaving the way clear for Dubrovin to sing an aria (andante) in which he expresses his agitation and apprehension: will Olyona still love him? Mariya and Olyona descend the staircase (No. 2). The couples embrace (andante), and launch into a quartet of rapt happiness (No. 3): 'The warm, still night covers us with its black cloak. . . .' As Bastryukov and Mariya pass into the garden, Dubrovin and Olyona are left alone (No. 4). She asks him how he has faced the trials of the past two years (allegro giusto). Surely, she says (bar 69), he has been comforted by a woman's caresses. He affirms (bar 75) that he has been true to her, and that only his faithful dog has shared his past trials and given him affection. Finally she is reassured: 'We will forget our sorrow: happiness is before us' (bar 127). In a duet (No. 5) they dwell on their future of eternal bliss together. Bastryukov and Mariya re-enter (No. 6) and the entire quartet is heard again. Suddenly the Voyevoda bursts in (No. 7). Dubrovin confronts him (allegro), draws a knife (bar 57), but is immediately overpowered by Shalïgin's servants. A crowd rushes in (bar 69): 'The Voyevoda has caught them! What will happen?' The couples join in farewells (No. 8), while Shalïgin reproaches Mariya, but says he will not detain her if she doesn't love an old man; instead she shall die. This ensemble continues into the first part of No. 9. As it finishes, Shalïgin orders the couples to be held (allegro moderato), and then drags Mariya offstage. The crowd are muttering apprehensively about the Voyevoda (bar 72), when Mariya's cries for help are heard (allegro molto). As the crowd fears the worse (bar 93), she suddenly appears and runs down the staircase as the new Voyevoda, sent to

replace Shalïgin, enters (No. 10). The couples tell of their injustices, the new Voyevoda orders them (bar 43) to be released, and goes off, taking Shalïgin with him. The couples and the crowd join in a finale of rejoicing (No. 11).

All the essentials of Tchaikovsky's operatic style are displayed in *The Voyevoda*. The basic narrative manner derives from that simple but flexible brand of accompanied quasi-arioso which Glinka had introduced into Russian opera in *A Life for the Tsar*. At the opposite structural extreme are the formal set-pieces, such as Bastryukov's arias in Acts 1 and 2, Mariya's beautiful, though inconsistent folksong setting in Act 2, and Dubrovin's markedly Russian aria in Act 3. In other cases the rigid structure is loosened or, at least, disguised to avoid the statuesque posture of such pieces. Scattered throughout the opera are occasional recollections of music heard earlier, though these are usually prompted by obvious factors within the plot, and there is only one theme that is associated extensively enough with a single character for it to assume something of the function of a leitmotif.

The stylistic sources are varied, and are often blended together. Laroche's identification of Schumann's influence must surely be mistaken, for though responsibility for some of the sounds that accompany the first meeting of Bastryukov and Mariya might be laid at his door, there is not much else in the opera that even hints at his style. In any case, in the mid-1820s Glinka had introduced something which sounds suspiciously like an anticipation of Schumann into his Viola Sonata and certain of his drawing-room romances, and Tchaikovsky, whose lyricism in this opera is often clearly marked by elements of this sentimental manner, is as likely to have got some of his 'Schumannesque' touches from that source. French grand opera must bear the greatest responsibility for the treatment of some of the more melodramatic moments, and it is certainly French operatic precedents that are responsible for the ballet, here excused as the dances of the hay maidens before Mariya in the second scene of Act 2. Some of the vocal manners are strongly Italianate, especially those of Bastryukov, though one must also recognise here a strong leavening from the sentimental drawing-room romance. Yet to all these alien elements (for the drawing-room romance was a naturalised import) is added a very strong infusion of native Russian music. Though only three authentic Russian folksongs[46] have been identified in *The Voyevoda*, there are a multitude of other moments when the melodic material sounds as though it might have escaped from the world of folk music. On the structural level the changing background method – that individual Russian solution which Glinka had evolved to the problem of building an extensive movement

[46] Also used as Nos. 23–5 of *T50RF*.

on material of a national character without doing violence to that
character – is found in the first section of the Overture and in the
khorovod which concludes Act 2. And even where it is not possible
to isolate the indigenous character by consistent demonstrable
relationships with folksong or other uniquely Russian practices, there
are passages or even whole scenes (the women's scene that opens the
opera, or the Bastryukov/Dubrovin dialogue in Act 2, for instance)
which have a character quite unlike that of any Western opera.
Significantly, perhaps, it is in those very places where the Russian
character is most pronounced that the best passages in the opera are
almost invariably found.

The Overture is crudely accumulated in a number of sections,
establishing its national character at the very beginning not only by the
changing background principle used in its first section, but also by the
thoroughly Russian sound of the opening theme itself, and by the
introduction of this theme without harmonisation. The last section,
with the chromatic progression which leads into it, provides the only
material relationship between the Overture and the opera.

The first act opens promisingly. The beautiful folksong setting sung
by an offstage women's chorus might appear to promise an enchanted
world like that of Glinka's *Ruslan and Lyudmila*; equally the presence of
two young sisters and a nurse anticipates by some ten years the opening
of *Eugene Onegin*. The folksong, 'Na more utushka kupalasya', had been
given to Tchaikovsky by Ostrovsky himself. In 1876 Tchaikovsky
recalled for Rimsky-Korsakov's benefit how he had received it. 'I
remember that essentially I made no changes in it, but only
"undiatonicised" it, for I recollect very well that he [Ostrovsky] had
adorned it with a sharpened leading note.'[47] The whole of this women's
scene is well handled; the nurse and chorus are capably treated, and
Mariya begins to emerge as something more than a cardboard love-lorn
girl, especially in the playful conclusion she invents to the sad tale she
had earlier begun to narrate – a racy little section in a mixture of $\frac{5}{4}$ and $\frac{6}{4}$
which is as national as the opening folksong itself. Mariya is a direct
descendant of Glinka's Lyudmila – a bright, lively character, sensitive
but unsentimental, extrovert, easily given to moods, but possessing an
engaging sense of mischief. The ancestry of this portion of *The Voyevoda*
is tangibly confirmed by Tchaikovsky's explicit echoing, during this
section, of Chernomor's spell of enchantment from Act 1 of Glinka's
Ruslan. Tchaikovsky's text elucidates why his thoughts should have
flown to Glinka's second opera at this point (Ex. 15).

No one could pretend that this first stretch is great opera, but it has

[47] *TLP*6, p. 67; *TZC*1, p. 500; *DTC*, p. 26.

[Instantly sleep fell on all]

much charm and, through Mariya, some real life. If what followed had been as good as this, then all would have been well. Unfortunately the ensuing chorus for Bastryukov and his servants (No. 3), though its furtiveness has some piquant attractiveness, possesses less real character, and the large aria (No. 4) which he sings when he is finally left alone is a conventional bel canto flood of soft-centred masculine seduction with pentatonic inclinations, a set-piece exuding a warmth which suggests Italy rather than Russia as its natural habitat, though the touches of dissonant tension effected by slow scalic orchestral movement in the D major section do something to suggest a different provenance, and add a little strength to its blandness. The preceding recitative, founded upon an incident which Tchaikovsky rescued from his orchestral piece, *The Storm* (the little 'scene by the Volga', just before the recapitulation), contains a good deal more of Tchaikovsky himself than most of the aria. Yet of its kind, the aria is a winning enough piece, and it was one of the opera's audience successes. The opportunities it provided for lyrical outpouring certainly found Tchaikovsky more at ease than in the type of situation that follows, where the demand for suitable musical agitation to accompany the meeting between Mariya and Bastryukov (No. 5) elicited from him, as such situations so often did, a stiff response which squeezes Mariya back into an operatic stereotype. For the opening section of their formal duet (andante non troppo) Tchaikovsky raided his graduation cantata, lifting the G major quartet bodily to provide all but the last half-dozen bars of the G flat section in this duet. Since in the cantata it had been composed for four voices, the vocal parts had to be rewritten, but the accompaniment was transferred little changed, except for modifications in the orchestral figuration and a considerable amount of rescoring. In the cantata it had been incongruous; here it is at home, but its lyricism is faceless and unredeemed by anything that follows in this very extensive movement – until suddenly, as Mariya is withdrawing after denying herself for the moment Bastryukov's love, there are heard from the orchestra brief recollections of the opera's very first scene, including that little sequential phrase to which Mariya had sadly declared: 'If there is no love in our own lives to give us delight, we shall be glad to rejoice in it even if it's only in a fairy tale.' It is a touching little moment which briefly lights up a vast area of otherwise drab music.

The movement which at last introduces the Voyevoda himself (No. 7) seems to have been modelled on the G major Scena and Chorus (No. 13) in Act 3 of Glinka's *A Life for the Tsar*. Both are concerned with preliminaries for a wedding, and they are in the same key; above all, each is based to a large extent on a relaxed and markedly Russian tune which is repeated in the orchestra while the voices unfold their dialogue freely. In fact, this is a delightful little scene, the orchestra suggesting the doggedly cheerful hospitality of Dyuzhoy as he endeavours to put on a genial face before Shalïgin, of whom he is scared stiff, to cope with a wife who is less silently submissive than he would wish, and not to be put out by the Jester's unwanted presence. It is too easily forgotten that Tchaikovsky had a marked gift for comedy, and the quasi-canonic protests of Dyuzhoy and his wife to the Voyevoda's demands to see his future bride provide a delicious little touch after which the tranquillo canon uncovers something of the earnest seriousness in their refusal.[48] Having achieved now a significant dramatic level, Tchaikovsky sought to maintain it by enlisting the whole of the admirable second subject of his C minor Overture, which serves well to underpin Mariya's precipitate entry, with the revelation of the Voyevoda's new infatuation nicely slotted into the broad cantabile tune in G flat.[49] For a moment, when he follows this with a declaration of his new feelings in a solemn Adagio (No. 8), Shalïgin sounds almost human, but the quartet which grows out of this quickly engulfs the characters in its dense and unrelenting vocal textures.[50] Tchaikovsky had none of his beloved Mozart's genius for

[48] Unfortunately this is a passage in which Tchaikovsky's own orchestral part is lost for eight bars.

[49] In this section Tchaikovsky's original vocal part is lost in bars 164–91.

[50] According to Kashkin, 'the composer himself considered this number if not the

ensembles that illumine the participants through their collisions with
one another. Instead he treated such movements simply as expressive
consolidation, conveying a consensus mood of joy or sorrow in which
the individual characters become mere ciphers.

Yet, that much said, it must be conceded that Tchaikovsky's quartet is
an affecting piece of music, better than what follows. The lovers'
farewells are more conventionally treated, and in the finale loud and
vapid tumult replaces genuinely inventive conflict. Yet there is one
precious moment of respite: Bastryukov's words of farewell as he
prepares to embark with his servants. 'We will wash away our grief on
mother Volga,' he sings, pouring out a pure Russian cantilena
supported by male chorus, as beautiful a melodic passage as any in the
opera (Ex. 16). Even here, however, Tchaikovsky cannot let slip the

Ex. 16

[We will wash away our grief on mother Volga]

opportunity for harmonic 'cleverness', and his sudden shift into
neapolitan regions in bar 4 of Ex. 16 compromises for a moment that
Russian world so clearly conjured up in the vocal part. In a number of

best, then at least just about the most effective in the whole opera' (*KVC*, p. 56; *TZC*1, p.
312). Unfortunately it proved too difficult for the performers, and had to be dropped
completely.

other places in this opera, and especially in chromatic contexts, Tchaikovsky is unable to resist the temptation to strive after harmonic effects which sometimes show more ingenuity than taste. Yet even if this neapolitan manœuvre in Bastryukov's interjection is questionable stylistic wisdom, the whole incident remains an affecting moment which emphasises the lifelessness of the flanking rowdiness.

Tchaikovsky raided his C minor Overture again to open the second act, taking the first fourteen bars, and then tacking on seven more to continue as he had done when this opening had been originally conceived to begin *The Storm*. The very Russian phrase that serves as subject for the concluding fugato of this introduction (Ex. 17a) becomes ubiquitously associated with the fugitive Dubrovin, and is the only instance of anything which might be termed a leitmotif in the whole opera. The first scene opens with a strangely haunting chorus of servants who are awaiting Bastryukov's return from hunting. Yet the expectations aroused by this arresting beginning are not fulfilled when the hero appears; conventional operatic gesture takes over and his aria (No. 2) is a formal expression of grief, impassioned but with little true melodic distinction, and ending with stiff choral support.

Then, suddenly, with Dubrovin's entry (No. 3), real life begins to stir. Of all the male characters in *The Voyevoda*, it is Dubrovin who, despite his belated appearance, creates the most substantial impression. Ever since Glinka's Susanin and Ruslan, it was the darker-voiced baritone far more than the lyrical tenor who drew the richest response from Russian composers, and Dubrovin is no exception. The phrase that introduces him (Ex. 17a), which might almost be a prototype of Russian folk melody, haunts the orchestral part in the rest of this first scene of Act 2, substantiating his quiet domination of these final pages. The range of

Ex. 17
Moderato assai

a.

Allegro

b.

treatment Tchaikovsky accords this phrase is quite remarkable. Ex. 17b–e set out the four harmonisations which occur in the next four pages of the vocal score; in the last it will be noted that Tchaikovsky has widened some intervals to fashion what is almost a new idea. This phrase is Dubrovin's companion in the last act, too, where it helps to consolidate that consistency of character which he always reflects, no matter what his predicament. The capacity which Dubrovin shares with both of Glinka's heroes (and, it seems, with the Russian people in general) for quiet, heroic endurance is one that transcends the triviality of this opera – and it is no surprise to find his music more consistently Russian than that of any other character. One need only compare the passionate wanness of the aria Bastryukov has just sung with the deep yet fully mastered agitation of that which Dubrovin delivers in the last act to sense which of the two men is the stronger, more rounded character. The simple solemnity which Dubrovin imposes upon the end of this first scene of Act 2 is almost Musorgskyan[51] and provides by far the most memorable piece of drama in the whole opera.

The second scene, for which Tchaikovsky salvaged his student *Characteristic Dances* to provide the introduction and a ballet for the hay

[51] Dubrovin's theme has close affinities with that used by Musorgsky at the opening of *Boris Godunov*.

maidens, opens excellently, announcing a six-bar phrase, as distinctive as it is Russian, which is then subjected to changing backgrounds. If all Tchaikovsky's invention in this opera had been as fine as the ravishingly chaste diatonicism he first fashions for this tune (Ex. 18), then *The Voyevoda* would have been a masterpiece. The set of dances that follows is

Ex. 18   Andante commodo assai

attractive, exposing that gift which was to make Tchaikovsky such a master of ballet. The brief dialogue of Nedviga and the female chorus opens the scene well, and Mariya's following aria (No. 5: cantabile), based on the twelve-bar folksong which Tchaikovsky had collected at Kuntsevo, is the real musical gem of the whole opera. Just as his sympathy for another heroine ten years later in *Eugene Onegin* was to produce the finest scene in all his operas, so his pity for Mariya's predicament, joined to the stimulus of this very beautiful folksong, seems profoundly to have stirred his musical fantasy. The little miracle he achieves in verse two with a relentless internal dominant pedal surrounded by slow scalic lines (Ex. 19) is worth all the other pages of stock musical posturing with the second-hand materials of Western opera. Only the conclusion, where the composer turns traitor to its essential Russianness by extending it with vocal sequence and operatic cadenza, mars a movement which, for poignant loveliness achieved with an apparently artless simplicity, is among the most affecting that Tchaikovsky ever wrote, and aroused an appropriate response from the audience.

It could hardly be expected that he would maintain this level, though much of what follows is admirable. Olyona, making her first appearance, declares her Russian provenance clearly in her opening

[Fly to me, nightingale, into my chamber: I will provide for you a golden cage]

phrases, and her narration of past misfortunes is finely impassioned, with unmistakable tones of Tchaikovsky's own voice. The first part of the duet in which she now joins with Mariya (No. 7) also does service to open the next act, where it can aptly recall that quiet, slightly nervous happiness aroused by the two women's expectations of deliverance. Tchaikovsky thought well enough of this entr'acte to use it again seven or eight years later in *Swan Lake*. As for the attractive second part of this duet, Tchaikovsky also borrowed from it much later in life when seeking for a second subject to his *1812* Overture. This was another movement which scored a success, though the duet cadenza with which Tchaikovsky adorned the end is exceedingly inept. The ritualistic khorovod (No. 9: allegro commodo) which closes the act is based upon the folksong, 'Za dvorom luzhok zelemyoshenek', a tune which is almost pentatonic, and whose tonal/modal ambiguity Tchaikovsky pointedly (and rather uncomfortably) demonstrates by following an unequivocal C major harmonisation with one equally firmly committed to G major (Ex. 20).

This khorovod's changing background commitment is an outspoken confirmation of the Russianness which has pervaded this act so much more fully than the first.

While Act 2 has given signs of far greater dramatic life and stronger musical character, Act 3 ultimately crushes these qualities beneath accumulating slabs of elephantine ensemble. Significantly Tchaikovsky thought nothing in this act worth reviving in a later context except for the prelude and the orchestral passage that accompanies the couples' reunion (No. 2: andante), both of which found a haven (still in their original keys) in *Swan Lake*, where the former became the entr'acte to Act

4, while the latter accompanied the reunion of the Prince and Odette.[52] In fact, the opening scene for Bastryukov and Dubrovin preserves a great deal of that impressive seriousness in which the first scene of the preceding act had ended. Though snatches of material associated with both men are heard in the opening recitative, it is the domination of Dubrovin that preserves the dramatic quality, and his aria (No. 1: andante) nicely blends manly dignity with an underlying agitation in music that is markedly Russian in character. The quartet (No. 3) in which the couples are reunited (another great success with the audience) is a concise and attractive movement.[53] The first eight bars might have been conceived south of the Alps, the next twenty-two bars were probably one of those contexts that reminded Laroche of Schumann, but the recurrent flattened submediant chord in the conclusion reveals Tchaikovsky as the composer of this rapt expression of blissful reunion (Ex. 21). Economy does not, however, mark the ensuing duet for Dubrovin and Olyona (No. 4), and though much of the earlier part is first-rate, it later becomes clear that a formal lovers' scene has developed, culminating in an extended grand climax in which everything is heard at least twice, and in which every trace of that Russianness which has been such an important factor in breathing life into the earlier part of this act is finally dissipated. The repetition of the entire quartet (No. 6: andante), while rounding off this segment of the act neatly, is dramatically inept, for the rapture that it had so well conveyed before can happen only once. With the entry of the Voyevoda (No. 7) conventional posturing holds sway. Unfortunately after the lyrical longueurs of the couples' reunions, Tchaikovsky permits them to indulge in equally long and loving farewells (Nos. 8 and 9). They start poignantly enough, and the national element returns, but then continually falters under the weight of extending techniques, so that the intervention of the new Voyevoda (No. 10) is deliverance, not only for the couples, but also for the audience. The final chorus (No. 11), with its alternation of $\frac{3}{4}$ and $\frac{5}{4}$ bars, and its repetitive melodic manner, brings a welcome reminder of that Russian element which has produced so much of the best in what has gone before.

It cannot be pretended that if Tchaikovsky had succeeded in

[52] Gerald Abraham has pointed out the close identity of scoring between *The Voyevoda* and *Swan Lake* versions: 'Hence we may assume with some confidence that the full score of *The Voyevoda* was not destroyed until after 1876 – perhaps not until after 1880, when *1812* was composed' (*Slavonic and Romantic Music* [London, 1968], p. 126). However, the following footnote ([53]) suggests that Tchaikovsky had a remarkably retentive memory.

[53] This was one piece in the opera for which Tchaikovsky retained a liking, and a fortnight before his death he told Kashkin that he could remember every note of it and would sometime write it out again.

Ex. 21

MARIYA ⎫
OLYONA ⎭ :   Eyes brighter than the dear light, heart warmer than the dear sun]

BASTRYUKOV ⎫
DUBROVIN   ⎭ : Heart of my beautiful one, brighter than light, eyes of my beautiful one, warmer than the sun]

eradicating *The Voyevoda* we would have been musically much the poorer, especially since he preserved a good number of the better pieces in his third opera, *The Oprichnik*. Yet for the student of Tchaikovsky *The Voyevoda* has great interest. It shows how far he had gained command of the basic craft of an opera composer, however deficient he may have been in creative dramatic response to its various types of situation.

Above all, it reveals that the most important roots for Tchaikovsky's musical personality were his Russian ones. The traveller through the scrublands and featureless dramatic plains of *The Voyevoda*'s landscape will remember with most pleasure coming upon those fresh springs of Russian inspiration which constantly break the surface. Sometimes the waters spread wide, at other times they produce a tiny trickle which will nourish no more than a simple musical phrase: yet wherever they well up, they enable living flowers to replace the artificial blooms with which Tchaikovsky, with varying degrees of success, endeavours to disguise the low fertility of so much of his operatic soil. *The Voyevoda* is further confirmation of Tchaikovsky's good fortune in his impending closer contacts with Balakirev and his nationalistic circle. Even without *Romeo and Juliet* and the Second Symphony, the relationship would have been invaluable, for it encouraged him to cultivate far more this precious Russian element in his next two surviving operas, making each a great improvement on its predecessor, and resulting, in *Vakula the Smith*, in some of the best music he ever wrote.

6

BALAKIREV AGAIN:

ROMEO AND JULIET

EARLY IN APRIL 1868 an Italian opera company, led by a certain
Eugenio Merelli, arrived in Moscow for a brief season. The singers were
indifferent, with the notable exception of a thirty-two-year-old Belgian
soprano, Désirée Artôt. Artôt had been a pupil of Pauline Viardot-
Garcia, and for the past ten years had been pursuing a distinguished
career in the opera houses and concert halls of Europe. In 1868 she was
at the height of her powers. According to Laroche, Artôt had a
remarkable range which enabled her to tackle an unusually large
number of parts. Though not particularly attractive in appearance, she
had much charm; above all, she was a great operatic actress.
Tchaikovsky made Artôt's acquaintance during this spring season, but
their contact seems to have been no more than casual. In the early
autumn, solely because of Artôt's success with the Moscow public,
Merelli's company returned, and Tchaikovsky saw their new production
of Rossini's *Otello*. He was impressed by the tenor, Roberto Stagno, but
it was still Artôt who dominated. She 'sang delightfully', he reported to
Anatoly the next day (22 September).[1]

Despite the threat this company's popularity posed to the production
Gedeonov was planning of *The Voyevoda*, Tchaikovsky delighted in the
presence of this prima donna. Within a fortnight he had forced
Gedeonov to postpone the production of *The Voyevoda* and, with his time
more free, had made Artôt's closer acquaintance, discovering that her
personality was as winning as her stage performance. 'Artôt is a
wonderful person. We are friends,' he informed Anatoly.[2] His esteem
for the lady was soon embodied in a practical service to her interests.
'I'm writing recitatives and choruses for Auber's *Le Domino noir* which
has to go on for Artôt's benefit performance. . . . I've become very
friendly with Artôt and am enjoying extremely marked favour with her.
I have rarely met such a pleasant, intelligent and sensible woman,' he

[1] *TLP5*, p. 139; *TZC1*, p. 298; *YDGC*, p. 55; *TPB*, p. 42.
[2] *TLP5*, p. 144; *TZC1*, p. 300; *YDGC*, p. 55; *TPB*, p. 44.

enthused to Anatoly a month later.[3] A yet more personal musical gift was a *Romance* in F minor for piano, Op. 5, which he wrote in November and dedicated to her.

Tchaikovsky was now in the middle of the only relationship of his whole life in which, it seems, a woman managed to rouse his sexual feelings. True, it is not absolutely certain whether it was Artôt the woman or Artôt the enchanting prima donna to whom he was really attracted. 'Ah, Modinka,' he exclaimed to his brother during November, '. . . if only you knew what a singer and actress Artôt is! Never before in my life have I experienced such a powerful fascination from an artist as now. . . . How you would be enraptured by her gestures and the gracefulness of her movements and her posture!'[4] Nevertheless the tantalising image of some feminine ideal, conjured from costume, wig and greasepaint, heightened by vocal allurement and consummate histrionics, and made enticingly remote by the barrier of footlights and make-believe setting, can all too quickly crumble when close contact reveals the human reality behind the illusion, and when passive indulgence in delicious fantasy is replaced by the demand for active participation in a human relationship. Yet the fact is that this did not happen in Tchaikovsky's affair with Artôt, and his attentions to her were outwardly ardent enough to excite the comment of independent witnesses. By the end of December she was the very centre of all his attentions – or so he reported to Modest: 'I have been devoting all my free time to one person of whom you, of course, have heard, and whom I love very, very much.'[5] So much did he love her that marriage was discussed between them, though nothing was yet decided. Nevertheless, for all his ardour, the Tchaikovsky who wrote to his father on 7 January 1869, admitting his intentions and asking for advice, was a very troubled lover:

Because rumours have, of course, reached you of my proposed marriage, and because maybe you are annoyed that I have written nothing to you about it myself, I shall straight away explain to you how the matter stands. I first became acquainted with Artôt as far back as the spring, but visited her only once when I went to supper after her benefit performance. When she returned this present

[3] *TLP5*, p. 145; *TZC1*, p. 302; *TPB*, p. 44. In fact, when Artôt's benefit took place on 7 Dec., the opera given was Gounod's *Faust*. Tchaikovsky's work (an introduction to a chorus in Act I and recitatives throughout to replace the spoken dialogue of the French original) had to wait for more than a year before the Auber opera was at last performed.

[4] *TLP5*, p. 146; *TZC1*, p. 303; *TPB*, p. 45.

[5] *TLP5*, p. 147; *TZC1*, p. 303; *TPB*, p. 46.

autumn I didn't call on her for a whole month. We met by chance at a musical soirée. She expressed surprise that I hadn't been to see her: I promised to visit her, but wouldn't have kept my promise (because of my characteristic slowness in making acquaintances), had not Anton Rubinstein, who was passing through Moscow, dragged me off to her place. From that moment hardly a day passed without me receiving from her a note inviting me to come, and little by little I got into the habit of calling upon her each evening. We were quickly inflamed with exceedingly tender feelings towards each other, and these were swiftly followed by mutual confessions of these feelings. It goes without saying that there arose forthwith the question of marriage, which we both very much desire and which should take place during the summer unless something prevents it. But this possibility cannot be discounted, for some obstacles do exist. In the first place her mother, who is constantly with her and who has considerable influence over her, is opposed to the marriage, finding me too young for her daughter, and in all probability fearing that I shall compel her to live in Russia. Secondly my friends, and [Nikolay] Rubinstein in particular, are employing the most energetic means to stop my proposed marriage. They say that, as the husband of a famous singer, I shall play the most pitiful role of being 'the wife's husband' – i.e., I shall travel with her all over Europe, live off her, shall lose the habit and the opportunity for work – in a word, that when my love for her has cooled a little, there will remain only the sufferings of pride, despair and ruin. The possibility of this misfortune might be forestalled if she decided to quit the stage and live with me in Russia, but she says that, despite all her love for me, she cannot resolve to throw up the stage, to which she is accustomed and which yields her both fame and fortune. She has already gone off to sing in Warsaw.[6] We have left it that in the summer I shall go to her estate near Paris, and there our fate will be decided.

Just as she cannot bring herself to leave the stage, so I on my part hesitate to sacrifice my whole future to her, for there is no doubt that I shall be deprived of the chance of going forward along my own road if I follow her blindly. And so, dear Papa, you see that my situation is very difficult. On the one hand, all the forces in my heart bind me to her, and at the present moment it seems to me impossible to live my whole life without her; on the other hand, cold reason compels me to ponder deeply the possibility of those misfortunes which my friends

[6] Artôt's last performance in Moscow before her departure had been at the concert of 20 Dec., in which Tchaikovsky's *Voyevoda* dances were performed. In this same concert Rubinstein also played Tchaikovsky's new *Romance*, dedicated to Artôt.

picture to me. I am waiting, dear father, for you to write to me about your view of this affair.[7]

Precisely how Tchaikovsky's courtship of this enticing singer had run its course we shall probably never know, but one thing at least is certain from this letter: his passion for her was not overmastering. He is rather embarrassed by the whole affair, tries to place the onus for initiating it upon the lady, and despite the attractions which he says she has for him (whatever their nature), he will not sacrifice all for the possession of her.[8] As for Artôt herself, we may only guess that, being now in her thirties and encumbered by a possessive and ever-present mother, she was actively seeking marriage. Tchaikovsky may have at first appeared a personable young man, but closer acquaintance probably revealed traits which made Artôt doubt her earlier assumptions of his fitness to be a bridegroom. Ilya's reply, which he lost no time in sending, proved irrelevant. Sensing his son's distress without understanding the real cause of it, this kindly man did his best to sound approving, but the arguments with which he attempted to brush aside the objections raised in Pyotr's letter were often hopelessly idealistic and begged many questions. 'Love will conquer all,' was the message of his reply, though Ilya did counsel that they should not rush into matrimony.

He need scarcely have bothered. The ravages of time were already taking their toll of the relationship, and within less than a month Tchaikovsky was confiding to Anatoly: 'It's very doubtful whether my entry into Hymen's bonds will take place; this affair of mine is beginning to disintegrate somewhat.'[9] It is in fact possible that Artôt had already actually taken the step which gave Tchaikovsky the most devastating proof conceivable of just how insubstantial were her feelings towards him: her marriage to a Spanish baritone, Mariano Padilla y Ramos. The news was broken to Tchaikovsky one evening by Nikolay Rubinstein, who made no attempt to disguise his satisfaction. 'Tchaikovsky didn't say a word,' de Lazari recalled. 'He simply went white and walked out. A few days later he was already unrecognisable [as the distraught lover]. Once again he was relaxed, composed, and had only one consideration in the world – his work.'[10]

Though Artôt's precipitate action sorely hurt Tchaikovsky's pride, his

[7] *TLP5*, pp. 149–50; *TZC1*, pp. 304–5; *TPB*, pp. 47–8.

[8] The facts as set out in Tchaikovsky's letter to his father are not always consistent with other evidence. For instance, Anton Rubinstein was not in Moscow until late October, but a letter from Tchaikovsky to his brother Anatoly makes it clear that he was already friendly with Artôt in early October (see p. 156).

[9] *TLP5*, p. 153; *TZC1*, p. 308; *TPB*, p. 49; *YDGC*, p. 58.

[10] *TPB*, p. 562; *YDGC*, p. 58.

more tender nerves seem to have withstood the shock successfully. 'The Artôt story has resolved itself in the most droll fashion,' he wrote to Modest on 13 February 1869. 'In Warsaw she fell in love with the baritone *Padilla* who had been the object of her ridicule while she was here – and is now married to him! What sort of woman is she? You would have to know the details of my relationship with her to understand just how comic this dénouement is.'[11] The apparent initial success of *The Voyevoda* helped to divert his thoughts, and even Modest admits that his brother showed little outward distress. Before the end of the year Tchaikovsky had to face Artôt again when she returned to Moscow to rehearse *Le Domino noir* with Tchaikovsky's own recitatives. His pride was still stung, but towards the lady herself he evidently felt no animosity. 'This woman hurt me greatly . . . but all the same some inexplicable sympathy draws me to her to such a degree that I am beginning to await her arrival with feverish impatience. Woe is me! All the same, this feeling is not love,' he told Anatoly.[12] To the end his admiration for the singer and actress remained unbounded, and his response to her first performance on the Moscow stage (as Marguerite in Gounod's *Faust*) at the end of 1869 was as strong as it had been during their intimate weeks a year before. 'On the artist's appearance on the stage,' wrote Kashkin, 'he [Tchaikovsky] hid himself behind his opera glasses and didn't remove them from his eyes until the end of the act, though he can hardly have seen much because tears, which he appeared not to notice, were streaming out from under the opera glasses.'[13]

During the last three months of 1868 the Artôt affair had far from monopolised Tchaikovsky's attention. With the production of *The Voyevoda* suspended, he resumed composition, and in addition to the *Romance* dedicated to Artôt, wrote during October a second piano piece, *Valse caprice*, which was published as Op. 4, dedicating the piece to the pianist Anton Door, a colleague at the Conservatoire, who was later to return to his native Vienna and become a member of Brahms's closest circle. More important were the piano duet arrangements of fifty Russian folksongs, commissioned by Jurgenson, upon which Tchaikovsky embarked in November or December, and which he completed the following autumn. The set was divided into two equal halves, and the first was finished before 1868 was out. The last three of this first volume were the folksongs Tchaikovsky had incorporated into *The Voyevoda*. Of these three the final one had come from Villebois's collection, *100 Russian Folksongs* (1860), and it was from this same source

[11] *TLP5*, p. 155; *TPB*, p. 50; *YDGC*, p. 58 (partial).
[12] *TLP5*, p. 182; *TPB*, p. 56; *TZC1*, p. 309 (partial); *YDGC*, p. 64 (partial).
[13] *KVC*, pp. 78–9; *TZC1*, p. 309; *YDGC*, p. 65.

that Tchaikovsky drew the remaining twenty-two tunes. When in 1869 he came to arrange the second batch of twenty-five, he resorted to Balakirev's collection of Russian folksongs (set, like those of Villebois, for voice and piano) which had appeared only three years before, and all but one were taken from this volume. The exception was 'Sidel Vanya' which he himself collected at Kamenka during the summer of 1869, and which was to become the basis of the famous Andante cantabile of his First String Quartet.

Whereas Tchaikovsky had borrowed freely from Villebois's collection, not only substituting his own harmonisations but also having no compunction about altering that editor's bowdlerised folktunes in an attempt to restore as much as possible of their former character, he approached Balakirev's volume with great circumspection. 'I should now like to take twenty-five [folk]tunes from your collection,' he wrote to Balakirev, 'and I am afraid that this may cause you some displeasure. Let me know (1) whether you want me to retain your harmonisation literally, and merely arrange it for four hands, or (2) whether, conversely, you don't want me to do this at all, or (3) whether you'll be cross with me either way, and are completely opposed to me taking your songs.'[14]

Balakirev responded generously. 'Do whatever is most to your taste,' he wrote,[15] adding, however, that for copyright reasons no acknowledgement should be made that his volume had been Tchaikovsky's source. This placed Tchaikovsky in a quandary, for he felt that he could not borrow Balakirev's work unless the debt were publicly declared – and in any case the relationship would become evident to anyone who acquired more than a superficial knowledge of the two versions. Thus he decided upon completely independent arrangements, though this proved very difficult to carry out in practice. 'I have got to know some of your songs so well that it has cost me an incredible effort to tear from them the harmonisations you have already grafted on to them,' he lamented on 14 October. 'As soon as they appear I'll send you a copy.'[16] This second half of Tchaikovsky's collection had just been completed, and it was published before the end of the year.

Tchaikovsky's accompaniments to these fifty folksongs show considerable variety. At one extreme he provides a thick, block-chord support, at the other he matches the tune with a melodic line of his own, often of considerable character, thereby exhibiting that same facility for decorative counterpoint amply displayed in his original compositions.

[14] *TLP5*, p. 151; *BVP*, pp. 123–4.

[15] *BVP*, p. 124; *TLP5*, p. 151.

[16] *TLP5*, p. 174; *BVP*, p. 135.

Sometimes this contrapuntal treatment veers to the canonic; more rarely an equal abrasiveness may result from the use of an ostinato. Pedals, too, occur on occasion. In treating any Russian folktune even the most scrupulous arranger runs two hazards: firstly, that a functional harmonisation generates a regularity of pulse inimical to the natural flexible flow of the tune, and secondly, that the presence of a Western-style accompaniment cannot but impose a certain harmonic interpretation upon something conceived without any such conditioning, thus in some measure contaminating the purely melodic properties of the original (though we must remember that a good many Russian 'folk-songs' are in fact town songs composed in the eighteenth century against a simple background of Western harmonic procedures). In consequence Tchaikovsky's chordal arrangements are rarely as satisfactory as those in which he biases towards a more contrapuntal treatment, where the harmonic tread is softened and the triadic element is less assertive, the tune being supported by a smooth decorative web of lines which may perhaps brush with it in occasional delectable dissonance. Such settings, especially when chromaticism infiltrates the texture, often remind the listener of Tchaikovsky's heavy debt to Glinka. Most of the tunes are very short, and Tchaikovsky normally plays each at least twice. When he states a tune several times, his varied treatments produce a tiny movement based on the changing background principle.

In borrowing from Balakirev, Tchaikovsky retained the original keys of his settings, and this must have posed some problems for Russia's amateur duettists. In only one of his settings (No. 46, second half) does he virtually duplicate Balakirev's treatment, and though fleeting moments do suggest that the memory of what Balakirev had done sometimes remained ineffaceable, he managed to make the majority of his settings commendably new, sometimes specifying a radically different speed, and occasionally introducing a minor modification or two into the melody itself. Balakirev's accompaniments are often exceedingly economical, and it may have been to guarantee something beyond what Balakirev had done that led Tchaikovsky to make some of the settings in the second half of his collection more complex. If at times this may overburden the texture (notably at the end of No. 32), at others it produces an extra richness which is undeniably attractive (as in Nos. 29 and 35, for instance). Yet such extra complexity was yet another factor that could compromise the character of the folktune. Forty years earlier Glinka had composed some folksong stylisations which demonstrated, amongst other things, that one of the surest ways of avoiding violence to the national characteristics of a tune was to restrict the accompaniment to the barest essentials, and Balakirev had followed Glinka's example in

many of his forty settings. True, he was not infallible, and his flair for
keyboard figurations did on occasion beguile him into patterned
accompaniments a little too redolent of Western musical manners.

Tchaikovsky is by no means always the less successful arranger. His
treatment of No. 31 ('Ne spasibo te'), for instance, is sturdier and far
more characterful than Balakirev's endless keyboard patter in his
setting; nor can Balakirev's heavy-handed treatment of 'Stoi, moy milïy
khorovod', with its ostinato evidently lifted bodily from the second
episode in Chopin's Polonaise in A flat, match the lovely contrapuntal
web which Tchaikovsky weaves above and below the same theme (No.
40). Yet it is generally true that Balakirev's arrangements, on the whole
much more sparing in their notes, far less laced with compositional
artifice, and sometimes 'ruder' in dissonance, marry more felicitously
with the Russian character of the folktune. Both composers set the so-
called 'Song of the Volga Boatmen', but whereas Tchaikovsky erected
above the tune a weighty edifice of keyboard ornament, Balakirev opted
for a leanness that exposes far better the natural strength of the tune,
permitting bare octaves, sometimes reinforced by parallel thirds, to
fortify the tune's epic properties. A fairer comparison is made in Ex. 22,
for both settings, though very different, have their particular virtues.
Balakirev first raps the tune with a naked G pedal and then roughly
engages it in canonic conflict with itself in a way that makes
Tchaikovsky's arrangement sound positively urbane, even though the
harmonic world of the first half is still heavily indebted to Glinka. Nor
can Tchaikovsky, in the second half (as sometimes elsewhere in his
settings), resist the temptation to devise a bit of invertible counterpoint.
In none of his settings does Balakirev ever add a melodic idea of his own
whose character might conflict with that of his folktune. As in so many
of Tchaikovsky's arrangements in the whole of this collection, this
one retains a genuinely Russian character, but one which is constantly
in danger of betrayal by procedures that stem all too audibly from Western music. Though Balakirev did criticise some of Tchaikovsky's
arrangements of songs selected from Villebois, there is unfortunately no
record of what he thought of Tchaikovsky's treatment of those songs
which he had himself also arranged. He can hardly, however, have
resisted pointing out to Tchaikovsky that here was a situation in which
conservatoire-acquired techniques could be a positive snare.

Even while embarking upon these folksong arrangements
Tchaikovsky was putting the finishing touches to an orchestral piece
which had been occupying him since his return to Moscow for the new
term. The symphonic poem *Fatum* had been begun on 22 September,
and the scoring was completed in December. Tchaikovsky was pleased

Ex. 22

with the finished work; 'it's not a bad piece, it seems, and it's very effectively orchestrated,' he informed Anatoly.[17] The first performance took place in Moscow on 27 February 1869 at an RMS concert conducted by Nikolay Rubinstein, and Tchaikovsky felt this confirmed the good opinion he had already formed of his newest composition. 'It seems to be the best thing I've written so far: at least, that's what other people say (it had a notable success),' he wrote to Anatoly within hours of the première.[18] At the last moment Tchaikovsky, who had evidently composed *Fatum* without any specific programme in mind (though Kashkin suspected it was in some way autobiographical), permitted an epigraph to be inserted in the concert programme. Nikolay Rubinstein had been worried that the title would be too indefinite for the audience, and Sergey Rachinsky, a professor of botany at Moscow University (and already one of Tchaikovsky's greatest admirers), happened to hear of Rubinstein's concern. He promptly suggested some lines of Batyushkov:

> You know that grey-haired Melchizedek, bidding farewell to life, declared: 'Man was born a slave, he goes to his grave a slave – and death will scarcely tell him why he traversed this sorrowful vale of tears, why he suffered, endured, wept, and vanished.'

Rachinsky had never heard a note of *Fatum*, and Tchaikovsky had reason to regret capitulating to Rubinstein's wishes, for these thoroughly inept lines were to produce more bewilderment than illumination. Laroche, who had little sympathy with programme music, fastened upon them when he came to review the piece in the Moscow press, and devoted a good deal of space to the incongruity of the verse and Tchaikovsky's composition. The one section of *Fatum* that Laroche warmly commended was the A flat section after the introductory material. Otherwise he recommended Tchaikovsky to study the classics more closely.

Since there appears to have been no definite programme for *Fatum*, it seems that Tchaikovsky's choice of a free periodic structure was a deliberate move to get away from the established sonata or rondo models which he had till now always used for large-scale instrumental pieces. The scheme (Ex. 23) is of some interest. Though centring upon C minor, *Fatum* opens in G minor, passes to a second introductory section in an ambivalent G minor/C minor (of which Tchaikovsky excised the first ten bars even before the première because he considered them 'ugly

[17] *TLP5*, p. 153; *TPB*, p. 49; *DTC*, p. 334; *TZC1*, p. 308 (partial).
[18] *TLP5*, p. 156; *TPB*, p. 50; *DTC*, p. 334.

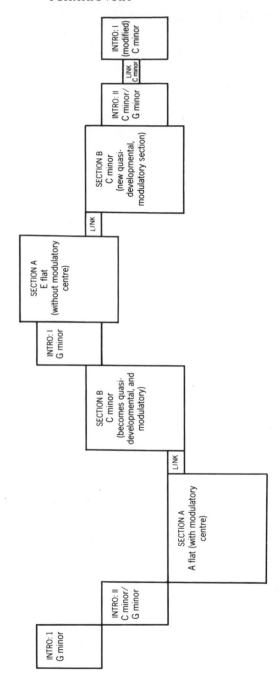

Ex. 23   Diagram of *Fatum*

both in music and scoring'),[19] and then settles on the other side of the tonic for the first main section (Section A) which is founded upon a broad cantabile tune, the opening motif of which has been anticipated in the previous section. With the ensuing molto allegro (Section B) the work finally commits itself to C minor in what might suggest the onset of a sonata exposition, and after the 'first subject' Tchaikovsky enters forthwith into a quasi-development of his material, a practice he was to follow a number of times in later sonata structures. In *Fatum*, however, no second subject follows; instead there is an abrupt return to the work's opening, and the remainder of the piece retraces all sections already heard with some rearrangements and modifications. Finally the work's introductory bars are heard for a third time, their actual pitch being closely preserved, though each brusque gesture is now directed to a C major conclusion, not one in G minor.

There is no particular reason why this plan should not have worked adequately. It provided for plenty of contrast within a scheme which, though unsubtle, was lucid and balanced, while the handling of the tonal strategy, both with regard to the placing of the main tonal landmarks and to the intervening sections of tonal flux, was feasible. Yet *Fatum* is a feeble piece, and when Balakirev, having performed it, compared it scathingly with Liszt's *Les Préludes*, which he happened to conduct in the same concert, he put his finger upon one of the work's fundamental flaws. 'Look what a miraculous form is there [in *Les Préludes*] – how everything flows naturally, one bit out of another.'[20] *Les Préludes* is not Liszt's masterpiece, nor does its form deserve Balakirev's epithet, but the simple inventiveness with which Liszt varies his material, and the sheer variety of guises in which it appears suffice to give at least the illusion of a developing experience, while in the opening pages the sense of one idea 'flowing' out of another is fluently realised. None of these compliments can be paid to *Fatum*. An even more crippling weakness lies in the basic material, none of which represents Tchaikovsky at his best, while some (the opening gesture [see Ex. 38e], or the 'first subject' of the molto allegro) is downright banal. Fundamentally the problem is one of phrase structure. Not only is the organisation almost invariably in four- or eight-bar lengths, but within these there are seemingly endless stretches of one- or two-bar phrases, each of which, once heard, is usually forthwith repeated. *Fatum* reveals none of that masterly variety within repetitive two-bar phrases which Tchaikovsky had already so precociously demonstrated

---

[19] *TLP5*, p. 158; *DTC*, p. 338; *BVP*, p. 126. These bars are still included in the score printed by Belaieff (Frankfurt) in 1972.

[20] *BVP*, p. 131.

in the first subject of *The Storm* (see Ex. 3). The result is diminishing interest at a local level, and gathering tedium in the short-winded, predictable manufacturing of whole sections. In the passages of quasi-development endless mounting sequences are all too often a substitute for any kind of organic growth or new illumination of the material. The A flat section (Ex. 24) is pleasant, and there are a few places where the

Ex. 24

listener's interest is suddenly a little stirred: the two bars of the intro-duction which must have been those that reminded Balakirev of Glinka's *Let him perish!* chorus from *Ruslan and Lyudmila* (see below, p. 170), an idea which, in combination with the opening motif of the cantabile tune, provides an arresting link back to the second statement of the C minor allegro molto – or the bold harmonic gesture that suddenly breaks in upon the literal repetition of this trite allegro (Ex. 25). This striking passage exemplifies that rigidly mechanistic type of har-monic structure to which the Russians were occasionally drawn, this one being built around a prolonged C sharp against which occurs, in every two bars, a two-stage stepwise resolution into a single pitch which is con-sonant with the C sharp (respectively A, F, and C sharp itself). The whole six-bar artifice is erected above a synthetic scale which descends in alternating tones and semitones. There is something rather haunting, too, in the final cor anglais allusion to the cantabile theme's opening motif, with its ensuing woodwind and harp chords, which provides the link to the disastrous last bars.

Tchaikovsky's liking for *Fatum* was short-lived, and he destroyed the score in 1870. Like *The Voyevoda*, it was reconstructed from the orchestral material after his death. However, its apparent success with the Moscow audience encouraged him to dispatch the piece forthwith to

Ex. 25

Balakirev in St Petersburg in the hope that the latter might conduct it there. The letter Tchaikovsky had written to Balakirev in early January, requesting permission to use material from the latter's folksong arrangements, seems to have been the first contact between the two men since the preceding Easter. Tchaikovsky knew perfectly well that he was submitting his latest piece to a stern and outspoken judge. 'I should like to dedicate this work to you, but before this I must know that the piece is not utterly repugnant to you,' he wrote in his covering letter.[21] The score of *Fatum* was circulated among the Kuchka before the first St Petersburg performance, which Balakirev conducted at an RMS concert on 29 March 1869. This time it was a failure. Nevertheless, when Cui came to review it, he was far kinder than he had been to Tchaikovsky's graduation cantata three years earlier. Though he considered a good deal of *Fatum* to be bad (notably the epigraph and the molto allegro), he complimented Tchaikovsky on his orchestration, even though he sometimes found it a little coarse. On the harmony he was equally equivocal, finding it 'bold and new', yet adding, 'but where it is new it is not beautiful'.[22] It was a work to which one listened 'with great interest from beginning to end'.[23]

We have already noted one of Balakirev's adverse criticisms; in fact, he thoroughly disapproved of the piece and, writing to Tchaikovsky the day after the performance, was merciless. His letter was long, and

[21] *TLP5*, p. 157; *BVP*, p. 125; *DTC*, p. 334; *YDGC*, p. 60.
[22] *TZC1*, p. 319.
[23] *TZC1*, p. 319; *DTC*, p. 339; *YDGC*, pp. 60–1.

contained criticism of specific points (like Laroche, he had a good word only for the A flat cantabile section). Having penned this damning document, even Balakirev had second thoughts about the wisdom of sending it. Instead he put it by for nearly a fortnight, and then made a paraphrase of it, retaining all the essentials of his critical views, but excising the comments on specific points. Since he was planning to be in Moscow for a memorial performance of Berlioz's *Requiem* at the beginning of May, he was obviously counting upon a lengthy man-to-man session with Tchaikovsky in which he could expose the work's faults bar by bar and section by section, as was his wont. It would also give him a chance of going over those of Tchaikovsky's Russian folksong arrangements of which he did not approve. In fact compression only renders the barrage of criticism the more concentrated. To Tchaikovsky almost every one of Balakirev's swift series of terse sentences must have been a stinging body blow, battering his self-esteem:

> Your *Fatum* has been played, and I dare to think that it was not badly done; at least, everyone was satisfied with the performance. There wasn't much applause, which I attribute to the hideous clatter at the end. I don't like the piece itself. It's not properly gestated, is written offhandedly, so it seems. The seams and unmatched stitching are everywhere conspicuous. Finally, the form is unsuccessful; everything has come out unco-ordinated. Laroche ascribes this to insufficient study of the classics. In my opinion this has happened for a completely different reason; you are little acquainted with new music. The classics won't teach you free form. You won't find anything new in them, anything you don't know already. All that you'll see in them you have already long known from when you sat on your school bench and reverently listened to Zaremba's learned treatise on the connection between rondo form and man's first fall. Liszt's *Les Préludes* was performed in the same concert. Look what a miraculous form is there – how everything flows naturally, one bit out of another. There's no motley assortment in that! Or look at Glinka's *Night in Madrid*; in how masterly a fashion are all the themes and sections of that overture linked together. There is no such inner organic linking in your *Fatum*. I deliberately cited the example of Glinka because you have apparently been studying him a lot, and throughout *Fatum* I saw that you couldn't get away from the influence of the chorus *Let him perish!* [from *Ruslan and Lyudmila*]. I've never seen anything like the verses you chose for an epigraph. It's a hideous jingle. If you really want to give yourself up to Byronism, then at least find a suitable epigraph from Lermontov, if not from Byron. . . .

I am writing to you with complete frankness, being fully convinced that you won't go back on your intention of dedicating *Fatum* to me. Your dedication is precious to me as a sign of your sympathy towards me – and I feel a great weakness for you.

M. Balakirev – who sincerely loves you.[24]

As it turned out, Balakirev was unable to attend the Moscow performance of Berlioz's *Requiem*, and for a whole month he waited for a reply with growing fears that Tchaikovsky's prolonged silence signified alienation. Then suddenly, from an unexpected quarter, came proof that the Moscow composer was not lost. The circumstances behind this confirming evidence were thus. Balakirev himself was having problems, for during his time as conductor of the RMS, his policy of broadening the programmes to include some of the newest and more radical music had been arousing increasing opposition led by the Grand Duchess Elena. Matters came to a head on 9 May when the royal lady relieved Balakirev of his post as conductor. Seven days later, under the heading 'A Voice from the Musical World of Moscow', *The Contemporary Chronicle* printed an article lauding Balakirev, enumerating his achievements, and deploring his removal. The eulogist was none other than Tchaikovsky, and his ardent support of Balakirev – and his full acceptance of the latter's strictures on *Fatum* – were confirmed in the letter he had written to Balakirev the previous day:

Dear Mily Alexeyevich,

I am very sorry to have taken so long to write, and perhaps my long silence has given you cause to think that I was offended by your letter criticising *Fatum*. Deep within me I am in complete agreement with your observations about this concoction – but I admit I should have been exceedingly happy if you had found but one thing in it to praise, albeit lightly. Your letter contains only criticisms, even though they are just ones; there's not a trace of sweetness in your pill. I admit your review didn't send me into raptures, but I wasn't in the least offended, and in my heart I salute that sincere uprightness that is one of the most attractive traits of your musical personality. Of course I shan't withdraw the dedication, and sometime I hope to write something somewhat better for you. . . .

The news of what the beautiful Elena has done to you filled Rubinstein and me with the utmost indignation. I have even decided to express myself in print about this extraordinarily base deed.[25]

[24] *TZC*1, pp. 320–1; *BVP*, p. 131.
[25] *TLP*5, pp. 162–3; *BVP*, p. 132; *DTC*, pp. 339–40 (partial).

Tchaikovsky's article was the more bold since he knew that on the very day of its appearance the Grand Duchess herself would descend upon Moscow to visit the Conservatoire. Balakirev was immensely delighted – and relieved – by Tchaikovsky's article and letter:

Dear Pyotr Ilich,
    Your letter could not have caused me more joy. I had already indeed begun to think that you had taken the huff at me (forgive me for having such an opinion of you), whereas now I love and respect you all the more. Now I'm convinced that you and I shall never part company, because all our relationships will be founded upon the most candid truthfulness.[26]

These letters prompted by *Fatum* are a microcosm of the musical and personal relationship which Tchaikovsky and Balakirev were to share during the next year or so. No one was ever to wield more influence over Tchaikovsky than the cham of St Petersburg. However much Tchaikovsky may have smarted under Balakirev's censure, the fact is that the latter's criticisms were right on the mark, and Tchaikovsky could not but recognise this. Yet Balakirev had wisely coupled criticism with expressions of respect for Tchaikovsky, and confidence in his talent. In consequence Tchaikovsky remained bound to him more closely than ever. But tension was always present and during the next year, until Tchaikovsky's early correspondence with Balakirev began to tail off as the two men drifted apart, there is constant evidence on Tchaikovsky's side of a touchiness which reveals his resentment of Balakirev's authority, so severe yet so richly beneficial to him. The idiosyncrasy of Balakirev's sympathies irritated him, and when Balakirev's own new piano piece, *Islamey*, was received in Moscow that autumn, Tchaikovsky was at pains to stress repeatedly that it was Albrecht, his colleague of German extraction, who was the work's most enthusiastic admirer (significantly he commits himself neither to censure nor praise of Balakirev's piece, despite a direct appeal from the composer). He is quick to respond, too, to what he feels has been a snub to Albrecht when Balakirev refused, not only on his own behalf but also on that of his colleagues, to contribute some male-voice pieces to a collection which Albrecht was compiling:

As for the matter of Albrecht, I am very surprised that you, rather loftily, don't admit even the possibility of the members of your company each composing a short choral piece for him. I do not think

[26] *BVP*, p. 133.

there is anything degrading for Borodin or Musorgsky to set down a little piece for three or four voices; neither Schumann nor Beethoven disdained to do so. If, in addition, they can by this be of great service to an honest and excellent fellow artist, then a refusal on their part will be nothing less than conceit. However, I think that [Rimsky-]Korsakov is so good and kind (the others I don't know so well), and is in addition so highly gifted that such a petty, selfish thing wouldn't enter his head, and it's wrong for you to take upon yourself to predict how he would react to Albrecht's proposal. As for you, there's nothing to be said. I know that with your commitments you have no time for trifles, but surely you'll give our German, your enthusiastic supporter, a Männerchor which you composed for the Free Music School.[27]

Earlier in the same letter there is an unmistakable undertone of satisfaction at the failure of Balakirev's recent Free Music School concerts. Outwardly Tchaikovsky is all sympathy, but then the inferiority complex of a citizen of Russia's second city breaks out:

No! Every day I am convinced that a peaceful life is possible only in Moscow, even if only because our old capital is not desecrated by that scabby paper of Famintsïn.[28] You ridicule our public because, though it understands nothing, it goes to the concerts of the [Russian] Musical Society. But do you know that, despite four performances a week at the Italian opera, we now already have 900 members, and by the end of the season will have 1200? Ah God, what a joy to live in Moscow![29]

The fact is that, for all its attendant irritations, Balakirev's advent in Tchaikovsky's life at this time could not have been more timely. During his three or four years in Moscow Tchaikovsky had been able to develop freely beyond the circumscribed techniques and attitudes inculcated into him by his training at the St Petersburg Conservatoire. He was now on the threshold of his full musical maturity, ready for his creative gifts to be subjected to the most rigorous standards and demands that would elicit from them for the first time their full individuality expressed through first-rate materials which were entirely characteristic, and which were deployed in a structure that provided a natural framework for their potentialities. Balakirev was just the man to impose these demands, and before the year was out the first version of *Romeo and Juliet* was to be composed under his catalytic power.

[27] *TLP5*, pp. 185–6; *BVP*, p. 144.
[28] A composer and critic violently hostile to the ideals of the Balakirev group.
[29] *TLP5*, pp. 184–5; *BVP*, p. 143.

In January 1869, while awaiting the first performances of *The Voyevoda* and *Fatum*, Tchaikovsky set to work on a new opera, *Undine*. The original story by the German writer, Friedrich de la Motte Fouqué, had been rendered into Russian hexameters by Zhukovsky, and in 1848 Vladimir Sollogub had fashioned from it a libretto for Alexey Lvov. The opera had been a failure, and it fared no better when it was revived in the mid-1860s. Inauspicious though this was, Tchaikovsky was drawn to the subject, for it satisfied two conditions. First, it was ready-made, and he could set it forthwith (he had no wish to risk the sort of librettist delays he had endured from Ostrovsky over *The Voyevoda*). Secondly, it contained no Russian scenes, and for some reason best known to himself, Tchaikovsky wanted none of these. Modest expressed understandable amazement that his brother should ever have been attracted to this ludicrous romantic tale of a water nymph, Undine, who is loved and deserted by a knight, Huldbrand, drowns herself, and who, after his renewed love has ended in his death, turns into a fountain. Tchaikovsky, however, was captivated by it. He laboured hard upon his new opera through the spring, hoping that he would be able to complete the orchestration during the summer.

The numerous emotional trials of his everyday life do not seem to have had any adverse effect upon his creativity. He had started the year with the disturbance of his disintegrating relationship with Artôt: he also had to give a good deal of time to members of the Davïdov family who were in Moscow at the time. Vera's yearnings for him had not faded, and he was particularly sensitive to her relatives' probings into his affair with Artôt. 'I have had to engage in confidential conversations about my marriage – and you know how communicative I am about everything touching myself!' he lamented to Anatoly.[30] By the end of February his nervous state was so overwrought that he was planning to escape from Moscow until the next autumn. Such an action would, of course, have created a very difficult situation at the Conservatoire and this finally persuaded him to abandon the idea. His moods were evidently fitful, for only a few days later he was again cheerful enough to turn up at a fancy-dress occasion dressed as a domino. Such events were rare in his private life, however. His assiduous work on *Undine* did not even allow him to attend concerts, except for the memorial performance of Berlioz's *Requiem* at a special RMS concert on 4 May ('What a good piece this is!' he wrote to Balakirev eleven days later).[31] He still found time, of course, to exert himself on behalf of his twin brothers, dealing out his customary exhortations to Modest to work hard, and taking

[30] *TLP*5, p. 154.
[31] *TLP*5, p. 163; *YDGC*, p. 61; *BVP*, p. 132.

vigorous, though unsuccessful steps to help Anatoly find a post in Moscow.

With single-minded application such as this to *Undine*, progress was so swift that by the end of April Tchaikovsky was already petitioning Gedeonov to accept the work for performance during the next season. 'He [Gedeonov] has replied through his secretary that my opera will be put on in November if I present him with the score by September. As a result of this I am now diligently busying myself with the orchestration of the first act. The remaining two are already written, and I shall score these during the summer,' he confided to Anatoly.[32] A fortnight later he could tell Balakirev that Act 1 was done. He had been planning to spend the summer abroad, for his doctor had advised him to visit a spa, and to bathe in the sea. He had had his fill of the Davïdov clan, and swore that he would not go again to Kamenka until Lev and Sasha were living on their own estate. Whether this independence had been achieved by the summer is not known; either way, his funds would not allow a trip to Europe, and he spent June and July at Kamenka, where he pressed ahead with the scoring of *Undine*, an activity interrupted only by Ippolit's wedding in June. He found some relaxation from the labour of orchestration in helping to make the fireworks that were part of the wedding festivities. 'Despite his 29 years, something of a childish, naïve joy constantly burst out in Pyotr Ilich. When in the company of his nineteen-year-old brothers and other young people, he sometimes seemed to be younger than they,' Modest recorded of this summer interlude.[33] It was during this visit that Tchaikovsky heard and noted down the folksong, 'Sidel Vanya', which he was to use in his First String Quartet.

In the middle of August, shortly after his return to Moscow, he entrusted the finished score of *Undine* to Begichev to hand over to Pavel Fyodorov, author of the vaudeville, *The Tangle*, for which Tchaikovsky had nearly two years before provided some music at the Lopukhins', and the man mainly responsible for the repertoire of the Imperial Theatres in St Petersburg. A two-month silence ensued. At last an irritated and anxious Tchaikovsky could contain himself no longer, and on 24 October he wrote to Gedeonov:

Not only do I have no news of when my opera will be given and when rehearsals will begin, but I do not even know whether my score has been received, and where it has now got to. I have read in the newspapers that several new operas are being prepared for

[32] *TLP*5, p. 161; *TPB*, p. 51; *DTC*, p. 36.
[33] *TZC*1, p. 322.

production, and that the intention is to produce my opera as well only if any free time remains. From this newspaper information I am led to the lamentable conclusion that there has as yet been no serious discussion of my opera, and that it is doubtful whether it will be staged. I find this most galling for, having declined all other work, I laboured diligently the whole summer, relying implicitly on Your Excellency's promise, and joyfully anticipating the realisation of my dream, so long cherished, of hearing an opera of mine in St Petersburg.[34]

Five weeks later he was at last told that time did not permit the mounting of *Undine* that season.

Undine was never to be produced, for the work had, in fact, been rejected as unsatisfactory. Three numbers (the Introduction, Undine's aria from Act 1, and the chorus, duet and finale from the same act) were performed at a concert in Moscow on 28 March 1870, but had no success. As with *The Voyevoda*, some movements found a haven in later works. The Introduction was transferred to fulfil the same function in the incidental music Tchaikovsky provided for Ostrovsky's play, *The Snow Maiden*, in 1873, while Undine's aria from Act 1, 'The waterfall is my uncle, the streamlet my brother', was provided with a brief orchestral introduction and, with some rewriting of the vocal part, became Lel's first song in *The Snow Maiden*. The wedding march for Huldbrand and Berthalda (Huldbrand's betrothed, whom he had deserted for Undine in Act 1, but to whom he has temporarily returned in Act 3) became the slow movement of the Second Symphony, and the theme of the final duet for Undine and Huldbrand was to achieve universal fame by being incorporated into the G flat dance (with solo violin and cello) for the swans in Act 2 of *Swan Lake*. In 1873 Tchaikovsky destroyed the score of *Undine*, and only three fragments (the pieces performed in March 1870) survive from the actual opera.

Though both the wedding march and the theme of the third-act duet were worth saving for service elsewhere, none of these three remaining pieces suggests that the destruction of the rest of the opera constituted much of a disaster. Undine's aria is notable for its use of piano in association with the harp, the precedent for which is to be found in the Bayan's songs in Act 1 of *Ruslan and Lyudmila*, where Glinka had used the combination to evoke the sound of the gusli, a folk instrument. Tchaikovsky's music has little character, however, for Undine's naïvety lures him into simplism, and her music distils a wan charm, no more. The finale to Act 1 is a three-part structure, the outer portions being

[34] *TLP*5, p. 178; *DTC*, p. 36.

choruses of desperate fisher-folk fleeing from a deluge, while the centre is an equally excited duet for Undine and Huldbrand, who are too submerged in their new love to care much about the storm. The one incident of real interest is the brief use of the whole-tone scale, the precedent for which is again to be found in *Ruslan and Lyudmila*. These two bars (Ex. 26) in *Undine* expose all too clearly Tchaikovsky's

Ex. 26

incapacity as a composer of operas in which the very stuff of the drama is embodied in the musical materials and the technical procedures of the music itself. In *Ruslan and Lyudmila* Glinka had hit upon the brilliant idea of suggesting Chernomor's magic power by introducing the whole-tone scale into contexts using the normal repertoire of major and minor triads and sevenths, thus subverting the tonality. Hence, in the final battle between Ruslan and Chernomor, the former's resolute E major is constantly assaulted by such whole-tone elements. The essential nature of this brilliant musico-dramatic conception was something Tchaikovsky completely failed to comprehend, and by wedding his whole-tone scale in *Undine* to equally non-tonal chromaticism, he produced a progression which is merely a little eerie. Nor does the concluding cadence of unrelated chords (Ex. 27) really succeed any

Ex. 27

better, for Tchaikovsky was as far from commanding that brilliant harmonic empiricism which Musorgsky exploited so boldly as he was from matching, or even understanding, Glinka's musico-dramatic insight.

If Tchaikovsky, on his return to Moscow early in August 1869, had reckoned upon giving his undivided attentions to furthering the fortunes of his newly completed *Undine* and to enjoying a brief respite before the onset of the Conservatoire's new session, his hopes were to be rudely disappointed. Installed in Moscow was Balakirev, who promptly descended upon him with demands upon his time and company which he found very wearying. '[Balakirev's] presence oppresses me, I admit. He insists that I should be with him every day, and I find this rather tiresome. He is a very good man and very well disposed towards me, but for some reason I just cannot get into full sympathy with him. I don't quite like the exclusiveness of his musical views, or his sharp tone.'[35] Eight days later, on 23 August, he again unburdened himself to Anatoly on this matter: 'Balakirev's still here. We see each other often, and I am more and more convinced that, despite all his qualities, his company would weigh upon me like a heavy yoke if I lived in the same city as he. . . . However, in certain respects he has been of some use to me during his short stay here.'[36] Together they paid a call on the poet, Pleshcheyev, several of whose verses Tchaikovsky was later to set. Borodin, too, visited Moscow, and Tchaikovsky included him with Balakirev and Pleshcheyev among the guests he entertained to a soirée at his own home. Then, on 31 August, Balakirev returned to St Petersburg, and the prospect of freedom from his perpetual demands helped to soften a little Tchaikovsky's opinion of this musical tyrant from St Petersburg. 'However exhausting he is, it must be confessed that he is a very honourable and good man, and immeasurably above the average as an artist. We have just parted in the most touching fashion.'[37]

Nor was Balakirev Tchaikovsky's only problem. Though, as Tchaikovsky had feared, the situation at Kamenka had been so fraught with tensions as to make him glad to be back in Moscow, he was still on his return constantly troubled by laments from Anatoly, who had been posted to the criminal court in Kiev, despite all his brother's efforts to find him a position in Moscow. Immediately after Tchaikovsky's return, when he and Rubinstein moved their quarters, Tchaikovsky made an attempt to escape into a flat of his own. Again his bid for independence proved abortive, but there were consolations in their new home: it provided him with a pleasant and convenient room of his own in which he could work, and there would be space for Anatoly when he at last managed to find a position in Moscow.

He visited Vladimir Shilovsky a good deal, but resisted the latter's request that he should accompany him in September to Nice, where Shilovsky proposed to spend two years for the sake of his delicate health. Quite apart from his obligations to the Conservatoire, whose new

[35] *TLP*5, p. 166; *TZC*1, pp. 327–8; *TPB*, p. 52; *YDGC*, p. 62 (partial).
[36] *TLP*5, p. 168; *TZC*1, p. 328; *TPB*, p. 53.
[37] *TLP*5, p. 169; *TPB*, p. 53; *TZC*1, p. 329 (where the letter is dated 30 Aug.).

session was about to begin, Tchaikovsky would have to travel at Shilovsky's expense, and he knew he would not be able to conceal for long his distaste for such dependence upon the bounty of another. Instead he agreed to go with Shilovsky to St Petersburg for a couple of days in September. During this visit his intention had been to remain incognito, but a distant relative spotted him on the Nevsky Prospect and his hopes were dashed, though he still resolutely confined his visits largely to his old school friends, Apukhtin and Adamov (whose help he sought to enlist on Anatoly's behalf) – and to Balakirev. This trip enabled him to clear the air with Modest who, perhaps jealous of the prolonged solicitations Tchaikovsky was making in Anatoly's interests, had written reproaching him for his 'coldness'. Conversely Tchaikovsky's failure to visit other members of his family so roused their resentment that he had to ask Sasha, for whom he was trying to find a governess for her young daughter, to intercede with them on his behalf. He had a chance of redeeming himself with his father and stepmother when they visited Moscow in mid-October. Tchaikovsky enjoyed having them with him in what was now very much his home city.

Another source of pleasure was his new acquaintance with Schumann's *Scenen aus Goethes Faust*, and especially with a symphony (which is unspecified) by Gounod. Again a French composer could conjure a special magic for Tchaikovsky – though in reporting this to Balakirev he was careful to show that he was not blind to the musical slenderness of this piece of 'pleasant prattle'.[38] By contrast Gounod's *Sappho*, which he heard at the newly opened Italian opera season, he considered 'vile', setting against it Rossini's *Semiramide* in which, 'despite all the stiltedness, falsity and incredible tedium, there are to be met flashes of talent, and in which the delicacy and skill in the treatment of some of the orchestration show that Rossini was a much greater natural artist than Mercadante, Pacini, Kashperov and all such-like.'[39] Even when writing to Balakirev, Tchaikovsky could not turn complete traitor to his partiality for Italian opera. Balakirev probably felt that Tchaikovsky had redeemed himself a little in matters of operatic taste when a month later he heard that Tchaikovsky had been going through Cui's recent opera, *William Ratcliff*, and had been amazed to find how 'remarkably good'[40] it was. But, with the Conservatoire term only a month old, he was already finding his work becoming unpalatable, while extra demands were being put upon his time by the need to prepare a new course on musical form. Added to this were the chores of correcting the proofs of his arrangements of Russian folksongs, of

[38] *TLP5*, p. 174; *BVP*, p. 136.   [39] *TLP5*, p. 175; *BVP*, p. 136.
[40] *TLP5*, p. 181; *BVP*, p. 141; *YDGC*, p. 64.

making a piano duet version of Anton Rubinstein's orchestral piece, *Ivan the Terrible*, for Bessel, and of translating Johann Lobe's *Katechismus der Musik* into Russian for Jurgenson. Yet, while engulfed by these, he was actually hard at work – and, by late October, making good progress – on his first masterpiece.

Balakirev may have been troublesome in August, but when Tchaikovsky conceded merely that he had been 'of some use', he was being less than generous, for (so Kashkin recalled) it was on one of the long walks which Tchaikovsky, Balakirev and Kashkin took together during this visit that Balakirev put into Tchaikovsky's head the idea for an orchestral piece based on *Romeo and Juliet*. The suggestion certainly emanated from Balakirev, and on 7 October Tchaikovsky set about his fantasy overture. For two months he had rested from all original composition, and he expected to find his creative faculties refreshed, yet after a week of toil he was lamenting that the subject had not prompted the anticipated flow of ideas. 'I had always expected that I should be favoured with inspiration,' he wrote to Balakirev in dismay:

> I didn't want to write to you until I had sketched at least something of the overture. But just imagine, I'm completely played out, and not one even mildly tolerable musical idea comes into my head. I'm beginning to fear that my muse has flown off to some distant place (perhaps she's visiting Zaremba), and perhaps I'll have to wait a long time for her to return – and that's why I have decided to write forewarning you that I have become a museless . . . musician like Gabrieli, Lassus and other composers known only to the one Lord God and his prophet, Laroche.[41]

Balakirev could scarcely contain himself, for here was a heaven-sent predicament in which he could take over the direction of another composer's creativity – and Tchaikovsky's mute appeal must have been the sweeter for its apostatical sorties against Zaremba and Laroche. By return Balakirev dispatched not only a full account of how he himself ten years earlier had approached the composition of his own overture to another Shakespearean subject, *King Lear*; he also set down the four bars with which *he* would launch *Romeo and Juliet* if he were to compose it:

> I've got your letter and I'm distressed that so far you've achieved nothing. . . . I think this is because you're not concentrating enough, despite your agreeable workshop. I don't know how your compositional process works, but with me it goes as follows. I'll cite

[41] *TLP5*, p. 174; *BVP*, p. 135; *DTC*, pp. 340–1 (partial).

you an example that is appropriate for you – how I composed my
overture to *Lear*. First, after reading the play, I was inflamed with a
desire to write the overture . . . but having as yet no materials, I fired
myself by means of a ground plan. I projected a maestoso
introduction, and then something mystical (Kent's prophecy). The
introduction fades away, and there begins a stormy, passionate
allegro. This is Lear himself, already uncrowned, but still a strong
lion. The characters of Regan and Goneril were made to act as
episodes, and finally the quiet and gentle second subject personified
Cordelia. Further on the development (the storm, Lear and the Fool
on the heath), then the recapitulation of the allegro. Regan and
Goneril finally outdo him, and the overture ends with a dying-down
(Lear over Cordelia's body). Then follows a repetition of Kent's
prophecy, now fulfilled, and then a calm, solemn death. I'll tell you
that at first, [even] with this plan, no ideas formed themselves, but then
afterwards ideas did begin to come and fit themselves into the frame I
had created. I think that all this will happen to you also if you first
inflame yourself with a plan. Then arm yourself with galoshes and a
stick, set off for a walk along the boulevards, starting at the Nikitsky,
inspire yourself with your plan – and I'm convinced that before you
reach the Sretensky boulevard you'll already have some theme or at
least some episode. At this very moment, while thinking of you and
your overture, I am somehow or other involuntarily fired, and I
conceive that the overture must begin straight away with a fierce
allegro with sword clashes like this

[Ex. 28]

. . . If I were writing this overture then, having inspired myself with
this germ, I should let it incubate – or, rather, would carry it around
deep within my brain, and then there would issue something alive and
feasible like this.[42]

Balakirev did not let the matter rest there, and subsequently
communicated to Tchaikovsky a more detailed and considered plan

[42] *BVP*, pp. 136–7; *TZC*1, pp. 330–1. The last part is quoted in *DTC*, p. 341.

which included suggestions for the key scheme. The scheme itself evidently no longer exists, but the letter Tchaikovsky wrote to Balakirev three weeks later does a good deal to clarify this further debt, and discloses just how effectively Balakirev's prescription had cleared the blockage in his creative channels. 'My overture is progressing quite rapidly,' he could write on 9 November:

> The greater part is already composed in outline, and if nothing happens to hamper me I hope it will be ready in a month and a half. When it's crept out of my womb you'll see that, whatever else it may be, a large portion of what you advised me to do has been carried out as you instructed. In the first place, the scheme is yours: the introduction depicting the friar, the struggle (allegro), and love (second subject). Secondly, the modulations are yours: the introduction in E,[43] the allegro in B minor, and the second subject in D flat.[44]

Predictably Balakirev was impatient. 'I beg you to send me what you've done so far, and I *pledge myself* not to write a word, favourable or unfavourable, about it while the piece remains unfinished,' he wrote a fortnight later,[45] not knowing that Tchaikovsky's steady stream of invention had in the meantime turned into a torrent, so that *Romeo and Juliet* was probably already completed. Five days later, on 29 November, Tchaikovsky could announce that the work had been passed on to the copyist. Yet just as he would not let Balakirev see the piece while composition was still in progress lest comment should impede the flow of ideas, so now he decided to continue withholding it from Balakirev's critical scrutiny until he had himself heard it performed:

> Now that it's ready but still unperformed, I know least of all what it's worth. I know only that, whatever it may be, it's not so bad that I'm afraid of it bringing shame upon me here in Moscow. . . .
>
> At the end of this letter I am sending you the main themes – and no more for the time being. Later I'll send you the score that's being copied out for you – with the dedication to you, of course.

[43] This was the key of the introduction in the first version of *Romeo and Juliet*. Later Tchaikovsky suppressed this introduction, replacing it by a completely new one (see below, p. 189).

[44] *TLP*5, p. 180; *BVP*, p. 140; *DTC*, p. 341.

[45] *BVP*, p. 142; *TZC*1, p. 331.

[Ex. 29]   I. Theme of the Introduction
[Andante non troppo]

II. Theme of the Allegro

After this comes some rushing about in the manner of that little sample which, you remember, you sent me.

III. Love themes

and so on

Even with no more than four snippets of the principal ideas from *Romeo and Juliet* before him, Balakirev could not refrain from giving Tchaikovsky the benefit of his critical views:

Because it's already finished and will even soon be performed, I consider it is permissible to give you frankly my opinion of the themes you've sent me. The first theme is not at all to my taste. Perhaps when it's worked out it achieves some degree of beauty, but when written out unadorned in the way you've sent it to me, it conveys neither beauty nor strength, and doesn't even depict the character of Friar Laurence in the way required. Here there ought to be something like Liszt's chorales (*Der nächliche Zug* in F sharp, *Hunnenschlacht* and 'St Elizabeth') with an ancient Catholic character resembling that of

[46] *TLP5*, pp. 185–7; *BVP*, pp. 143–5.

Orthodox [church music]. But instead your E major tune has a completely different character – the character of quartet themes by Haydn, that genius of petty-bourgeois music, who arouses a strong thirst for beer. . . . On the other hand, it's possible that in its working out your theme gains a completely different character – and then I'll recant my words.

As for the B minor theme you've written down, this isn't a theme but *a very beautiful introduction to a theme*, and after the C major rushing about there is surely need for a strong, energetic melodic idea. I assume that it is there. . . .

The first D flat theme [it will be noted that Tchaikovsky quoted his second-subject themes to Balakirev in the reverse order] is very beautiful, though a bit overripe, but the second D flat tune is simply *delightful*. I play it often, and I want very much to kiss you for it. Here is tenderness and the sweetness of love. . . . When I play

[Ex. 30]

then I imagine you are lying naked in your bath and that the Artôt-Padilla herself is washing your tummy with hot lather from scented soap. There's just one thing I'll say against this theme; there's little in it of inner, spiritual love, and only a passionate physical languor (with even a slightly Italian hue) – whereas Romeo and Juliet are decidedly not Persian lovers, but Europeans.[47]

Despite the reservations, Tchaikovsky was delighted – and reassured – by Balakirev's first reactions, for he had gone on to predict confidently that it would prove to be Tchaikovsky's best work to date. Still having no wish to hear Balakirev on the complete work until after the first performance, he contrived to withhold *Romeo and Juliet* from him when the latter and Rimsky-Korsakov visited Moscow for a fortnight at the turn of the year. Nevertheless the score followed hard on Balakirev's heels when he returned to St Petersburg, though he did not sit down to write out his verdict to Tchaikovsky until 28 March 1870, twelve days after Nikolay Rubinstein had conducted the first performance at an RMS concert in Moscow. This event was not very encouraging. 'My overture had no success here and passed quite unnoticed,' Tchaikovsky

[47] *BVP*, pp. 145–6; *TZC*1, pp. 331–2 (slightly shortened; the reference to Artôt is pointedly omitted); *YDGC*, p. 68.

wrote to Klimenko some two months later.[48] As for Balakirev, he found
that the impressions he had formed from Tchaikovsky's earlier thematic
samples were confirmed by the completed work. 'I received your
overture a long time ago, and only illness has prevented me from
replying to you straight away to tell you how delighted everyone is with
your D flat bit – including Vladimir Stasov, who says: "There were five
of you; now you've become six!" The beginning and the end . . . are to
be strongly censured,'[49] and would need to be rewritten. Yet the
enthusiasm for *Romeo and Juliet* within the Balakirev circle was
enormous, and that winter, whenever they met at the home of Glinka's
sister, Lyudmila Shestakova, there was always a demand that Balakirev
should play it through at the piano, a feat he learned to perform from
memory.

Though Tchaikovsky, having heard his new work performed, still
felt that it was his best piece to date, he was aware of the piece's
inadequacies, and during July and August 1870 he revised it. On 18
September he summarised the results of his labours to Balakirev: 'I
think that the end is now respectable. The introduction is new, the
development almost new, and the recapitulation of the second subject
(in D major) has been completely rescored.'[50] The new introduction and
development delighted Balakirev, but he still found that the last part of
the piece contained a good deal that was routine, though the very end
'isn't bad', he thought. 'But what is the point of the sudden sharp chords
in the very last bars? This is against the sense of the drama. . . .'[51]
However, Tchaikovsky, whose response to Shakespeare was a good deal
less exact than Balakirev's (he confessed that in his revised introduction
Friar Laurence had become no more than 'a solitary soul, with spiritual
aspirations for heaven'),[52] had had enough of the work, and he allowed
Nikolay Rubinstein to use his good offices in persuading Bote & Bock of
Berlin to publish it. By now he felt that he had done all he could with
Romeo and Juliet, and when in May 1871 Balakirev tried to cajole him into
making further revisions which Jurgenson might in due course

[48] *TLP*5, p. 214; *DTC*, p. 342. This may not reflect a very considered judgement on the
part of the audience. Nikolay Rubinstein had been involved in a lawsuit over the
expulsion of a student from the Conservatoire. Though he won the case, the decision was
reversed on appeal. This revised verdict was pronounced only two days before this
concert, and the strong feeling of sympathy for Rubinstein found expression on this
occasion. The demonstration of support for the conductor probably distracted attention
from the works being performed.

[49] *BVP*, p. 151; *DTC*, p. 342. This letter was never sent, but was found amongst
Balakirev's papers after his death.

[50] *TLP*5, p. 231; *BVP*, p. 154; *DTC*, p. 343.

[51] *BVP*, p. 158; *TZC*1, p. 333; *DTC*, p. 343.

[52] *TLP*5, p. 237; *BVP*, p. 156; *DTC*, p. 343.

incorporate in another edition, he declined. The revised *Romeo and Juliet* was first heard on 17 February 1872 in St Petersburg at an RMS concert conducted by Nápravník. In 1880 Tchaikovsky substantially rewrote the end of the piece.

After the disaster of *Fatum* Balakirev can have had no difficulty in persuading Tchaikovsky not to try his hand at 'free form' again – at least, not for the time being – and from the beginning the new work was cast as a sonata structure. There is no better way to an appreciation of the merits of the definitive *Romeo and Juliet* than through a comparison with its preliminary version, not merely because such a study demonstrates the invariable superiority of Tchaikovsky's second thoughts, but also because it reveals a considered shift in the whole thematic balance of the piece so as to project a more weighty musical climax. In addition, it shows a growing perception of how the very core of the drama – the destruction of young love through the hatred of two warring clans – might be more powerfully played out in musical terms, a perception which only became fully focused in the final revision made to the end of the work in 1880. In the drastic first revision of 1870 Tchaikovsky scorned all half-measures, either retaining what he had written just as it stood or else rejecting it completely. When he came to review the earlier parts of the work, where the drama's protagonists are exposed, he concurred with Balakirev's verdict on the introduction and composed it afresh. On the other hand, he left intact the whole exposition with its excellent musical ideas and commendably taut structure, as well as the greater part of the recapitulation.

The exposition consolidates the principles already clearly declared in the First Symphony's opening movement, for once again the two subjects are massive paragraphs joined by a transition which is no more than a brief dominant preparation for the new key – though since, in *Romeo and Juliet*, Tchaikovsky is intending to follow Balakirev's advice and place his second subject in the distant key of D flat (really C sharp), this promise of the relative major (D major) to come enables him suddenly, and with ravishing effect, to melt his prolonged dominant into this remote key for the first statement of the broad love theme (see Ex. 29d). Yet the most remarkable part of the exposition is the first subject (Ex. 31). While possessing certain clear features in common with that of the First Symphony, this could not repeat the same kind of magisterial growth from the interaction of two thematic elements, if only because Tchaikovsky had decided to make it represent peremptory conflict, unleashed precipitately in invention which brims over with tensions. The violent rhythms, the unprepared and unresolved ninth of the second crotchet beat, the leap in bar 4 on to the neapolitan

Ex. 31

(Balakirev's 'C major rushing about') which is explored for a further four hectic bars before an abrupt return to the opening rounds off this nucleus of the first subject – all vividly represent the 'pernicious rage' which is to crush the lovers. Yet, splendid as this is, it posed major problems, for despite all its store of motivic material, it was a proposition so fully evolved that it made genuine organic extension difficult, especially when it closed with such finality in the tonic. The situation paralleled exactly that of the First Symphony after the opening theme had been stated; indeed, the overall design of the first subject of *Romeo and Juliet* (a key-enclosed paragraph with a shift to a distant tonal region in the centre) is equally like that of the earlier movement. But whereas the symphony had employed a second, chromatic agent to engineer the key shifts, the main theme of *Romeo and Juliet* had no such ally. Tchaikovsky's response to this problem of tonal and thematic inertia was as simple as it was novel and bold: to break out of the tonal confines in the most uncompromising fashion, extract some material from the opening proposition, and proceed to instant development. Thus he swiftly takes the opening phrase canonically through D minor and an even more distant G minor before leaping to a frenetic dominant of B minor in preparation for a full balancing restatement of the opening ten bars. Ex. 32 charts the structure of the entire first subject. It was a

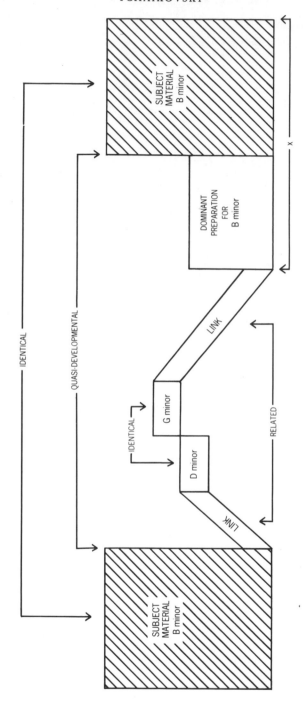

Ex. 32

basic pattern which Tchaikovsky was to repeat several times, most notably on a vastly extended scale in the Fourth Symphony.

The whole exposition of *Romeo and Juliet* is as admirable as the original introduction had been dreary. As one of Balakirev's letters has already shown, the first version of the latter had begun with a slow unaccompanied theme (see Ex. 29a) set (at Balakirev's own suggestion) in E major. Tchaikovsky had twice repeated this with different accompaniments in a way that signified some debt to Glinka's changing background technique, and which anticipated the way in which he was to open his Second Symphony some three years later. A modulating section concentrating melodically upon the first four bars had followed, and after a formal return to the opening theme in the tonic, this introduction had ended with sixteen bars of conventional dominant preparation into which was worked a foretaste of the first couple of bars of the broad love theme.

If Balakirev had done no more than persuade Tchaikovsky to abandon this lame beginning, their relationship would still have been worthwhile. It is not only that in the new introduction the 'chorale' in F sharp aeolian is far better than the faceless E major tune which it replaced: it is succeeded by three further quite distinct ideas which give this fresh beginning a diversity and richness of character quite lacking in the first. When composing this material Tchaikovsky may have paid little heed to Balakirev's counsel to take Liszt as his model except in the chorale, but he followed exactly that master's common practice of repeating the entire succession of ideas starting in another key (here everything is a semitone lower). The ensuing link to the first subject is far more imaginatively handled, too, for this time Tchaikovsky settles on to the initial chord of the allegro giusto itself, and by asserting it for some eight bars with ever-increasing obsessive force, portends the fast approaching eruption of uncontainable forces in a way which makes the sedate poise of the former dominant preparation sound merely decorous.

With the development *Romeo and Juliet* enters the first of the two structural divisions in which the drama is to be played out; significantly it was in these sections (the other is the last stage of the recapitulation) that Tchaikovsky's main revisions were to be made. Quite apart from making the basic miscalculation of launching the original development with an extensive fugato, as he had done in his student work, *The Storm*, Tchaikovsky simply does not appear to have perceived the deeper dramatic possibilities within his materials until he had lived with them for some time. As we have already noted, to think in terms of variation is one of the most deeply rooted instincts of Russian musical creativity. It is

seen at its simplest and clearest in certain Russian folksongs which
extend themselves by devising constant variations against an initial
prototype; it is also seen, in a brilliantly sophisticated form, in
Kamarinskaya, which is based on Glinka's perception that two outwardly
dissimilar tunes were related, and that through a series of linking
variations he might demonstrate that relationship. From the beginning
the musico-dramatic technique of *Romeo and Juliet* had included a
similar process, and one that was made possible by Tchaikovsky's
doubtless unconscious fashioning of certain similarities between
different materials.

Thus, close comparison reveals an identity of outline within the
openings of the violently contrasting subjects, the first depicting the fury
of the Montague–Capulet feud, the second portraying radiantly the love
of Romeo and Juliet in two quite separate themes; in addition, the
second of these themes (see Ex. 29c) has a characteristic rocking
movement anticipated in bars 7 and 8 of the first subject (see Ex. 31). Of
these two inter-subject relationships Tchaikovsky certainly quickly
perceived the former, clarifying it in the development where four bars
making prominent use of a shape extracted from the broad love theme
follow hard upon six bars in which a similar contour has been sifted
from the first subject (Ex. 33). It is significant that Tchaikovsky
determined not to sacrifice these ten bars in his revision, though all the
rest of the development went. As for the other relationship, Tchaikovsky

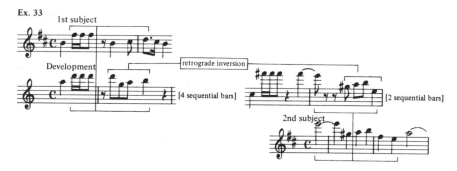

Ex. 33

offers no evidence in the first *Romeo and Juliet* that he had spotted it, but
in the revision he inserted two new incidents in which the oscillation
between two chords which is the feature common to both is employed,
though in such a way as to make it impossible to say to which subject
either of these new derivatives is more closely related. The first of the
new insertions (Ex. 34a) appears in the development; in fact, an equal
progenitor of this passage could be found in a conflation of two
incidents in the exactly corresponding section of Glinka's overture to

Ex. 34

Ruslan (Ex. 34b and c): the second of these recurs in the abduction scene (see Ex. 15a). The other insertion occurs in the coda, where the new rocking derivative is twice slotted into the original (now turned into the major key), greatly enriching it. As Ex. 35 shows, Tchaikovsky expanded his original seven bars to more than twice this length. Even more

Ex. 35

important, as we shall see, was his decision to make a completely new integration of the first subject and the broad love theme serve as a fundamental agent in the work's climax.

Whether Tchaikovsky rejected the opening fugato of his original development on any grounds of quality we do not know; what he can hardly have failed to perceive is that, while the vigorous contrapuntal deployment of a single theme may suggest forceful activity, it will scarcely convey conflict. For purely musical reasons it was natural that Tchaikovsky should now turn to a favoured alternative method of launching a development – that is, by dexterously combining different materials. Add to this that there is no better way of matching the tensions of the drama than through the collision of those musical ideas that embody the diverse conflicting elements in the tale, and it comes as no surprise that Tchaikovsky engineered an immediate engagement of representative musical ideas, deploying the work's new first theme against bustling lines originating in the former fugal opening of the development (these were derived from the first subject), passing subsequently to his new Ruslan-related invention (see Ex. 34a). Having repeated all this first stretch of the development a semitone higher, he clipped in the ten bars which he had decided to preserve from his first attempt.

The Tchaikovsky family (1848); l to r: Pyotr, Mrs Tchaikovskaya,
Alexandra (Sasha), Zinaida (standing), Nikolay, Ippolit,
Mr Tchaikovsky

Tchaikovsky (1860)

Sasha (née Tchaikovskaya) and Lev Davïdov (1860)

Nikolay Kashkin

Pyotr Jurgenson

Karl Albrecht

Herman Laroche

Nikolay and Anton Rubinstein

Tchaikovsky (1868)

Tchaikovsky (1874)

What follows heralds one of the most significant changes in the whole work. Formerly these last ten bars had been followed by the broad love theme set against peremptory reiterations of the ♪♪♩ figure extracted from the first subject. Now, instead, Tchaikovsky embedded the new Friar Laurence theme in this accompaniment, thus enabling him to remove almost all trace of this love theme from the development. By so doing, he changed the entire expressive balance of the piece. This love theme was by far the most powerful emotional weapon in his thematic armoury. So far he had confined complete statements of it to the exposition where its restrained wind scoring had ensured that its full force had been held in reserve; now, by postponing its explicit recurrence, he also ensured that when it did at last reappear during the recapitulation, its impact would be the greater. In the first version of *Romeo and Juliet* this love theme had also been an ingredient in the final part of the development. Here Tchaikovsky had at last combined ideas extracted from the introduction and both subjects, following this with six bars of naked timpani F sharps to provide the most rudimentary of dominant preparations for the recapitulation. There were three reasons for excluding all this from the revision: it alluded to the broad love theme, the revised development had already adequately played out the drama in some intensive thematic encounters, and the timpani passage simply would not do. It could all be sacrificed, Tchaikovsky decided: to herald the recapitulation he need do no more than slot in the hectic dominant preparation which had been part of the first subject in the exposition, and the truncated first subject would follow naturally (see the portion bracketed *x* in Ex. 32).

The recapitulation of the first subject and the first part of the second were left as they were in the original, for the reversal of the order of the two love themes suited Tchaikovsky's new intentions excellently. From the point at which the broad love theme turns flatwards the first version had merely extended this theme for some further four bars, had referred briefly to the first subject, and had then musically embodied the ultimate catastrophe in sixteen bars of frenetic string-and-woodwind semiquavers over a bass descending stepwise in minims, with trumpets and horns hammering out the rhythm of the first subject's initial bar. This had terminated abruptly in a diminished seventh, to be followed by an allusion on trombones and tuba to the rocking love theme, counterpointed by fragments of the broad love theme. The coda had opened with a funeral march based on a new, even more undistinguished version of the work's E major opening over tonic and dominant timpani crotchets with attendant chromaticism. Ex. 35a, followed by some solemn tonic chords, had closed the piece.

If the new development had been based mainly on thematic

confrontation, the new conclusion laid far more emphasis on drastic thematic integration. It was a splendid intention, but Tchaikovsky's first revision left the process only half completed, and the motivation for his second assault on this last stretch in 1880 was clearly an urge to fulfil what he had begun ten years earlier. When in 1870 Tchaikovsky rescored the first part of the broad love theme in the recapitulation (from bar 419), and then extended it by some twenty bars, his intention was not just to avail himself further of its full emotional potential, but also to prepare the ground for a climax that expressed, in terms as profoundly musical as they were expressively heightened, the final fateful collision between the unequal forces of a frail young love and an old inter-family feud. Up to this point the various materials had merely brushed with one another; now there follows a melodic fusing which signifies the ultimate catastrophe as elements of the conflict music infiltrate destructively into the broad love theme, swiftly overwhelm it, and leave the first subject to occupy the field. Then, with Friar Laurence powerless to intervene (and from this point [bar 461] we hear Tchaikovsky's final thoughts of 1880, in which he again availed himself of that inter-subject relationship he had uncovered in his very first version [see Ex. 33]), the rampaging first subject finally winds itself down sequentially, and from its fury the love theme again issues (Ex. 36),

Ex. 36

twisted, broken, and accompanied by a lacerating dissonance which looks forward to the even more tragic end of Tchaikovsky's last major work, also in B minor.

Tchaikovsky did one thing more. This masterly transformation which he devised in 1880 had not merely involved composing some twenty-four bars of new music before the moderato assai; it had also necessitated the shedding of nearly twice as much existing music. The excision of most of this was no great sacrifice, but the last eight bars, where the broad love theme has ridden majestically above a strong, darkly chromatic bass, were too good to lose. Their new habitat was brilliantly chosen; Tchaikovsky resited them in the coda between the end of the wind 'chorale' and the four concluding bars of abrupt chords, where they could assume the character of an apotheosis of the lovers.

One wonders whether Tchaikovsky himself quite realised what an admirable musico-dramatic concept had 'crept out of his womb', even by 1870. As for the four concluding bars, it was typical of Balakirev's essentially literal mind that he should have missed their point. Their succession of fierce tonic chords harshly recalls that fatal feud on which these young lives have been broken; the warring families now stand transfixed, the grim B minor chords no longer suggesting, as at the end of the introduction, an imminent explosion of ferocious strife, but a stunned horror at what has been done. Through them Tchaikovsky drove home the fatalism of a musical masterpiece which is likely to remain unsurpassed as an expression of young and tragic love.

Even as Tchaikovsky was engaged on *Romeo and Juliet*, the conditions affecting his relationship with Balakirev were beginning to change. Balakirev's musical fortunes were declining. Having earlier in 1869 lost his position as conductor of the RMS in St Petersburg, he organised that autumn a series of five subscription concerts which, as his correspondence with Tchaikovsky has already shown, proved financially disastrous. In September 1870 he returned to his home town of Nizhni-Novgorod to give a recital, hoping that the fame he had acquired in Russia's musical life would gain him a hero's welcome and a handsome profit. Instead the event was largely ignored, and the material gain was negligible. To restore his shattered finances he was forced to do more and more teaching, which left little or no time for concert organisation, even if his funds had permitted such costly enterprises. The first performance of the revised *Romeo and Juliet*, which Balakirev himself had hoped to conduct at one of the Free Music School's concerts, did not take place through lack of money, and he had to endure the mortification of hearing this work which he had nursed into the world, and of which he was the dedicatee, receive its first performance at a concert of the now rival RMS. During 1871 his fortunes sank still lower. Despair nearly drove him to suicide, he suddenly became deeply and morbidly religious, and his behaviour antagonised many of his friends. Then in the autumn of 1871 he appeared to regain abruptly his former energy and enthusiasm, planning five concerts at the Free Music School, and again turning his thoughts to directing Tchaikovsky's creative destiny. Among the works Balakirev was proposing to perform was a 'Chorus of Flowers and Insects' which Tchaikovsky had composed in December 1869/January 1870 for an abortive opera, *Mandragora*. On receiving the score Balakirev saw how a new home might be found for this little operatic waif. Characteristically he provided a full plan for Tchaikovsky:

> Write a cantata to be called *Night* and include [with the 'Chorus of Flowers and Insects'] a few more similarly fantastic choruses. Have a chorus of water nymphs, a forest chorus of wood sprites, an aria to the night after the fashion of 'O belle nuit' in Félicien David's *Le Désert*, of which I'm very fond. . . .
>
> Then have an instrumental scherzo after the manner of *Queen Mab* [from Berlioz's *Romeo and Juliet*], imitating the buzzing of midges, moths and their nocturnal darting hither and thither; somewhere a frightful owl is perched ready to gobble them up (the element of terror); the babbling of a brook, glow-worms, or something of that sort.
>
> A cantata mustn't have a definite subject, but let it be lyrical and descriptive, for then it will be a cantata and not an opera, and let it finish with a valedictory chorus of spirits. As dawn approaches the spirits depart, taking their leave of one another until the next night (a gradual diminuendo). Finally the orchestra alone depicts the dawn, rises later in a crescendo, getting lighter and lighter; then finally orchestral chords depict the rising sun, with which the whole work ends.
>
> Let the cantata be preceded by a short orchestral prelude. Throughout the whole work the atmosphere of fantasy must be maintained. If you should think fit to add a Russian or an oriental character, this would add to its charm; in particular the oriental type with its grace and delicacy is far better suited to fantasy than the Russian.

And, as an afterthought, he added: 'A Russian character can be useful where an element of strength is required – for instance, in the chorus of wood sprites.'[53]

Tchaikovsky replied that he liked Balakirev's idea very much and would certainly use it – though not yet, because his time was being completely absorbed by his new opera, *The Oprichnik*. In fact he never composed the cantata. Balakirev's concerts were not the hoped-for success, and the fifth had to be cancelled. In utter financial ruin he took

[53] *BVP*, pp. 161–2.

a post with a railway company, and for four years withdrew completely from Russia's musical life. With this proposal for the cantata, *Night*, his contact with Tchaikovsky ceased abruptly, and for ten years there appears to have been virtually no further relationship between them. It was probably as well. Balakirev had certainly done Tchaikovsky splendid service, for he had subjected him to a rigorous supervision which had drawn from him his first masterpiece, but what Tchaikovsky now needed was independence. Yet thirteen years later, when the two men were briefly brought together for a second time, Balakirev extracted from Tchaikovsky the Manfred Symphony which, if less consistent than *Romeo and Juliet*, also contains some of Tchaikovsky's very best invention. Even though Tchaikovsky had by 1884 become an international figure with an impressive list of compositions to his credit, the old despot's persuasiveness and catalytic power remained undiminished.

A Note on Désirée Artôt, *Fatum*, and the First Piano Concerto

In addition to the *Romance* for piano, Op. 5, and the Six Romances, Op. 65, all of which were dedicated to Désirée Artôt, there are two substantial pieces by Tchaikovsky which seem to have less explicitly acknowledged connections with the singer: namely, the symphonic poem, *Fatum*, and the First Piano Concerto. The former was written during the very weeks when the composer's affair with Artôt was in full swing, while the latter employed in its slow movement a French chansonette which is said to have been a popular item in her repertoire. The evidence I offer below that the singer's presence is embodied in cipher-generated motifs within each of these works is too inconclusive for it to be accorded the authority which might seem to be implied by an examination in the main text of this book; nevertheless, it seems to me substantial enough to merit this supplementary note.

In deriving musical pitches from words, Russian composers were prepared to widen the possible range of derivatives by mixing both French and German pitch nomenclatures. By such means DÉSIRÉE ARTÔT yields a six-note pitch series (Ex. 37a). Taking also the single pitches which may be derived from the first letter(s) of the singer's name, we may extract Ex. 37b.

Ex. 37

Tchaikovsky composed *Fatum* without admitting to a programme, though, as already noted, Kashkin thought it was in some way autobiographical. Unfortunately we do not know the exact condition his personal relationship with Artôt had reached by 22 September 1868, when he had already begun work upon this symphonic poem, but it was certainly developing rapidly within less than a fortnight. Nor do we know anything about the order in which Tchaikovsky composed the constituent parts of *Fatum*. Nevertheless, if we take the four consecutive pitches at each end of the above six-note series, reading outwards – and, in addition, inverting the first of these four-note series (see Ex. 38a and d) – we have the precise outlines of the work's opening motif (Ex. 38e) and of the ostinato bass of the second section (Ex. 38b) which, in turn, furnishes the first two bars of the main A flat theme (Ex. 38c).

Ex. 38

The First Piano Concerto was composed six years later, in the last weeks of 1874. The massive introduction, which is so often alleged to be unrelated to anything that follows, in fact immediately and exactly foretells the distinctive harmonic progression at the beginning of the second subject (Ex. 39b and c), thus bestowing an extra significance upon the very place where there is to occur a theme launched with notes which may be derived from Artôt's initials (Ex. 39a and b). The upward move to B flat in the first bar of Ex. 39b was the obvious melodic resolution in this harmonic context; it also reproduced exactly the contour outlined by the last three of the four notes in Ex. 38a. This might occasion little comment, were it not that it would explain a melodic inconsistency in the slow movement upon which earlier commentators have

Ex. 39

[P] E [t] E [r T s]C   H   A [ikowsky]

remarked without being able to offer any explanation. The main theme of this slow movement (which contains the Artôt-associated song) occurs six times, opening in the same way every time (Ex. 40a) except the first, when it occurs as in Ex. 40b. Conceivably Tchaikovsky modified his preferred version of this

Ex. 40

theme in order to impress the secret 'Artôt contour' upon the beginning of this movement.

It is also provocative to note the four-note pitch series which may be extracted from Tchaikovsky's own name, using the Western transliteration of his surname normally employed during his lifetime (but omitting Schumann's

liberty of taking 's' as 'Es') (Ex. 39d). Transposed to B flat minor, this series
yields the imperious horn phrase which opens the First Piano Concerto,
punctuated by the chords which later support the twice-heard 'Artôt contour'
of the second subject (Ex. 39c). Could it be that he wished to symbolise for
himself the one 'affair' of his own life? It is a curious fact that the 'Artôt contour'
and the thrice-heard 'Tchaikovsky contour' appear in exactly the same structural
locations in the first movement of Tchaikovsky's next major work, the Third
Symphony of 1875, though this time their positions are reversed (Ex. 39e and f).

The fact that the 'Artôt contour' is also incorporated in the first few notes of
the *Romance* dedicated to Artôt is probably coincidental (Ex. 41).

Ex. 41

7

FIRST QUARTET AND

THE OPRICHNIK

TCHAIKOVSKY'S HUNDRED OR SO songs remain, like his country's songs in general, largely unknown in the West. Though the reason is partly linguistic, it is equally true that the nature of the genre is not such as to win it a ready popularity outside its native land, for nineteenth-century Russian song is dominated by the romance, a sentimental and soft-centred species which closely parallels the Victorian drawing-room ballad. Nor can it be claimed that the song output of late-nineteenth-century Russian composers matched their instrumental and operatic works. Admittedly Balakirev and Borodin each produced a handful of masterpieces, but Musorgsky was the only composer whose songs, both in quality and quantity, add up to a major corpus of work. Even so, only a small number even of his finest songs has gained any sort of fame outside Russia, and it is futile to pretend that Tchaikovsky could in any way equal Musorgsky in this field. Nevertheless he was better as a song composer than our neglect would suggest.

As a serious art form Russian song begins with Glinka, who elevated the romance to an unprecedented level, and also provided the first really worthy examples of three other types: the folksong stylisation, the dramatic ballad (spectacularly in 'The Midnight Review'), and the song epigram (exquisitely in 'Where is our rose?'). Which of these four types was to dominate Tchaikovsky's song output is established in his very first set of songs, the Six Romances, Op. 6, composed in November and December 1869, immediately after completion of the first version of *Romeo and Juliet*. His decision to write these was determined, at least in part, by his wish to make some money, but this should not lead us to conclude too readily that their musical currency is debased. Nevertheless, as a song writer, Tchaikovsky had his limitations. He has been especially faulted for overgeneralisation – that is, for showing a disregard both for the individual phrase and for the shifts within the psychological state which may be reflected in a lyric. He has been accused, too, of unsympathetic and even faulty declamation, and of using verbal repetition prompted solely by musical considerations, often prejudicial to the verse. There is a good deal to support these charges. He had no hesitation in modifying verbal details (in the present set the first song's opening should read 'Do not believe me, friend'), exchanging the order of lines, and even adding extra words (like the 'no' in the refrain of 'A tear trembles'). In the first two songs he repeated the whole of the opening stanza at the end to permit a ternary structure, while in the last, in which Goethe had already provided him with a common opening and closing couplet, he broke the middle of the lyric for yet another delivery of these two lines. Nor, elsewhere, did he have any hesitation in cutting down his text (as in 'It's both bitter and sweet', where the deletion of the penultimate stanza does nothing to aid the sense of the whole).

In fact Tchaikovsky conceived most of his songs as balanced musical entities furnished with a formal piano prelude and postlude which neatly frame, but usually add nothing essential to the whole. Those contemporary critics whose view of musical truth was restricted to the maximum-of-realism and minimum-of-stylisation principle so compellingly evinced in many of Musorgsky's best songs can have found little to admire in Tchaikovsky's. Yet while the latter's may not particularly illumine the lyric, as musical responses to the intensity of feeling which lies behind the words they are sometimes powerful and apt. Nor should it be assumed too readily that they are always obtuse in more precise textual response. In the very first song of this set, for example, the opening vocal phrase setting words of disavowal ('Do not believe, my friend [, when . . . I say I have ceased to love you]') breaks urgently into the piano part in the central section in a way which both braces the musical structure and resonates with significance for the poetic content.

The texts used in these six songs are Russian translations of a lyric each by Goethe, Heine and Moritz Hartmann, and three verses by contemporary Russian writers, Evdokiya Rostopchina and Alexey Tolstoy, the latter a distant relation of the great novelist and one of the minor poets to whom Tchaikovsky was to turn frequently in his search for suitable texts. The majority of these six lyrics are highly charged, even desperate expressions of frustrated or troubled love; common to all six is a strong personal emotion which Tchaikovsky could match freely and passionately. The most poised is the fourth, 'A tear trembles'. One might wonder, from the accompaniment, whether Tchaikovsky had already heard Borodin's 'The Sea Princess', composed the previous year (but not published until 1873), though he does not hazard the emancipated dissonance which Borodin so boldly paraded in that song.

His declamation, too, is closer to Borodin's measured manner in 'The Sea Princess' than to that used in the five remaining songs.

The set opens splendidly with 'Do not believe, my friend', which employs a harmonic palette, rich in fervid sevenths and telling chromaticism, as support for a passionate melody infected with a nervousness which breaks it into short urgent phrases, knit tightly together by the insistent momentum of the accompaniment. In the second song, 'Not a word, O my friend', the vocal phrases are even shorter and more separate; even more, therefore, the harmony is used to keep the piece in motion, supporting each phrase-end with a dissonance whose tensions ensure a continuing drive towards the next vocal entry. The climax of the central section must have been cited by Tchaikovsky's critics as a blatant example of disharmony between the composer and his text, for the musical phrase rides roughshod over the natural break in the verbal sense (Ex. 42) – though the disconsolate verbal reiteration, followed by

Ex. 42   [Andante ma non troppo] Poco più mosso

[Not a word, O my friend]

the return of the song's opening, is beautifully judged. The third song, 'It's both bitter and sweet', returns to the agitated world of 'Do not believe, my friend', but the growing overemphasis on the opening words whenever they return seems finally to transport the piece out of the drawing room into the opera house, and what Tchaikovsky doubtless intended should express the height of excitement topples over into something closer to hysteria.

The distinction between the aria and the romance is frequently blurred in nineteenth-century Russia, but even without this there was especial danger of an over-blown response from a composer like Tchaikovsky who, for all his zeal in preserving a balanced musical structure, could so easily succumb to an emotional summons. And when the text employed a repetitive device, like the chain of questions framed into couplets in the lyric Tchaikovsky chose for his fifth song, 'Why?' (from Heine's 'Warum sind dann die Rosen so blas?'), there was the added danger that the equally restricted melodic world which might initially seem so apt for matching this literary device would ultimately circumscribe even more the scope for amplifying feeling by a genuinely musical evolution, thus leaving increasing dynamic force as the most obvious agent for suggesting the swelling of emotion. Of all German song writers it was Schumann who had the strongest influence upon Russian composers, and it may have been the use of a lyric by one of Schumann's compatriots that inclined Tchaikovsky a little towards that composer in 'Why?', notably in some of the chromatic moves and the bass progressions in fifths. Tchaikovsky was, however, incapable of matching Schumann's subtle musical distillation of the very essence of lyrics such as Heine's, and the end of 'Why?' suggests frenzied petulance rather than an access of emotional pain.

Following upon this outburst, the success of the last song, also dwelling on the agony of love in separation, is the more striking. Very curiously, Mey's translation of Goethe's 'Nur wer die Sehnsucht kennst' puts it into the mouth of the Harper, but Tchaikovsky must have been aware that it was Mignon's plaint, for the lyric had already had an irresistible attraction for many composers. Beethoven set it four times, though only one of these settings suggests that he had the slightest interest in burdening the music with the weight of Mignon's sorrow. Schubert attempted it on no less than six occasions. Tchaikovsky's 'None but the lonely heart' (to give it its usual English title) is a significant achievement in which text and music are joined in a felicitous union to unfold a truly developing experience. The treatment of the crucial 'Ah! the one who knew and loved me is far away' projects a sudden tender pathos more touching than anything in the companion songs, and which cannot but colour the prompt return of the opening music (made possible by Tchaikovsky's rearrangement of the text, and which he might more wisely have marked *p* instead of *f*). The most affecting moment is still to come; this impassioned outburst is cut off abruptly, and as the voice quietly resumes, evolving its line further with the last fragment of Goethe's middle section ('My whole breast burns'), the piano slides in yet again with the opening melody, drawing the singer back to the opening words, and leading the song tenderly towards its end (Ex. 43).

Yet this moment, for all its beauty, is wistful, perhaps, rather than sad.

[. . . and how I suffer. My whole breast burns . . . The one who has known the yearning for the tryst will grasp how I suffered, and how I suffer]

In any case, feeling itself is not sufficient, since it is less the intensity of the suffering than the degree of defencelessness of the victim that determines the strength of our response. For that very reason Schubert's A flat setting of 1815, in which the constantly shifting keys seem designed to reflect the tensions of torment itself, is inferior to his solo setting of 1826, which conjures up the very image of this gentle person, a solitary figure uttering her sorrow softly in the simplest of $\frac{6}{8}$ andantes, only once, and very briefly, releasing the full force of her distress before retreating into her resigned misery. Tchaikovsky's Mignon (for surely, despite Mey's translation, this should be *her* song) is an habituée of the drawing room, able at moments to bawl her grief and, in self-dramatisation, to find a release which eases her sufferings. Because she is less vulnerable, she can never touch us like Schubert's waif.

Tchaikovsky was already engaged on these romances when he received the news that *Undine* would not be performed that season. This blow might reasonably have been expected to scatter any other operatic intentions that were lurking in his head; yet no sooner were these romances complete than he began applying himself to a new opera, *Mandragora*. The story, by Tchaikovsky's botanist friend, Rachinsky, who had provided the unfortunate epigraph for *Fatum*, had some features strikingly like those of *Undine*. Modest quoted Rachinsky's own summary of the tale:

A knight is enamoured of a lovely lady who rejects his love. A feast in a castle: a minstrel sings of the all-powerful mandragora, an enchanted root which is actually mentioned in the Bible. The knight sets out for the secret garden to get the mandragora. Night. An incantation. The mandragora bursts into bloom. The knight tears it from its roots – it turns out to be an enchanted beauty who, of course, immediately falls in love with him and, in the guise of a page, attaches herself to him. After a whole series of varied fortunes, the knight falls in love with another woman, and the unfortunate Mandragora once again turns into a flower.[1]

One cannot but wonder whether Tchaikovsky, sensing that *Undine* was unsatisfactory and might never be performed, was attracted by a similar story which could, if need be, absorb the best music of his second opera. He composed only one piece for *Mandragora*, a 'Chorus of Flowers and Insects', completed on 8 January 1870, for his enthusiasm for this new opera was short-lived. Kashkin, to whom he showed not only this chorus but also the proposed scenario, approved strongly of the former but

[1] *TZC*1, p. 336.

opined that, while the latter might make a good ballet, it was quite unsuitable for an opera, and finally persuaded Tchaikovsky to abandon it.

The 'Chorus of Flowers and Insects', presumably intended to open the scene where the knight goes into the secret garden, was scored for unison boys' voices, mixed chorus and medium-sized orchestra. Nikolay Rubinstein conducted it at an RMS concert given in Moscow on 30 December 1870, where it was described as a 'Chorus of Elves'. According to Tchaikovsky the performance was bad and the work enjoyed no success, but Laroche reviewed it enthusiastically, detecting in the instrumentation some influence of Berlioz (especially of the 'Chœur de Gnomes et de Sylphes' in *La Damnation de Faust*). Yet there is also a strain of Glinka's magic idiom – of the slightly brittle world of Naina in *Ruslan and Lyudmila*, where the harmonies, textures and colours have a harder edge than in Berlioz's exquisite, but always warm delicacy. Cast as a ternary structure, Tchaikovsky's chorus is a little essay in atmosphere with a quite magical coda which draws up the greater part of its substance from its Russian root, most obviously in the treatment of the chromaticism and in the final rotation around the three major chords which have in common the A which the boys hold in the last bars (the major triads on D, A and F). It is not surprising that Balakirev, who conducted this charming trifle in St Petersburg at a Free Music School concert exactly a year after its Moscow première, should have wished Tchaikovsky to explore this world on a larger scale (see above, p. 196), though he felt the melody of the E flat middle section was trivial, a view which the composer came to share.

Nothing daunted by the demise of *Mandragora*, Rachinsky promptly proffered an alternative. This was *Raimond Lully*, a melodrama set in Spain, and concerning a medieval Don Juan-like character whose beloved, Donna Inez, is horrified at his debauched living, and retreats to a nunnery. In a mad passion Raimond (on horseback) bursts into the nunnery chapel during service, scattering everyone, and joins in a duet with Donna Inez, in the course of which he is converted to a life of contemplation. He sets out for Africa as a warrior-missionary, where he is struck down by an old accomplice who has become alarmed at the improvement in his character, and dies in the arms of Donna Inez who happens to be in Africa buying the freedom of some Christian prisoners. It was, as Modest put it, 'in a highly mystical style'.[2] It may seem surprising that Tchaikovsky could ever for one moment have considered such a ludicrous tale, let alone have found it 'very interesting' (as he informed Modest).[3] When we criticise his choice in the libretti he did

[2] *TZC*1, p. 337.   [3] *TLP*5, p. 202; *TPB*, p. 61; *YDGC*, p. 66.

actually set, it is as well to temper our judgement by reflecting on the far more horrifying temptations which he was offered, and which he rejected. If *Mandragora* had been unsuitable, *Raimond Lully* was ten times more so, and Tchaikovsky rapidly lost interest in it, side-stepping any further proposals from Rachinsky, and within less than a month settling down to be his own librettist for the subject which did become the basis of his third opera: Lazhechnikov's tragedy, *The Oprichnik*.

Tchaikovsky's social life during the last weeks of 1869 had been blighted by a visit to Moscow of Vera and members of her family. Artôt's return had presented its own peculiar strains, and the added presence of this unsuccessful rival for Tchaikovsky's affections did nothing to make the position easier. Vera and some members of her family actually attended Artôt's reappearance on the Moscow stage on 11 December, but would have nothing favourable to say of her, and Vera herself left after the third act. During her three weeks in Moscow, Tchaikovsky sensed that Vera was trying to pretend her affection had passed, but behaviour like this left him unconvinced and uncomfortable. The New Year started much more pleasantly with the visit of Balakirev and Rimsky-Korsakov. Tchaikovsky particularly enjoyed the evident respect which Balakirev now accorded him, while Rimsky-Korsakov paid his homage with the dedication of a new romance, 'Where you are, there are my thoughts'. Congenial as such friendships were, however, he was very much aware of his longing for a more intimate kind of relationship, for there was no one in Moscow to whom he felt really close. As usual Sasha was the recipient of such confidences: 'I feel a strong need for the clamour of children, a need to share personally in some trivial domestic interests – in a word, for a family situation.' There was always marriage, of course, 'but I haven't enough courage for that'.[4] To Balakirev he confessed that his nerves were in a bad way. 'Why this should be I don't know,' he wrote on 7 March, 'but an inexpressible melancholy oppresses me. I should like to go off somewhere and hide myself in some impenetrable backwood.'[5]

During the spring there were one or two brighter spots. One of his new romances, 'It's both bitter and sweet', was performed to great acclaim at an RMS concert on 26 March, and the whole Op. 6 set was published a fortnight later, to be greeted with enthusiasm by Laroche, and equally predictable censure from Balakirev's group. Within the month two piano pieces composed in February, the *Valse Scherzo*, Op. 7 (dedicated to Sasha), and the *Capriccio*, Op. 8, were printed. His

[4] *TLP5*, p. 203; *TZC1*, p. 338 (with the reference to marriage omitted); *TPB*, p. 61 (partial).

[5] *TLP5*, p. 205; *YDGC*, p. 66; *BVP*, pp. 150–1.

translations from the German of the texts of Anton Rubinstein's Twelve Persian Songs, Op. 34, had appeared earlier in the year. But otherwise there was little to cheer him. *Romeo and Juliet* was tepidly received at its première on 16 March, the *Undine* extracts given at another concert twelve days later fared no better, while *Fatum*, heard in St Petersburg the very next day, was a failure. The cumulative effect was to make him feel that no one was interested in his work.

Added to this was his inability to make much headway with the new opera. After a month he was still stuck at the first chorus, he reported to Anatoly. The next few weeks saw some progress, and he could write to his brother-in-law, Lev Davïdov, that he had composed several numbers. 'From time to time, as before, an inexpressible fit of the blues descends on me. Nevertheless this doesn't prevent me working; on the contrary, I find the best antidote to it is work.'[6] Yet he was disappointed with his rate of work, attributing this to the fact that 'though the subject is very good, somehow it's not one after my own heart. Despite the fact that the libretto of *Undine* is rough and ready, composition went very quickly because it matched my sympathies.'[7] To crown it all, the delay in producing *Undine* had upset his financial calculations. On 13 May he summarised his woes to Klimenko:

1. Illness. I am getting inordinately fat; my nerves are in shreds.
2. My financial affairs are utterly chaotic.
3. I am sick and tired of the Conservatoire. I am more and more convinced that I'm not fitted to teach the theory of composition.[8]

With his funds so straitened Tchaikovsky had little choice about where he might pass the summer. The previous year, when Shilovsky had pressed him to be his travelling companion in Europe, he had resisted. Since then Shilovsky had bombarded him with further invitations; it seems also that alarming reports on Shilovsky's health had reached him, and this doubtless influenced his decision finally to capitulate. It was, in any case, financially expedient, for the wealthy Shilovsky would pay all his expenses. Nevertheless he did not intend to stay with the invalid for more than a month. Shilovsky might be ill, but this did not prevent him from engaging periodically in a riotous life which would allow Tchaikovsky little of that peace and quiet he was so desperately seeking. He might also have to endure the religious fanaticism of Konstantin Ryumin, who had been appointed to try to

---

[6] *TLP5*, p. 211; *TPB*, p. 64.
[7] *TLP5*, p. 212; *TZC1*, p. 341; *TPB*, p. 65; *YDGC*, p. 70 (partial); *DTC*, p. 41 (partial).
[8] *TLP5*, p. 214; *TZC1*, p. 342; *YDGC*, p. 70.

keep some control over Shilovsky's affairs, and who had already, while in Russia, heaped a pile of religious books upon Tchaikovsky, extracting a promise that he would read them. Evidently Tchaikovsky felt he would be able to equal the minimum standards that might satisfy Ryumin: 'In general I have taken up such things as would please God. In Holy Week Rubinstein and I fasted,' he reported to Anatoly,[9] no doubt hoping, with the concern he always showed for the twins' welfare, that the example of his own good behaviour would not be lost on his brother. On 29 May he left for St Petersburg. There he remained for two days, during which he saw Balakirev and was informed of the unanimous decision by the committee of the Imperial Theatres that *Undine* did not merit production. On 1 June he left for Paris where Shilovsky awaited him.

'I travelled non-stop from St Petersburg to Paris; I was terribly tired, and approached my destination in frightful agitation. I feared I should find Shilovsky dying. However, although he's very weak, I had yet expected something worse. His joy on seeing me was indescribable. We spent three days in Paris, and then set out hither [to Bad Soden, near Frankfurt-am-Main]. Because I love Paris, these three days of course passed pleasantly for me. I went to the theatre three times, and did a lot of walking.'[10] Tchaikovsky had arrived in the small German spa town of Bad Soden on 11 June, two days before writing this letter to Anatoly. He found it a pleasant place, but the sight of so many consumptives immediately brought on a terrible fit of depression, though the need to relieve another's troubles probably helped him forget his own a little. It is difficult to say just how ill Shilovsky was, for while the doctor (according to Tchaikovsky) had declared that it was touch-and-go whether he would die of tuberculosis or live, he could still find the strength to accompany Tchaikovsky on a donkey ride, an experience Tchaikovsky did not enjoy. Their mode of living was normally more quiet and orderly. 'We get up at six, take the waters and stroll until eight; we drink coffee, dine at one; then we walk or go for a drive right up until evening. At eight we drink tea, and go to bed at nine,' he informed Avdotya Bakhireva, the former governess to the twins.[11]

The summer of 1870 was a relatively unproductive one for Tchaikovsky. There can be no doubt about his overwrought state when he left Russia, and the rejection of *Undine* was a parting blow which can have done nothing to stimulate him to composition. His five weeks in

[9] *TLP5*, p. 212; *TZC1*, p. 341; *TPB*, p. 64.

[10] *TLP5*, p. 219; *TPB*, p. 65; *TZC1*, p. 345 (which significantly omits the phrase 'His joy on seeing me was indescribable').

[11] *TLP5*, p. 221.

Bad Soden were therefore spent mostly in idleness and in taking the baths, which proved very beneficial to his nerves. Although there was a considerable number of Russians in the town, he avoided them as much as possible, partly for fear of encountering someone he might know, partly because he found his fellow countrymen insufferable when abroad. 'You can recognise them instantly from their loud and brazen voices, from their pretentious dress and generally impertinent behaviour,' he complained to Sasha.[12] Shilovsky's was the only company he tolerated; otherwise he preferred to be alone. 'Each morning I walk over to a place called *Drei Linden*, and there I read or compose by myself,' he informed Modest a week after his arrival.[13] He told Balakirev that he intended to revise the central portion of the 'Chorus of Flowers and Insects', but this was never done; the only composition upon which he is known to have engaged while abroad that summer was the revision of *Romeo and Juliet*. His main musical nourishment was provided by the spa orchestra, a tolerable group which played each afternoon. Their programmes, however, were frightful, and before he left Tchaikovsky had persuaded them to give a performance of Glinka's *Kamarinskaya*. The other memorable event of his Bad Soden sojourn was a concert by a prize-winning Prussian military band. 'It's amazingly good. I've never heard anything like it before,' he enthused to Modest.[14] Often the routine of Bad Soden induced a feeling of boredom, and he found visits to surrounding places provided a welcome relief. During June he journeyed to Wiesbaden to see Nikolay Rubinstein who was busily engaged in losing all his money at roulette, though remaining convinced that he would break the bank. Despite Rubinstein's gambling obsession, Tchaikovsky spent a pleasant day with him. Even more memorable was a trip to Mannheim for some of the Beethoven centenary celebrations. These included a performance of the *Missa solemnis* which Tchaikovsky had never before heard, and which impressed him profoundly. 'It's one of the greatest musical works of genius,' he told Anatoly.[15]

Then, on 14 July, war broke out between France and Prussia. It had always been Tchaikovsky's intention to leave Bad Soden with Shilovsky after about five weeks, but this event certainly speeded their departure. As it was, there ensued an immediate exodus of foreigners from the spas near Germany's western frontier, and the two men decided upon a detour via Stuttgart, Ulm, and across the Swiss border by Lake Constance in order to avoid the worst of the congestion. The journey

[12] *TLP*5, p. 225.
[13] *TLP*5, p. 223; *TZC*1, p. 346; *TPB*, p. 67; *YDGC*, p. 71.
[14] *TLP*5, p. 223; *TZC*1, p. 346; *TPB*, p. 67; *YDGC*, p. 71.
[15] *TLP*5, p. 226; *TZC*1, p. 347; *TPB*, p. 68; *YDGC*, p. 71.

was still uncomfortable, unnerving and hungry, but on 22 July they arrived safely in Interlaken.

If Tchaikovsky had been delighted by the situation of Bad Soden, that of Interlaken overwhelmed him. Indeed, the view was 'so majestic and astounding that on the day of our arrival I experienced a kind of vague feeling of fear'.[16] The violence of Tchaikovsky's reaction was so evident that Shilovsky, who was quite indifferent to the wonders of nature, teased him about it. But, Tchaikovsky added in this report to his father, there was one thing that 'infuriated him a little';[17] if Bad Soden had been filled with Russians, Switzerland was saturated with Englishmen scurrying all over the country. For all his detestation of such rushing hither and thither by 'the sons of Albion', as he called them, he himself quickly found his thirst to discover all the beauties around Interlaken so strong that he could spend the whole day energetically engaged on such quests and still arrive home without feeling tired. All this walking had an excellent effect upon his weight.

On his doctor's advice he spent six weeks in this glorious place, during which he completed the revision of *Romeo and Juliet*, though the utter impossibility of obtaining manuscript paper prevented him from scoring what he had done, and this operation had to wait until he had returned to Moscow in September. The improvement in his health, begun at Bad Soden, was consolidated amid the beauties of Switzerland, and towards the end of August a much stronger Tchaikovsky bade farewell to Shilovsky and set out for Munich. The parting from his companion afforded Tchaikovsky great relief, for the emptiness and triviality which Shilovsky had displayed throughout so much of the summer had finally sickened him. In Munich he spent a day with his old school friend, Alexey Golitsïn, and proceeded thence to Vienna, a city which he then felt pleased him perhaps more than any other in the world, and where he ran into brother Nikolay, with whom he passed two days. On 5 September he arrived back in St Petersburg, where he was able to consult further with another old school friend, Adamov, about the future careers of Anatoly and Modest. After a pleasant week in the Russian capital, he returned to Moscow.

And so the autumn routine began all over again. An indisposition immediately after his return quickly passed, and the perpetual work at the Conservatoire (where he now also taught instrumentation) was offset by the usual visits to friends, and by dining out. He was delighted to find in Moscow Alexandra Davïdova, the old 'Decembrist' widow and friend of Pushkin, and also her eldest daughter, Elizaveta. The old lady 'has changed a lot; she's grown very thin and aged,' he confided to Modest,[18]

---

[16] *TLP*5, p. 227.   [17] *TLP*5, p. 227.   [18] *TLP*5, p. 234; *TZC*1, p. 362.

little dreaming of the further twenty-five years she had to live. However tiresome the duties that encumbered him, or the problems that beset him, there was one thing that now always gave him pleasure: living in Moscow. His circle of friends had become quite extensive yet close, and he was constantly in demand as a guest. 'In general everybody adores me so much that even I can't think why,' he wrote happily to Modest soon after his return.[19] As usual there were plays to see, and concerts and operas to attend. He was one of the ten signatories to a letter published in the Moscow press protesting at the public's hostile reception for the Italian tenor, Enrico Tamberlik, at his Moscow début in Verdi's *Il Trovatore*.

Tchaikovsky was still hoping that Anatoly could be found a post in Moscow before the winter was out, and he continued to worry over Modest who had left the School of Jurisprudence in May and been posted to Simbirsk (Ulyanovsk) where his capricious behaviour, moods and debts were a perpetual torment to his composer brother. He worried, too, that Modest would be cold, offered to buy him a fur coat, and finally rushed out to purchase a beaver fur costing fifty roubles to send to him. Constantly throughout the winter he sent the improvident twin sums of money when he could, adding always a liberal allowance of sound advice which, it seems, Modest rarely heeded. At the very end of December the miscreant passed through Moscow on his way to St Petersburg, and doubtless a good deal of verbal counsel, as well as kindness, flowed from the elder to the younger brother. Then there was Vera. She was presenting a new kind of anxiety, for it seems that, through Sasha's machinations, a match was being engineered for her with a certain Apollon Krivoshein, whom Tchaikovsky now met and found thoroughly detestable. Fortunately the affair came to nothing.

He did a little work on *The Oprichnik*, only to be deflected in the middle of October by a project for a four-act ballet of *Cinderella*. This enterprise evaporated as quickly as it had materialised. It is not known who had hatched the idea, but it had to be ready by the beginning of December, and two months would have been quite inadequate for a work of this magnitude, even if ideas had come readily.

Nor would the circumstances of Tchaikovsky's life at this time have permitted the completion of such a mammoth project, for he constantly bewailed the multitude of demands upon his time. Anton Rubinstein appeared in Moscow to open the new season of the RMS on 4 November with performances of the Schumann Concerto and some piano pieces, including in a second programme his own Piano Trio in A minor, Op. 85. Tchaikovsky enjoyed seeing Rubinstein daily, but the visit did nothing to dispel his reservations about his former teacher as a

[19] *TLP5*, p. 234; *TPB*, p. 70.

composer, though when he heard Rubinstein's new orchestral piece, *Don Quixote*, tried out at a specially arranged rehearsal, he could pronounce it 'very interesting and, in places, splendid',[20] and he agreed to make a piano duet arrangement of it for Bessel. He noted that Rubinstein's habitual compositional facility seemed to be undiminished; by contrast, all he could report were three inconsequential piano pieces, to be published in 1871 as Op. 9 (the last, *Mazurka de salon*, drawing its main theme, as we have noted, from his unpublished music to Ostrovsky's *Dmitry the Pretender and Vasily Shuisky*), and a romance, 'To forget so soon', to words by his friend, Apukhtin. Even this may have been merely a completion of a piece begun in 1867 or 1868. A long-winded and platitudinous trio, 'Nature and love', for two sopranos, alto and piano followed in December. With a few unspecified bits for *The Oprichnik*, this completed the total of Tchaikovsky's original achievement for the last months of 1870. It had, indeed, been a pretty lean year.

With the arrival of the New Year his creative urges evidently began to stir themselves more strongly. By now they had had time to recover from the stunning blow of *Undine*'s rejection, and had no doubt been challenged by the recent display in Moscow of Anton Rubinstein's assiduous activities as a composer. In addition Tchaikovsky had heard Rimsky-Korsakov's orchestral piece, *Sadko*, performed in Moscow on 23 December, and he cannot but have compared the success of this piece with the failure of his own 'Chorus of Flowers and Insects' at another RMS concert exactly a week later. Then only four weeks passed before Balakirev's symphonic poem, *1,000 Years* (subsequently revised and published as *Russia*), was given at yet another RMS concert. It was nearly a year since there had been a performance of any of Tchaikovsky's own major works, and he must have felt there was some danger he might be forgotten as a serious composer. These various considerations probably commended to him all the more strongly the idea of a concert devoted to his own works, though an even more pressing argument for it was the need to make some money. The suggestion for such a project originated from Nikolay Rubinstein. To arouse sufficient public interest it would be desirable to include a brand-new piece in the programme, and he would have to enlist the co-operation of performers whose reputations would draw an audience.

In the event the star of the evening was Elizaveta Lavrovskaya (Lawrowska), a twenty-six-year-old contralto who had already scored a great success on both the operatic stage and the concert platform. Nearly a year earlier she had introduced Tchaikovsky's 'None but the

[20] *TLP5*, p. 238; *TZC1*, p. 363.

lonely heart' to Moscow audiences; now she agreed to repeat this performance, and the equally eminent Nikolay Rubinstein undertook to play the *Rêverie* and *Mazurka* from Tchaikovsky's new set of Three Piano Pieces, Op. 9. In addition, there was the duet for Mariya and Olyona from the second act of *The Voyevoda*, another of the successful Op. 6 romances, 'It's both bitter and sweet', the new Apukhtin setting, 'To forget so soon', and the evening was rounded off by the pupils of Berthe Valzek singing the trio, 'Nature and love', which Tchaikovsky had recently composed for them. Yet the most momentous item was the new work. Tchaikovsky's resources did not permit him to engage large forces, but he could muster a string quartet led by his colleague, the eminent Ferdinand Laub, and which included the young cellist, Wilhelm Fitzenhagen, another of Tchaikovsky's fellow teachers at the Conservatoire, who was to be both the first performer and the dedicatee of his Rococo Variations for cello and orchestra, Op. 33. For this group he composed a quartet to open the concert.

Fortunately the New Year seems to have brought some respite from the welter of activities which had swamped Tchaikovsky during the last months of 1870. It brought some sad things, too. In February Uncle Pyotr died, and Tchaikovsky wrote a tender letter of condolence to his father on the loss of this brother who, with his family, had shared three years of their lives during St Petersburg days. Tchaikovsky was also upset by Anatoly's sudden decision to remain in Kiev, though he had finally to admit that a transfer to Moscow, for which he himself had longed so much and worked so hard, was not now in his brother's best interests. On the credit side there was a visit from Klimenko, who had moved his permanent base from Moscow, and Tchaikovsky happily accommodated his architect friend during his stay. Then Adamov suddenly appeared in Moscow, and Tchaikovsky spent a delightful day with him. Exactly when he got down to work on the new quartet is not known. As late as 15 February he was still tinkering with *The Oprichnik*, and the concert took place only six weeks later, on 28 March 1871. The quartet was therefore composed very swiftly.

Though the hall was not full, the size of the audience was gratifying. A late arrival was Turgenev, who had already heard of Tchaikovsky while living in western Europe. The personal interest shown by this great writer gave Tchaikovsky particular pleasure and, Kashkin suggested, raised Tchaikovsky's prestige in the eyes of some persons. As for the new quartet, which was dedicated to Rachinsky, this proved to be the first of Tchaikovsky's larger works to achieve any wide currency. Its success was largely due to the second movement, the Andante cantabile which Tchaikovsky based upon the folksong he had noted down at Kamenka nearly two years earlier. Within two years Leopold Auer was playing this movement in a transcription for violin and piano, and among the many other arrangements by Laub, Fitzenhagen and others, there is one by Tchaikovsky himself, made some fifteen years later for cello and string orchestra. At times the popularity of this Andante cantabile exasperated him. 'They don't want to know anything else!' he lamented to Modest after hearing it in Berlin in 1884. 'This Andante was also advertised on a poster for another concert on the evening of my departure.'[21] Yet it was a performance of this same movement that was to afford him one of the most memorable incidents of his whole life. What Turgenev thought of it we do not know, but when another, and greater, writer heard it in December 1876, he was overwhelmed. Ten years later Tchaikovsky could confide to the pages of his diary: 'Perhaps I was never so flattered in my life, nor was my pride as a composer so stirred as when Lev Tolstoy, sitting beside me listening to the Andante of my First Quartet, dissolved in tears.'[22]

While the orchestra was certainly a far more apt medium through which to express that brand of colourful and extrovert music which came most naturally from Tchaikovsky and his fellow countrymen, they often showed a fine understanding of the quartet medium, readily shedding the bolder gestures and generous rhetoric which befitted their symphonies and symphonic poems in favour of a more refined and purely musical train of thought. This sometimes involved a very radical shift in manner, resulting in a far wider gap between their symphonies and quartets than that which divided the equivalent works of the classical masters. In his String Quartet in D, Op. 11 – in fact, the very first major quartet by a Russian composer – Tchaikovsky approached as close as he could to absolute music without risking the complete effacement of his own identity. Eclectic it may be, but Russian eclecticism has always incorporated a flair for a brand of pastiche that is genuinely alive. Nor is the apparent time-travelling in which Tchaikovsky here engages merely a pleasant diversion from more important personal matters; rather it is the first manifestation of an urge which was to recur with increasing strength in some of his later music – an urge to return to a realm of purer expression from which were purged those features of his own style which he felt to be blemishes, and in which he could achieve a degree of structural equilibrium beyond what was possible within his own heated, often eruptive, personal language.

The foundation of Tchaikovsky's almost fanatical reverence for Mozart was a sense that the world of this classical giant was chaste and

[21] *TLP*12, p. 479; *TZC*2, pp. 674–5; *TPB*, p. 321; *DTC*, p. 490 (partial).
[22] *DTC*, p. 489; *TD*, pp. 210–11; *TZC*1, p. 519.

poised in a way his own could never be. To attempt to re-enter that world was not simply an agreeable amusement but a profoundly serious undertaking which could elicit from him a flow of living invention that evoked a little of the radiance of (as he heard it) bygone musical innocence. But the real world of Mozart, with, on the one hand, its rich subtleties of detail and, on the other, its magisterial command of musical space, was quite beyond Tchaikovsky's grasp. Schubert's simpler handling of such matters was more within his capabilities, and the innocent listener, hearing the first few bars of this quartet (Ex. 44),

Ex. 44

might be forgiven for attributing them to the Viennese master. There are other features that recall common Schubertian practices – for instance, employing exactly the same transition in the recapitulation as in the exposition with only the minimum adjustment needed to ensure arrival at a new tonal destination; extending the development by simply repeating in transposition a very substantial stretch of music; and, in the minor-key scherzo, shifting for a period to the tonic major (shortly after the double bar) before reverting to the minor. And just as Schubert had allowed a figure from the end of the development to persist into the recapitulation in the first movement of his great C major Quintet, so Tchaikovsky permits the semiquaver figure, which had first appeared in the exposition's codetta, and had subsequently saturated the development, to spill over into his recapitulation.

The structure of the first movement is modelled scrupulously on classical proportions, with carefully equated dimensions for the major sections of exposition, development and recapitulation, and a notably democratic allocation of space for the subdivisions of the exposition. There is thus not a hint of the principles or proportions of the First Symphony's first movement, or of *Romeo and Juliet*. The tonal behaviour is strictly classical; so, too, is the marked emphasis in both subjects upon chords and pedals of the tonic and dominant, and upon typically classical harmonic mechanisms elsewhere, especially in the transition. Yet into this elegant mould Tchaikovsky has poured material of notable freshness – and most critics seem to agree that the medium is, for the most part, excellently handled. Much of the movement's richness comes from the abundant contrapuntal decoration of fundamentally simple harmonies, with Tchaikovsky amply exploiting that facility he had always shown for devising fertile counterpoints of running semiquavers. While the broader phrase structure is mostly regular, even square, there is much asymmetry in detail, whether it takes the form of nervous syncopation (as in the first subject) or of adjustments of metre that cut across the basic pulse (as in the second subject, Ex. 45).

Ex. 45

It is again Schubert rather than Mozart who is the father figure of the attractive third movement. If the freshness of much of the scherzo stems from its wide rhythmic variety and alternation of triple and duple metres, the trio is marked by the opposite traits: rigid restriction of the rhythmic content, and simultaneous engagement of the two metres. The first movement's view of sonata structure is reproduced in the finale, though here the second subject is set in the remote key of B flat (felicitously recalling the key of the slow movement), and the recapitulation does reproduce exactly one procedure from *Romeo and Juliet* by beginning at the tutti restatement of the first subject (where the tune was treated canonically between the first violin and viola), leading into it with the same dozen bars of dominant-based preparation. Despite the grace of some passages, the finale is squarer rhythmically than the first movement, and its material is less attractive. Even more than at the end of the first movement, the frenetic scrubbing and cadencing of the coda stretches the sonorities of the four instruments beyond what they can comfortably supply.

There remains the second movement, the famous Andante cantabile. Some unkind things have been said of this piece, above all of the handling of the folksong (Ex. 46a). Before fretting about any violence

which Tchaikovsky may have done it by compounding it with more sophisticated musical techniques, we might well question whether the folk culture which produced this beautiful tune had shown any stronger discrimination when it coupled it with words such as these:

Upon the divan Vanya sat
And filled a glass with rum:
Before he'd poured out half a tot,
He ordered Katenka to come.[23]

The weakness of this movement lies less in anything to do with the folksong than in the subsidiary theme over the pizzicato cello ostinato, which is charming but relatively commonplace. As for the folktune, Tchaikovsky had already incorporated it nearly two years before into his piano duet arrangements of fifty Russian folk songs,[24] and he had no intention of wasting his earlier double harmonisation which is reproduced almost literally when the tune recurs at bar 98. At the Andante's opening it is treated rather differently, and is forthwith repeated in yet another harmonisation. This done, the opening paragraph is extended in a freely composed section (Ex. 46b) which uses material derived from the tune, passing it imitatively between the four instruments, adding turns, melodic intervals, and cadential formulae which have no part in folksong. To the purist all this is bound to give offence. What must be recognised, however, is that there is all the difference in the world between a folksong arrangement (as in Tchaikovsky's set of fifty for piano duet) whose central purpose is the commendation of the folksong, and the incorporation of folksong as just one element within a far larger strategy (as in this movement), where it must accept subsumption under a broader musical purpose. In fact, these first forty-nine bars are one of the most successful of all attempts to merge folk material into a train of thought which does not deny itself the vaster technical resources of a more sophisticated musical language, yet applies these with such tact and taste that no intolerable violence is done to the original; its bounds are merely extended into regions it could never have conquered by itself. If Katenka had been adorned with crown, ermine robe and sceptre, her identity would certainly have been destroyed; but if she merely exchanges her peasant tunic for a silk dress, and her rougher country manners for the courtesies of a more polite society, there is no reason why her personality or her beauty should be compromised. Changed they will be; they may even be enhanced.

The success of the concert was a great boost to Tchaikovsky's morale. There was encouragement also on the publishing front. In March

[23] This was the version which Tchaikovsky communicated to Rimsky-Korsakov in 1876. The version quoted by Modest in his biography differs in substance, thought not in banality. Kashkin suggested that these words were spurious, and had been made up by the Kamenka singer himself.
[24] No. 47.

Jurgenson brought out his Three Piano Pieces, Op. 9, while in St Petersburg Nadezhda Purgold, who a year later was to become Rimsky-Korsakov's bride, was labouring over a piano duet version of *Romeo and Juliet*, with Balakirev himself taking a hand in arranging the introduction. At the same time in Moscow, Karl Klindworth, a professor of piano at the Conservatoire, and the man whom Wagner had already charged with making the vocal scores of his operas, was engaged in preparing a two-piano transcription of the same piece. Simultaneously Bote & Bock were preparing publication of the full score.[25] Best of all, Tchaikovsky's enthusiasm for *The Oprichnik*, which had never done more than smoulder damply, suddenly caught fire. 'I have now given myself up wholeheartedly to composing the opera,' he could write to Balakirev on 10 June,[26] the very day of his departure from Moscow for his summer break. His first stop was at brother Nikolay's home at Konotop. From there he sped to Kiev to collect Anatoly, and then headed for Sasha's home at Kamenka.

This visit to Kamenka was a particularly pleasant one. Sasha, realising that her brother had sometimes felt oppressed by being unable to escape from the host of relatives who invaded her home during the summer, had arranged that he should have two rooms of his own with a private entrance into a little attic where he could be quite alone if he wished. For Tchaikovsky this arrangement was ideal, and from this moment if anyone in Moscow were to ask him whither he was travelling, and he replied 'Home', it meant he was off to Kamenka. Besides, his nephews and nieces were growing in size and numbers, and could satisfy those very needs which, a year earlier, he had confided to Sasha: 'the clamour of children . . . trivial domestic interests . . . a family situation.' The three oldest were all girls. Tatyana was now nearly ten, Vera eight and Anna seven – every one old enough to share in all sorts of games and activities in which the eternal child in Tchaikovsky could readily join. It may have been on this visit that the composer, who as a child had proved to be such a fertile inventor of games, dreamed up a ballet for his young nieces. The subject was one which he was to use four years later for his first full-length ballet, *Swan Lake*. Modest danced the Prince, Tatyana participated, apparently as Odette, and Anna was a cupid. The décor was by Uncle Vasily Davïdov. Tchaikovsky's nephew, Yury, Sasha's youngest son, preserved the family's memories of their Uncle Pyotr's role in this

[25] This firm had already commissioned solo piano and piano duet versions of *Romeo and Juliet* from Karl Bial, and these were issued simultaneously with the full score in May 1871. Nadezhda Purgold's and Klindworth's arrangements were published by Bessel in 1872.

[26] *TLP5*, p. 256; *BVP*, p. 160; *DTC*, p. 41; *YDGC*, p. 75.

domestic creation. Not only did he write the music, he arranged almost everything else:

> The staging of the ballet was done entirely by Pyotr Ilich. It was he who invented the steps and pirouettes, and he danced them himself, showing the performers what he required of them. At such moments Uncle Pyotr, red in the face, wet with perspiration as he sang the tune, presented a pretty amusing sight. Yet in the children's eyes he was so perfect in the art of choreography that for many years the memories of this remained with them down to the finest details.[27]

Among the properties were some large wooden swans which long remained favourite toys with the Davïdov children. The success of this one-act *Swan Lake* was such that it sparked off a whole series of similar theatrical enterprises in later years, including renditions of Gogol's *The Marriage* and scenes from Molière's *Le Misanthrope*, in all of which Uncle Pyotr again acted as producer, designer, choreographer when needed, and prompter. His delight in such homely diversions was unbounded. Nor was this little *Swan Lake* without its musical benefits to him, for though none of the music for it has survived, Yury Davïdov stated that one tune from it was employed by his uncle in the music for the swans when he settled down to his full-length ballet in 1875.

Tchaikovsky remained at Kamenka until after the middle of July, and when he left, the first act of *The Oprichnik* was finished and scored. His destination was the estate of Nikolay Kondratyev at Nizy near the town of Suma. Like Tchaikovsky, Kondratyev had been trained as a lawyer. They had first met in 1864 at Trostinets, the estate of Prince Golitsïn, where Tchaikovsky had passed the summer composing *The Storm*, that precocious student work which caused such offence to Anton Rubinstein. Close friendship did not begin until the last months of 1870, when Kondratyev, with his wife and daughter, settled in Moscow for the winter. Outwardly Kondratyev was a wealthy, worldly dandy, but he had more substantial qualities, including an unfailing optimism and a capacity to see a bright side in even the most desperate and painful situation, a quality Tchaikovsky was to observe some sixteen years later

[27] Y. L. Davïdov, *Zapiski o P. I. Chaykovskom* (Moscow, 1962), p. 26. There is some difference of opinion over the year in which this domestic *Swan Lake* was mounted. According to Anna it was in 1867, when she would have been only three, but Tchaikovsky did not visit Kamenka that year. As for 1871, though Anatoly was at Kamenka that year, Modest makes no mention of his own presence – though Anna may have been mistaken in saying that he danced the Prince. It has also been suggested that the Kamenka production was simultaneous with or a little after the mounting of the real ballet, but this seems improbable.

when he shared in the care of Kondratyev during the latter's final agonising illness. Modest believed it was this buoyancy of spirit in Kondratyev which attracted his brother to him, for it infected his own mood in a way that facilitated work. During the past winter he had often been entertained by the Kondratyevs, and the ten days he now spent at Nizy were certainly productive, though he had to lay aside the opera and apply all his energies to writing a textbook on harmony which Jurgenson was to publish. On 27 July, five days after his arrival, he could send the first instalment to Jurgenson with an assurance that all would be finished by the middle of September. He was devoting some five hours a day to the work – and if Kondratyev's catalytic cheerfulness was aiding progress, so also was the desperate need for an excuse to escape from the throng of people which filled his host's house. The estate at Nizy was very beautiful and the entertainment lavish, but the endless human bustle frayed his nerves, and he considered that Kondratyev's servants were insubordinate. He was glad, therefore, to be able to flee to Shilovsky's home at Usovo for the remainder of the summer. Though it was less beautiful and less luxurious, and the cooking was plain, it was peaceful, and Shilovsky had the tact to leave his guest very much to himself. There, on 14 August, Tchaikovsky signed the preface to his textbook. On 10 September he was back in Moscow.

There was one great difference about his return that autumn: he was at last able to break with Rubinstein and live for the first time in his own flat. In 1870 Laroche had given up teaching at the Moscow Conservatoire, and in 1871 he moved to St Petersburg where he became professor of the theory of composition at the Conservatoire. Nikolay Hubert, also a former student at the St Petersburg Conservatoire, who had recently resigned his post as second conductor of the Kiev Opera to replace Laroche in Moscow, was delighted to take over Tchaikovsky's lodging with Rubinstein, and this eased Tchaikovsky's conscience about leaving the companion with whom he had shared five and a half years of daily living. The new flat had three rooms, and Tchaikovsky's furnishings were very modest: a large ottoman, a few cheap chairs, a portrait of Anton Rubinstein, and an engraving of Louis XVII with the shoemaker Simon. But Tchaikovsky's delight – and pride – in this new home were great. 'I am overjoyed that I have had the courage to undertake what I have so long wanted. . . . I am living a new life and (O wonderful!) I have spent my second consecutive evening at home. That's what it means to feel that one is in one's own home!' he wrote to Anatoly five days after his return to Moscow.[28] Nevertheless he continued his dining arrangements with the Albrechts. Now that he was by himself he

[28] *TLP*5, p. 258; *TZC*1, p. 372 (partial).

immediately engaged as servant a twenty-three-year-old from Klin, near Moscow, a certain Mikhail Sofronov, who had been employed by Laub. As a country-loving peasant, Mikhail insisted on returning home for the summer, an arrangement which initially suited his new master well. When, however, Tchaikovsky also required service during the summer months, Mikhail sent his young brother, Alexey, and after the former had left Tchaikovsky's service in 1876, the seventeen-year-old Alexey stayed on to serve Tchaikovsky to the day of his death. In his will Tchaikovsky treated Alexey generously, and the latter became a staunch ally to Modest in the scheme to make the composer's last home at Klin into a museum to its illustrious occupant.

Tchaikovsky's new domestic arrangements created a mode of living far more favourable to composition than the one he had shared with Rubinstein, and as soon as he had settled himself into his new home, he set about *The Oprichnik* vigorously. 'It must be ready by the end of the year,' he informed brother Nikolay on 10 October.[29] Within a month he had realised that, with his other commitments, he had little hope of finishing it so soon. 'I suppose that this unhappy opera will suffer the same fate as my *Undine*,' he wrote gloomily to Balakirev, 'but nevertheless I want to finish it, for until I do I shan't be in a state to undertake another composition with enthusiasm.'[30] Six weeks later he had to admit to Anatoly that the opera was still going slowly. For the first time in his life he spent Christmas and the New Year outside Russia. Shilovsky had pressed him to come to Nice, and the relative freedom of his three weeks in the south of France refreshed his creative faculties. Certainly he must have resumed his dogged labours during the first months of 1872, for on 1 April *The Oprichnik* was finally done. On 17 May Tchaikovsky sent the score to the Imperial Theatres' directorate in St Petersburg.

It is a sign of Tchaikovsky's growing prestige as a composer that Bessel should have wanted to conclude forthwith a contract for the publication of the new opera. Such an arrangement had strong practical advantages for Tchaikovsky. Bessel undertook to publish the vocal score ahead of the opera's production, and also to do what he could to further its fortunes in the Imperial Theatres; in return Tchaikovsky agreed to his receiving one-third of the royalties from performances, and assigned to Bessel all rights over both the libretto and the music. On 4 November 1872 the music committee of the Imperial Theatres met, went over the score with Tchaikovsky, and almost unanimously gave the work its blessing. It might have seemed that the way ahead to production was now clear. In fact, it was not. Little more than three weeks later

Tchaikovsky bitterly narrated to Klimenko an unfortunate coincidence that had arisen: 'Two composers are simultaneously submitting their operas to the directorate of the Imperial Theatres: Famintsïn his *Sardanapalus*, and I my *Oprichnik*. Everyone recognises that Famintsïn is utterly ungifted; they write and say of me that I have talent. Yet they are going to put on Famintsïn's opera, while the fate of mine is quite unknown, and there is a lot of evidence that during the summer it will sink into oblivion just like *Undine*.'[31] If *The Oprichnik* were not taken, he swore he would never again put pen to manuscript paper. Fortunately his worst fears proved groundless. By mid-December formalities with the first two censors had been completed, and the decisive committee meeting was fixed for early January. Tchaikovsky himself was summoned to attend and play through the whole of his opera to the assembled members. It was a terrible ordeal. 'I was so convinced that I should be rejected,' he wrote to Sasha, 'and I was in consequence so downcast that I even decided not to go straight to Papa, fearing that my distraught appearance would upset him.'[32] Again he need not have worried. The committee unanimously approved *The Oprichnik* for production. As for Famintsïn's *Sardanapalus*, that opera was not to be produced until a year after Tchaikovsky's.

It was too late to mount *The Oprichnik* that season, and in the meantime Tchaikovsky laboured over the preparation of the vocal score,[33] revising the words of Basmanov's arioso on the insistence of the censor. Then, in the middle of September 1873, Tchaikovsky was told that the management of the Bolshoy Theatre in Moscow also wished to produce the opera in the spring of 1874. The satisfaction of having this new work given in the city which he now felt was really his home outweighed his apprehensions about the Moscow company's limitations. A Moscow production would be an added financial bonus to that in St Petersburg: meanwhile he urged Bessel to continue exercising himself on the opera's behalf in the Russian capital. Seven weeks passed, and still there was no news of when that production would take place. Tchaikovsky's spirits sank, and on 30 October he poured out to Bessel all his gall, comparing the fate of *The Oprichnik* with that of Musorgsky's *Boris Godunov*, three scenes from which had at last been performed in February. 'It [*The Oprichnik*] will never be given because I'm not acquainted with any of the powerful men of the world in general, or of the St Petersburg theatrical world in particular. Judge for

[31] *TLP5*, p. 289; *DTC*, p. 42; *TZC1*, p. 394.
[32] *TLP5*, p. 297; *TZC1*, p. 397.
[33] According to Kashkin, he and Hubert each prepared one act of the vocal score because Tchaikovsky was too pressed to be able to complete it himself in time.

yourself: isn't it ridiculous? The committee doesn't take Musorgsky's opera – but Kondratyev [the chief producer of the Maryinsky Theatre] gives it for his benefit performance, and now Platonova is fussing about it: mine is accepted – but no one wants to know about it.'[34] For a third time his anxiety proved to be unnecessary, and less than a fortnight later he heard that *The Oprichnik* would definitely be mounted in the spring.

Tchaikovsky was singularly fortunate in the man who was to prepare and conduct his new opera. Eduard Nápravník was Czech in origin, and though only a year older than Tchaikovsky, he already had formidable experience as an opera conductor. In 1869 he had been appointed chief conductor at the Maryinsky Theatre, and during his forty-seven-year regime the reputation of the theatre stood high. He had a remarkable range of talents: highly gifted as a conductor, firm but tactful in his dealings with the staff of the theatre, he was also a very capable administrator. Nápravník had conducted the first performance of the revised *Romeo and Juliet*, and he was to play a major role in Tchaikovsky's creative life, conducting the premières of five of his operas. The production of *The Oprichnik* was the first occasion on which the two men had met and worked together. Even before consulting Nápravník, Tchaikovsky had been applying his mind to the casting of the opera. He had been much taken by a young soprano, Wilhelmina Raab, and he wished her to sing the main female role, Natalya. Through Bessel he put forward additional suggestions for filling some of the other roles, but when these were passed to Nápravník, he rejected all except Raab. His reasons, which he explained fully to Tchaikovsky in a letter, were practical and made good sense. In addition he required Tchaikovsky to revise some of the vocal parts, rescore portions of the accompaniment where he considered the orchestration was too heavy for the singers, and make cuts in the interests of the drama and to avoid overtaxing the performers.

Such implied criticism of what he had suggested and done might have been expected to antagonise Tchaikovsky. But Nápravník, like Balakirev, knew how to sugar the pill. 'I hope you will take all my observations as from a benevolent partner who is well disposed towards you, and whom fate has now compelled daily for eleven years to devote himself to the art of opera,' he concluded, combining friendliness and goodwill with a little reminder that he was far more experienced in the practicalities of the opera house than Tchaikovsky.[35] The latter was completely disarmed. He agreed wholeheartedly to carry out Nápravník's requirements, and in late January or early February he travelled to St Petersburg to meet the conductor and sort out some of the

[34] *TLP*5, p. 331; *TZC*1, p. 418.   [35] *TZC*1, p. 422.

problems of the opera. 'I spent all the four days on making cuts and revisions in the score,' he told Anatoly on 5 February,[36] immediately on his return to Moscow. The censor had objected to the implied portrayal of Ivan the Terrible in part of the last act, but finally the original text had been allowed to stand. Tchaikovsky felt his part in the preparations was now finished. Daily rehearsals were soon to begin, and he had absolute faith in Nápravník's zeal and expertise.

The première of *The Oprichnik* took place in St Petersburg on 24 April 1874. It was Tchaikovsky's first real triumph. At the end of the second act there were already calls for the composer, and the applause was unanimous. Nikolay Rubinstein and some of Tchaikovsky's other Moscow colleagues had travelled to St Petersburg specially to see the new opera (though Tchaikovsky had already warned several of his friends that he did not think it was worth the journey), and after the performance the directorate of the RMS gave a supper in Tchaikovsky's honour at which he found himself the first recipient of the Kondratyev prize, a newly founded award of three hundred roubles instituted under the will of a retired army officer for the encouragement of Russian composers. After the comparative failure of *The Voyevoda* and the disaster of *Undine*, Tchaikovsky might have been expected to revel in his success. He did not. '*The Oprichnik* torments me,' he wrote to Modest a fortnight after the première:

This opera is so bad that I fled from all the rehearsals (especially those of Acts 3 and 4) so that I shouldn't hear a single sound, and at the performance I would willingly have vanished. Isn't it strange that when I'd written it, it seemed to me initially to be such a delight. But from the very first rehearsal, what disenchantment! There's no movement, no style, no inspiration! The calls and applause at the first performance signify nothing, but mean (1) that a lot of my friends were there, and (2) that even beforehand I had gained a secure reputation. I know the opera won't last out six performances, and this simply finishes me off.[37]

To the end of his life this dislike of *The Oprichnik* never faltered. And if Laroche praised it, and thus made amends for his harsh words on *The Voyevoda*, Cui liked it no better than Tchaikovsky. His review was consistently scathing, and Tchaikovsky admitted that Cui was right. The public continued to think otherwise. Despite the composer's gloomy prediction, *The Oprichnik* was given fourteen times before the end of

[36] *TLP*5, p. 341; *TZC*1, p. 423; *TPB*, p. 85.
[37] *TLP*5, pp. 353–4; *DTC*, p. 45; *TZC*1, p. 431; *TPB*, p. 89.

1875, when it was withdrawn from the repertory. Its fame travelled swiftly. On 7 August 1874 it was produced in Odessa, and on 21 December in Kiev.[38] The latter opera house mounted a splendid production, and Tchaikovsky had to admit that he enjoyed the ovation, and being fêted to his hotel by a large group of students. The Moscow production at last materialised on 16 May 1875.

The Oprichnik is not a great opera; neither is it a bad one. At times it is third-rate, sometimes cheap, yet it is a good deal better than either Cui's or the composer's own unqualified damnation would suggest, and the first audiences recognised this quickly enough. Lazhechnikov's play, upon which it is based, possessed the attraction of having been until only recently forbidden fruit. Suppressed by the censor in the 1840s, it had at last been published in 1867. The tragedy is set against the background of the *oprichnina*, the personal, paid bodyguard which Ivan the Terrible had set up in 1565 and maintained for seven years until the abuses of its powers and the enormities of its atrocities finally forced its disbandment. Ivan, whose own ruthlessness was offset by a religious fervour which amounted to mania, spent much of his time isolated in a new settlement he had established outside Moscow at Alexandrovskoye. There, surrounded by his oprichniks, including his favourites Basmanov and Vyazemsky (in Tchaikovsky's opera Vyazminsky), he would alternate orgies of feasting and drunkenness with the practices of a 'religious' life, assuming the robes of an abbot, and compelling his oprichniks to don monkish habit. The action of *The Oprichnik* is set in both Moscow and Alexandrovskoye. In planning the scenario Tchaikovsky was very free with Lazhechnikov's play. The plot of the opera is as follows:

ACT 1. *Evening in Zhemchuzhny's garden.*
Prince Zhemchuzhny, Natalya's father, entertains Molchan Mitkov (No. 1), who asks for Natalya's hand in marriage. Although Mitkov is old, Zhemchuzhny readily agrees. When they have left, an offstage women's chorus is heard singing a folksong (No. 2). The women enter with Natalya and her nurse, Zakharevna. Natalya is bored. Enjoined by the nurse, the chorus sing the second verse of their song (bar 58). Natalya is dissatisfied; she wants a still sadder song – the one that was sung by their neighbour Mashenka, 'the one they married to a grey-haired old man: the one who pined away, and afterwards died' (bar 77). Reproved by Zakharevna, she says she will instead lament her own plight, and sings a folksong (Natalya's song) which tells the tale of an imprisoned maiden and a nightingale. When she has finished, the chorus ask for a fairy story (No. 3). They approve when Natalya says she will sing a song

[38] In this production the part of Vyazminsky was sung by the young Fyodor Stravinsky, father of the composer.

about love, but the nurse upbraids them all for their frivolity (bar 17). Natalya takes their part (bar 61): 'If there is no love in our own lives to give us delight, we shall be glad to rejoice in it, even if it's only in a fairy tale.' Slowly the stage empties and the voices fade.

Andrey Morozov, in love with Natalya, enters with Basmanov and oprichniks (No. 4). These last undertake to keep watch while Andrey and Basmanov confer and, if necessary, come to their aid. When the oprichniks have withdrawn, Andrey tells Basmanov (No. 5) that he has himself decided to join the ranks of the oprichniks. Basmanov extols the benefits of being an oprichnik: feasts and beautiful women – but Andrey confesses (bar 85) that Natalya has all his love. However, her father has appropriated all his and his mother's possessions, and driven them from their home. He now proposes to apply to Ivan the Terrible himself for justice. To help alleviate Andrey's plight, Basmanov gives him the money he has on his person, knowing that when Andrey is an oprichnik he will be able to pay him back. Andrey would wait to see Natalya, but Basmanov persuades him (molto meno mosso) that such pleasures must wait on more urgent business. He must seek his mother's blessing upon his intention to join the oprichniks. Andrey agrees (bar 126), swears he will gain Natalya by force if necessary, and goes out with Basmanov (allegro giusto). After they have left, Natalya rushes in (No. 6). She has heard the sounds of the men, and thinks that Andrey must have come. Finding herself alone, she sings (bar 13) of her love and longing for him. As she finishes she seats herself sadly (bar 37). It is now night. Soon after (allegro moderato) Zakharevna and the maidens begin to return to the stage. Finally Zakharevna spots Natalya and, unable to draw any answer from her about the reasons for her sad silence, instructs (moderato) the maidens to sing a song. They form a circle, and the act ends with a khorovod (allegro con moto).

ACT 2, SCENE 1. *A peasant hut.*
The Boyarïna Morozova is alone, lamenting her misfortunes (No. 7). She is worried on behalf of her son Andrey, though for her own part she is prepared to endure her sorrows. 'Before God's will I bow my submissive head, and will bear my suffering with resignation' (andante sostenuto). '. . . Pride is my terrible sin' (bar 50). Her thoughts turn (bar 66) to Zhemchuzhny and the wrongs he has done her, and she shudders at the temptation Satan has laid for her (bar 89). But she regains her self-control, and repeats her submission to God's will (bar 99), ending (poco più mosso) with a plea that He will protect Andrey from evil. Andrey enters (No. 8), and shows his mother some money. She is horrified (bar 29) when she hears that it has come from Basmanov, the Tsar's favourite, and denounces Basmanov and the oprichniks as robbers. However, when Andrey tells her (bar 61) that Basmanov had received the money from his father, she agrees to accept it, and she begs Andrey (andante non tanto) to remain pure. He reassures her, reaffirming (moderato quasi allegro) his faith in Basmanov, but she remains unconvinced, and fears that Basmanov will persuade Andrey to join the oprichniks. He conceals from her his intention, declaring he will either obtain justice or flee with her. She tries to detain him, but finally lets him depart, giving him her blessing (bar 258) as he repeats his assurances.

Act 2, Scene 2. *The Tsar's mansion at Alexandrovskoye.*

The oprichniks enter solemnly, singing (No. 9). They are to be entertained by the Tsar, and they praise him (bar 128). As Prince Vyazminsky, their commander, tells them (bar 145) that they should withdraw elsewhere to avoid disturbing the Tsar, who is praying near by, Basmanov enters to say that he comes from the Tsar with news that His Majesty has agreed to take Andrey as an oprichnik. Vyazminsky is enraged (bar 187) and opposes the admission, for Andrey is the son of a deadly enemy, but Basmanov points out (bar 211) that the elder Morozov is dead. Vyazminsky agrees (bar 219) that he has no quarrel with the son, but secretly hopes (bar 238) that he may still have his revenge through Andrey. Andrey enters and declares (bar 272) that he seeks justice for his mother through joining the oprichniks; he accepts that if he breaks his vow he will die. Vyazminsky, echoed by the oprichniks, begins (bar 338) to administer the oath to Andrey, which demands that he forsake absolutely all except the Tsar and his fellow oprichniks. Andrey is stunned (bar 366) by the thought that this ban includes his mother and Natalya. Vyazminsky resumes (bar 379) giving the oath. Again the conditions appal Andrey (bar 425), and Vyazminsky secretly gloats (bar 431) at the prospect of having Andrey in his power. The oath is continued (bar 447), and yet again Andrey is aghast at the complete renunciation demanded of him. The struggle is prolonged, the oprichniks adamant, Basmanov persuasive, and Andrey torn. Finally Vyazminsky declares (bar 574) that Andrey must take the oath or die, and in wild desperation he agrees (bar 591). The scene ends with the oprichniks glorifying the Tsar.

Act 3. *A square in Moscow.*

A crowd are recalling past misfortunes (No. 10), and how the Tsar delivered them from these troubles. Now, however, he has again left them, and they pray (bar 115) to God for mercy. The Boyarïna laments (No. 11) her loneliness, and worries over Andrey. As she goes off to pray, a group of boys starts to abuse her (allegro), but they are driven off by five men (bar 64). The Boyarïna thanks them. As she is again leaving, Natalya rushes in (allegro giusto) and falls into her arms. She can no longer bear to live at home where her father and her betrothed are hateful to her. The Boyarïna knows of her love for Andrey, and comforts her (bar 141), but counsels her to return home for her own safety. Natalya refuses. Again the Boyarïna advises her (bar 203) to return and marry the rich Mitkov, and again she refuses (bar 236). Natalya urges (No. 12) the Boyarïna to go away with her. As they are about to seek sanctuary in the church, Zhemchuzhny enters with his servants, and demands to know where Natalya has been and whom she has seen. She falls on her knees before him (bar 37) and confesses (allegro tranquillo) her love for Andrey whom both Zhemchuzhny and Andrey's father (once Zhemchuzhny's friend) had hoped she would marry. 'I am his: God himself has joined us,' she pleads (andante), adding that she will renounce her father if he does not agree to her marriage with Andrey. The Boyarïna pleads for her (bar 109), and calls upon Zhemchuzhny to repent before God. He refuses, and orders Natalya home. When she defies him (No. 13), he commands his servants to take her by force, but at that moment Andrey, Basmanov and the oprichniks burst in, and Andrey and Natalya embrace passionately (bar 32). The Boyarïna asks him (bar 47) why he is in the company of oprichniks. Andrey tells her (bar 68) not to worry, and assures her (andante) of his love. The oprichniks remind him (bar 87) of his vows, and Basmanov reinforces their warning. But Andrey insists that his mother must know the truth and, against the continued warning of the oprichniks (bar 110), he reveals that he has joined their ranks to gain justice for his father, that they are now rich again, and that Zhemchuzhny is humbled. The furious Boyarïna condemns him (bar 143), and solemnly disowns and curses him (bar 185). Natalya is horrified. Andrey, Natalya, Basmanov and Zhemchuzhny, all stunned at the turn of events, lead off a gigantic ensemble (andante non tanto) in which the oprichniks and the people join, all aghast at Andrey's predicament under his mother's curse. Basmanov exhorts Andrey (allegro giusto) to go immediately to the Tsar at Alexandrovskoye, and ask to be released from his vow. The Boyarïna is taken away. All join in a chorus of hope and exhortation.

ACT 4. *The Tsar's mansion at Alexandrovskoye.*
A wedding chorus (No. 14) is sung in praise and honour of Andrey and Natalya, who are to be married, and the women and oprichniks join in a series of dances (No. 15). Andrey rejoices (No. 16) in his release from his oprichnik's vows, the humiliation of Zhemchuzhny, and his freedom to marry Natalya, but is sorrowful (bar 33) that he will no longer have the comradeship of the oprichniks. He vows (bar 48) continued fidelity to the Tsar. Basmanov reminds him that he is still an oprichnik until midnight, and Andrey reaffirms his absolute devotion to the Tsar, and proposes his health, a toast in which the oprichniks join (bar 78). Part of the wedding chorus is heard again. Natalya is apprehensive and wishes the feasting to end (bar 146). Andrey tries to calm her. Her sense of impending disaster increases (bar 194), and Andrey can do nothing to dispel her fears. She sings of her love for him (bar 237), but returns to her forebodings (bar 252), and again he tries to allay her dread. Finally they declare that they will share together whatever the future holds, even death. More of the wedding chorus is heard again (No. 17). Suddenly Basmanov rushes in (bar 72), draws Andrey aside, and darkly warns him of some terrible impending disaster. Andrey cannot fathom Basmanov's meaning. 'You will understand. You are not a child!' replies Basmanov (bar 148). Thereupon Vyazminsky enters (No. 18). Andrey greets him cordially. Vyazminsky reveals his business: the Tsar has heard of Natalya's beauty, and wishes to see her immediately – and alone. Andrey is bewildered and angry. Basmanov (bar 53) and the chorus attempt to persuade him to consent, but he is adamant. Natalya is horrified, Vyazminsky quietly triumphant. When (No. 19) Andrey challenges them to separate him and Natalya by force, Vyazminsky orders him to be restrained. Natalya faints into the arms of the oprichniks. Andrey curses them – and then the Tsar himself (bar 22). He is arrested, and Natalya is carried to the Tsar. Basmanov rushes out (bar 30) to plead with the Tsar for mercy, but in vain. Returning quickly, he throws himself on Andrey's breast, and tells him his doom is decided. Andrey shouts a farewell to Natalya (bar 40), and is led out. Vyazminsky prepares triumphantly (bar 53) to bring the Boyarïna 'to a splendid feast'. He leaves to fetch her. When he returns with her, he shows her through a window the

execution of her son taking place. She screams, and falls lifeless. Outside the oprichniks are heard praising the Tsar.

Tchaikovsky set about *The Oprichnik* determined to salvage whatever he could of the best music in *The Voyevoda*. The testimony of Modest, who witnessed the production of the new opera, contains critical observations which are well to the point:

> The violent intrusion of Ostrovsky's text into Lazhechnikov's tragedy gave rise to a distortion of the scenario which had a very harmful effect upon the whole libretto. The exposition became unclear, the characters of the dramatis personae were completely annihilated, beginning with the crafty and greedy Zhemchuzhny. As Pyotr Ilich has it, he is chatting genially with Mitkov when the curtain goes up, and does not display any of that malice and brutality which justify Morozov's enlistment in the *oprichnina*. In this act everybody else engages in actions which are completely inconsequential, and unnecessary for making sense of what is happening; sometimes these actions are utterly senseless, and distort the characters. Thus Andrey Morozov, in imitation of Bastryukov, breaks down Zhemchuzhny's garden fence with the oprichniks' help (and in so doing, recommends himself as being in sympathy with them), an action which makes no sense in the tragedy, since he does not do this with the slightest intention of carrying off his beloved (or, at least, of seeing her) as Bastryukov had done, but solely in order to borrow money from Basmanov. And, having accomplished this, which was hardly in character, he goes off, carefully setting the fence back in order. . . .[39]

Modest added a good deal more in this vein. To be fair to Tchaikovsky, he did in fact remove Bastryukov's instruction to break down the fence, but there was still no earthly reason why Andrey had to meet Basmanov in someone else's garden. Tchaikovsky showed an almost obtuse reluctance to alter anything pillaged from *The Voyevoda*, and it is a sign of his continued pride in parts of his first opera (so different from his total aversion to *The Oprichnik*) that he was determined to preserve what he could quite untouched. Modest might have added that when his brother took the music to which Dyuzhoy had entertained Shalïgin in Act 1 of *The Voyevoda* and assigned it to the opening scene of *The Oprichnik*, where Zhemchuzhny entertains Mitkov,[40] he was

[39] *TZC*1, p. 389; *DTC*, p. 40.

[40] Tchaikovsky did recognise that the music which had accompanied the Jester's first vocal entry in *The Voyevoda* scene, and which had actually characterised the Jester, would be inept in *The Oprichnik*, and he substituted a new passage at this point.

depriving it of its irony, for formerly its cheerfulness had deliciously pointed up a situation of outward conviviality and underlying tension. He might have observed, too, that when his brother, before transferring the opening scene of *The Voyevoda* to *The Oprichnik*, ripped out the whole of Mariya's A minor song with its little appended scena and substituted the folksong-aria from Act 2, he badly weakened the character of his heroine, for he deprived Natalya of that delightfully mischievous $\frac{5}{4}/\frac{6}{4}$ conclusion which had added a quite new element to Mariya's personality.

The Oprichnik begins, then, with three large slabs of *Voyevoda* music to set the scenes of Zhemchuzhny with Mitkov, of Natalya with her nurse and maidens, and of Andrey with Basmanov and the oprichniks in Zhemchuzhny's garden. The first act ends, too, with material from the earlier opera. As the nurse and maidens return, so does some of their music heard earlier, and the concluding choral dance, ostensibly designed to raise Natalya's spirits, was really no more than an excuse for using again the khorovod which had rounded off Act 2 of the earlier opera. Fortunately, in the rest of *The Oprichnik* there is relatively little recourse to existing music. During the duet in the first scene of Act 2 Andrey borrows a four-bar phrase from Bastryukov's aria in the corresponding *Voyevoda* scene, and the duet ends with the whole last stretch of that same scene, where Bastryukov and Dubrovin had concluded their plans for rescuing Mariya and Olyona. There the sombre tread of this music had married well with the plot; here it sounds like the gratuitous addition it is, even though Tchaikovsky has excised the first part of the phrase which derived from Dubrovin's motif and substituted a bit from the Boyarïna's plea (see bar 3 of Ex. 55). The third act is entirely new; in the fourth, one of the most Russian passages in the whole of *The Voyevoda*, Bastryukov's farewell in the Act 1 finale, becomes Andrey's farewell to the oprichniks.

The single remaining piece of second-hand music was not from *The Voyevoda* at all, for to round off the love duet Tchaikovsky resurrected the cantabile theme from *Fatum*. The lyricism of the preceding portion of this duet is less than Tchaikovsky's best, and he probably hoped that this theme, the one portion from that ill-starred piece of which Balakirev had anything good to say, might redeem the situation. Finally, to complete this record of music which Tchaikovsky did not compose specifically for *The Oprichnik*, it should be noted that the entr'acte before the second act is not by Tchaikovsky at all. His Russian contemporaries showed a curious readiness to allow others to participate in their creative projects (as Balakirev's activities so readily demonstrate), and Tchaikovsky himself did not feel so proprietary about *The Oprichnik* that he was not prepared to let Shilovsky compose this entr'acte, a brief piece which speaks well for the harmonic competence of his pupil.

The national quality is stronger and more consistent in *The Oprichnik* than in *The Voyevoda*. All the major borrowings from the earlier opera are of scenes, movements or sections which are markedly Russian in character, and the freshly composed music for *The Oprichnik* contains a number of movements in which the national flavour is very deliberately cultivated – the folk chorus which opens Act 3, for instance (a movement whose relative stiffness renders it, nevertheless, a hopeless competitor with the great crowd spectacles of *Boris Godunov*), and the bridal chorus and dances in Act 4 (the latter incorporate six Russian folksongs, five of which Tchaikovsky had already arranged in his *50 Russian Folksongs*).[41] In addition there is an infusion of the idiom of Orthodox church music, which is used explicitly in the oprichniks' chorus at the opening of the oath scene, and again in the brief prayer at the end of the Act 3 folk chorus. More important still, however, is the infiltration of such native musical elements, both secular and sacred, into Tchaikovsky's own style. The ecclesiastical idiom penetrates the Boyarïna's splendid aria at the beginning of Act 2, while certain of the proto-shapes of Russian folk melody underlie a number of Tchaikovsky's own phrases. It was this latter feature which had contributed most to the specifically national quality of Glinka's two operas. Yet such melodic conditioning could have wider ramifications, for in *Ruslan and Lyudmila* the proliferation of a whole fund of material which had been moulded upon a folksong-derived contour, and then dispersed throughout the opera, had also served to consolidate both the stylistic consistency and the structural integrity of the piece.[42] In *The Oprichnik* we may see Tchaikovsky using the same sort of process, though less intensively than Glinka. For instance, a particle of the actual folksong upon which is founded the khorovod that ends the first act (Ex. 47a) lingers over into the very first phrase heard after the curtain has risen upon the next act (Ex. 47b). True, when the Boyarïna passes to her aria, she moves into completely new territory both in her opening phrase (Ex. 47c) and in another which emerges later (Ex. 47d); yet when Andrey enters, to be introduced by a new phrase (Ex. 47e) synthesised from Ex. 47d coupled to the second bar of Ex. 47c, we move back towards the melodic world of Ex. 47a and b. And when, later, the formal duet begins, Andrey's first utterance is a high elaboration of this same phrase (Ex. 47f).

Nevertheless, the importance of such techniques in *The Oprichnik*

[41] *T50RF*, nos. 10, 17, 29, 32, 34.

[42] See my *Mikhail Glinka* (London, 1974), pp. 202–3. For a fuller examination of certain of the characteristics of Russian folksong, see also pp. 113ff. of that book.

Ex. 47

must not be exaggerated. Tchaikovsky used the process less naturally than Glinka, relying for thematic integration more upon a body of reminiscence-themes which crop up in different parts of the score. Unlike the introduction to *The Voyevoda*, which had contained only one quotation of material heard subsequently in the opera, that to *The Oprichnik* is largely an anthology of such reminiscence-themes shuffled among six sections to foreshadow in very simple terms some of the principal persons and events of the tragedy. After an abrupt explosion containing all the signals that a strong-situation drama is to follow, there comes a theme associated with the oprichniks (Ex. 48), a part of the

Ex. 48 Allegro giusto

Boyarïna's contribution to the duet in the first scene of Act 2 (Ex. 49; it is interrupted by Ex. 48 to prefigure the most extreme conflict of interests

Ex. 49

in the opera), and Andrey's declaration to the assembled oprichniks in the second scene of the same act (Ex. 50). To portend the final event of

Ex. 50

the whole tragedy, there is a stretch of music from the very last scene, where the execution is witnessed; here Ex. 49 is distorted and used in diminution. Finally the oprichniks' theme peals out brazenly, with much emphasis in the last cadential stretch on those mediant relationships to which Tchaikovsky shows considerable favour in the opera.

Tchaikovsky's operatic language in *The Oprichnik* is a consolidation of that established in *The Voyevoda*. There are set-pieces, but these tend to be shorter and to merge more naturally into the flow of the main body of music, which treats the action in a species of recitative-arioso of wide variety. At its simplest the accompaniment is merely chordal, the orchestra either punctuating the singers' phrases or providing a sustained harmonic background. More normally the accompaniment is animated by motifs or whole melodic phrases, often placed in a striking, sometimes very beautiful, harmonic setting, and garnished, where the action may require it, with appropriate dramatic gestures and effects. The commendable skill which Tchaikovsky had now acquired for marshalling all these resources to match efficiently a strong dramatic situation is perhaps best exemplified in the second scene of Act 2. This is a well-paced and tightly organised musical entity, in which the most powerful unifying agent is the oprichniks' theme, first heard in the opera's introduction (see Ex. 48), remembered in Basmanov's solo in Act 1 (see Ex. 53), reintroduced in the entr'acte before this scene,[43] and which now roves freely throughout the whole scene. So, too, the chorus plays a crucial structural role. The music of the oprichniks' opening chant (whose key and style recall the opening of *Romeo and Juliet*) persists in the orchestra until some way into the act, their new chorus in praise of the Tsar acting as a neat frame for the Basmanov/Vyazminsky dialogue

[43] Here its opening is four times provided with a different harmonisation in a way strikingly similar to that of the eclipse music which Borodin was composing for *Prince Igor* at the very time when Tchaikovsky was finishing *The Oprichnik*.

early in the scene, while throughout the lengthy oath-taking they provide refrains which function as structural cornerstones.

While such procedures help to give a clear shape to broad expanses of the scene, the incorporation of motifs from elsewhere in the opera provides longer-range links with more distant regions. The entr'acte employs a phrase used briefly in the preceding scene when Andrey is admitting to his mother Basmanov's liking for the pleasures of this world, and Basmanov's 'persuasion' motif, first used in Act 1 when he is exhorting Andrey to forgo the joy of seeing Natalya to attend to more pressing business, now influences Vyazminsky to drop his opposition to Andrey's enrolment in the *oprichnina*. Most telling of all is the moment when part of the Boyarïna's share in the earlier duet with her son (see Ex. 49) recurs as Andrey broods upon the mother and the bride he must now renounce. And quite apart from the abundance of abrupt and forceful vocal utterance, the wealth of striking harmonic detail, and the fertile store of rhetorical imagery presented in vivid orchestration, there is a brief but admirable representation of the struggle within Andrey himself, as part of the monologue in which he had supplicated to the oprichniks engages roughly with the oprichniks' own theme (Ex. 51).

Ex. 51

All this is musically an extension of what had been begun in *The Voyevoda*; what has been conspicuously absent right up to this scene in *The Oprichnik* is any movement in which a whole group of soloists (perhaps with the chorus) shares. The most painful lesson Tchaikovsky carried away from his first opera was of the dangers inherent in that most tricky of operatic forms, the dramatic ensemble, and there are only two such ensembles in *The Oprichnik*, occurring at the ends of the last two acts. The second of these[44] is the weakest part of the whole opera, but the Act 3 ensemble, which arises after the Boyarïna has uttered her curse, is an impressive movement, and a great improvement upon anything of the kind in *The Voyevoda*. It is clear that Tchaikovsky has been examining with profit the quartet which occurs after Lyudmila's

[44] It is in fact followed by the execution scene.

abduction in Act 1 of *Ruslan and Lyudmila*. The dramatic situations are parallel; both sets of characters are stunned by a sudden catastrophic turn of events, and Tchaikovsky uses the same basic mechanism as Glinka to suggest paralysis – an unrelenting pedal note against which the slowly paced harmonies eternally pull, and a nervously whispered delivery of the text (though he forgoes Glinka's strictly canonic vocal relationship). And as the chorus joins in, Tchaikovsky demonstrates that he has well grasped two conditions for satisfactory ensemble writing: the need for a clear lucid strategy in deploying the participants so as to avoid textural turgidity and maintain dramatic clarity, and the advantages of a musical foundation which consists of simple and very clearly carved ideas whose melodic outlines are bold enough and whose harmonies firm enough not to be engulfed in the performers' huge sonorities, and around which the constituent parts of the massive vocal forces may continue to exercise their own appropriate dramatic functions. A noteworthy detail of the conventional harmonic heightening towards the very end of this finale is the brief use of the whole-tone scale in the bass.

Enough has been said already to show that, for all its inconsistencies and miscalculations, *The Oprichnik* represents some very positive advance in Tchaikovsky's skill as an operatic composer. In the end, however, an opera surely stands or falls upon the degree to which the protagonists of the drama may engage our interest, making us believe that the drama flows from their strengths and weaknesses, their loves, hates, loyalties and ambitions. On this point Modest was scathing: the characters in *The Oprichnik* were mere marionettes. In fact, he did rather less than justice to his brother's work. Even the oprichniks themselves emerge as a group of some real, if limited substance. Of course, Tchaikovsky's treatment of them is highly idealised. Even if he had been prompted to a more veracious representation of their cruelty and ruthlessness, it would never have got past the censor who, in any case, objected to Ivan the Terrible himself being portrayed on the stage, with the result that Vyazminsky had to take over the Tsar's role in the proceedings. Instead the oprichniks are seen as a band of stern servants and protectors of the Tsar, living under a rigorous law which permits them easily to assume the guise of a quasi-religious community. Tchaikovsky assigns them music dug from that heroic vein which has its origins in *Ruslan and Lyudmila* and which, usually with some special emphasis on its modal solemnity or enrichment with some particularly striking and strong harmonic progression, can easily pass into the vaguely numinous – and, in so doing, confirm by a kind of reverse process that the idiom of Russian church music itself is a prime source for this heroic musical manner.

As for Andrey, Basmanov and Natalya, the short stretch of newly composed music which Tchaikovsky inserted into Act 1 would in itself suffice to define each of them as some sort of individual. Andrey starts his confession of love unremarkably (Ex. 52), but by bar 4 his phrase

Ex. 52

[No, my friend: my compliments to your beauties and your feasts. There's only one feast for me – to wash away the bloody insult. Natalya alone is my betrothed unto the grave.]

is blossoming, its rhythmic structure displays admirable flexibility, and its passions are abetted by considerable harmonic tensions. Basmanov's more manly[45] strength is equally disclosed in the opening of his arioso, which is prefaced by a transformation of the oprichniks' theme (Ex. 53). His phrases are succinct and resolute, clear in outline, firmly paced, and seated upon simple, strong harmonies. As for Natalya, to what she had already borrowed from Mariya of *The Voyevoda* she now adds a

[45] In fact Tchaikovsky wrote this part for a contralto, as Glinka had done with Vanya and Ratmir in his two operas.

[There's life with us — there is no need to die! By day, a sumptuous feast: at night, a beautiful woman. There's life with us — there is no need to die!]

revelation of capacity for a more mature passion, embodying her longing for Andrey in fine, strongly profiled phrases which are unmistakably from the creator of *Romeo and Juliet* (Ex. 54a). Indeed, the central subsidiary motif of her arioso (Ex. 54c) is very much akin to the broad love theme of the earlier work (see Ex. 29d); it may have been this that the very first thematic germ of the opera's introduction had

[Ah, tempestuous winds, bear to my beloved tidings of my sorrow and pain, of my love and sighing, how I pine and languish.]

foreshadowed (Ex. 54d). There can be little doubt that the love duet in the last act of Meyerbeer's *Les Huguenots* (Ex. 54b) had a very direct influence upon Natalya's passionate utterance, also in G flat.

Yet none of these three characters develops further. In the end it is difficult to believe that Andrey is driven either by a really overmastering passion in love, or by an absolutely unflinching resolution in that pursuit of justice which leads him into the ranks of the oprichniks; set beside Glinka's Ruslan, he is positively pallid. Basmanov, who starts even more promisingly, is never given the chance to attain the substance of Dubrovin in *The Voyevoda*, nor can Natalya match Mariya, except perhaps in her duet with the Boyarïna in Act 3, where she seems to draw

Ex. 54
b.   [MEYERBEER]

some character and colour from the older woman's presence. Left to her own devices in the confession to her father, she loses substance as her pleading becomes couched in the musical terms of the drawing-room romance (the most striking feature of this slightly pale music is the notable way in which it foreshadows something of Tatyana's musical world in *Eugene Onegin*).

One character remains who has all the substance that these three lack: the Boyarïna. This old woman retains the vulnerability of her sex, for she is all too susceptible to pain; yet she also commands that special capacity for endurance that seems to be such an attribute of Russian women, searching within herself even more than within Zhemchuzhny's guilt for the seeds of her own misfortunes, devoted to her son yet prepared to curse him to all damnation for what she sees as his recourse to evil. It might have been hoped that in Act 3, when she and the oprichniks at last come face to face, a fusion from the best of her musical world and theirs might have crowned Tchaikovsky's achievement in this opera. Unfortunately this could not be, for such a result would have required a situation which permitted either a dialectic or else some kind of Orpheus-and-Furies encounter; given the inflexibility of the oprichniks, there was scope neither for argument nor for persuasion, only for a head-on collision of diametrically opposed ideals. The Boyarïna can only curse, and though this may make good theatre, it is also a measure of the characters' impotence to influence at all the events of this contrived plot. Here, of course, is the really damning indictment of *The Oprichnik* as a piece of drama. In the end all that Tchaikovsky could do to articulate musically the conflict of these opposing forces was to engage the oprichniks' theme and the Boyarïna's melody (see Exs. 48 and 49) in the final scene of the opera.

Yet despite all this, the Boyarïna does come very much alive. The secret of Tchaikovsky's success with her, as some years later with Tatyana, lies in the obvious sympathy he conceived for this heroic yet helpless woman. From her first appearance at the beginning of Act 2 she draws from him some of the best music in the opera. We hear this both in her recitative and in the splendidly dignified aria that follows, and her character unfolds further during the dialogue that precedes the formal duet with her son. It is she, embodied in the motifs carried over from her scena and aria, who dominates this dialogue. For all its transparent simplicity, her exhortation to Andrey to remain unblemished is not the pathetic pleading of a weak woman but an injunction backed by moral authority and declared with chaste eloquence; observe how her line, which had started nervously with one-bar phrases, burgeons into an integral eight-bar span of manifest strength (Ex. 55), and is the signal for some pages of fine, if inconsistent music. When Andrey thinks of his mother and bride in the oath scene, it is the Boyarïna's, not Natalya's music that is heard. In Act 3 her sorrows draw from Tchaikovsky some of his richest harmonic pathos, and even Natalya rises to some finely impassioned lyricism in her presence. And if the last scene of the opera can move us at all, it is because we have really come to believe in this old woman as a living being who, despite her capacity for enduring monumental suffering, is unable to bear this ultimate horror, and is destroyed by it.

Gerald Abraham categorised *The Oprichnik* well when he described it as 'Meyerbeer translated into Russian'.[46] As the complete operatic

---

[46] G. Abraham, *Tchaikovsky: a Symposium* (London, 1945), p. 136, and *Slavonic and Romantic Music*, p. 130.

Ex. 55

[Let my son be whiter than the snow, brighter than the sun, clearer than the azure skies, firmer than the crag amid the tempestuous waves. I pray you, bring peace to your father's ashes in his damp tomb.]

craftsman Tchaikovsky was no match for that expert purveyor of smoothly streamlined operatic situations; as a composer he was vastly superior. *The Oprichnik* will never become a repertoire piece, nor does it deserve to. Its drama is bogus and a good deal of its music is simply well-contrived dressing for crude melodrama – though even here Tchaikovsky far outstrips his German-Jewish confrère in musical inventiveness. Yet there are some real delights in the score. Meyerbeer, for instance, was probably incapable of anything quite as memorable as the deliciously characterful urchins' chorus near the beginning of Act 3, with its piquant oscillation between two tritone-related dominant seventh chords (Ex. 56a), an harmonic trick which originated with Naina in *Ruslan and Lyudmila* (Ex. 56b), and which Musorgsky also used for the coronation motif in *Boris Godunov* (Ex. 56c) – though to very different

[I am the enchantress Naina!]

effect. And there are patches in *The Oprichnik*, above all when the Boyarïna occupies the stage, that penetrate to a level of human feeling which transcends the rather sordid context they are required to inhabit. For such passages especially, *The Oprichnik* deserves an occasional revival. Those companies who specialise in the resurrection of operatic museum-pieces which have long lain neglected might with profit occasionally blow the dust off this flawed but fascinating, torrid yet, at times, touching piece.

8

HIGH NATIONALISM I:

SECOND SYMPHONY

MOST OF TCHAIKOVSKY'S friends who wander in and out of this book were beings of importance either as fellow musicians or as persons of substance who in some material way contributed to his career and well-being. But the circle of Tchaikovsky's acquaintances extended beyond such people, for there were a number of men in whose society he delighted, whose company was precious to him, who had no importance whatsoever for his career or livelihood, yet without whom his world would have been duller, and he less contented. One such man was Nikolay Bochechkarov, an old man with old-fashioned aristocratic manners, antiquated turns of speech larded with stock French words (though in fact he was quite ignorant of the language), who cleaned his icons three times a day in expiation for having had their metal coverings in pawn from time immemorial, whose religion consisted of so many little private rituals that Tchaikovsky jokingly called it 'cabalistic', who was in fact a penniless beggar, yet who contrived to get invited out to dine every day on the strength of his pleasant personality and the fund of gossip he had acquired from his previous day's round and the pages of the *Police Gazette*. Bochechkarov was one of those eccentrics who, like the composer's Uncle Pyotr, seem to be peculiar to Russia. Tchaikovsky first met him in 1869 when Bochechkarov was in particularly dire circumstances, and took to him immediately, loved his talk and his tales, and from that moment helped to ensure that his body and soul did not part company. When Tchaikovsky, on his return to Moscow towards the middle of September 1871, detached himself from Rubinstein and moved into his own quarters, Bochechkarov became a daily visitor whose chatter quickly dispelled the tensions of the day and restored Tchaikovsky to an equable frame of mind. Though Bochechkarov could never be, like Laroche, Kashkin or Jurgenson, a member of Tchaikovsky's closest circle of friends, his death in 1879 was a terrible blow to the composer. Bochechkarov will scarcely be mentioned further in these pages, but to ignore him completely would be ungrateful to this man who quietly and perhaps unwittingly contributed so much to Tchaikovsky's well-being in his Moscow years. It would also mean ignoring yet another pointer, like Tchaikovsky's delight in his nephews and nieces at Kamenka, to his great and enduring need for simple, whole-hearted relationships with ordinary human beings.

Yet he needed solitude, too, and he was able to enjoy this now that he had severed his domestic ties with Rubinstein and established himself in his own quarters. The trouble was that independence proved costly. Though his annual income from the Conservatoire was 1,500 roubles, and from composition some 500 roubles, his new situation made it desirable that he should supplement these resources, and to do this he embarked on a subsidiary career as a music critic for *The Contemporary Chronicle*. Laroche had for some time acted in this capacity for the journal, and when he left Moscow to take up his new appointment at the St Petersburg Conservatoire, Hubert had replaced him, but because the latter proved too indolent for the paper's requirements, Tchaikovsky and Kashkin agreed to write notices. Tchaikovsky told Anatoly that he had undertaken the job solely out of selflessness, and he probably felt some relief when *The Contemporary Chronicle* ceased publication at the end of December 1871, only one month and four reviews after his début as a critic.

In fact, the loss of this remuneration was a problem greatly exacerbated by the serious uncertainties that were then surrounding the Conservatoire. The institution's finances were in such a bad way that there was even talk of closure. Yet, calamitous as this would have been for Tchaikovsky, it was something he almost welcomed, as he admitted to Anatoly: 'For the cause [that the Conservatoire represents] I shall be regretful, and if it does fail I shall be outraged. But for myself I shall be glad. My duties have become so loathsome to me, I am so tired and distraught that I shall be glad for any change. I shall not, of course, die of hunger. It is most probable that we shall organise classes in Moscow for people to attend, or I shall move to St Petersburg if they offer me a better salary at the Conservatoire.'[1] His confidence in his ability to stand on his own feet, if need be, is clearly apparent. There was, indeed, increasing evidence to justify this self-assurance. In October Cui's pen had informed St Petersburg of the high qualities of *Romeo and Juliet*, which the Russian capital was soon to hear for itself at an RMS concert conducted by Nápravník. This fresh sign of esteem from Balakirev's group warmed further Tchaikovsky's feelings towards the St Petersburg composers; 'make Borodin hurry up and finish his superb symphony [No. 2],' he added when asking Balakirev to convey his thanks to

[1] *TLP5*, p. 265; *TZC1*, p. 373; *TPB*, p. 73; *YDGC*, p. 78 (partial).

Cui.[2] Meanwhile Balakirev himself had started rehearsing the 'Chorus of Flowers and Insects', and had been so taken by it that, as we have seen, he had suggested to Tchaikovsky the plan for a cantata, *Night*, in which the inspiration that had produced this little piece might be deployed more impressively (see above, p. 196). Tchaikovsky's own failure to achieve the hoped-for progress on *The Oprichnik* rendered even more hateful those Conservatoire commitments that devoured time which he might otherwise have given to composition. And as he was leaving for Nice to spend Christmas and the New Year with Shilovsky, there came a commission for a cantata to be performed in Moscow at the opening of the Polytechnic Exhibition arranged to celebrate the bicentenary of the birth of Peter the Great. For this 750 roubles would be paid. There was certainly no shortage of remunerative work to occupy his creative faculties.

Nevertheless, it was not only the frustration of his compositional drives that was giving him torment, for there are signs of agonising emotional stresses within his own personal life. 'Now I must inform you that, at Shilovsky's persistent request, I am going abroad for one month about 27 December,' he confided to Anatoly on 14 December 1871. 'But because no one must know about this, and because in Moscow everyone (except Rubinstein) must think that I'm going to Sasha's, please don't tell anyone.'[3] Tchaikovsky's close association with Shilovsky had clearly begun to occasion gossip which this extended trip would fortify. Nor is this the only strong hint that Tchaikovsky's homosexual proclivities were active. In October he had written an urgent letter to brother Nikolay about a certain Eduard Zak, a cousin of one of his Conservatoire pupils. Nikolay had been showing some kindness to the youth, and Tchaikovsky now proposed that the boy should come to stay in Moscow. Having set out fully his reasons for thinking this would be good for Zak, he begins to sound a note which has a more pressing, slightly frantic ring:

I beg you, old chap, if you find that my view is sound, to let him – and even order him – to travel to Moscow; in doing this you'll cause me great pleasure. I have missed him a great deal, and I'm fearful for his future. I fear that manual work will kill all higher aspirations in him. I'll tell you frankly that, if I notice in him a moral and intellectual decline, I shall take steps to find alternative employment for him. But whatever happens, it's absolutely necessary that I see him. For God's sake, arrange it![4]

[2] *TLP5*, p. 263; *BVP*, p. 161.   [3] *TLP5*, p. 265; *TZC1*, pp. 372–3; *TPB*, p. 73.
[4] *TLP5*, p. 262.

Such intemperate terms scarcely suggest a natural thirst for the presence of this seventeen-year-old. Beyond this there is no evidence that might illumine this relationship, and Zak himself remains a shadowy figure. Finally he did come to Moscow, where he associated with both Tchaikovsky and Shilovsky before committing suicide in 1873.

Whatever anxieties Tchaikovsky may have felt about the constructions others would put upon his mid-winter excursion, the visit itself was beneficial. Leaving Russia at the end of December by way of St Petersburg, he travelled via Berlin and Paris to Nice, where he arrived on 5 January 1872 for a three-week stay. He was a little alarmed by the violence of the torrential rains and high winds that sprang up on some days, but enjoyed the longer periods of spring-like weather which had already roused to life the flowers and trees, and he found it difficult to resist being drawn into the bright social life of the resort. Yet a restless melancholy remained with him. 'I awaited the moment of leaving Moscow with such wild impatience that towards the end I couldn't sleep,' he wrote on 13 January:

> But on the very day of my departure I was enveloped in a burning melancholy that didn't leave me for a moment during the whole of my journey, and which remains with me even now amid all these wonders of nature. Of course, there are pleasant moments, especially when, in the morning, I'm sitting alone by the sea beneath the rays of a burning though not intolerably hot sun. But even these pleasant moments are not without their melancholy tinge. What follows from all this? That old age has come, when nothing pleases any more. You live on memories or hopes. But what is there to hope for?[5]

Sasha had normally been the beneficiary of such world-weary sentiments, but this time it was to Anatoly that he confided them. His closeness to this twin was greater than ever; by contrast his relationship with Modest was still fraught with tensions, and he was both hurt and angry to discover that this brother had chosen to come and stay in his new flat in Moscow at the very time that he himself was away in Nice.

Despite the despondency expressed in this letter, in Nice Tchaikovsky stirred himself to compose two piano pieces, Nocturne and Humoresque, which were published as Op. 10; the second of these used for its middle section a popular song he heard while in the Mediterranean resort. The composition of these trifles cost little effort and gave him little sense of fulfilment, however; virtual inactivity finally produced boredom, and when he set out on the return journey to Russia, it was with some real

---

[5] TLP5, pp. 271–2; TZC1, pp. 373–4.

pleasure at the thought of resuming work. His journey took him through Genoa, Venice and Vienna, and on 10 February he arrived back in Moscow, where Rubinstein was now awaiting his return with some impatience. Immediately on his return he provided some little couplets, with accompaniment of two violins, for Count Almaviva to be incorporated into a performance on 24 February of Beaumarchais's *Le Barbier de Séville* given, in Sadovsky's translation, by students of the Conservatoire.

Nor were his Conservatoire duties the only thing that urgently needed his attention. The newly commissioned cantata was to be performed in barely four months' time, and he had only just received the prescribed text from Yakov Polonsky (who was also to provide the libretto for Tchaikovsky's next opera). From St Petersburg Laroche had already warned Tchaikovsky that his collaborator's text was 'most anti-musical',[6] and however much, as a Russian, Tchaikovsky may have admired the achievements of Peter the Great, it is obvious that he could find no interest in his subject; as with the graduation cantata of some six years earlier, he dashed it off hurriedly, in this case even resorting to existing material to hasten the work. To frame the piece he took two chunks from the finale of his First Symphony, opening with the whole of that movement's slow introduction played twice (with some modifications in the repetition), followed by the lead into the allegro, and closing the whole cantata with two statements of the folksong used in this introduction,[7] on to which was tacked a straightforward choral-orchestral transcription of the entire coda. To be fair, just as these appropriations signified a debt to the past, so the piece also provided a legacy to the future, for Tchaikovsky rounded off the orchestral intro-duction with a new section which three years later was to form the basis of the trio in his Third Symphony's scherzo.

Between these second-hand flanks came new music, much of it quite featureless. Little in the bland opening movement for tenor and chorus even hints at Tchaikovsky as its composer, while pompous anonymity

[6] *DTC*, p. 279; *YDGC*, p. 79; *TZC* 1, p. 375.
[7] There was a great deal of national awareness in these celebrations of Peter the Great. Nikolay Rubinstein, who was the first chairman of the music section of the organising committee, had proposed that Tchaikovsky, Laroche and Kashkin should spend the summer of 1871 scouring Russia both for folksongs, which they were to collect, and for folk singers, who would come to Moscow during Exhibition time to perform their native music. Tchaikovsky seems to have been sufficiently interested to be prepared to sacrifice a precious summer's composition for this project, but it foundered when the committee refused to allocate the 1,000 roubles of expenses which Rubinstein claimed for each of the collectors. The inclusion of folksong in Tchaikovsky's cantata was probably determined by the prevailing spirit of the Exhibition.

allies itself with pedantry in the obligatory fugal movement to manufacture as dull a piece as Tchaikovsky ever wrote. Elsewhere there is one brief section where the attention is caught: an unpretentious dozen bars (Ex. 57) which occur four times during the work as a kind of refrain, and which also provide the link to the final chorus. The conversion of the last part of the introduction into a tenor solo works well, and when the little martial phrase that was to find a haven in the Third Symphony lingers on to punctuate the halting phrases of Ex. 57 on its third occurrence, there seems some prospect that genuine organic life is at last stirring. Sadly these hopes are dashed by the new tenor solo, which filches an idea from Natalya's arioso in Act 3 of *The Oprichnik* (and badly weakens it in so doing). Before the coda Tchaikovsky inserted a full statement of the Russian national anthem; in the published Soviet edition this is primly excised. As in the graduation cantata there is a wide tonal range between the different movements. Compared to the earlier work, this second specimen shows a far more assured technique, but that is the sum of the progress it does represent, and since its best new invention was resuscitated in another context, its oblivion is well merited.

During February and March 1872 Tchaikovsky was remarkably busy, for within these two months he not only composed the entire cantata, but also completed *The Oprichnik*. Already the bridal chorus which opens the last act of the opera had been heard at an RMS concert in Moscow (2 February), and further signs of the increasing esteem in which he was held as a composer were afforded by other performances of his works. The First Quartet was played in Moscow in January, while the première in St Petersburg of the revised *Romeo and Juliet* on 17 February was followed a fortnight later by a performance in Moscow, for which he received 200 roubles. This must have been as beneficial to his morale as to his pocket, and the abrupt three-month break in his letter-writing is probably a reflection of the total absorption of all his free time by composition. With these two large undertakings completed, he set about providing harmonisations for an anthology of children's songs on Russian and Ukrainian folktunes made by Mariya Mamontova, an enthusiastic crusader for the cause of children's musical education. This task can have caused him little effort, for his harmonisations were of the most functional.

By the middle of May, with the score of *The Oprichnik* dispatched to St Petersburg, he began to resume his usual social contacts. On 12 June the cantata was given an open-air afternoon performance on the Troitsky Bridge. Despite the awning erected for the occasion, the sound was so dissipated that much of its effect was lost, even to those who sat quite

Ex. 57

N.B. This text is a substitute by a Soviet writer for Polonsky's original, which has been suppressed.

[Our nation grew its cherished cornfield, the countless horde trampled it down. Burial mounds sprang up, Russia was bathed in blood, her seed quietly broke through into the world.]

close to the performers; to those who were in the gardens below it was virtually inaudible. Since the composer himself, in order (characteristically) to avoid being an object of curiosity, had chosen to sit in these gardens, it is improbable that he can have gained much of an impression of the effect produced by his new piece. His self-effacement also caused him to miss meeting for the first time his collaborator, Polonsky – though he probably had no regrets at being spared an interview with the Grand Duke Konstantin, who had expressed a wish to see him after the performance. On the very same day he left Moscow for the summer and headed, via Kiev, for Kamenka. Thus he also missed hearing a second performance of the cantata at the Bolshoy Theatre twelve days later.

Tchaikovsky stayed with Sasha for a month, enjoying the added pleasure of his father's company. Among the other guests was Sergey Donaurov, a civil servant in the Foreign Office, a composer of popular romances, and now a friend of Tchaikovsky. Later Donaurov was to be responsible for the French translations of some of Tchaikovsky's songs. On 14 July Tchaikovsky bade farewell to Sasha and her family and, with Donaurov, travelled by steamer to Kiev, where he was joined by a very amenable Modest. Tchaikovsky had a great liking for Kiev, and he spent two days visiting friends and seeing the sights, including St Sofiya's Cathedral and the monastery. Then, on 17 July, he, Modest and Donaurov set out for Kondratyev's estate at Nizy, where they stayed some ten days. Tchaikovsky's third and final call that summer was to be on Shilovsky at Usovo. It was now time for the three men to go their separate ways, Donaurov to Moscow, and Modest back to Kiev. The two brothers were still able to share the first part of the journey, and this they did in style. But when they reached the railway at Vorozhba, where their ways parted, Tchaikovsky discovered with alarm that he had left behind his baggage, which included all his money and papers. Amongst these was the beginning of the work which was to prove his most important composition since *Romeo and Juliet* – his Second Symphony.

However much Tchaikovsky's spirits may have been taxed by the drudgery of the Conservatoire and the torments of his sexual urges, composition was never anything but a blessed relief. Even when progress was difficult (as with *The Oprichnik*), or the product of his labours merely functional (as was the cantata), the deep satisfaction of having shaped a new creation far outweighed the tensions and sheer effort which had attended the process of composition. Normally his newest child enjoyed his critical favour, and while he perhaps felt no great pride in the cantata, he still believed during the summer of 1872 that *The Oprichnik* was an opera in which he could take deep satisfaction. Exhausted he may have been when he left Moscow for Kamenka, but tormenting thoughts and dulled spirits seem to have been mastered for the time being, and the symphony he began at Sasha's home sounds not one tragic note nor contains one clouded phrase. Of all his major works, it is the most joyous and extrovert. The mishap with the luggage containing all he had so far composed of the piece might have been expected to fill him with alarm and despondency; instead it played a part in a little episode which reveals something of his spirits' good condition, as well as confirming that his inclination to practical jokes, this one born of the exigency of the moment, had not deserted him.

The brothers had travelled part of the way from Nizy in a carriage they had hired, and after wining and dining at a staging post, Tchaikovsky had ordered the horses to be harnessed, only to be told that this was impossible. A heated altercation developed with the unco-operative postmaster, until Tchaikovsky, fortified by the wine he had drunk, called for the complaints book and signed his entry 'Prince Volkonsky, gentleman of the Emperor's bedchamber'. The effect was magical; within a quarter of an hour an abjectly apologetic postmaster reported that their carriage was ready, and that they could continue their journey to Vorozhba. It was here that the loss of Tchaikovsky's baggage was discovered. While Modest gave his brother the few roubles he had on him and then proceeded on his way, Tchaikovsky, having no wish to confront the postmaster who might now have investigated the baggage and discovered the true identity of its owner, arranged that another should return for it. After a sleepless night in a rat-infested bedroom, Tchaikovsky had his misery increased when his emissary returned to say that the postmaster would not release the baggage of so eminent a person as 'Prince Volkonsky, gentleman of the Emperor's bedchamber' except to His Highness in person. Thus a very apprehensive Tchaikovsky was forced to return to the staging post where, however, he found his possessions unopened. Relieved beyond measure by this discovery, he talked affably with the postmaster, did his best to clear the air, and finally asked him his name. 'Tchaikovsky' was the reply. A stunned, mystified composer, dimly suspecting that this might be some sharp-witted revenge on the part of his former adversary, was not satisfied until Kondratyev's enquiries had confirmed that this was indeed the post-master's name. After this he took special delight in recounting the story.

Tchaikovsky returned to Moscow earlier than usual, leaving Usovo on 26 August. It is possible that his early return had something to do with his resumption of work as a music critic. The journalistic labours of the next four years, enough to fill a stout volume, made heavy inroads into the time he might otherwise have devoted to composition. The reward was extra income, and since the Conservatoire's financial crisis had been resolved by a government grant of 20,000 roubles a year over a five-year period, while his own salary had been increased by over 50 per cent to 2,300 roubles per annum, he felt he could safely move to a better flat. 'I have fixed myself up very luxuriously,' he enthused to Anatoly, 'and spent a pile of money,'[8] regretting that he was unable to satisfy Anatoly's request for a loan to help cover the expenses of a recent illness. Nikolay was in Moscow and came to Anatoly's aid, as well as treating Tchaikovsky to a splendid dinner. Nikolay's expansiveness on this occasion impressed Tchaikovsky as much as it surprised him; what he did not know was that his brother was about to marry. His relationship with Nikolay was never as close as with the twins, and it was only via the Davïdovs that a few weeks later he heard that the marriage, to a certain Olga Denisyeva, had actually taken place.

Despite his journalistic and teaching duties he had no intention that the momentum of his work on the symphony should be lost that autumn, and every spare moment was devoted to it. '[It] has so absorbed me that I'm not in a state to undertake anything else,' he wrote to Modest on 14 November, apologising for not having answered his brother's letter. 'This work of genius (as Kondratyev calls my symphony) is close to completion. . . . I think it's my best composition as regards perfection of form – a quality for which I have not been conspicuous.'[9] A fortnight later he informed Klimenko that he was 'frenziedly' engaged in scoring it. One more week, and he could report it finished.

None of Tchaikovsky's works found greater favour with the Kuchka than this symphony. At Christmas, when negotiations for the acceptance of *The Oprichnik* took him to St Petersburg, he introduced them to his new piece. 'I played the finale at a soirée at Rimsky-Korsakov's, and the whole company almost tore me to pieces with rapture – and Madame Rimskaya-Korsakova begged me in tears to let her arrange it for piano duet. Let her do it!' he added, rather ungraciously, to Modest.[10] Tchaikovsky offered the dedication to the Moscow branch of the RMS, who demonstrated their gratitude by a gift of three hundred roubles and by promptly arranging for the symphony's performance, which would have taken place on 24 January 1873, had not the Grand Duchess Elena finally taken her revenge on Tchaikovsky for his quondam defence of Balakirev and died, thus plunging everyone into official mourning and forcing the cancellation of the concert. The new work was at last heard on 7 February. '[It] enjoyed a great success, so great that Rubinstein

[8] *TLP5*, p. 286.

[9] *TLP5*, p. 287; *DTC*, p. 348; *TZC1*, pp. 393–4; *TPB*, p. 76; *YDGC*, p. 84 (partial).

[10] *TLP5*, p. 303; *DTC*, p. 349; *TPB*, p. 81; *YDGC*, p. 86 (partial); *TZC1*, p. 398 (partial).

wants to perform it again at the tenth concert [of the RMS's season] as by public demand. To tell the truth, I'm not completely satisfied with the first three movements, but "The Crane" ["Zhuravel"] itself [the finale which employs this Russian folktune] hasn't come out so badly,' he reported to Vladimir Stasov the next day.[11] Rubinstein was as good as his word, and on 9 April it was heard again. It was even more successful this time: Tchaikovsky received an ovation after each movement, and at the end was garlanded with a laurel wreath and presented with a silver cup. In the meantime, on 7 March, Nápravník had introduced it to St Petersburg, where it was received with sufficient warmth to ensure a repetition in the next season's concerts, even though this time Cui accorded the symphony a very unfavourable review. As for Moscow, two performances in one season were still not enough, and the symphony was heard for a third time at a special RMS concert on 27 May.

The Second Symphony was yet another of Tchaikovsky's works with which he later became dissatisfied, and seven years after completing it he borrowed his manuscript score from Bessel and set about a revision. Bessel should have published the first version, but he had procrastinated over issuing the full score, and only printed the arrangement for piano duet devised by Tchaikovsky himself after illness had prevented Nadezhda Rimskaya-Korsakova from making it. Tchaikovsky, who had for long badgered Bessel to print the full score, now felt nothing but relief about his publisher's inaction, and on 2 January 1880 he summarised for Bessel the results of his labours during the previous three days. '1. I have composed the first movement afresh, leaving only the introduction and coda in their previous form. 2. I have rescored the second movement. 3. I've altered the third movement, shortening and rescoring it. 4. I've shortened the finale and rescored it.'[12] This done, he destroyed the score of the original version, which was reconstructed after his death from the orchestral parts.

The Kuchka's rapture over this piece, and especially over the finale, was predictable, for the Second Symphony embodied Tchaikovsky's most whole-hearted identification so far with some of the most fundamental musical attitudes of this nationalist group, not simply because it incorporated three folktunes from the Ukraine ('Little Russia': hence the name by which Kashkin later suggested the symphony should be known, and which has stuck to it), but because it made more use than any of his previous works of those techniques and structural methods which they particularly favoured. Yet not all the work is

[11] *TLP*5, pp. 299–300; *DTC*, p. 349; *TZC*1, p. 401.
[12] *TLP*8, p. 476; *DTC*, p. 351. In fact, the scherzo's length finally remained unaltered – except that, by adding in the scherzo itself the conventional repeats he had omitted in the first version, he actually lengthened it!

notably Russian. The slow movement afforded a new home for the wedding march in Act 3 of the ill-fated *Undine*, and there is little in the outer portions of this ternary movement to identify the nationality of its creator, even though the lightness of this graceful confection far removes it from the more solid, portentous examples by Mendelssohn and Wagner. However, if these flanks are scarcely Russian, the central section is unmistakably so, for it both employs one of the Ukrainian folktunes and extends itself by using the changing background method that Glinka had evolved.[13] What Tchaikovsky so markedly lacks in the central portion of this movement is the freshness and sheer variety of which Glinka's fertile imagination was capable, and the scoring finally takes on a more thickly Germanic sound. For all its charm, this slow movement is less impressive than its predecessor in Tchaikovsky's First Symphony. Though, as already observed, it is in its broadest outlines a ternary structure, it may be further subdivided to disclose a rondo organisation ABACABA, on the face of it more complex than that of the earlier movement. Such a conclusion is illusory; all the A sections are in E flat, none of the last three adds anything to what has been heard when the section had first occurred, while the B passages are absolutely identical (C is the most substantial section, and uses the folksong). Thus, instead of the vastly spanned experience which Tchaikovsky had essayed in the First Symphony, this slow movement remains a procession of sections acceptably strung together, providing a respite after the far more concentrated fare of the first movement, especially in its original form. In this it foretells the tendency of Tchaikovsky's later symphonies to make the central portion of the total conception markedly lighter than the outer movements.

What this slow movement may lose beside that of the First Symphony is more than compensated by the gains of the scherzo. The danger of generating a movement from a single rhythmic figure, as Tchaikovsky had done in the scherzo of the First Symphony, is that the metrical repetitions will lace into a straitjacket, constricting invention and inducing monotony. The scherzo of the First Quartet had shown Tchaikovsky avoiding this pitfall by exploiting simple metrical switches within regular phrase lengths to vitalise the rhythmic life, and the process is carried further in the Second Symphony's scherzo, where a far wider variety of metrical irregularities provide constant foreground dislocations against the regular background of three- and six-bar phrases. To take just two examples of this rhythmic inventiveness: after the first double bar (Ex. 58) the second six-bar phrase, which promises

[13] The tune had already been used in *T5oRF* as No. 6, and Tchaikovsky drew upon his earlier arrangement in this slow movement.

Ex. 58   [Revised version]

to echo its predecessor, breaks off at the beginning of the fifth bar, slips
in the semiquaver figure which had been the movement's anacrusis, and
promptly re-uses it as an anacrusis to another phrase, as well as turning
it subsequently into a counterpoint to more fundamental things in the
next twelve bars. Later, again, it serves as the anacrusis to another phrase
(Ex. 59) which suddenly divides its six bars into three divisions of two
bars each, heightening the rhythmic surprise by simultaneously
speeding up the harmonic rate of change to three chords in every two
bars.

Perhaps an explanation of the special rhythmic verve of this scherzo
may be found in its ancestry, for it is the corresponding movement of
Borodin's First Symphony (and, some way behind that, Berlioz's *Queen
Mab*) that is unmistakably the model for Tchaikovsky's. There is an

Ex. 59

identity of harmonic language: both movements have a spicy piquancy, even pungency, with much use of seventh chords and of a discreet chromaticism that is utterly uncloyed. Yet the differences are perhaps even more instructive. The most notable one is in the decorative counterpoint, for Borodin has none of those little darting semiquaver lines such as Tchaikovsky so characteristically uses in the last four bars of Ex. 58. Throughout Borodin's scherzo the quaver momentum is more single-minded, and his rhythmic pulse more naked. Instead of flickering counterpoints there are lean motifs with many tritone tensions, all paced out in measured dotted crotchets. Because its creator lacked the sheer expertise of the professionally trained Tchaikovsky, his work is fundamentally simpler, and his invention is couched in terms of a more basic texture. Yet, for all the fertile rhythmic resourcefulness and rela-tive textural intricacy of Tchaikovsky's scherzo, the discipline – and attendant inhibitions – of the former conservatoire student holds everything on a tighter rein than in Borodin's. Tchaikovsky's trio may abruptly jolt the triple pulse into duple, and take on a positively folky character, but it still remains within regular six-bar periods, with none of the endless rhythmic flexibility of Borodin's mêlée of two-, three- and four-crotchet bars, and more freely ranging key-course. As in the First Symphony, the coda embraces elements both of the scherzo and the trio.

Tchaikovsky's revision of the first movement resulted in what, to all intents and purposes, was a completely new piece. Considering the scope of the labour, it went remarkably quickly. 'Today I set about revising my Second Symphony, the first movement of which I want to compose afresh, and the work went so well that by lunch I had managed to compose in rough nearly half of the first movement,' he wrote to Nadezhda von Meck on 30 December 1879.[14] On 16 January 1880, with the work completed, he assessed the results of his labours for his friend and former pupil, Sergey Taneyev. 'This movement has come out compressed, short, and is not difficult. If the epithet "impossible"

[14] *TLP*8, p. 471; *TPM*2, p. 283; *DTC*, pp. 350–1.

applies to anything, it is to this first movement in its original form. My God! How difficult, noisy, disjointed and muddle-headed this is!'[15] Nineteen years later (and some five years after Tchaikovsky's death), Taneyev, who in the meantime had developed into one of the finest craftsmen among all Russian composers, as well as one of the best teachers of composition that Russia has ever known, compared the two versions again. His verdict (and Kashkin's, too) was an unequivocal contradiction of the composer's.

And basically Kashkin and Taneyev were right. The original first movement is one of the most solid structures Tchaikovsky ever fashioned. From *Romeo and Juliet* he took the idea of integrating the introduction (based on another of the Ukrainian folktunes) with the main body of the movement by using material from it in the allegro. As in *Romeo and Juliet*, too, the original first subject consisted of two tonic statements of the main theme with a central section of a quasi-developmental character. The first subject itself was a splendid idea, spacious, with a restless momentum deriving from almost constant tensions between the melody and the bass – tensions which were often heightened by elements within the syncopated accompaniment (Ex. 60;

Ex. 60 [First version]

the extract begins at bar 17 of the subject). As for a transition, this was completely abandoned in this movement; instead Tchaikovsky halted the tutti restatement of the first subject on its emphatic neapolitan (see bars 7 and 8 of Ex. 60), reinterpreted this chord as the subdominant of A flat (the key in which the second subject was set in the first version), and proceeded forthwith with the second subject. This, like the first, was a

[15] *TLP*9, pp. 15–16; *DTC*, p. 351.

tonally restless idea with a good measure of decorative chromaticism, and almost constant contrapuntal interplay (Ex. 61). The natural kinship between these two subjects made it easy to reintroduce elements of the first subject while the second was still running its course, and the opening bar of Ex. 60 was incorporated into the latter before the exposition was rounded off by the sudden intervention of the folktune from the introduction, now accompanied by the quaver motif in the second bar of Ex. 61, a motif which is clearly related to first-subject material (see bars 2–4 of Ex. 60).

Ex. 61   [First version]

This was a skilfully wrought exposition, limited in expressive range, maybe, but rich in inventive detail, and constituting as monolithic a slab of symphonic music as Tchaikovsky had yet composed. But by 1879 these points were lost on the composer himself, whose ideals of musical truth had undergone much change in the preceding few years. His attraction to those qualities of lightness and grace which he saw as the embodiment of the musical eighteenth century had already manifested itself several times, most overtly in the Rococo Variations for cello and orchestra, and the powerful appeal in the lucidity, refinement and good taste of French music, to which he had always been powerfully drawn, had now been fortified by his exposure to Delibes's *Sylvia*, and by the devastating impact of Bizet's *Carmen*. Against the musical values such works epitomised, the textural complexity, massive scale and involved structure of the symphony's first movement must have seemed suffocating to the Tchaikovsky whose most recent vision of the sonata ideal had been incarnated in the Violin Concerto. The revision of the symphony's first movement represented a clarification of structure and texture, achieved partly by compression (over one hundred bars are shed), and partly by using more abrupt contrasts in the material, thus introducing a more obvious element of drama, and making it possible to define more sharply the structural divisions of the compressed and far more orthodox sonata movement which Tchaikovsky now built. The slow introduction and postlude remained untouched; of the main body of the movement there were left only the first twenty-eight bars of the development, and the coda.[16] There had been little contrast between the two subjects and so the second was sacrificed, its place being taken by the original first subject, which was completely rewritten (Ex. 62), and which

Ex. 62

[Revised version]

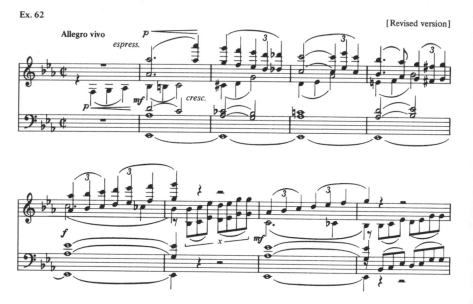

acquired a new string countermelody. In addition, if Tchaikovsky was to justify the retention of the first part of the original development, he had

---

[16] In the revised version bars 158ff. (these were transposed down a fifth and some running semiquaver lines in bars 174–81 were dropped) and 303ff. (here a sizeable repetition was excised).

to preserve somewhere in the exposition the quaver motif in the discarded second subject (see *x* in Ex. 61). To this purpose he incorporated it into the new second subject, as Ex. 62 shows.

Where the first subject had once been there was now a void, and to fill this Tchaikovsky devised a brand-new paragraph of marked brevity, and with a sharply articulated rhythmic/motivic life (Ex. 63a). As in the first

Ex. 63

version there is no transition as such; the first subject simply manœuvres itself to the dominant of E flat (the orthodox key in which Tchaikovsky now sets his second subject), and the second subject emerges immediately. This new first subject, like its predecessor, recurs towards the end of the exposition, but this time it crowds out not only the second subject but also the folktune which is not allowed to re-enter until the beginning of the development. For one new detail at the exposition's end Tchaikovsky must be given full credit: the shifting, by one crotchet, of the accent in the original first subject is neat and effective (Ex. 63b).

Though both developments use identical music initially, the thematic changes in the exposition compel them finally to part company. Except for these fundamental changes in the thematic material, the most marked single difference between the two versions concerns the role of the introduction's folktune in the main body of the movement. In the revised version it is confined exclusively to the first part of the development and to the coda (i.e. to those sections which Tchaikovsky took over bodily from his first version);[17] in the first version it had operated freely within the main movement, sometimes engaging on equal terms with the allegro's own indigenous material, at others even assuming briefly a fundamental structural role in a way that was bold and quite unprecedented. After reappearing to complete the exposition, it had continued as a constant ingredient of the entire development, and when the recapitulation had arrived, had paraded itself in its entirety before retiring to permit the official first subject its allotted role. And, whereas in the exposition there had been no transition, in the recapitulation one was provided by a resurgence of the folktune in combination with a fragment of the first subject.

The revised version reduced all this to the simplest and most regular of terms; hence the speed at which Tchaikovsky was able to work. The maverick folktune was expelled from all places where it might cause structural confusion in the listener's mind, the new second half of the development was no more than enough to do duty by the new first subject, and the recapitulation was orthodox, the last three bars of the first subject being tonally modified to enable the second subject to be recapitulated forthwith in the tonic.

To be fair to the second version, it is certainly attractive, and structurally as clear as anything that Tchaikovsky could wish for. There is an undeniable heaviness in the original, but its imposing scale, and its richness of content and detail make it a far more impressive piece that ought to be restored to the place which is still permanently usurped by its slighter and far less enterprising successor. Equally impressive, though in a very different way, is the finale. Here it was that Tchaikovsky aligned himself more closely than ever before with the nationalists' ideals and practices. In the first movement, even in its original, bolder version, the folktune, once it had entered the allegro, had become simply a thematic ingredient, subordinate to a broader symphonic purpose; in the finale a folktune is not merely allowed to take almost sole possession of an entire major portion (the first subject) of a symphonic structure, but even to bring with it into that section the particular treatment that had been found most favourable to its nature – a treatment quite unlike anything a Western symphonist would have dreamed of using. It cannot be claimed that Tchaikovsky invented this novelty in this symphony, for Glinka had used it in his First Spanish

---

[17] Thus it plays almost exactly the same role in the main body of the movement as the Friar Laurence theme in *Romeo and Juliet*.

Overture, and Balakirev had consolidated it in his first Overture on three Russian themes. To build a whole symphonic subject from a folksong treated with the changing background method may have been new to Tchaikovsky, but the inescapable lack of structural advancement within multiple repetitions of one theme presented no real problem to him, since in all his most important symphonic movements to date his practice had been to close the first subject exactly where it had begun. And so, after a portentous introduction which ushers in the folktune, 'The Crane', in a manner anticipating by two years both the *Promenade* and *The Great Gate of Kiev* from Musorgsky's *Pictures from an Exhibition*, the tune becomes not simply the point of departure for a freely constructed first subject, but constitutes the very vertebrae from which is built the backbone of this huge paragraph of more than 170 bars. A diagram may, perhaps, make Tchaikovsky's procedures, and their relationships to a classical precedent, clearer. Ex. 64 (overleaf) summarises in the very simplest terms the expositions as far as the second subjects of Beethoven's Eroica Symphony, first movement, and Tchaikovsky's Second Symphony, first movement (initial version) and finale. These may usefully be supplemented by Ex. 32, relating to *Romeo and Juliet*.

The second half of 'The Crane', as set out in the Mamontova collection[18] of children's songs which Tchaikovsky had just harmonised, differs from the version in the symphony. The discrepancy is obviously due, at least in part, to Tchaikovsky himself, but the butler at Kamenka, who was evidently exasperated by what he thought was a faulty delivery of the tune, also made a contribution which Tchaikovsky cheerfully acknowledged. 'Credit for the success [of the finale with the audience at the first performance] I do not ascribe to myself, but to the real composer. . . . Pyotr Gerasimovich who, while I was composing, and strumming through "The Crane", constantly came up and hummed:

[Ex. 65]   '19

a version which was presumably in Tchaikovsky's mind when he composed bars 113–16.

Yet Tchaikovsky's greatest debt was not to Pyotr Gerasimovich, nor even, perhaps, to Glinka's First Spanish Overture, but to *Kamarinskaya*. No one believed more fervently than Tchaikovsky that it was in this slight orchestral piece that there lay the origins of the entire Russian

¹⁸ M. A. Mamontova, *A Collection of Children's Songs on Russian and Ukrainian Melodies*, harmonised by Tchaikovsky, No. 18.
¹⁹ *TLP*5, p. 302; *DTC*, pp. 349–50; *YDGC*, p. 90; *TZC*1, p. 402.

Ex. 64

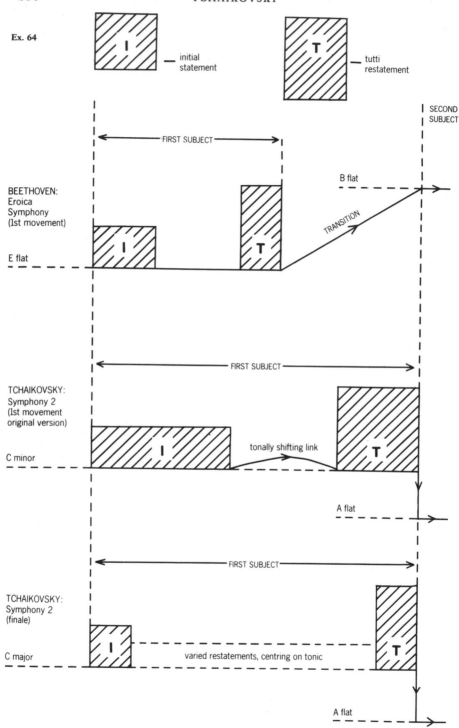

symphonic school, 'just as the whole oak is in the acorn', as he confided to the pages of his diary in 1888.[20] To Madame von Meck eight years earlier he had been even more explicit about his own debt. 'What a stunningly original piece is *Kamarinskaya*, from which all later Russian composers up to the present day (and I, of course, among them) draw, in the most obvious fashion, contrapuntal and harmonic combinations as soon as they have to develop a Russian dance tune.'[21] Without *Kamarinskaya*, that little prodigy of wit and sparkling invention in treating a trivial thematic fragment, this first subject, with its twenty-four statements of the equally slight opening phrase of 'The Crane', could never have been written. The pungent little appoggiatura figure that accompanies one statement of the theme (Ex. 66b) is patently suggested by the obstinate 'wrong note' pedal of one *Kamarinskaya* variation (Ex. 66a), a model which is copied even more explicitly and at far greater length in the development (Ex. 66c). Not that this first subject

Ex. 66

[20] *TD*, p. 215; *YDGC*, p. 450.
[21] *TLP*9, p. 176; *TPM*2, pp. 369–70; *TZC*2, pp. 400–1.

is completely single-minded, for in addition to using the second part of 'The Crane', there is a passage in which Tchaikovsky takes a couple of bars from the coda of his long-forgotten Overture in C minor (see Ex. 6) and fully exploits its whole-tone ramifications (Ex. 67).

Ex. 67

This first subject is a perfect riposte to any who would assert that Tchaikovsky was incapable of composing music of immense vitality which is also abundantly inventive in decorative detail and joyful to its very roots. There is virtually nothing by way of transition, and the second subject, set (as in the original first movement) in A flat, is a gentler creature with a kind of catchy 'rumba' rhythm (Ex. 68a), a theme

Ex. 68

which is quickly ousted by yet more variations on 'The Crane' to complete the exposition. As for the development, this is an almost bizarre mélange of the two subjects tangling with a vastly-stepping bass which rises and falls in huge intervals like the enormous strides of some sportive colossus, leading the two subjects in strange directions (see Ex. 66c); the way in which it twists the second subject within half a dozen bars from D major into a remote tonal region is positively weird (see Ex. 68b). With ever-mounting abandon these ingredients are mixed to ferment the most heady potion Tchaikovsky ever brewed. Musorgsky must have looked with secret envy upon it, especially since Tchaikovsky was able to build it over a time scale which would have been beyond that relatively untutored composer, despite all the marvellous brilliance of his basic conceptual faculties. It is one of the greatest causes for regret in all Tchaikovsky's work that he never again attempted something of the same sort.

The original recapitulation had returned, as expected, to 'The Crane', repeating some old variations, devising some new ones, and exploiting a wider tonal range than in the exposition, before ending firmly in E major. C major is restored with the second subject, and the course of the rest of the movement is straightforward, finishing with a vigorous coda. When revising this finale, Tchaikovsky excised the entire recapitulation of the first subject. It would not be difficult to restore this for modern performances; the effort would be well worthwhile.

With the Second Symphony completed by the beginning of December, Tchaikovsky undertook a modest little labour of love, the composition of a miniature one-movement serenade for Nikolay Rubinstein's name day. This insignificant morsel, scored for flute, two clarinets, horn, trumpet and strings, was performed at Rubinstein's home on the appropriate day, 18 December. Work on the symphony had left Tchaikovsky drained, his eyes were giving him trouble (he had taken to wearing pince-nez which, he was told, suited him admirably), and his nerves were edgy, though he had to admit that his general health was good. 'At the moment I'm surrendering myself to idleness because of the absence of any inspiration or urge to compose,' he reported to Modest on 22 December. 'I was on the point of trying to compose some little romances, but somehow everything came out commonplace, and I can't find any words that really please me.'[22] He did not abandon the search, however, and before the year was out, some at least of his second set of songs, the Six Romances, Op. 16, had been written. As in the first set, each is dedicated to a different person, the first two being offered to the Rimsky-Korsakovs. If the 'Cradle Song' (No. 1) was dedicated to Nadezhda in anticipation of the birth of her first child, it can hardly have been written before January, since this happy event did not take place until 1 September 1873. Perhaps, too, Tchaikovsky felt there was still some appositeness in addressing to her recent bridegroom a song, 'Wait a while' (No. 2), in which a lover begs the departing beloved to remain and revel in the ravishing beauties of the night. There seems no earthly

[22] TLP5, p. 293; YDGC, p. 86; TZC1, p. 396.

reason, however, why he should offer to Nikolay Rubinstein, except in a
moment of mischievous whimsicality, a desperately amorous verse
which he actually wrote himself, and which began 'Thy bright, angelic
image is always with me day and night'.

In the three years since his first set of songs Tchaikovsky had
composed only one other romance, the limp Apukhtin setting of 1870,
'To forget so soon', one of those songs in which the listener is aware
of the strength of feeling in Tchaikovsky's response, yet where he
simultaneously senses something of the wateriness of a written-down
improvisation in which the composer's fingers have too easily slid into
cliché. Though there are better things than this in the Op. 16 set, it is of
less general interest than its predecessor. Always Tchaikovsky has a
ready facility for stringing together a succession of tremulous or
impassioned phrases, an unfailing adroitness for lacing stock harmonies
with appealing dissonance (inner appoggiaturas are a favourite device),
and impeccable skill in forming a shapely, neatly packaged structure
with a carefully devised climax. Yet rarely will the listener immediately
ascribe the melody to Tchaikovsky or, when the song is done, carry away
the memory of some touch that has really illumined the poem. To be
fair, there are some very nice things in these songs – the quiet asymmetry
of the seven-bar vocal phrase, and its following six-bar variant, at the
beginning of the tender 'Cradle Song', for instance, or the sudden
agitated switch from triple to duple pulse for the repeated return of the
song's opening word in 'Wait a while' (No. 2; Ex. 69a) before the

Ex. 69

[Wait awhile! You hasten to bid farewell as the East catches fire with the rays of the sun.]

[The air is filled with the scent of the rose. Beloved! This is life, not daydreams! Life flies away. Wait awhile!]

singer's line moves urgently on above a little patch of appealing chromaticism. Yet the following bar, with its bald seventh chords arranged over a circle of fifths, is a disappointing decline towards formula: Tchaikovsky manages this moment much better when the incident recurs towards the end of the song. Indeed, this whole last stretch is ravishing (Ex. 69b). But the next three songs are uniformly undistinguished. For all its surface passion and the tumult of its piano part, 'Accept but once' (No. 3), with its endless stepwise-descending bass, platitudinous melody, and grossly overwritten accompaniment, is commonplace, while the materials of the next two songs, 'O sing that song' (No. 4), a translation by Pleshcheyev from the English of Felicia Hemans, and 'Thy radiant image' (No. 5), are too slight for Tchaikovsky's resourcefulness to be capable of making anything of real substance from them – though Tchaikovsky himself thought the fifth one the best of the bunch.

By far the most interesting song in this set is the last one, 'Modern Greek Song'. Perhaps it was not altogether coincidence that Tchaikovsky had only recently, at an RMS concert on 22 November, heard a performance of Liszt's *Totentanz* based on the 'Dies irae' theme. A week later he had enthused over it in *The Russian Gazette*. 'With great and amazing mastery Liszt exploits this superb theme, which is characterful to the highest degree, by means of variation form,' he observed[23] – and that is precisely what he himself now did in this sixth song, a lament of women in hell yearning for the joys and blessings of the upper world. Some dozen times the tune, or the first part of it, stalks through the texture, on one occasion advancing its entry by one beat, thus transforming its rhythmic structure, and widening the possibilities at Tchaikovsky's disposal (Ex. 70, bars 1–2), on another shrinking itself, in thoroughly Lisztian fashion, into semiquaver figuration, and embellishing its own stately progress (Ex. 70, bar 3). Unlike Musorgsky,

Ex. 70

[. . . and golden ikons, and, as before . . .]

Tchaikovsky could not command the macabre or satanic on equal terms with Liszt, and set beside his compatriot's *Songs and Dances of Death*, Tchaikovsky's 'Modern Greek Song' cannot but sound a little tame. Yet the variety within this strange and unexpected experiment is impressive.

[23] *TMKS*, p. 86.

If, as a finished and distinguished creation, it cannot compare with the best of Tchaikovsky's Op. 6 songs, such as 'Do not believe, my friend', 'Not a word, O my friend', or the Mignon song, it possesses one attribute they do not: its world lies right outside the walls of the drawing room.

9

TCHAIKOVSKY AS MUSIC CRITIC:
SNOW MAIDEN TO SECOND QUARTET

WHEN, AS REPRESENTATIVE of *The Russian Gazette,* Tchaikovsky attended the revival of Serov's *Rogneda* on 8 September 1872, he was embarking on a stint as music critic that was to last four years, ending sonorously with five articles connected with the opening at Bayreuth in 1876 of the new opera house with the first performances of the *Ring* cycle. Tchaikovsky felt no attraction to musical journalism, and his notices were efficient, readable, but would be of no more than ephemeral worth, were it not for the light they shed upon his values as a mature musician – his sympathies and antipathies, his insights and his blind spots. For this they are invaluable – above all because they reveal his attitude towards many major composers, both past and contemporary. It is not, therefore, simply for completeness of the record that we will break the biographical narrative to scrutinise more closely this corpus of critical writing.

The Russian concert/operatic season lasted from the early autumn to Easter, with a particularly hectic phase during the last few weeks when the theatres and opera houses closed for Lent, and concerts of all sorts proliferated. There is, of course, no way of testing the validity of Tchaikovsky's judgements on performers, though nearly all his criticisms have the marks of discrimination and honesty. If his innate gentleness made him charitable, his honesty could compel him to sternness. He encouraged the young in whom he saw more promise than, as yet, fulfilment, was generous to the ageing artist through whose failing physical accomplishments still shone those precious insights of a deep and abiding artistry, and was as capable of limitless enthusiasm in the presence of great performers like Patti, Christine Nilsson, the Rubinsteins, Laub or von Bülow, as he was possessed by a remorseless spirit of condemnation when confronted by incompetence, self-admiration or plain charlatanism. Like any keen-eared enthusiast for Italian opera, he was a knowledgeable critic of singing, noting precisely a performer's quality of voice, intonation, technique, musicality, gift for characterisation and so on, and passing final judgement in terms which sound truthful, even when denunciatory. He waged a constant battle against the debased standards of the resident Italian opera company, still run during his first season as a critic by that same Merelli who had brought Artôt into his life. Russian musical journalism was boisterous, even rough, and it is against such a background that Tchaikovsky's sometimes devastating verdicts must be set. 'Now in her stentorian voice she will scream out some high note resembling the cry of some great owl, now she'll rattle out a low, almost bass note which makes your flesh creep – and all this out of time with the orchestra, extremely out of tune, wildly, oddly, absurdly . . .'[1] is just one sample of Tchaikovsky's pen at its sharpest, jabbing into the entrails of some dreadful singer in the hope of driving her as rapidly as possible from the boards of the Bolshoy. His predictions for the future of singing in Russia were pessimistic, and this fortified his determination to damn those who, so often winning the enthusiastic approval of undiscriminating fanatics for Italian opera, both symbolised this decline and actively contributed to it. As for Moscow audiences themselves, they were cajoled, castigated and condemned for their mindless support of the deplorable resident Italian opera company, and for the constant failure of the majority to recognise and support real talent. When he himself and so many of his friends were associated with the RMS it can hardly be expected that his notices of the Society's concerts would sound a note of uncorrupted impartiality, though even here he was prepared to fault a colleague and friend.

Despite his merciless attacks on Merelli and his brood, the enduring place in Tchaikovsky's affections of Italian opera itself is clearly apparent. True, he rarely utters more than the briefest comment upon the actual works of Bellini, Donizetti and the like, and there is no doubt that, as a musician, he was aware of the severe limitations of their art. Nevertheless the constant careful attention he pays to the performers in such works is sufficient to show that he did not despise the ends to which their talents were being applied: that is, the revelation of the grace, brilliance and pathos within the melodic gifts of such composers. Rossini he recognised as far more significant. *Il Barbiere di Siviglia* was his supreme achievement, and would 'remain for ever an inimitable model of its own kind'.[2] However, when Rossini attempted the loftier conception of *Guillaume Tell*, Tchaikovsky's enthusiasm faded, and he disagreed with the general consensus of his time that it was Rossini's best work. One suspects that he was attracted to the lighter, less complicated of early-nineteenth-century operas because they possessed for him something akin to that innocence he believed was embodied also in the

[1] *TMKS*, pp. 62–3.   [2] *TMKS*, p. 117.

relatively simple world of late-eighteenth-century music, a world he was soon to begin exploring on his own terms in his own music. *Guillaume Tell* worried him; even more did Verdi. Like Glinka before him, Tchaikovsky felt that the later Italian had somehow desecrated and cheapened this world by capitulating too readily to the demands of Italian audiences – that his works, 'despite the occasional flashes of inspiration which break through, abound in most places with every kind of baggage belonging to composers of the Italian school in general'.[3] To acknowledge that a composer could have his occasional moments of beauty seems to have been Tchaikovsky's way of coping either with someone whose compositions he fundamentally disliked, yet whom he suspected of being of major significance, or else with a composer (often a personal acquaintance) whose severe limitations he could not but recognise, yet whom he did not wish to wound or discourage. In the recent *Aida* he saw signs of redemption, though at the time he feared that it confirmed a trend, already apparent in *Don Carlos*, towards that operatic Antichrist, Wagner. Many years later, after he had come to know *Otello* and discovered his fears to be unfounded, his recognition of Verdi's greatness was to be less clouded.

Of non-Italian operas, Weber's *Der Freischütz* he had loved from boyhood, and it remained for him 'a great product of German art',[4] over which he repeatedly enthused. About Meyerbeer he was divided, rating *Les Huguenots* and *Le Prophète* highly, but judging *L'Africaine* 'unsuccessful in every respect'.[5] For operas by native Frenchmen he already had a particular sympathy. He devoted a large part of one article to Auber, including a summary of those qualities he shared with his race in general. 'Like all good composers of the French school, Auber is distinguished by the elegant purity of his harmonic technique, the abundance of nice, rhythmically striking melodies, by his judicious economy with surface effects, and by his beautiful scoring. Don't expect passion, stormy upsurges, strong spontaneous inspiration from Auber. In his works, as in his life, he is the deft, cheerful, intelligent, worldly-elegant Frenchman.'[6] Does one detect a note of envy sounding through Tchaikovsky's lengthy account of this composer whose uncomplicated career, untroubled by any summons to grapple with novel expressive demands or by any need to go beyond Paris, could be devoted simply to producing, in collaboration with a librettist who was ideal for his needs, a succession of attractive operas, and to quietly receiving the rewards and honours which accrue with prolonged success? Tchaikovsky recognised, of course, the narrow bounds of the French operatic manner, and when Thomas set *Hamlet* he was quick to censure its superficiality. Gounod he

[3] *TMKS*, p. 68.   [4] *TMKS*, p. 45.   [5] *TMKS*, p. 60.   [6] *TMKS*, p. 68.

greatly admired, though not uncritically. It is unfortunate that his regular work as a music critic finished just before he was exposed to the force of a work which was to remain ever after a passion with him – Bizet's *Carmen*.

Unlike the nationalists around Balakirev, Tchaikovsky had no special conditioning towards the major representatives of the German-Austrian tradition, and his response to the music of each was largely a matter of personal idiosyncrasy, hedged round by the limitations to his knowledge of each composer's work. Of pre-classical composers he clearly knew few except by repute. Bach and Handel always elicited respect, but he found them handicapped by the restrictions of the technique available to them. His view is summed up succinctly in his verdict on Bach's Chromatic Fantasia, where 'the splendid fantasy of the old master struggles in vain with the conventional procedures of the compositional routine of that time'.[7] Living in a period in which an awareness of the panorama of musical history was growing, but in which the stage had not been reached when, as today, the work of a long-past composer might be accepted on its own terms, Tchaikovsky could only accord respect, not understanding, unless the music could in some way satisfy the expectations of mid-nineteenth-century aesthetic fashions. (Thus he could only be overwhelmed by Handel's music when performed by mammoth forces such as he experienced at the Crystal Palace in London in 1861.) Haydn fared no better than Bach or Handel. Of course he deserved honour; he had paved the way for Mozart and Beethoven, but his music was merely light and pleasant. Yet Haydn merited a reprieve for services rendered, and should certainly not be entirely excluded from concert programmes, 'for, especially in Russia, Haydn's work is something which our public must experience before it can grow to a full understanding of Beethoven. It is desirable [that Haydn should be played] simply so that his slight, superficial idiom may be used as a standard against which to set the major works of later composers.'[8]

By contrast Tchaikovsky worshipped Mozart – or, more precisely, certain of that composer's works. He thought he understood him, though in fact much of his awe-struck admiration was based upon misunderstanding. One work above all was responsible for his Mozart worship: *Don Giovanni*. Though he was capable of recognising the dramatic weakness of the longer concert-type arias, he could only wonder at the gallery of characters Mozart had created in this opera. Significantly it was to the passionate Donna Anna, pouring out her feelings of sorrow and anger in an uninhibited flood, that he responded

[7] *TMKS*, p. 186.   [8] *TMKS*, p. 124.

most of all. In *Don Giovanni*, with its strong emotions, tense situations and supernatural elements, he was able to find traits which seemed romantic and 'profound', which could match up to contemporary musical expectations, and thus give it a special validity. Little else in Mozart could rouse anything like the same enthusiasm. Works that did were the Jupiter Symphony ('one of the wonders of symphonic music'),[9] especially the quasi-contrapuntal finale, the overture to *Die Zauberflöte*, and the 'Requiem aeternam', that 'marvellous, poetic introduction with the double fugue at the end' which opens the *Requiem*.[10] But in other respects the dramatic gestures of this mass offended against his sense of the propriety essential for church music, though he could not remain unmoved by the 'Lacrymosa'. All these favoured instrumental pieces (and the first movement of the *Requiem*) are notable for demonstrating a high degree of contrapuntal skill. Here, however, there was none of the struggling in vain with 'the conventional procedures of the compositional routine' of an archaic baroque, but a parade of contrapuntal wizardry within the full drama of the classical idiom (for the double fugue of the *Requiem* avails itself of all the tensions of the sonata situation). It was this that commanded Tchaikovsky's admiration; simpler pieces left him unimpressed, and even the D minor Quartet he judged 'rather watery'.[11]

Like all the leading composers of his generation Tchaikovsky was overawed by Beethoven, though it is apparent that he neither properly understood him, nor had much real liking for his works. *Fidelio* did not grip him at all; he completely missed its blazing idealism, judging it a 'rather watery subject, smacking of bourgeois sentiment'.[12] Beethoven might be 'the greatest genius among composers',[13] the Mass in D 'one of the greatest musical works of genius',[14] but such pronouncements could all too easily be mere slogans. When he turns to a work at greater length, as he does with the Eroica Symphony, Tchaikovsky's words sound like a regurgitation of something heard in a history lecture, with little of affection in them. On other occasions he will simply side-step any comment upon the work, even when it is a major piece, like the Appassionata Sonata, or the C sharp minor Quartet. The late string quartets and piano sonatas were evidently beyond his comprehension (he once confessed privately to Kashkin that he could not bear the former), though still subject to his bewildered admiration. His pronouncement on the Ninth Symphony devastatingly reveals his romantic misunderstanding of at least one of these late pieces, for in it he heard 'the cry of hopeless despair of a great creative genius, who has

[9] *TMKS*, p. 234.   [10] *TMKS*, p. 143.   [11] *TMKS*, p. 112.
[12] *TMKS*, p. 84.   [13] *TMKS*, p. 72.   [14] See above, p. 211, note 15.

irrevocably lost his faith in happiness, who has quit life for a world of impossible day-dreams, for a realm of unattainable ideals'.[15] His dutiful comments on other pieces should be set in the context of a revealing remark dropped in one of his later articles: 'It is known that Chopin had an odd, invincible aversion to certain of Beethoven's works which are universally recognised as the very highest examples of art. However, if he had had to write musical notices in a widely distributed journal, he would, of course, have refrained from publishing these idiosyncratic minutiae of his musical make-up. . . .'[16] The works that could appeal to Tchaikovsky were those which came closest to the radiance he saw in a 'rococo' work like Mozart's Jupiter Symphony. Beethoven's Fourth Symphony, for instance, conjured up a serene and joyful world ('Yes, such music so distracts you from the prose of everyday life that for long afterwards you do not believe that war, illness and poverty exist in this world'),[17] and to each movement he could fit a little picture. He liked the Seventh Symphony, too – especially the slow movement – and the Eighth even more. And there is no doubt that wide-eyed respect passes into deep enthusiasm before the slow movement of the Fourth Piano Concerto, simply because he felt it had something to do with fate.

In dealing with composers nearer his own time, who had to grapple with problems he himself could recognise from his own experience, he was sometimes more perceptive. When he wrote of Berlioz that, although he had 'attained in some spheres of his art such a level on the road to his ideal as few artists attain, yet he did not create one work which revealed that balance, that range of technical perfection, that correspondence between depth of content and beauty of form which are characteristics of the greatest works of art,'[18] he was declaring nothing but the truth. This insistence that a composer needed both a musical imagination and a capacity for purely musical invention (i.e. craft) was a cardinal belief underlying all Tchaikovsky's criticism. Not that he always judged composers well with regard to their possession of one or other of these faculties; in making a list of those with an abundance of musical invention, but deficient in imagination, he cites Dargomïzhsky, Chopin (at times) – and, of all people, Schubert, while those with an inverse endowment he lists as Berlioz, Liszt, Balakirev – and Mendelssohn. Yet if he misjudged Mendelssohn here, he redeemed himself with a clear-headed perception of the fundamental weakness of Mendelssohn's works when, speaking apropos the E flat Quartet, Op. 12, he observed that 'in fact the exquisite roundness of his form and the fluidity of his harmonic progressions have been brought to such an ideal purity by Mendelssohn that, strange to say, they have led to sickly sweetness and to

[15] *TMKS*, p. 237.   [16] *TMKS*, p. 271.   [17] *TMKS*, p. 284.   [18] *TMKS*, p. 131.

slickness, if one may so call it.'[19] This, surely, is impeccable. He admired Schumann vastly, even hazarding the bold assertion that 'the music of the second half of the present century will be, in the future history of art, the period that coming generations will call "Schumannesque".'[20] Yet, he added, he did not mean this as a verdict on the quality of Schumann's works. He was highly critical of Schumann's orchestration, though he had great admiration for the content of both the Second and Third Symphonies. Yet it was the piano pieces that won his warmest approval. He had no time for Schumann's verdict on another and younger German composer whom Schumann had seen as the Messiah who would come after Beethoven. Brahms, Tchaikovsky snorted, 'is one of those mediocre composers in which the German school is so rich; he composes smoothly, skilfully, clearly – but without the slightest glint of individual talent.'[21] Many years later the two men were to meet, and Tchaikovsky was to revise, if not completely recant this opinion.

The fact is that all the principles governing the Austro-German symphony – that it was a purely musical organism evolving according to purely musical dictates, framing its structure upon mighty corner posts and stout cross-beams of related keys, braced by the carefully placed cross-stresses of more remote tonal areas – were completely beyond Tchaikovsky, as his own symphonic works – sectionalised, at their best producing a satisfying cumulative experience because he has ordered his elements judiciously, not because he has fused them into an organic whole – bear witness. Equally revealing is his judgement as to who were the two leading symphonists of his own time; they were, of all people, Rubinstein and Raff. As far as a classical composer like Haydn was concerned, he could pity him for having had the misfortune to work in a circumscribed and now obsolete style. In any case Haydn was dead, but a living composer with a different creed was a very different matter. He was a factor in Tchaikovsky's own world, at best a threat, at worst an open enemy. To a certain extent this was Brahms's status; even more it was Wagner's. Tchaikovsky recognised Wagner's position in the vanguard of European music, but was repelled by his egotism and ideals. He condemned him for having abandoned melody and subordinated the singers to the orchestra in his music dramas, rendering them almost superfluous. For Tchaikovsky the singer and melody must remain supreme, and it was this that led him to reject Dargomïzhsky's *Stone Guest*, as well as all composers who sought realism at the expense of musical values. He believed that Wagner had become trapped in his own ideals – and he claimed to have heard, through some unnamed source, that Wagner had confessed a wish to compose symphonies and string

[19] *TMKS*, p. 74.   [20] *TMKS*, p. 38.   [21] *TMKS*, p. 76.

quartets. Over Wagner's purely instrumental works he could enthuse: over the prelude to *Lohengrin*, for instance, or the *Faust* overture, 'one of the most outstanding achievements of German symphonic music. I do not know a single lyrical artistic creation in which the tortures of the human spirit, doubting its own aims, hopes and beliefs, are expressed with such irresistible pathos,' he wrote,[22] perhaps suspecting, with sly glee, that this overture might be a Wagner self-portrait. Certainly he believed that the German had lost his way. 'By virtue of his rich, original gift, Wagner could stand at the head of contemporary symphonists, had not the theoretical cast of his mind and his falsely directed self-esteem deflected him from his real calling.'[23] We shall hear more of Wagner when Tchaikovsky visits Bayreuth in 1876.

In treating the Kuchka his journalistic writings are less useful. His direct dealings with them obstructed the relative objectivity he could achieve in recording his views on other major composers, and his attitudes towards the group changed sharply during these four years of critical activity. In any case, the simple record of his contacts with them yields clearer evidence than all his public pronouncements upon their work. His relationship with the Kuchka was never closer than at that soirée at the Rimsky-Korsakovs' on 7 January 1873, when he played them the finale of his as-yet-unperformed Second Symphony. Yet it would be utterly wrong to conclude that their apparent unanimity on this piece signified at last a complete and united acceptance of Tchaikovsky and his work into their fold. Quite apart from Tchaikovsky's own ambivalence towards the nationalist stream in contemporary Russian composition (and this ambivalence will emerge very clearly by the end of this chapter), the Kuchka itself was a group of widely differing individuals, and was itself changing – indeed, beginning to disintegrate. Already Balakirev had virtually gone. Worn down by the failure of his concert schemes, and driven by necessity to working during the day in the goods department of the Central Railway Company's Warsaw line and to teaching at night, he had sunk into a depressed and self-imposed isolation from which few of the persuasions and encouragements of his friends could draw him. The evening before the Rimsky-Korsakovs' soirée Bessel had arranged a similar event at his own home, and Balakirev had dropped in to hear Tchaikovsky's First Quartet, stopped to play through with Musorgsky the piano duet version of Dargomïzhsky's *Fantasy on Finnish Themes*, and had then left. He was, according to Musorgsky, overwrought, and it seems improbable that either he or Musorgsky was at the Rimsky-Korsakovs' the next evening to share in the enthusiasm for Tchaikovsky's new

[22] *TMKS*, p. 91.   [23] *TMKS*, p. 91.

symphony. As for Cui, who had always viewed himself as the joint leader with Balakirev of the Kuchka, he was growing ever more cantankerous. Enjoying little success as a composer himself, and having at his disposal a regular column in a St Petersburg paper, he increasingly vented his spleen on new works that came into his court for judgement. Almost inevitably Tchaikovsky's journalistic toil in Moscow brought him into open conflict with Cui, which did nothing to improve their relationship. Tchaikovsky was soon to find that Cui's approval of *Romeo and Juliet* did not signify the tone of things to come.

Nor did he find any greater approval with Musorgsky, though this was based less upon Musorgsky's personal animosity towards a composer more successful than himself than upon their fundamentally opposed musical attitudes. Just as Tchaikovsky found repugnant the brand of operatic realism espoused by Musorgsky, so the latter poured scorn upon *The Oprichnik* which Tchaikovsky had written, so Musorgsky believed, 'with the intention of winning public fame and making a name for himself. The composer has ingratiated himself with the public's taste (O Pasha!),[24] and at the same time has applied himself to his work very ardently and sincerely (O Sadïk!). First, the public's tastes are fickle; secondly, the public wants something Russian from Russian artists; thirdly, it is shameful to play with art for personal ends. It emerges that Sadïk, like a true Pasha, is not without cynicism, and openly preaches the religion of unconditional beauty,' he wrote to Stasov on the very day of the Rimsky-Korsakovs' soirée.[25] That Tchaikovsky should have applauded the slender little song about the parrot in Act 2 of *Boris Godunov*, when it was performed at Cui's soirée the night before Bessel's, only increased Musorgsky's contempt for Tchaikovsky's operatic values. As for Tchaikovsky, although he later admitted to Nadezhda von Meck that he suspected Musorgsky of being the most gifted of all the Kuchka, yet he could not accept work that, to his ears, was all too often wrong-headed, rough – even illiterate, and shapeless. 'I whole-heartedly commit Musorgsky's music to the devil,' he roared to Modest in November 1874[26] concerning *Boris Godunov*, which had at last been published and performed earlier in the year. There was no hope of accommodation between the musical tastes and attitudes of two such men.

Tchaikovsky's relationship with Borodin is more clouded. The very

[24] Pasha Sadïk was the nickname Musorgsky gave Tchaikovsky. It was the title by which a certain Polish writer, Mikhail Tchaikovsky (Czajkowski), who had joined with Mickiewicz at the time of the Crimean War to raise forces to fight against the Russians in Turkey, became known after he had embraced the religion of Islam.

[25] A. Orlova (ed.), *Trudi i dni M. P. Musorgskovo* (Moscow, 1963), p. 268.

[26] *TLP*5, p. 372; *TPB*, p. 91; *YDGC*, p. 109.

dearth of information suggests that it was not very close, though it is difficult to believe that there was not always some mutual respect, despite the infamous verdict Tchaikovsky was to deliver in 1877 to Nadezhda von Meck on Borodin and other members of the Kuchka. Tchaikovsky was certainly drawn to Borodin as a man. 'I have the most cordial memory of the deceased,' he wrote to Vladimir Stasov in May 1887, some two months after Borodin's death. 'I liked very much his gentle, subtle and refined nature. It is distressing to think that he is no longer of this world.'[27]

Borodin must surely have approved the finale of Tchaikovsky's Second Symphony, and if the Rimsky-Korsakovs were in raptures over it, so was Vladimir Stasov. Stasov, being no composer himself, had no compositional axe to grind. Standing thus apart from the clash of conflicting musical creeds, he could assess each talent objectively and foster it as best he could by providing material upon which its creative impulses could feed and grow. If leadership can consist in offering a group of composers a succession of irresistible suggestions for subjects upon which their works might be written, then Stasov had become, now that Balakirev had withdrawn, the real leader of the Kuchka. Yet he saw no reason why he should confine the bounty of his liberal fund of ideas to this circle. Confronted at the Rimsky-Korsakovs' with this new confirmation of Tchaikovsky's gifts, Stasov that very evening talked with him about what his next composition might be, and on parting from Tchaikovsky, applied his fertile mind to scouting for suitable topics. Within an hour he had one, to which he added two more before dispatching a letter hard on Tchaikovsky's heels when the latter returned home on 8 January 1873. The three suggestions in it were Shakespeare's *The Tempest* ('You'd be able to do a most wonderful overture on this subject'),[28] Scott's *Ivanhoe* and Gogol's *Taras Bulba*. 'I think you'd be able to cook up something even more filled with poetry, passion and strength than your incomparable overture, *Romeo and Juliet*,' Stasov wrote apropos his last suggestion.[29]

Tchaikovsky pondered these proposals for a fortnight, trying to recall *Ivanhoe*, and re-reading both *The Tempest* and *Taras Bulba*. Then he announced his choice: it was to be *The Tempest*. He hoped that sometime he would do a piece on *Taras Bulba*, but since both *The Oprichnik* and the Second Symphony, his two most recent major works, were very Russian in character, he preferred now to tackle something foreign. His faith in Stasov's judgement was already firm, and he straightway sought his

[27] *TLP*14, p. 103; *YDGC*, p. 412.
[28] *TZC*1, p. 398; *DTC*, p. 354; *YDGC*, p. 86.
[29] *YDGC*, pp. 86–8.

counsel on a point that was troubling him. 'Does there need to be a tempest in *The Tempest*? That is, is it essential to depict the fury of the elements in an overture written on a piece in which this incidental circumstance [the tempest] serves simply as the point of departure for the whole dramatic action? . . . If a tempest is necessary, where should it go: at the beginning or in the middle? If it's not necessary, why not call the overture *Miranda*?'[30] Stasov did not fail him, and a further fortnight later Tchaikovsky was thanking him profusely for sending 'a superb programme, enticing and inspiring to the highest degree'.[31] He had no intention of hurrying the work, however, and for the moment all his time was being taken up in making the vocal score of *The Oprichnik*, and in writing a series of articles, 'Beethoven and His Time', for the periodical, *The Citizen*[32] – as well as, of course, by his regular teaching and journalistic commitments. In any case, before he could find time to start upon *The Tempest*, he was suddenly pressed to undertake another task: the provision of incidental music to a new play by Ostrovsky, *The Snow Maiden*.

During the earlier part of 1873 the Maly Theatre was closed for substantial renovations, and only the stage of the Bolshoy was available for the dramatic, operatic and ballet companies. With facilities so restricted, it occurred to Vladimir Begichev, who was in charge of the repertoire of the Imperial Theatres in Moscow, that he might mount a production of some new 'spectacular' involving all three companies. To this end he approached Ostrovsky, who responded enthusiastically, choosing as his subject a fairy tale, *The Snow Maiden*. Music was, of course, required, and this was commissioned from Tchaikovsky in the middle of March. If Ostrovsky had to work quickly, even more haste was needed of the composer, who could not set about some at least of his music until he had received Ostrovsky's text. Yet, Kashkin recalled, the composition of this very substantial score weighed lightly on Tchaikovsky:

Spring had already begun, and her approach always put Pyotr Ilich in an enthusiastic, poetic mood. . . . The spring of 1873 was, I believe, quite early, so that the composition of the music to this 'spring tale' coincided with the arrival of spring itself. Pyotr Ilich laboured with unusual enthusiasm, and because he had to proceed very rapidly, he even worked during the evenings, contrary to his usual habit. Thus in

---

[30] *TLP5*, p. 298; *DTC*, p. 354.

[31] *TLP5*, p. 299; *TZC1*, pp. 400–1; *DTC*, p. 356; *YDGC*, p. 88.

[32] The series was never completed since, after four of Tchaikovsky's instalments had been printed, *The Citizen* ceased publication.

three weeks he managed to finish this bulky score, at the same time continuing with scrupulous regularity to give his lessons at the Conservatoire. If you bear in mind that there were twenty-seven hours of these lessons each week, then the speed with which this work was written will seem almost incredible.[33]

Yet on 6 April Tchaikovsky could already report the composition finished and request payment of the 350 roubles that had been agreed as his fee. He had, in fact, completed his share ten days ahead of Ostrovsky. The première took place on 23 May. That *The Snow Maiden* was not particularly successful was not the fault of Tchaikovsky's music, for this seems to have pleased everyone except Cui, who was scathing. 'The most banal ideas, the most trite harmonies, rough finish – or rather, absence of finish or form – clumsiness, lack of taste or refinement; these are the characteristic features of the music to *The Snow Maiden*,' he vituperated.[34] Nikolay Rubinstein, the conductor at the first performance, was so taken by Tchaikovsky's contribution that after the play had been taken out of the theatre's repertoire, he insisted upon performing the music uncut at one of the RMS concerts. Even more significant, Tchaikovsky himself retained his affection for it, and thought of using it as the basis for an opera. When Rimsky-Korsakov forestalled him by bringing out his *Snow Maiden* in 1882, Tchaikovsky was so upset that for some years he avoided making that work's acquaintance.

Ostrovsky's tale of the young enchanted Snow Maiden, daughter of Frost and Spring, is known outside Russia solely through Rimsky-Korsakov's opera, but since this keeps very close to the original drama, it gives a very fair idea of the piece for which Tchaikovsky was the first to provide music. The Snow Maiden can survive only so long as her heart is unwarmed by love. Drawn by a wish to live as other girls do, she enters the human world, unwittingly disrupts the wedding of Kupava and Mizgir when the latter falls in love with her on sight, is accused by Kupava and brought before Tsar Berendey for judgement, is told she must marry, and is finally destroyed when the warmth of the love that grows in her heart for Mizgir makes her vulnerable to the rays of Yarilo, the sun god. Tchaikovsky provided nineteen separate numbers for this fantastic tale – an introduction before the Prologue, an entr'acte apiece before three of the four acts, two very substantial dance movements (a dance and chorus for the birds in the Prologue, and a tumblers' dance in Act 3), a march for Tsar Berendey in Act 4, a couple of melodramas (the second essentially a repetition of the entr'acte before Act 2), and an orchestral passage to support the appearance in Act 3 of the wood sprite

[33] *KVC*, p. 85; *TZC*1, p. 405; *DTC*, pp. 264–5.   [34] *DTC*, p. 266.

and the apparition of the false snow maiden (one of the devices to thwart Mizgir's advances, for which the Snow Maiden is not yet ready). The remaining nine numbers were vocal pieces of various lengths, including a monologue for Frost, a chorus to accompany the procession with the maslenitsa (the carnival effigy), three songs for Lel, the shepherd who is the first to touch the Snow Maiden's heart but who finally makes a match with Kupava, and a khorovod which Ostrovsky required to be founded on the folksong, 'Ay, vo pole liponka', and which also acts as the entr'acte before Act 3.

Signs of haste may be expected in a work composed as swiftly as *The Snow Maiden*. In particular one notices moments when the endings do not match up to a good beginning – like, for instance, the limp conclusion to Ex. 71. That Tchaikovsky never used his music as the basis

Ex. 71

[Greetings to thee, O most wise, great Berendey, silver-haired sovereign, father of thine own land.]

for a full-length opera is not a matter for much regret. He himself admirably assessed his own work when, some six and a half years later, he wrote to Nadezhda von Meck: '*The Snow Maiden* is not one of my best works . . . [but] it is one of my favourite offspring. . . . I think the happy, spring-like mood with which I was filled at the time must be audible in the music.'[35] Yet it was not only his buoyancy of mood, but also his pleasure in the fairy tale that carried Tchaikovsky through the work so expeditiously. *The Snow Maiden* captivated him – and if, from among the subjects that Stasov had set before him at the beginning of the year, he had preferred to choose something Western, his response to Ostrovsky's utterly Russian play was as deeply and consistently national as in any of his works. Not only do the more substantial instrumental

[35] *TLP8*, p. 434; *TPM2*, pp. 262–3; *DTC*, p. 266.

movements tend to grow by repetitive procedures rooted in Glinka precedents; the score also incorporates at least a dozen folksongs. Half of these were from the Prokunin collection Tchaikovsky had edited the previous year, and a further three had appeared in his earlier fifty arrangements for piano duet.[36]

The composer confessed that he had 'somewhat modified' these melodies (at least, the Prokunin tunes),[37] but in some instances this is an understatement. In *The Snow Maiden* the very least he did to any of them was to compose a continuation to make a larger entity (as in 'Brusila's Song' [No. 15, bars 13ff.]), while on other occasions he took only a small part of the tune, squaring it up rhythmically to suit his purpose, as in the birds' dance of No. 2 (Ex. 72), or in the 'Chorus to Accompany the

Ex. 72

Maslenitsa' (No. 4), where a $\frac{7}{4}$ bar is expanded into a three-bar phrase (Ex. 73; in the tenor/choral continuation the first two solo phrases are folksong, the third Tchaikovsky's own – and quite admirable – extension). In fact, nothing reveals more clearly Tchaikovsky's attitude towards folksong than his treatment of these borrowed melodies in *The*

[36] The folksongs identified (there are more than Tchaikovsky disclosed to Rimsky-Korsakov) are as follows:
'Vot sizïy orol' (Prokunin, No. 31) in 'Dances and Chorus of Birds' (No. 2, bar 58)
'Davno skazano' (Prokunin, No. 19) in 'Chorus to Accompany the Maslenitsa' (No. 4)
'U knyazya Volkonskovo' (Prokunin, No. 6) in ibid. (bar 18)
'U vorot' (Prokunin, No. 23) in 'Lel's Second Song' (No. 7, bar 13)
'Ne khmel moyu golovushu klonit' (*T5oRF*, No. 14) in 'Chorus of the Blind Gusli Players' (No. 9)
'Ay, vo pole liponka' (Prach's collection, No. 126) in 'Khorovod' (No. 12)
'Ya po berezhku pokhazhivala' (Prokunin, No. 2) in 'Lel's Third Song' (No. 14a)
'Ne shum shumit' (*T5oRF*, No. 21) in 'Lel's Third Song' (second version, No. 14b)
'Gde zh tï bïla' (Prokunin, No. 25) in 'Brusila's Song' (No. 15)
'Oy, utushka moya lugovaya' (*T5oRF*, No. 36) in 'Tsar Berendey's March' (No. 18, bar 46)
'A mï prosu seyali' (Prach's collection, No. 121) in ibid., (bar 120)
'Vo gornitse' (Villebois's collection, No. 99) in the finale (No. 19)
[37] Letter to Rimsky-Korsakov of 19 Sept. 1876. *TLP6*, p. 67; *DTC*, p. 266.

Ex. 73

[Early the cocks began to crow.]

Snow Maiden. For him the people's musical artefacts were not sacred, even if they were precious. If folksongs needed modification or supplementation to suit their broader function in his work, then modified or supplemented they would be, for he had faith enough in their capacity to retain a recognisable character of their own, even when so changed. And mostly they do. The most impressive example of supplementation is in No. 7, the second song for Lel, where the folksong (converted from the minor to the major) is placed, not at the beginning, but in bars 9 to 16 as the continuation of Tchaikovsky's own initial eight bars, which marry so well with it that the whole sixteen-bar stretch sounds like a single conception. By contrast, Lel's third song (No. 14a) is a disaster. Not only is the tune (Ex. 74a) violated; the harmonisation of the first phrase is weak, while the contrived modulation to the dominant adds a final injury to insult (Ex. 74b).[38] For Lel's first song (No. 6) Tchaikovsky avoided folksong altogether, turning to redundant music from his ill-fated *Undine*, and adapting the heroine's aria, 'The waterfall is my uncle', to Ostrovsky's text. From the same opera he also transferred the Introduction to serve as Introduction to this new piece.[39]

If performances of Rimsky-Korsakov's opera are rare in the West, the chances of Ostrovsky's play ever being performed may be counted negligible. Yet some of Tchaikovsky's music would be well worth rescuing for the occasional concert performance, especially if a choral society and orchestra (with, perhaps, a tenor soloist) is seeking some effective but not very demanding material with which to complete a

[38] It is significant that there exists a second, completely different setting of this text using another folktune whose original form is preserved almost intact. Whether this was done at the request of the theatre (who had a right to require such changes) is not known. Tchaikovsky himself, however, did not renounce his earlier version, and both appeared in the Jurgenson catalogue.

[39] It is not impossible that other movements in *The Snow Maiden* may be appropriations from *Undine*.

Ex. 74

Tu - cha so gro - mom...

programme. Most of the better movements in *The Snow Maiden* are near the beginning. Clearly Tchaikovsky's inspiration began to flag under the intensive demands being made upon it, and there are some unremarkable, even weak movements in the last three acts: the 'Chorus of Blind Gusli Players' (No. 9),[40] the 'Chorus of People and Courtiers' (No. 11), the 'Tumblers' Dance' (No. 13), 'Lel's Third Song' (No. 14: both versions), and 'Brusila's Song' (No. 15). Nor does the finale (No. 19) show much enterprise. But even in these last acts there are some good things, notably the delightful 'Khorovod' (No. 12), the monologue (No. 17b) in which Spring, supported by a chorus of flowers, grants her daughter's wish to be able to feel love, and (intermittently) 'Tsar Berendey's March' (No. 18), especially the first part of the concluding chorus, which is based upon a folksong traditionally associated with the millet-sowing ceremony which it accompanies in the play. However, all

[40] It was at Ostrovsky's special request that the first three lines of each verse were sung by a solo voice, the remaining three by the men's chorus.

the Prologue would be worth doing: the attractive Undine-derived Introduction, the colourful and substantial 'Dances and Chorus of Birds' (No. 2), the striking 'Monologue of Frost' (No. 3) with its oboe melody which could as easily be folk-derived as any of Tchaikovsky's borrowed material, and the 'Chorus to Accompany the Maslenitsa' (No. 4), perhaps with the melodrama (No. 5a) tacked on. All three entr'actes contain some charming music – above all the first (No. 5b), in which two clarinets duet freely and freshly on a soft cushion of strings. Lel's second song (No. 7) is an attractive piece, too – and there would be some justification for including his first song (No. 6), which Undine should once have sung.

With his regular income supplemented by the bonus of 350 roubles for the *Snow Maiden* music, Tchaikovsky decided he could travel abroad that summer. His memories of Switzerland were still vivid, and his first intention was to devote a whole month to exploring further the beauties of that country. He knew the trip would be expensive, and from Bessel he requested an advance of 250 roubles against the royalties of *The Oprichnik*, while from Jurgenson he also collected another 200 or so roubles owing to him. Even Bessel could scarcely deny him such a favour, for Tchaikovsky's own attitude towards both his publishers was marked by that same generosity he showed to all his friends and family. Realising that, as yet, he could have no great commercial value to them, he gave Bessel without any charge not only his Op. 16 romances but also his Second Symphony, and when *The Snow Maiden* proved to be less of a success than had been hoped, he voluntarily halved his fee from Jurgenson. On 6 June he left Moscow. Before setting out for Europe he visited both Nizy and Kamenka, staying about a fortnight at the former, and enjoying not only Kondratyev's but also Apukhtin's company. While there he caught a chill – from bathing, he believed – and for some days after his arrival at Kamenka he remained indisposed. This upset did not prevent him from suddenly conceiving, on the way from Nizy to Kamenka, an embryo for the first theme of a new symphony, to the composition of which he promptly determined to devote the summer. Though this project evaporated as quickly as it had materialised, the theme soon found a home in the *Capriccioso* for piano, Op. 19, No. 5. While in Kamenka he was flattered to hear that Liszt had expressed a wish to meet him if he should be in Europe, and he decided he would add Weimar to his itinerary. This intention was never fulfilled, however, and when he left Kamenka on 8 July, he headed via Breslau to Dresden, where he spent five days in the company of Jurgenson and his wife, proceeded with them to Cologne, and thence to Zurich.

Tchaikovsky spent only ten days in Switzerland, for his travelling schemes had now become more wide-ranging. The impressions of his journeys were recorded in a diary covering a period of little more than a month (23 June–30 July), and which is the earliest of his journals to survive. Many of the jottings in it are trivial, but they are enough to show that he suffered minor internal disorders over which he fussed, that his moods were changeable, and that he found much in Switzerland that gave him pleasure. His travels took him first to Zurich ('the Rhine falls are magnificent . . . Zurich's a charming place'),[41] and Lucerne, from which he visited Mount Rigi, ascending by the new mountain railway whose 'rack-and-pinion' mechanism was a source of wonder to him. Thence he sped to Bern, Vevey (where he was overcome by a longing for his homeland – though he did add 'but, then, distance lends enchantment'),[42] Montreux, and finally Geneva. On 28 or 29 July he left for Italy, passing through Turin, stopping briefly in Milan, and enjoying greatly a trip on Lake Como. He had planned to explore Italy quite widely, but the heat proved unbearable and drove him northwards to Paris, where he arrived on 2 August. Paris he always found enchanting and marvellously rejuvenating, and he remained about a week, as long as his funds permitted. In the middle of August he arrived at the last destination of his round of summer visits: Usovo.

The whirlwind rapidity of his European excursion had left no time for composition, even if he had felt inclined to work, and when he arrived on Shilovsky's estate, his creative faculties were thoroughly refreshed. Shilovsky himself was away, and the absolute peace and freedom at Usovo – and the fact that his return to Moscow was barely a month away – encouraged him to turn his thoughts to purposeful composition. On 19 August he set about *The Tempest*. As already recorded, Stasov had at the beginning of February set out in detail a suggested scheme for the work, developing the plan he had sketched when first proposing the idea to Tchaikovsky, and resolving unequivocally Tchaikovsky's doubts about the need for 'a tempest in *The Tempest*'. 'Of course there must be!' Stasov exclaimed:

Certainly, certainly, certainly! Without it the overture won't be an overture, and the whole programme will be changed! [In my earlier letter] I weighed every moment, both for their continuity and their contrasts. I think, therefore, that it would be a pity to spoil it. I had thought of presenting the sea twice, at the beginning and at the end – only at the beginning it would be *introductory*, quiet and gentle, and Prospero, uttering his magic words, would break this calm and raise a storm. But I think that this storm should differ from all preceding

[41] *TD*, p. 6; *TZC*1, p. 411.   [42] *TD*, p. 7; *TZC*1, p. 412.

ones in that it should *begin suddenly*, at full strength, in utter turmoil, and should not grow or arise *by degrees*, as normally happens. . . . Let your storm rage and engulf the Italian boat with the princes in it, and immediately afterwards subside. . . . And now, after this picture, let another begin – the enchanted island of wonderful beauty, and Miranda passing across it with light tread, a creation of even more wonderful beauty – all sun, with a smile of happiness. A moment of conversation between her and Prospero, and immediately afterwards the youth, Ferdinand, who fills her with wonder, and with whom she immediately falls in love. I think a motif of someone who is falling in love, a substantial crescendo that bursts into bloom, [stemming from what is] plainly drawn in Shakespeare at the end of Act 1, should exactly match the requirements of your talent and your whole nature. After this I would suggest the appearance of Caliban, a bestial and base slave, and then Ariel toying with the Italian princes: the inspiration for him is the lines which Shakespeare himself wrote at the end of the first act, to my mind a whole picture in themselves:

> Come unto these yellow sands,
>   And then take hands:
> Curtsied when you have, and kiss'd –
>   The wild waves whist, –
> Foot it featly here and there;
> And, sweet sprites, the burden bear.

– two strophes in all.

After Ariel, Miranda and Ferdinand should appear for a second time, but now at the height of their passion; then the majestic figure of Prospero, renouncing his magic power and sadly bidding farewell to all his past: finally a picture of the sea, now calm and quiet, lapping the desert and deserted island, while all the former brief inhabitants fly away in their boat to distant happy Italy.

Taking all this in such an order, I consider it quite impossible to omit the sea at the beginning and end, and to call the overture *Miranda*.[43]

Tchaikovsky thanked Stasov very warmly for his programme, but declared that he had no intention of attempting the piece until circumstances permitted him the freedom to do it justice. At Usovo, with Shilovsky absent, he now found conditions of work ideal to a degree that he had never before experienced. 'I can't convey to you my state of bliss

[43] *TZC*1, pp. 399–400; *DTC*, p. 355.

during those two weeks,' he wrote to Nadezhda von Meck in 1878, recalling this time. 'I was in a kind of exalted, blissful frame of mind, wandering during the day alone in the woods, towards evening over the immeasurable steppes, and sitting at night by the open window listening to the solemn silence of this out-of-the-way place – a silence broken occasionally by some indistinguishable sound of the night. During these two weeks I wrote *The Tempest* in rough without any effort, as though moved by some supernatural force.'[44] Composition of the work took, in fact, only eleven days. However, the return of Shilovsky shattered this peace, and the scoring was delayed until after Tchaikovsky's return to Moscow early in September.

The first performance took place on 19 December 1873 at an RMS concert conducted by Nikolay Rubinstein, the Society paying Tchaikovsky 200 roubles as fee for the work. It enjoyed sufficient success to be repeated at a special concert later in the season. St Petersburg – and Stasov – heard it in November 1874, when it was conducted by Nápravník. Stasov and Rimsky-Korsakov attended the first rehearsal. 'What a delight your *Tempest* is!' the father of Tchaikovsky's invention enthused:

> What an incomparable piece! Of course the storm itself is inconsequential and isn't marked by any originality, Prospero is unremarkable – and finally, near the end, there is a very ordinary cadence just like something out of an Italian operatic finale – but these are three tiny blemishes. All the rest is wonder upon wonder! Caliban, Ariel, the love scene – all these belong among the *loftiest* of musical creations. In both love scenes, what beauty, what languor, what passion! . . . Then that magnificently wild, ugly Caliban, Ariel's miraculous flights and sporting – all these creations are absolutely capital! And, again, the orchestration in these scenes – wonderful! Both of us, Rimsky-Korsakov and I, send you our profound, most profound compliments, and firmly shake your hand.[45]

Even Cui was won over: 'a most fine, most impassioned, talented composition, wonderfully, sonorously and beautifully scored,' he judged it to the readers of the *St Petersburg Gazette*.[46] *The Tempest* was also to enjoy Balakirev's approval.

Yet the chorus of praise was not unanimous. Tchaikovsky was particularly upset by Laroche's review, which detected the influence of certain specific composers (Glinka, Schumann – and Litolff) in his work, and faulted the structure of *The Tempest*, though it warmly approved the

[44] *TLP*7, p. 232; *TPM*1, pp. 307–8.   [45] *DTC*, p. 356–7; *TZC*1, p. 450.
[46] *DTC*, p. 357.

love music, and the characterisations of Ariel and Caliban. 'I'm not offended that he doesn't particularly like *The Tempest*: I didn't expect him to, and I'm glad that he does praise at least some details. What I find unpleasant is the way he has generally characterised me, from which it appears that I have pilfered from every living composer,' he complained bitterly to Modest.[47]

Stasov never fully grasped what Tchaikovsky had achieved in his earlier treatment of a Shakespearean theme. 'Unfortunately in your first overture, *Romeo and Juliet*, you cut out the nurse . . . and the picture of the early Italian dawn during the love scene,' he lamented in the same letter that set out *The Tempest* programme.[48] Stasov was attracted more to the participants than to their actions. His approach was essentially picturesque and catholic (hence his criticism of Tchaikovsky for the missed opportunities in *Romeo and Juliet*), and his programme for *The Tempest* was a panorama which denied Tchaikovsky the opportunity for close dramatic engagements, demanding instead a wide range of contrasted and precisely characterised invention to be distributed among a succession of almost unconnected sections. These were given an overall shape by being organised in a mirror structure, with the portrayals of Ariel and Caliban at the centre. Tchaikovsky followed Stasov's plan closely.[49] The sea frames the piece. Prospero's utterance is a solemn chordal phrase alternating with darting fragments of music for Ariel, whom he dispatches to raise the storm; the whole of this section is underpinned by a long-sounding horn note clearly signifying (as in the canon in Act I of *Ruslan and Lyudmila*) the binding spell of enchantment. The storm itself follows, rising and falling a little less abruptly, perhaps, than Stasov had envisaged, and the magic island appears (again a long horn note is heard). There is no dialogue between Miranda and Prospero, however; instead the lovers commune forthwith in richly romantic tones. Ariel appears ahead of Caliban; then the lovers return, signifying the 'height of their passion' by ending with the most tempestuous (and loudest) emotional declaration that had so far erupted anywhere in Tchaikovsky's music. Prospero pronounces his renunciation (this time symbolically breaking the horn note), and the gently undulating sea closes the piece.

[47] *TLP*5, p. 381; *TZC*1, p. 452; *TPB*, p. 93; *DTC*, p. 357.

[48] *TZC*1, p. 400; *DTC*, p. 355.

[49] Tchaikovsky himself briefly summarised the plan of the work at the beginning of the score: 'The sea. The magician Prospero sends his obedient spirit Ariel to raise a storm, of which the boat carrying Ferdinand becomes a victim. The enchanted island. The first timid stirring of Miranda's and Ferdinand's love. Ariel. Caliban. The pair of lovers surrender to the exultations of passion. Prospero casts away his magic power and leaves the island. The sea.'

Because *The Tempest* was patterned as a procession of neatly ordered but essentially self-contained chunks of representative material, rather than compounded, as *Romeo and Juliet* had been, by isolating the basic forces of conflict within Shakespeare's play and embodying them in a sonata structure, thus permitting the tensions, clashes and resolutions of the sonata principle to articulate the drama, this new work could not hope to match the achievement of the earlier one. And if the very nature of the piece was of a lower musical order than *Romeo and Juliet*, so, regrettably, was some of the musical invention. When Stasov faulted the storm section he was absolutely right, but his judgement carried none of the imperative that was implicit in Balakirev's critical utterances, and Tchaikovsky made no attempt to revise the piece. Its defects are the sadder when set against the larger quantity of good, sometimes excellent music it contains.

The opening, which Tchaikovsky informed Rimsky-Korsakov was influenced by the beginning of Wagner's *Rheingold* (though Rimsky-Korsakov said that he could see no resemblance),[50] is solemn and arresting, starting with a slow succession of six chords hinging on the single note they hold in common (thus, maybe, signifying the binding power of magic), decorated by the magisterial undulations of the strings and the flickering lights of the woodwind playing on the surface. Through this texture stalks a solemn brass phrase, the one thematic element which crosses the boundaries between the constituent sections of the piece, and which thus affords some thematic integration. And if Ariel is portrayed in little more than fleet, colour-contrasted figuration which might seem more at home in a ballet divertissement than in a work with symphonic pretensions, Caliban leaps magnificently out of the score (Ex. 75). Surprisingly, Mendelssohn's name does not occur among those cited by Laroche as influencing Tchaikovsky, for the 'Bottom-as-ass' theme in the overture of the *Midsummer Night's Dream* music, which Tchaikovsky so much admired, surely suggested the plunging seventh which is such a prominent feature of this vigorously earthy portrayal of Shakespeare's man-monster. As for the lovers' music, the paragraph is one of the most perfectly wrought passages in all Tchaikovsky's music. The phrase from which it grows (Ex. 76a) has been censured for triviality – but surely it could be no more than the most

[50] Kashkin probably shed a clearer light upon Tchaikovsky's relationship to the beginning of Wagner's tetralogy when he quoted the composer thus: 'Here is a true man of genius who had the courage to go through with his conception in all its purity. I had exactly the same intention at the beginning of *The Tempest*, but I was afraid this would be too monotonous, and so added the little wind phrases which were quite superfluous.' (*KVC*, p. 95.) Tchaikovsky was thus recognising a similarity of intention, rather than admitting a direct influence.

Ex. 75

slender and ingenuous of conceptions if it was to capture at all the child-like innocence and hesitancy of the first stirrings of passion when one of the lovers is a girl who has never before encountered any man, save her own father. Once stated, however, this phrase shows remarkable powers of growth, first widening its intervals and strengthening its contours (Ex. 76b and c); then, by incorporating elements from bars 2 and 4 of the first phrase into a new, broader melodic line (Ex. 76d), it swells in emotional force and scope to burst into as open-hearted an

Ex. 76

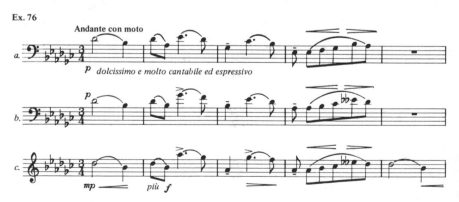

expression of fresh young passion as is to be found in any music. Harmonically there are some lovely touches, too: the sudden re-entry, at the end of Ex. 76d, of the cadential bar of the first phrase, now set in a neapolitan harmonic region, for instance. Yet the most striking moment of all comes at the end, when the melodic figure of bar 2 of the original theme descends to the bass to support a chromatic configuration as tender and unforgettable as anything Tchaikovsky ever wrote (Ex. 77). It would almost have been worth composing *The Tempest* for these four bars alone.

After the charms of Usovo, the return to Moscow that autumn must have seemed particularly harsh to Tchaikovsky. Troubles with his teeth,

Ex. 77

worries over the fortunes of *The Oprichnik* – and, of course, his weighty work as Conservatoire teacher and music critic – beset him. Yet he could still find time for some relatively undemanding composition, and work on scoring *The Tempest* alternated with the composing during October of two romances, 'Take my heart away' and 'Blue eyes of spring', for inclusion in two issues of the periodical *Nouvelliste*, and the compiling of two sets of piano pieces, the Six Pieces, Op. 19, finished early in November, and the Six Pieces on a Single Theme, Op. 21, completed a month later. The second of these sets was dedicated to Anton Rubinstein in gratitude for the latter's inscription of one of his recent piano pieces to Tchaikovsky. True to his general aversion to his former pupil's music, Rubinstein neither acknowledged the dedication nor ever played these pieces in public. Fortunately others appreciated the two sets of pieces more readily, and their swift publication (by Jurgenson and Bessel respectively) provided, with the fee for the performance of *The Tempest*, a much needed relief in Tchaikovsky's financial affairs. Some of his other compositions were also giving him more cause for joy. Not the *Snow Maiden* music, if judged by Cui's withering review – but this at least was balanced by news that *The Oprichnik* would be produced in St Petersburg in the spring. A month later came the successful première of *The Tempest*.

It was probably this upward turn in his compositional fortunes which roused his creative morale, stimulating him to a major undertaking: the composition of a second string quartet. He began it early in the New Year, and composed the entire piece at remarkable speed. 'None of my pieces has ever flowed out of me so easily and simply,' he later wrote to Modest.[51] 'I wrote it almost in one sitting.' Completed on 30 January 1874, the work was heard at a soirée at Nikolay Rubinstein's in the middle of February. Anton was present, and expressed himself with his customary mercilessness towards Tchaikovsky's music,[52] but the rest of the company were delighted by it, as was the audience at the first public performance on 22 March in Moscow.

The Second Quartet consolidates many of the practices and principles instituted by its predecessor. The scherzos of both works gain much of their character from the alternation of duple and triple rhythms, but whereas the variable metres of the First Quartet are flexible alternatives within four-bar phrases built from consistent three-beat bars, those of the Second Quartet operate at a deeper structural level, mixing bars of two and three beats, thus constantly dislocating the basic metre to generate a series of limping three-bar phrases ($2 + 2 + 3$ beats; Ex. 78),

[51] *TLP*5, p. 372; *TZC*1, pp. 442 and 449; *TPB*, p. 91; *DTC*, p. 494; *YDGC*, p. 109.

[52] It is possible that Tchaikovsky did heed some of Anton Rubinstein's criticisms, and made some revisions to the quartet after this private performance.

Ex. 78

later twice expanded by the incorporation sequentially of one or two extra two-beat bars (thus building phrases of $2 + 2 + 2 + 3$, or even $2 + 2 + 2 + 2 + 3$ bars). With its harmonic language whose simple sturdiness is garnished with some arresting touches, it is an attractive piece. If the scherzo itself may seem to conceal a waltz, the trio exhibits this dance explicitly, inverting the final cadential motif of the scherzo as its point of departure. The movement gains further structural bracing when the coda compresses into a harmonic microcosm the two tonal poles of the entire movement (D flat and B double flat [written A]) by oscillating between chords generated solely from these two roots.

As in the First Quartet, the slow movement is the most overtly Russian, and certainly the one most characteristic of its composer. Since it is the expressive centre of gravity of the entire piece, and far more extensive than either the scherzo or finale, Tchaikovsky reversed the normal order of the central movements, placing this very substantial elegy between its two slighter companions. The copious pathos of the opening promises well, but too much of what follows leans upon a single four-bar phrase (Ex. 79), itself internally repetitive, whose perpetual

Ex. 79

reiterations finally border on the wearisome. If the principle of continuous variation upon which the middle section of the movement is built recalls *Kamarinskaya*, the continuous tonal shifts of this section are clearly designed to balance the relative tonal stability of the flanking sections, a stability which finally passes into inertia through the addition of a very extensive tonic-restricted coda. This, like that of the Andante cantabile in the First Quartet, recalls the material of the central section. The quiet resourcefulness with which Tchaikovsky extends this movement's most ubiquitous phrase into five- or six-bar lengths is commendable, as is the decorative variety of the accompaniments he devises for it, but it is scarcely strong enough to sustain the span of music assigned to it. In the end its repetitions become almost obsessive, bordering on the pathological; it is as though, by the constant reiteration of one expressive phrase, may be exorcised some emotional devil within the composer's own soul. If the Andante cantabile of the First Quartet can touch our more sensitive nerve-ends, this slow movement may make them a little raw.

The movement with which the quartet opens could scarcely exhibit more differing values. As in the First Quartet, here are precisely balanced symmetries and nicely poised expression – at least, as far as the main body of the movement is concerned. By contrast, the adagio introduction is extraordinary. Wagner, we have noted, had no enchantments for Tchaikovsky, yet for a moment the latter takes a little of the German composer's fundamental chromaticism; indeed, it is difficult to believe that the opening was not composed under the explicit shadow of the beginning of *Tristan* (Ex. 80a and b). The principle is certainly the same; start with a moment of arresting dissonance and then drift into relative consonance through a series of stepwise movements. Yet the differences are even greater. Tchaikovsky had none of Wagner's harmonic sophistication, where a widened repertoire of harmonic materials included altered chords which were not simply the incidental by-product of a web of counterpoint, but entities in their own right with an autonomous function in the broader harmonic structure. Tchaikovsky's opening has no equivalent to the 'Tristan chord', merely a cluster of three adjacent notes which demands and receives resolution into the diminished triad at x as a stage on the road to the relative stability of the B flat first inversion in bar 2. Nor, when the imitative passage follows in bar 3 (and especially when it recurs from bar 9 [Ex. 80c] with an unusual succession of pitch entries), is there that sense of harmonic substructure which Wagner always maintains, no matter how involved the contrapuntal workings. Tchaikovsky's normal harmonic thinking was in simple, broad diatonic terms; in a situation where

Ex. 80

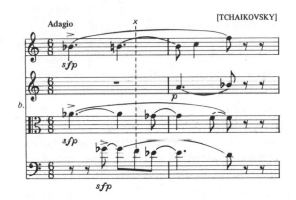

this was not possible, as here, he thought intervallically, relating the simultaneously sounding pitches acceptably in formations of various types of seventh chords, but abandoning all sense of harmonic movement except for a general downward drift. Such music seems almost to leap past Wagner towards the early world of the Second Viennese School or Bartók's First Quartet until, in the fourth and fifth bars of Ex. 80c, G minor emerges from the mists and the tonal orientation becomes clear.

This introduction is certainly one of the most unconventional passages in all Tchaikovsky's music, more than can be said of the Moderato assai that follows. If faultless craftsmanship, fluent invention and good taste could suffice to produce a masterpiece, this would be one. As in its counterpart in the First Quartet, here are precisely balanced proportions and simple, clear harmonic structures well bastioned by tonics and dominants. The texture is even more consistently linear and filled with a greater abundance of detail, especially rich in tiny chromatic touches. There is the same sequential repetitiveness in the development; indeed, as the diagram of Ex. 81 shows, this whole 45-bar stretch is fabricated by doing little more than shuffle and transpose a couple of four-bar, and four one-bar phrases, and the section incorporates near the end that most 'academic' of techniques – a complete trip down the circle of fifths. As in the First Quartet, too, the recapitulation reproduces the exposition almost exactly with only the minimum of modification to ensure the restatement of the second subject in the tonic. And, to balance the undisguised compartmentalisation of the total structure, there is a quiet but assured thematic integration. Thus, for example, the repeated-fifth motif in the third bar of Ex. 82a is again taken up at the end of the transition (Ex. 82b), is inverted and then rhythmically restructured to grow three bars later into the opening bar of the second subject. If this has produced a neat thematic linkage between the two subjects, the development carries the process further, incorporating a particle of the first subject, y, into the first two bars of the second subject (Ex. 82c). A blend of elements from the two subjects also plays a part in the coda.

Yet, for all its impeccable skill and fertile detail, the movement is too bland. There is no solving of a problem simply because there is no problem. It has all come out too easily, is written to an easy structural formula, and it contains little that comes from Tchaikovsky himself, even though the repetitive second subject does have some Russian flavour to it. The movement's fluency is that of Tchaikovsky's idol, Mozart, composing a divertimento which seeks to do no more than please with a flow of attractive sound. The response of the first audiences to the quartet confirms this. Whereas for years the merits of *Romeo and Juliet* were not to be fully appreciated by the wider public, the evidence suggests that the success of this quartet was instantaneous, even though Tchaikovsky himself was somewhat disappointed by its reception. Above all, it seems, the weakest movement, the facile rondo finale, with its fluent but faceless fugue, won enthusiastic plaudits. This audience response to such cordial chatter may not be difficult to understand; more puzzling is Tchaikovsky's own enthusiasm for the whole work. Six months after the first performance he could still feel that it was his best piece yet; two years later, when Laroche criticised the first movement for being cold, Tchaikovsky had retorted: 'If I have written anything during

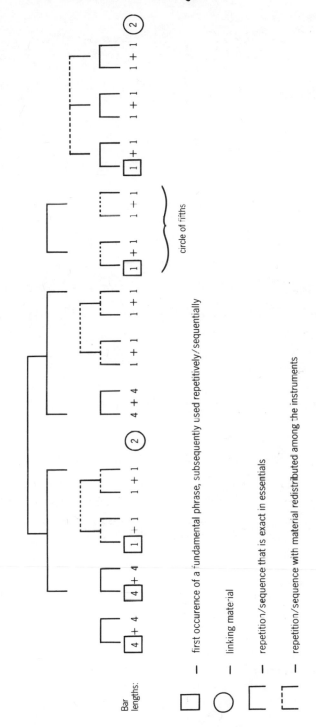

Ex. 81

Ex. 82

my life that is really heartfelt and flowing straight from the depths of the inner me, then it is just this first movement of this quartet.'[53] Perhaps, however, this quartet's attraction for him was not so strange, for it

[53] *TLP*6, p. 56; *TPB*, p. 110.

certainly contained a wide variety of those qualities he might well wish his work to exhibit. If he looked to the slow movement he could find in it a patent declaration of himself; if he turned to the mixed metres of the scherzo or the striking chromaticism of the work's opening he could find novelty; if he observed the first movement or the finale he could find expressive poise and elegant technique. The trouble was that these qualities were all separated. In the First Quartet he had at least managed some sort of amalgam of these elements; in the Second a deep cleavage is appearing between the music which represents Tchaikovsky himself and that which embodies those ideals which his nature would never allow him to attain fully on his own stylistic and expressive terms.

This dichotomy is clearly bound up with the continually developing trends in his private life. Modest observed significantly that from the autumn of 1873 his brother's fits of depression became longer, stronger, and more frequent. In early December Tchaikovsky himself had confided to this same brother his own feeling of personal isolation. He saw Shilovsky much but was finding him increasingly uncongenial company, and there was still something missing in his relationship with all his remaining Moscow friends. Whether this feeling of loneliness was a cause or an effect of the flaws, divisions and contradictions in his character it is not possible to say, but the deepening crisis in his personal life is surely evident in the extreme expressive antipodes of this quartet where, on the one hand, there is music in which he shows a rigorous determination to exclude anything of himself while, on the other, there is a slow movement which is a most naked exposure of his stress-filled personality, less brutally emotional than some that were to come later, perhaps, but the most self-declaring piece he had yet composed. In Tchaikovsky's musical biography, the Second Quartet is of much significance.

IO

HIGH NATIONALISM II:

VAKULA THE SMITH

IN 1870 THE Grand Duchess Elena, a great admirer of Serov's music, had commissioned that composer to write an opera on a libretto prepared for him by the poet Polonsky from Gogol's *Christmas Eve*. Early the next year Serov had suddenly died, the opera scarcely begun. Some eighteen months later, in September 1872, the Grand Duchess instructed the RMS to arrange a competition for an opera on Polonsky's text, offering two prizes of 1,500 and 500 roubles respectively, and assuring the winning work of production at the Maryinsky Theatre, and of publication. Having set the matter in motion, the Grand Duchess in January 1873 made her own exit from this world, leaving the responsibility entirely in the hands of the RMS. Now that the formidable spirit of its patroness had departed, the Society felt free to seek advice before deciding the final terms of the competition, and among those it consulted in March was Tchaikovsky, who observed that the great diversity of attitudes among contemporary opera composers could well prove a problem to the jury when attempting to reach a decision. Might it not be better if the RMS specified what sort of music was preferable in this instance, and whether it should be a number opera or one that was through-composed? In the end, however, the Society decided to give the competitors the utmost latitude, even permitting them not merely to modify Polonsky's libretto as they wished, but even to substitute a completely new one on the same subject if they so desired.

When Tchaikovsky replied to the RMS in March 1873, he made it clear that his personal interest in the competition was already aroused, but he made no move to begin work on his entry when the conditions were finally published in May. *The Tempest* occupied him during the summer, and after completing the Second Quartet in January 1874, he seems to have become so preoccupied with the impending production of *The Oprichnik* that all thoughts of composition were banished from his head. As we have noted, he turned violently against his most recent opera when he was confronted by it in production, found little satisfaction in its public success, and on 25 April, immediately after its première, he left Russia for Italy, where he intended to review the first Milan performance of Glinka's *A Life for the Tsar*. His spirits were low.

Four days later he was in Venice, a city whose decaying magnificence did nothing to cheer him; 'if I had to spend a week here, I should surrender to despair on the fifth day,' he wrote to Modest.[1] He surveyed the buildings along the Grand Canal, saw the Palace of the Doges but passed it by, and salved his conscience by visiting 'two or three different churches with a whole pile of pictures by Titian and Tintoretto, statues by Canova, and other artistic objects of great value. But, I repeat, it is a city that is as gloomy as if it were dead.'[2] Hearing that the production of *A Life for the Tsar* had been postponed, he decided to venture further afield, and after only one day in Venice, headed south for Rome. The Italian capital itself he found uninteresting and lifeless, but he was fascinated by its historical remains, the Coliseum and Capitol, the Vatican and, above all, by that 'triumphal summit of human genius', St Peter's.[3] His main objective, however, was Naples, to which he directed himself on 2 May. His six-day stay was marred by bad weather, but he found some pleasure in wandering about the city, and he doggedly made the tourist's obligatory round of visits. The one place that impressed him profoundly was Pompeii. 'I cannot express in words the force of the sensation I experienced as I wandered among these ruins,' he wrote to his cousin, Anna Merkling. 'I did the tour first with the inevitable guide, but later I detached myself from him and went round the whole town again by myself, going into nearly every house, surrendering myself to dreams, and trying to imagine to myself life in this place that was buried alive.'[4] This was one of the few genuine pleasures of his trip. All the time he was haunted by *The Oprichnik*, and his whirlwind tour and indefatigable sightseeing were less joys in themselves than a desperate attempt both to divert his thoughts from that work whose faults rose up so starkly before him, and to smother the loneliness he so deeply felt. 'You are thinking to yourself "There's a happy man!"' he wrote to Modest on 9 May from Florence, where he passed a night after leaving Naples. 'Now he writes from Venice, now he's been to Rome and Naples, and now he suddenly sends a letter from Florence. But all the while, Modya, you cannot imagine a sadder man than I am at this time. In Naples I got into such a state that each day I shed tears of longing for our homeland. . . . Everything to do with Moscow seemed to me especially dear. . . . It is St Petersburg that is the

[1] *TLP*5, p. 347; *TZC*1, p. 432; *TPB*, p. 87.
[2] *TLP*5, p. 348; *TZC*1, p. 432; *TPB*, p. 87; *YDGC*, p. 104.
[3] *TLP*5, p. 349; *TPB*, p. 87; *YDGC*, p. 104.   [4] *TLP*5, p. 352.

root cause of my melancholy. *The Oprichnik* torments me.'[5] While in Rome he had heard that the new production of *A Life for the Tsar* was to be adapted to suit Italian taste. Unable to face such mutilation to his favourite Russian opera, he abandoned his special mission to Italy. Nor did he fulfil his intention of visiting Sasha at Vevey. Instead, his conscience uneasy about the classes he should be giving at the Conservatoire, he directed himself straight back to Moscow.

Tchaikovsky returned to Russia more settled than when he had left it. Whatever his aversion to *The Oprichnik*, he could not but be flattered that the opera had drawn full houses in St Petersburg and was to have immediate productions in Kiev and Odessa. The rehearsals had taught him much, too, about the weaknesses in his operatic technique, and he had to admit that these lessons had been invaluable. His faith in his own ability to write a good opera remained undiminished, as he had confided to Anna Merkling while still in Italy, and on his return he straightway refocused his attention on the opera competition, urgently requesting Bessel to send him a copy of the rules governing entry. On 13 June, immediately after the end of the Conservatoire term, he set out for Kondratyev's at Nizy, intending to set about *Vakula the Smith* (as the opera was to be called) without further delay. According to Modest, the prize was only a secondary consideration to the subject itself. Polonsky's libretto 'completely captivated him. The novel colour of the tale, its originality, and the variety required of the music, the beautiful lines and deep poetry of this tale by Gogol caught Pyotr Ilich's imagination to such a degree that he was drawn irresistibly to setting this libretto to music.'[6] Not, nevertheless, before he had checked that major figures like Balakirev, Anton Rubinstein and Rimsky-Korsakov would not be numbering themselves among his rivals for the prize. None of these proposed to take the field, however, and when Tchaikovsky left for Nizy he was eager to begin, the more so since he was misinformed about the closing date. The RMS had changed this more than once before finally setting it, at Rimsky-Korsakov's suggestion, as 13 August 1875. When he left for the country Tchaikovsky believed it to be 13 January 1875. It was therefore essential to have the work virtually complete before the onset of the next Conservatoire session and concert/operatic season.

At Nizy he straightway settled into a regular routine which ensured systematic progress with his formidable task.

I get up at six-thirty, drink five glasses of water [mineral water from Karlsbad], the first at seven; from tea at nine until midday I read and

[5] *TLP*5, pp. 353–4; *TZC*1, p. 434; *TPB*, pp. 88–9.
[6] *TZC*1, pp. 438–9.

play the piano (mainly Schumann); at noon[7] lunch, from then until three, work – that is, composing *Vakula*; from three to five the first session of bezique (to which I have taken a great liking), then a bath and dinner; after dinner a walk by myself, lasting about two hours, then I sit outside in the porch; at nine tea, and soon after that a second session of bezique, and at eleven or eleven-thirty bedtime. This routine has now been going on essentially unchanged for a fortnight,

he wrote to Modest on 30 June. '. . . I am *exceedingly* content with this mode of living and I am expecting that it, together with the waters, will greatly benefit my health.'[8] Even the brief presence of an odious iconoclastic youth who, amongst other things, scornfully dismissed Beethoven and Schumann, could only impair, not destroy his contentment.

Tchaikovsky remained at Nizy about six weeks, and when he moved on to Shilovsky's at Usovo at the end of July the composition of almost the entire opera was, incredibly, already done, even though he had devoted no more than two or three hours a day to it. At Usovo he had to engage in more prolonged work if the scoring was to be completed before he returned to Moscow. Yet on 2 September, little more than three weeks later, everything was finished. Never before had he composed so much music so quickly, enjoyed such a flow of inspiration, or experienced greater pleasure in his work. 'In consequence he always retained a particularly soft spot for *Vakula*,' wrote Modest, 'and till his death he remained convinced that it was the best of his operas.'[9]

Happy in the successful completion of the new work, Tchaikovsky promptly submitted it to the RMS. The competition rules required that each entry should be received anonymously, and Tchaikovsky chose the motto 'Ars longa, vita brevis est' as the identifying mark to place on his score – though since he wrote it in his own characteristic handwriting well-known to most of the judges, it scarcely masked his identity. It was only after he had returned to Moscow in September that he discovered his error about the competition's closing date, and realised that any plans for a production of his opera would not be started for over a year. It was a severe shock. Naturally he wanted this new work, in which he could take such pleasure, mounted as soon as possible to prove to everyone, himself included, that he could write a *real* opera and not just a meretricious potboiler like *The Oprichnik*. His reputation abroad was

[7] Modest states 'at one o'clock'.

[8] *TLP*5, p. 358; *TZC*1, pp. 439–40; *TPB*, p. 90.

[9] *TZC*1, p. 440. Tchaikovsky's own judgement was, in fact, a little less emphatic (see p. 313).

growing, too. In particular his First Quartet had already scored considerable success outside Russia, and his confidence in himself and his self-assertion on behalf of his own music were becoming stronger. Suspecting that *Vakula* could gain immediate acceptance for production on its own merits, he made approaches to Kondratyev, the chief producer at the Maryinsky, to have the opera withdrawn from the competition and submitted for production forthwith.

Unfortunately for Tchaikovsky, Kondratyev consulted not only Nápravník, but also the Grand Duke Konstantin, the president of the RMS, who was not amused. On 31 October, a very embarrassed Tchaikovsky wrote to Nápravník a defence of his action:

> Today I found out through Rubinstein that you and the Grand Duke were very displeased at my attempt to advance my opera's cause in the theatre outside the competition. I regret very much that my completely private communication to you and Kondratyev was brought to the notice of the Grand Duke who thought that I wanted, as it were, to show my unwillingness to submit to the rules of the competition. In fact, the matter can be very easily explained. I had imagined that the competition's closing date was 13 January, and therefore hastened to finish my score. When I arrived in Moscow from the country, I discovered that I should have to wait more than a whole year. In my impatience to secure the opera's production (which, in fact, I value more than the money), I wrote in a purely private capacity a letter in reply to one that Kondratyev had sent me, asking whether my opera would be accepted outside the competition. I asked him to talk with you when an opportunity arose, and to give me a reply. Now I see that this was a blunder on my part because the text of the opera is not in my control. But you are unjust in writing to me, or in instructing Kondratyev to write to me, to tell me that I am very foolish, and moreover you are unjust in suspecting me of some crafty designs: such were not in my head. I beg you very much to put this out of your mind, and equally to disabuse the Grand Duke who, Rubinstein says, was very displeased with my action.[10]

If Tchaikovsky had shown no more than bad judgement in his approach to Kondratyev, he committed an inexcusable blunder in allowing the overture to *Vakula* to be publicly performed at an RMS concert in Moscow on 4 December, when it was conducted by Nikolay Rubinstein who was to be one of the competition judges. Though the actual identity of the opera was not revealed in the concert programme,

[10] *TLP*5, pp. 370–1; *TZC*1, p. 447.

any pretence of anonymity was now effectively destroyed. Nor were Tchaikovsky's open dealings, during the first half of 1875, with Bessel and Jurgenson over the matter of the opera's future publication within the spirit of confidentiality laid down by the RMS. His passionate love for his new opera, and his agony at the possibility that it might not win the first prize seem to have unbalanced his judgement in all matters concerning his 'beloved child', as he called *Vakula*. By May he was actually planning to play it through to Rimsky-Korsakov, who was to be another of the judges. The final affront to impartiality was delivered by Rimsky-Korsakov himself, who wrote to Tchaikovsky a fortnight before the judging was to take place, not only offering critical comment upon Tchaikovsky's entry, but virtually pre-empting the judgement: 'I don't doubt for a moment that your opera will get the prize.'[11]

Both composers should long since have been disqualified from having any part in the competition; yet when the jury sat in final judgement on 28 October, Tchaikovsky's entry was still among the scores before them. Even less might the impartiality of their verdict be believed, considering that the seven judges included Laroche and Nápravník, as well as Nikolay Rubinstein and Rimsky-Korsakov. Their decision could hardly be doubted, though the terms in which it was expressed still endeavoured to maintain a pretence of innocence. 'We have decided (1) to award the first prize (1,500 roubles) to the composer of the opera with the motto "ars longa, vita brevis est" . . . Footnote: the opera with the above-mentioned motto is deemed worthy of the prize not as *relatively the best* but as *the only one* that measures up to the artistic demands of the competition.'[12] Perhaps, after so many improprieties, this codicil was felt necessary to confirm just how complete and unequivocal had been their verdict. Years later Rimsky-Korsakov was to confess that the management of the competition had been irregular, though he claimed it had made no difference since Tchaikovsky's entry was indisputably the best.

Vakula was safe; now came the period of waiting for production. This, at least, was attended by neither the uncertainties nor delays that had beset *The Oprichnik*, and by May 1876 arrangements were well in hand. Tchaikovsky was delighted by the enthusiasm of his friends and colleagues. '*Vakula* is a sensation with all those who are close to me,' he wrote to Modest. 'Taneyev already knows it by heart from cover to cover.'[13] By mid-August rehearsals were taking place, and a foretaste of the new piece was provided four days before the première when some of

[11] *DTC*, p. 57; *YDGC*, p. 119; *TZC*1, p. 475.
[12] *DTC*, p. 57.
[13] *TLP6*, pp. 37–8; *TZC*1, p. 486; *TPB*, p. 108; *DTC*, p. 58.

the opera's dances were conducted by Nápravník at an RMS concert in St Petersburg. On 6 December 1876 the opera was performed.

It was a bitter irony that Tchaikovsky, having seen the *Oprichnik* he despised accorded an audience success which he knew it did not deserve, should now see the *Vakula* he loved denied the public honours he so confidently felt it merited. '*Vakula* has failed triumphantly,' he wrote to Taneyev a week after the première:

> With the exception of the overture and the first duet, which were applauded, the first two acts passed off in deathly silence. There was a lot of laughter during the Mayor's scene and especially that of the clerk,[14] but there was no applause and no curtain calls. After the third and fourth acts (the third was divided into two) I took a lot of curtain calls, though amid strong hissing from a significant part of the audience. The second performance went somewhat better, but it may still be said quite definitely that the opera has not pleased, and will scarcely survive more than five or six performances. What is remarkable is that, at the dress rehearsal, everyone, including Cui, predicted that I would enjoy a great success; the more painful and distressing to me has been the opera's downfall. I confess that I'm badly shaken and disheartened, above all because I cannot complain about either the performance or the production. Everything was done with care, intelligence, even opulence. The décor was simply magnificent. Of the performers, Raab alone dissatisfies me. . . . In a word, I am responsible for the opera's lack of success. It is too clogged with details, too thickly scored, too thin in vocal effectiveness. Only now do I understand why, if you remember, you were all so cold and reserved when I played *Vakula* for the first time at Rubinstein's. *Vakula*'s style is utterly unoperatic: there's no breadth or sweep to it.[15]

By contrast Cui considered that the opera enjoyed a marked, though not undivided success, and he maintained his good opinion of it in his published review. Nor was Laroche the only other critic to praise it. Despite its less than unanimous reception, *Vakula* was revived in each of the next three seasons, and even Tchaikovsky had to admit that the audiences, though lukewarm, were good. Yet each time it was revived, what he saw as the opera's faults stung him to the quick. 'I have done everything to neutralise the good effect of all those bits that might by themselves have pleased, had I restrained more my purely musical

---

[14] The censor, presumably objecting to the possible ecclesiastical implications of 'clerk', insisted that this character should be made into a schoolteacher.

[15] *TLP*6, pp. 88–9; *TZC*1, pp. 509–10; *DTC*, p. 59.

inspiration, and been less forgetful of the conditions needed for that *theatrical* and *scenic effectiveness* peculiar to the operatic style,' he declared to Madame von Meck on 11 November 1878.[16] A year later he returned to the subject again: 'I wearied the listener with a superfluity of detail, harmonic complexity, and absence of any sense of moderation in the orchestral effects. Further, I did not let the listener *have any respite* – I gave him forthwith too much spicy musical fare. The operatic style must be marked by breadth, simplicity, and some scenic effectiveness. *Vakula*'s style is not operatic but symphonic, even chamber-like.'[17]

Yet despite his recognition of what he felt to be the opera's glaring faults, Tchaikovsky lost neither his love for *Vakula* nor, paradoxically, his faith in it, and in 1884 he carefully planned a revision of the whole piece. This operation was carried out between 28 February and 3 April 1885, and the result was renamed *Cherevichki*.[18] The revision was drastic; about one-eighth of the original *Vakula* was cut, and nearly twice as much new music substituted, Tchaikovsky himself providing the libretto and all but one of the new scenes the opera now acquired. The exception was Vakula's arioso in the third act, for which Nikolay Chayev wrote the text, and it appears that this addition was composed towards the end of 1886 at the request of Dmitri Usatov, who sang Vakula in the revised opera. This was first given on 31 January 1887 at the Bolshoy Theatre in Moscow, Tchaikovsky himself conducting. By now his fame was enough to ensure at least a respectful reception for the piece. Nevertheless, for all the applause, Tchaikovsky recognised it was not the sort of work that would ever command a large and fervent following. 'For the moment the opera arouses interest rather than affection. . . . I think that *Cherevichki*, like *Onegin*, will be performed without much audience clamour – but that, little by little, people will come to love the opera,' he confided to Modest after the third performance.[19] This time it lasted only five nights, and the two performances planned for the next season were abandoned. Thus it was withdrawn from the repertoire, never more to be heard in the composer's lifetime. Yet, as Modest noted, Tchaikovsky's faith in it remained, and in 1890 he could still write to Jurgenson: 'I believe unreservedly in *Cherevichki*'s future as a repertoire piece, and I consider it musically well-nigh my best opera.'[20]

Pushkin described Gogol's *Evenings on a farm near Dikanka*, from which

[16] *TLP*7, p. 440; *TPM*1, p. 467; *TZC*2, pp. 216–17; *DTC*, p. 60.

[17] *TLP*8, p. 390; *TPM*2, p. 232; *TZC*2, p. 326; *DTC*, pp. 60–1.

[18] 'Cherevichki' were the high-heeled leather boots worn by Ukrainian women; the new title is therefore virtually untranslatable. The opera is sometimes known in the West as *Les Caprices d'Oxane*. I have preferred to retain the original title for the revision.

[19] *TLP*14, p. 35; *TZC*3, p. 158; *TPB*, p. 374; *DTC*, p. 138.

[20] *TPJ*2, p. 171.

Christmas Eve was taken, as a 'truly happy book'.[21] Published in two parts in 1831 and 1832, these tales laid the foundation of their author's reputation with their vivid, sometimes fantastic, even macabre portrayal of Ukrainian peasant types and life. Tchaikovsky was as strongly captivated as Gogol's readers had been forty years before by the mixture of realism and fantasy in these tales, by the brilliant yet simple charm of their world, and by the varied sharp outlines of the characters which inhabit it, even when their edges were blunted and the colouring softened by transposition into an opera libretto. *Christmas Eve* is set out as a series of clear, simple scenes which only required a little pruning and reshuffling to provide an admirable scenario. In its revised form of 1885 the plot of Tchaikovsky's opera is as follows (the major additions which appeared in this second version are given in italics):

ACT 1, SCENE 1. *A street in Dikanka on a moonlit Christmas Eve.*
Solokha, a witch and the mother of Vakula, comes out of her cottage (No. 1) and muses upon how she might ensnare some man to visit her home. The Devil, dressed much like an ordinary person, enters and creeps up behind her so that she jumps with surprise when she turns and sees him (bar 53). They tease each other, he commenting on her age and she retorting (bar 87) that everyone is still in love with her. A comic love scene develops. How does the Devil know that Solokha is a witch? There are many signs, replies the Devil, especially her little forked tail (bar 141). 'How did you come to see that?' asks Solokha with arch alarm. 'What am I a little imp for?' cheekily retorts the Devil. Solokha declares her intention of going into the cottage and flying, in true witch's fashion, up the chimney to the stars. After a lively duet (allegro vivo) she runs (No. 2) into her cottage, leaving the Devil to reveal that he is furious with her son, Vakula, for having painted a picture of him which makes him look ridiculous so that the other devils laugh at him. Knowing that Vakula wants to visit Oxana, the peasant Chub's beautiful daughter, he plans to steal the moon and raise a great snowstorm so that Chub will not drop in on a friend, but stay at home instead. In a noble andante the Devil invokes the snowstorm. Solokha suddenly shoots out of the chimney, calling upon the Devil to follow her (bar 71). The Devil hastens into the cottage and appears from the chimney in his natural form. Blanketing the moon and plunging the street into darkness, they ride off (allegro vivace) as the storm gathers and then breaks. Chub and another peasant, Panas, come out of a cottage (bar 128). Finding it pitch-black, they are in two minds about returning indoors, but the thought of the fare at the inn persuades them to proceed and finally, after some groping, they reach their destination.
ACT 1, SCENE 2. *Chub's cottage.*
Oxana enters (No. 3), clearly out of spirits because her father has gone off to greet Christmas with his friend, the clerk, instead of staying at home with her. She sings to herself (andante) a melancholy song about an apple tree which has

---

[21] In a letter to No. 79 of *The Russian Invalid* (1831), quoted in T. Wolf, *Pushkin on Literature* (London, 1973), p. 299.

blossomed and withered, and about a young girl who sings to her departed nurse of her longing for love. Then she gazes at her own reflection in the mirror. 'People say that I am beautiful as a white swan,' she reflects (moderato), and plunges into a welter of self-admiration, not noticing Vakula's entrance (bar 95), nor his disapproval of her vanity (No. 4). Suddenly aware of his presence (bar 34), she greets him ungraciously and demands to know whether the trunk he is making for her is ready. He replies that it is nearly made, and that all he now wants to do is to talk with her and look at her. Despite some unkind remarks about him, he breaks into a passionate declaration of love (bar 104); even if the Tsar were to offer him half his kingdom and other riches, he would reply: 'I need nothing. Give me only Oxana!' When he finishes, Oxana predicts (No. 5) that her father will marry Vakula's mother; having delivered this blow, she goes off into the partitioned portion of the room. Immediately afterwards her father enters (allegro), so covered with snow that Vakula does not recognise him and ejects him back into the street. Oxana reappears (No. 6) and, having discovered her father's plight, upbraids Vakula who is crestfallen.[22] *Seeing that the storm is abating (bar 38) she expresses her impatience for the arrival of the village girls and lads with whom she intends to join in celebrating the arrival of Christmas, and tells Vakula how bored she is with him. He makes as though to leave (bar 68), but she detains him and sings (allegro ma non troppo) of the young man whom she pretends to love: 'He's not an old woman like you!' she taunts Vakula (bar 88). Angry and hurt, he reproaches her (poco meno mosso), but she continues her tormenting, rousing him to a great passion of rage and misery. As the finale (No. 7) begins, she laughs mockingly at him, and he makes one more bid to persuade her to withdraw her words, but as the girls and young men are heard approaching, she rejects him. 'Is it possible that such a beauty as I should love such a bumpkin? Be off with you!' (bar 30) 'You're not a girl — you're a snake in the grass!' he cries (bar 39) as he leaves. Left alone, Oxana is torn by remorse, and when the revellers joyfully enter, she refuses to join them. After their departure she confesses her love for Vakula.*

ACT 2, SCENE 1. *Solokha's cottage.*
Solokha is just closing the front door (No. 8) as the Devil emerges from the stove. She has had a hectic ride with him during which her broomstick has been broken, and she is vexed with him. The Devil flirts playfully with her (moderato), but she says (bar 62) that she is weary, yawning twice (bars 60 and 65). Nevertheless she rouses herself to join with him in a gopak (allegro vivo), accompanied by strange creatures who come out of the stove and corners of the room to play on various instruments. Suddenly a knocking is heard at the door (bar 147), and the creatures disappear. The Devil is worried that it might be Vakula — and is particularly alarmed in case it is the Mayor who, when drunk, constantly crosses himself, a habit the Devil naturally finds disconcerting. When Solokha declares (bar 190) her intention of opening the door, the Devil hides in one of the coal sacks along the wall, and the Mayor enters (No. 9). Solokha takes little pleasure in this new arrival, but gives him (bar 32) a glass of pepper brandy. The Mayor's spirits are threatening to become a little high (allegro),

[22] In the original *Vakula* only four pages of vocal score remain for Act 1. In these Oxana dismisses Vakula angrily, then reveals the ambivalence of her feelings towards him before the curtain falls. The revision begins at bar 31 of No. 6 in the revised version.

when another knock is heard. In a panic the Mayor jumps into another of the sacks Solokha has hurriedly emptied, and the schoolteacher enters (No. 10). Solokha reproves him for his visit, reminding him that he is married. Under the pretext of bad eyesight, he contrives to paw her hand, neck and shoulder before she cuts short his tactile investigations. *Then, to her further annoyance, he insists on singing a ditty (bar 61) he has specially composed for her.*[23] *As he finishes* further knocking is heard. Fearing the Day of Judgement has come, he begs a reluctant Solokha to hide him, and he slips into another of the sacks before Solokha opens the door to admit Chub, whom she greets warmly (No. 11), and to whom she straightway offers a drink. A little love scene follows, but when at last he kisses her, knocking interrupts them, and Vakula's voice is heard outside. It is now Chub's turn to hide, and he unwittingly chooses the sack already occupied by the schoolteacher. *The latter's head appears from the neck of the sack calling out in alarm to Solokha, as a quintet begins. Other heads poke out, Chub and the Mayor complaining of their stifling predicaments, and the Devil enjoying the whole situation. All the heads abruptly disappear as* Vakula enters (bar 81).[24] He is pensive and sad: left alone by Solokha, he notices the sacks and decides to take them off to the smithy so as to leave the cottage unencumbered for the Christmas festival. He sings (No. 12) of his passion and grief, and as he does so he mechanically fastens the necks of the sacks and attempts to pick them up, noting with some surprise their weight. He is further depressed (bar 15) to find that he seems to have lost his strength, and again he pauses (bar 25) to reflect on his dejected condition at Oxana's treatment of him. 'You snake in the grass, how you dry up my heart, poison my spirit!' he cries (bar 38). Then, wearily gathering up the sacks, he goes out.

ACT 2, SCENE 2. *The street in Dikanka as at the beginning of the opera.*

Groups of girls and lads are heard singing as they approach (No. 13). Old folk gather to listen to them, and then join in. When the stage is filled, they look for Oxana (bar 89). Not seeing her, they call out for her, and finally she appears with another girl, Odarka, in a sleigh drawn by two young men (No. 14). The centre of universal attention, Oxana jokingly asks the crowd the identity of the young man who has been serenading her beneath her window; then, spying Vakula, who has entered with the sacks, she obliquely torments him (bar 43) by alluding publicly to the way he had ejected her father from his own house. As she gets out of the sleigh she notices Odarka's feet. 'What beautiful new *cherevichki* you have!' she exclaims (bar 78). 'You have some man who buys you all you need. But I've no one!' Vakula immediately offers to get her a pair of these shoes, but she insists that hers must be like those of the Tsaritsa herself. Warming to the crowd's reaction, she utters her challenge (moderato): 'If Vakula the smith will get me the shoes that the Tsaritsa herself wears, then I give my word that I'll marry him forthwith!' Having merrily delivered this promise, she summons the young men and women to a game of snowballs, leaving Vakula alone on the forestage to give vent to his sufferings and the desperate passion he feels for her. The young people return, and Oxana, while pretending not to notice Vakula, cruelly torments him (bar 174), abetted by the crowd.

[23] The newly interpolated material is bars 61–105.
[24] The newly interpolated material ends on the first beat of bar 82.

Then she addresses him directly (No. 15), repeating her condition for marrying him. He is now so distraught that the crowd beg her (bar 14) to stop; in his desperation he believes (andante sostenuto) that the torment will destroy him, while Oxana realises with alarm what may happen: 'If he can fall in love, he can surely fall out of love!' The chorus try to persuade him that she was only joking. Vakula departs, carrying one of the sacks (bar 64), followed by the young women, leaving Oxana to her fears. Then the attention of all is suddenly taken by the two sacks Vakula has left behind. The young men prod them and they begin to wriggle. Calling back the girls, the young men untie the sacks, and the Mayor, the schoolteacher and Chub jump out to universal amazement. The Mayor retreats with as much dignity as he can command, and the schoolteacher scuttles off. Only Chub remains. 'See what a splendid joke I played on you!' he shouts (bar 104), and all burst out laughing.

ACT 3, SCENE 1. *Moonlight on the bank of a river.*
A chorus of disconsolate rusalkas is heard lamenting in the distance (No. 16), their singing disturbing a wood goblin who finally notices Vakula's approach and discerns his desperate state. Vakula enters (No. 17), still carrying the sack. His opening phrase-ends are echoed by an offstage chorus. He is tempted to throw himself into the river, *and he sings of his sorrow: 'Maiden, does your heart hear bitter grief, my sorrow?' (bar 25). As he finishes despairingly,*[25] he puts down the sack and the Devil jumps out, leaps on his back, and demands his soul in return for Oxana. The oath must be written in blood, the Devil insists, and as Vakula reaches into his pocket (bar 107) on the pretext of getting a nail with which to scratch himself, he grabs the Devil by the tail and pins him to the ground. The Devil concedes defeat and promises him anything he wants. 'Take me forthwith to the Tsaritsa,' commands Vakula (bar 129). 'So be it! Sit on my back,' replies the Devil, and in an aerial ride (allegro giusto) Vakula is transported to St Petersburg.

ACT 3, SCENE 2. *A reception room in the royal palace.*
The Devil flies in with Vakula still clinging to his back (No. 18). The Devil hides behind the fireplace as some Cossacks enter and inform Vakula that they have been summoned to a soirée of the Tsaritsa. Vakula asks them (bar 28) to let him join their party, but their leader refuses as they have personal business with the Tsaritsa. Vakula invokes the aid of the Devil who emerges from behind the fireplace and points out enigmatically that Vakula's presence might be helpful to them. The Cossacks agree to take him. An official enters (allegro moderato) to tell the Cossacks that they are to be taken straightway to the Great Hall, and are to receive gifts. All leave.

ACT 3, SCENE 3. *The Great Hall in the palace.*
A grand polonaise (No. 19) is in progress. During it the Cossacks enter with Vakula, who is dazzled by the splendour of it all. A master of ceremonies instructs them in the proper etiquette for the occasion. Then the Prince[26] enters and announces a great victory; all join in the rejoicing and glorify the Tsaritsa.

[25] The newly interpolated material is Vakula's arioso, bars 21–86. This was composed in 1886.

[26] The Prince deputises throughout for the Tsaritsa, since the Russian censor would not permit the representation of either the Tsar or the Tsaritsa on the stage.

Before the dances resume, the Prince delivers an ode (No. 20, bar 26) written by a humble poet on the Russian victory.[27] *When the applause has subsided,* the Cossacks are requested to approach as the other guests begin a minuet (No. 21). The Prince tells them that their petition will be answered in a couple of days. As he is about to leave, the Cossacks confer (bar 13) and then one of them nudges Vakula who blurts out his request for the Tsaritsa's shoes for his own bride. The solicitation causes general amusement, but the Prince whispers (bar 35) to one of the courtiers who goes out and returns almost immediately with a pair of elegant shoes on a silver tray. They are given to Vakula who is overwhelmed by the gift (moderato), to more general amusement. The Prince orders more dancing, and there follow a Russian dance (No. 22A) and a Cossack dance (No. 22B). When these are finished the master of ceremonies announces (No. 23) the performance of a comedy in the Tsaritsa's own theatre, and invites all to attend. The stage begins to empty. The Devil reappears, and having diverted everyone's attention, summons Vakula to return with him to the Ukraine. Vakula jumps on his back, and they fly off.

ACT 4.[28] *A sunny Christmas morning in the square at Dikanka.*

Solokha and Oxana are bewailing Vakula's disappearance, and are fearing the worst (No. 24). The church bells are heard, and the villagers emerge from Mass (No. 25). They invite Oxana to the Christmas feast, but despite all their persuasions she will not go. 'I have made my beloved angry, and I have destroyed him,' she laments (bar 66) as she goes out weeping. The young men excitedly exhort everyone to repair to the inn (allegro vivace). The Mayor, Panas and Chub enter, the last inviting all the men to feast at his house. He looks round for his daughter (bar 148), is cross at her absence, and repeats his invitation. The Mayor and Panas accept, but the others opt for the inn. Suddenly (allegro giusto) Vakula is seen approaching. When he enters, the crowd question him. Solokha greets him emotionally, and goes off to fetch Oxana. Vakula turns to Chub (bar 208), kneels before him (bar 216), and invites Chub to chastise him for his misdemeanour of the previous night. Chub immediately forgives him, and asks him what he wants. Vakula straightway begs for Oxana's hand (bar 239). He is vociferously supported by the young men, and Chub readily agrees as Oxana enters and Vakula offers her the shoes. 'I don't need them. I don't want them. Without them I'm . . .' she stutters (bar 259). Chub gives the young couple his blessing and some advice, and orders the kozba players to praise the betrothed pair. This they do (allegro non troppo), and all join in.

As is evident from this summary of the plot of the revised opera, Tchaikovsky made some significant additions to his original *Vakula*. To balance this a little he made a few excisions. There was a small one in the Overture, a movement which, like that to *The Oprichnik*, exposes a

[27] The whole of No. 20 is a new interpolation.
[28] Although in the published score of the first version it appears as Scene 4 of Act 3, the four-act division was made before the première.

selection of material to be heard in the subsequent opera. All the main participants are represented; Oxana's aria at the beginning of the second scene of Act 1 provides the material for the opening, while in the third section, a substantial sonata movement, the second subject is derived from Vakula's arioso in the same scene (with, it seems, some interference from the Devil),[29] the first subject from the Solokha/Devil gopak early in Act 2. A little of the music that follows upon this in the opera (after the first knocks have been heard) is used to begin the development. The remaining two sections of the Overture are based on the kozba players' music at the close of the opera; in the fourth and final section this kozba music leads into the sounds of general rejoicing, just as at the end of the opera itself. In the revised opera Tchaikovsky chopped half a dozen bars from the first subject in the Overture's allegro giusto exposition[30] (all bar numbers in the footnotes refer to the revised opera), and in Act 1 he also dropped the repetition of the B major allegro vivace in the snowstorm during the first scene.[31]

Nevertheless, far more extensive than excisions were the substitutions he made for existing music. As he had noted to Madame von Meck in 1878 (see above, pp. 312–13), he had been too much of a musician in *Vakula*, too engrossed by detail, too unthinking of the needs of his characters. Thus (to take only the substitutions he made in Act 1) the last fifty-one bars of the Solokha/Devil duet were new;[32] even more drastically rewritten was the entire Chub/Panas dialogue at the end of the first scene.[33] Originally Tchaikovsky had set their conversation against an orchestral background of persisting snowstorm music, but the new version abandoned this elaborate accompaniment with its bass moving mainly in crotchets, using instead an economical string-tremolando support, pointed by tiny pungent wind interjections, thus distracting attention less from the vocal parts, allowing the singers more flexibility, and opening the way for a more vivid characterisation from them. This new scene was typical of the textural pruning and general simplification that marked the majority of Tchaikovsky's substitutions, including the modifications made to the exchanges between Vakula and Oxana before

---

[29] The little motif which enters in bar 107, and persists against the repetition of Vakula's aria, may originate from the allegro in Act 2, Scene 1, No. 8 (especially bars 189ff.), while the concluding exposition phrase (bars 136ff.), with its prominent augmented triads, seems to anticipate the whole-tone passage at the end of the first scene (No. 2, bars 177ff.).

[30] These had occurred in the middle of bar 82.

[31] This passage had occurred in F sharp major between bars 110 and 111 of No. 2.

[32] From bar 208 of No. 1.

[33] Bars 128–67 of No. 2.

the former's arioso in the second scene of Act 1,[34] and the rewriting of the little Chub/Vakula scene that follows.[35]

Vakula retained the same division into set-pieces linked by quasi-arioso as its two predecessors, though the revisions made to the dialogue passages in 1885 turned the arioso into plainer recitative. From the beginning the musical language was less complicated than in *The Oprichnik*, less laced with studied musical gesture, fresher and more direct. Though there were choruses, there were no formal ensembles involving more than two solo singers, for the Quintet was an addition in the revised version; even here, Tchaikovsky ensured that it was an economical and dramatically apt movement which in no way clogged the action. Of reminiscence themes there are virtually none. Such labels had been of particular value in an opera of strong situations and violent deeds like *The Oprichnik*, but *Vakula* was not a drama of aggression, and except for the brief Vakula/Devil struggle in Act 3, personal battles have no part in it. Instead there were tense, sometimes fraught emotional situations which demanded – and received – from Tchaikovsky an issue of deeply felt, sometimes highly charged invention.

Not that Tchaikovsky had grown indifferent to the emotional power of long-range recall, for there are some judicious recollections of music heard earlier in the opera. The most important source of these are

[34] Bars 58–71 and 87–102 of No. 4.
[35] No. 5, bar 23–No. 6, bar 2. The first seven bars of Oxana's part in No. 5 were also rewritten.
The following are the most significant substitutions and excisions made in the remaining acts (additions are not included if they have been indicated in the summary of the plot above). Bar numbers refer to the revised version of the opera:

Act 2, Scene 1
The last portion of the Chub/Solokha scene rewritten (No. 11, bars 25–47) before the newly interpolated quintet.
Scene 2
Six bars in the centre of the first chorus (No. 13) rewritten and expanded to twenty-six bars (bars 67–92); concluding nine bars rewritten and expanded to twenty-one bars (bars 133–53); Oxana's address to Odarka rewritten (No. 14, bars 78–88); background chorus and part of Vakula's recitative rewritten (bars 144–57). Molto più lento interpolated (bars 173–81).

Act 3, Scene 1
Vakula's recitative before his new arioso rewritten (No. 17, bars 9–16).
Scene 3
The end of the scene rewritten (No. 23, from bar 25). The original had concluded with another statement of the Devil's gopak which had transported Vakula to St Petersburg.

Act 4
The men's chorus in the finale expanded from eight bars to sixty-four (bars 82–137 are new). The last eight bars of choral writing in the finale were also new.

Vakula's first two ariosi. The first, in Act 1, Scene 2, recurs thrice in the same scene (just before the new ending begins, again as Vakula finally curses Oxana in the new addition, and, very fragmentarily, as Oxana is preparing to admit her love); more significantly, it indicates Vakula's continuing love-lorn state as he makes his entrance in Act 2 – a condition which immediately prompts his second arioso. This becomes, it seems, an embodiment of his rejected love, and is recalled in the next scene as Vakula broods upon Oxana's cruelty after her first challenge to him. In the ballroom scene it is again heard as he gazes dazedly at the shoes that will soon adorn his beloved's feet, without yet, perhaps, fully grasping the promise of future happiness this new acquisition brings. On the other hand, his first arioso, the one he had sung before Oxana had so thoroughly crushed his hopes, is the one with which he addresses Chub to make his peace with him in the last act before asking for his daughter's hand. Finally, and with gentle irony, the music through which Oxana had delivered her challenge to Vakula is used by him to present the shoes to her.[36]

From its first incarnation *Vakula* must rate among Tchaikovsky's best works. Unlike *The Voyevoda* and *The Oprichnik*, it started with the inestimable asset of an excellent subject. Here was no contrived melodrama peopled with ciphers; instead Gogol afforded a real, picturesque human community engaging in acts and events that were credible because they sprang from the impulses and relationships of real people. There was a pair of lovers whose pangs one could truly credit, a fine gallery of minor characters, and a witch and a devil. the former as much of the village as the ordinary humans, though a little more spicy, the latter scaled down to integrate into the community, feeling and behaving in many respects like any ordinary mortal, a tease and a prankster, susceptible to human emotions of annoyance and discomfort, vulnerable to human guile, yet clearly capable of absolute evil if he got the upper hand. It was a world that simply cried out for national colour in its musical realisation.

Tchaikovsky responded fully. Some of the nationalism derives directly from the idioms and methods that Glinka had fathered. Not surprisingly, it was *Ruslan* rather than *A Life for the Tsar* that provided

---

[36] Excluding repetitions within single scenes, the following are the main recurrences of material in the opera:

1. Music from the snowstorm in Act 1, Scene 1 persists into the following scene.
2. Opening of Solokha's teasing of the Devil in Act 1 (No. 1, bar 87 [see Ex. 86]) recurs momentarily near the opening of her scene with the Mayor in Act 2 (No. 9, bar 12).
3. Chub's theme in Act 1, Scene 2 (No. 5, bar 19) recurs in Act 2, Scene 1 (No. 11, bar 6). Oxana, being his daughter, has a closely related melody in Act 1, Scene 2 (No. 4, bar 80). See also Ex. 89 t–x.

Tchaikovsky's precedents in *Vakula*. Admittedly the chorus that opens Act 2, Scene 2 comes equally close to the world of Glinka's first opera, but the chorus of rusalkas that opens Act 3 is in direct descent from the chanting of seductive maidens in *Ruslan*. Also straight from Chernomor's magic world is both the opening of the preceding prelude, with its held horn E flat against which pull tiny harmonic cells little related except for holding this note in common (Ex. 83), and also the intrusion of the whole-tone scale into the bass of the orchestral passage which rounds off the snowstorm in the opera's first scene (Ex. 84). Although

Ex. 83

Ex. 84

the aria with which Tchaikovsky in 1886 furnished Vakula after the rusalkas' chorus takes a Ukrainian folksong as its point of departure, it develops into a movement patently composed against the background of the largo from Ruslan's great Act 2 aria. This was one of the finest of Tchaikovsky's additions to the opera. The pathos of Gorislava's cavatina in Act 3 of *Ruslan* seems to condition the plangent Solokha/Oxana duet (also in A minor) that opens the last act of *Vakula*; compare, for instance, the chromaticism of Ex. 85a and b. Even when Tchaikovsky seems to have in mind a less specific model from Glinka, there are hosts of incidents which echo the idioms of the father of Russian music – for instance, the similar brand of chromaticism that supports Vakula's cry of despair near the end of Act 2 (Ex. 85c).

Ex. 85

[Is it really possible for me, in the prime of life and love, to say: "Farewell!"?]

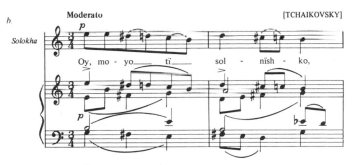

[Oh, you are my sun!]

[No, I cannot, I cannot, I have no more strength, no strength to breathe!]

Elsewhere Tchaikovsky draws his local colour more directly from national prototypes, both Russian and Ukrainian. There are, for instance, the gopaks with which the opera abounds. Mostly Tchaikovsky makes these only miniature movements with dimensions which match appropriately the pithy two-beat metres and clipped phrases characteristic of the dance, thus allowing them to be digested into the drama – though in the case of the Russian and Cossack dances in Act 3 he multiplies the sections and turns them into set-pieces. One concludes the very first scene between the Devil and Solokha, and then, rewritten,

carries them on their ride to the stars, also serving later to transport
Vakula to St Petersburg – and, in the original *Vakula*, to whisk him back
to the Ukraine. A second rounds off the Devil/Solokha scene at the
beginning of Act 2, and yet another threatens to break out at the end of
the Mayor's flirtation with Solokha. Even the schoolteacher's song is a
kind of gawky gopak. The most notable example in the rest of the score
(besides the Russian and Cossack dances) is the men's allegro vivace
chorus in the last act. On other occasions the dance nudges itself less
formally into the music: at the very beginning of Act 2 Solokha sings to a
kind of distorted gopak whose $\frac{2}{4}$ is disrupted into $\frac{3}{4}$ and then $\frac{6}{8}$. Metrical
switches of this sort occur elsewhere in music of a quite different
character, notably in the opening chorus of the next scene and in the
rusalkas' chorus (which incorporates $\frac{5}{4}$ bars), stamping such movements
with a rhythmic character that removes Tchaikovsky's invention still
further from a Western milieu.

As for the melodic content of the opera, the four identified
folksongs[37] in it are supplemented by some original material which
sounds like deliberate folksong pastiche, especially the carollers' theme
in the Act 1 finale and the old folks' first contribution to the chorus
which begins Act 2, Scene 2. Far more pervasive, however, is the national
colouring of Tchaikovsky's own characteristic melodic invention. We
are made aware of this in the melodic consistency of the opening stretch
of the opera. It is a genuine Ukrainian folksong we first hear (see Ex.
89b) even before the curtain has risen, yet it is quickly subsumed into
Tchaikovsky's own invention which seems to take its whole character
from this borrowed tune, amplifying it, adding new yet never
incongruous phrases, and thus producing a flow of fresh, unaffected
melody which is borne along on a stream of pastel chromaticism to
conjure within some twenty-five bars a world that is grounded in simple
reality, yet touched by enchantment. During all the ensuing scene
between witch and Devil Tchaikovsky never sounds a false phrase; only
at the end does something of the formality of the set movement appear
when both join in a lively gopak in which Tchaikovsky's invention
applies itself, *Kamarinskaya*-like, to devising a swift series of changing
backgrounds for the reiterations of this five-bar tune.

This is an enchanting beginning. The Devil's taunts are a challenge to
Solokha's powers of seduction, and if age has taken its toll of her natural

[37] These occur in:
1. Solokha's song, Act I, No. 1 (Rubets, *216 pesen*, No. 134).
2. Vakula's arioso, Act 3, No. 17 (Rubets, ibid., No. 66).
3. Russian dance, Act 3, No. 22a, bars 47 and 63 (Prokunin (arranged Tchaikovsky), No.
   5, and *T50RF*, No. 11).

charms, experience has done much to balance the wear and tear of time. Certainly she can produce none of the ravishing fullness and luxuriance of Oxana's phrases, but her little utterances, with their archly drooping phrase-ends cooingly echoed by flute and oboe, betray the old campaigner who still has power to inflame Satan himself (Ex. 86).

Ex. 86

[Everyone loves me, everyone wants my caresses. Even the moon grows warm, tickles the frost.]

Perhaps we may underestimate the Devil from this scene; if so, his invocation of the storm quickly reveals the strength of the forces at his command, for the magnificent melody in which he rouses the elements has a resolution equal to anything Glinka or Borodin devised in their heroic strain. Rarely did Tchaikovsky invent so strong a tune or, by curbing his support to a single inexorable pedal (another debt to *Kamarinskaya*), so enhance its naked power (Ex. 87). The snowstorm envelops the whole second half of this first scene, but abates briefly to permit a delightfully vivid cameo of the peasants, Chub and Panas – two sons of earth caught up in the Devil's magic in a way that seems quite natural in Gogol's blend of the real and the fantastic.

With the ravishing transition to the second scene, *Vakula* moves from the world of spells and elemental forces into one of warm-blooded humanity. The shift in this scene towards the solo set-piece was perfectly reasonable, for it was natural that the strong, forthright feelings of Oxana and Vakula should find expression in broad lyrical phrases

Ex. 87

[Ho, you tempestuous winds, you snowstorms and winter blizzards, break out of your frosty chain, rush across the steppes to the sea.]

organised in musical sweeps which coalesce into larger, but never ponderous entities. In any case, the forthright self-declarations of Oxana's opening aria and of Vakula's arioso that follows hard upon it perform the useful service of swiftly establishing the personalities of these two central figures of the whole opera. Both are passionate beings, yet very different. Oxana is wilful yet uncertain of herself, vain yet insecure, unthinkingly cruel not because she lacks a capacity for love but because she is too young and inexperienced to recognise the nature of her own emotions or know how to control or channel them. As for Vakula, he is a man of fewer words yet equal feelings, his phrases as strong as hers, admirably matching the strength without roughness of this abrupt declaration of love. Take the openings of their respective arias and already the difference between them begins to emerge (Ex. 88).

Ex. 88
a.

[An apple tree blossomed in a garden, blossomed, then shrivelled; a nurse played with a daughter, played with her and brought her up, and then deserted her.]

b.

[O, what is my mother or father to me! For me you are both father and mother, and everything that is lovely in this world. Let the Tsar himself summon me!]

Oxana's phrases are as firm in outline as Vakula's, yet more separated, and are initially cushioned on a double pedal; when the bass does move, its progress is, for all its definition, wayward in rhythm and direction. Vakula's phrases are less demonstrative, perhaps, but equally firm; like

Oxana he is first supported by a pedal, but the harmonic structure above it already has a momentum and purposefulness which is quickly transmitted to the bass to set in motion a measured downward tread that admirably complements the growing strength of the young smith's utterance.

Yet these two young people share more than they divide. Both are the prey of powerful feelings; both have a common nationality, for native intonations are fundamental to the music of both, not because Tchaikovsky has deliberately exploited folksong pastiche, but because, like Glinka before him, he has bedded the roots that draw up nourishment for his own melodic blooms in a richly national soil. Witch, Devil, beauty and lover: all are defined not merely by their individual traits but by the stamp of the clan to which they all belong. Which brings us back to the nationalism of this most national of Tchaikovsky's works. It is, indeed, the consistency of its nationalism, supported by the intensity of Tchaikovsky's inspiration and his certainty about the kind of opera he was trying to create, that accounts more than any consciously devised procedures for the integrity of the whole. True, formal movements like the Polonaise sound a more cosmopolitan-national note, but in the ballroom scene Tchaikovsky was bowing to the dictates of an audience which expected a formal ballet within an opera. All this music is at least very efficient, and the Russian and Cossack dances are rather more than this – and also more truly national. Nevertheless, this scene was already the most unsatisfying in the whole opera, even before Tchaikovsky made matters worse by interpolating the dreary, and quite superfluous couplets for the Prince.[38]

As for the rest of *Vakula*, it is remarkably of a piece. We may perceive one small, doubtless unconscious way through which stylistic integrity was pursued if we study the interrelationships of a number of the themes in the earlier part of the opera (we have already observed some evidence of the same sort of thing between Acts 1 and 2 of *The Oprichnik*, significantly in one of the most national stretches of that opera). Perhaps the real source theme is the Ukrainian folksong that opens Act 1 (Ex. 89b). The contour of the first four notes (two notes framing a lower auxiliary, followed by a drop, and marked *x* in the examples) is evident in Ex. 89a, the Overture's very first theme, which Tchaikovsky derived from Oxana's Act 1 aria. Not that this figure in itself could confer a national character on the music, for it is, after all, also a cliché of Western figuration; it is simply the most obvious of a whole complex

---

[38] Tchaikovsky was here embodying a hint given by the Tsaritsa to the court poet in Gogol's tale suggesting that Vakula's request (not, as in the opera, a Russian victory) deserved immortalising in verse.

of tiny characteristics which recur from theme to theme in a variety of guises and combinations, thus giving diverse melodic ideas a certain kinship. This theme of Tchaikovsky's own creation betrays its creator's nationality by extending in bar 2 with a distant variant of the opening bar, a variant that is picked up in bar 5 before the thoroughly Russian candential shape (Ex. 89 p–s shows a few more instances of this type of ending in *Vakula*). Ex. 89 demonstrates these relationships more widely; Ex. 89 t–x sets out another little family of themes which substantiates the father–daughter relationship of Chub and Oxana. Curiously the intense emphasis upon the thematic particle x ceases abruptly just before the new extension Tchaikovsky provided for Act 1, recurring subsequently almost exclusively in contexts where Vakula is singing (most of Ex. 89 i–o), though the Mayor's scene with Solokha is somewhat infected by it.

The annexe to Act 1 was the largest of Tchaikovsky's additions. He was right to feel that he had cramped the relationship of Vakula and Oxana, but there is an immediate loss of freshness in the new musical invention. Far worse, Tchaikovsky could not in 1885 avoid the pitfall of the set-piece. The duet he devised for Oxana and Vakula ends with the most wooden of farewell conclusions, an appalling piece of attitudinising which drains the life from both. The addition of the carollers' chorus brings a more conventional weight to the last stages of the act, but the impression grows of a master craftsman building an efficient artifice rather than of the joyful creator who eleven years earlier had revelled in fashioning the world of Dikanka. Nor, in view of the way Oxana is to treat Vakula in Act 2, can her explicit, if private, declaration of love at the very end sound other than oddly.

Fortunately such doubts have no place with regard to the music of Act 2. Again it is Solokha and the Devil who begin; again there are the same playful, teasing exchanges supported by the same brand of attractive, economical invention. Sidling up to Solokha with a tender leer, the Devil woos her with a little phrase whose coy pathos is a little too ingenuous to be safe (Ex. 90). Twice Solokha yawns delectably (Ex. 91),

Ex. 90

but cannot resist the temptation to dance. Badinage yields to a spirited gopak, interrupted by the knocking of the first of her aspiring lovers. As in the first act, the second scene dwells upon the relationship of Vakula and Oxana, amplifying it against the active background of the village community, Oxana's vanity responding irresponsibly and uncontrollably to the admiration she receives, her challenge to Vakula

Ex. 91

[I am terribly tired! Let me rest a bit!]

more a burst of impetuous exhibitionism than a serious enjoinder (Ex. 92), her music radiating a lyrical freshness which confirms her motive as wilfulness, not malice. This is very much Oxana's scene, and

Ex. 92

[If Vakula the smith will get for me cherevichki such as the Tsaritsa herself wears . . . .]

Tchaikovsky makes her sparkle as the dazzling coquette in her brilliant exchanges with the chorus – until, suddenly perceiving how deeply she has pierced Vakula's feelings, and fearful of the extremity to which she may so thoughtlessly have driven him, her self-assurance collapses. For all Oxana's bid to hold the limelight, it is Vakula's pain that dominates in the end, caught into a cantilena which matches grief with fortitude (Ex. 93) and which winds unbroken through the finale until he leaves the

Ex. 93

[No, I cannot endure it, my breast is oppressed, I have not the strength to breathe. God, may my foe not have to bear what I have borne! Her smile, voice, her glance are so scorching that they seer my heart and spirit.]

stage. It is a very different Oxana who appears in the final scene of the opera. Chastened and apprehensive, aware now of her folly and cruelty, she shares an equal grief with Solokha in a duet, one of the most touching pieces in the opera. The brittle Oxana who glittered so perversely in Act 2 has far less power to steal our hearts than the tearful girl who, to the music in which she had once mockingly challenged Vakula, now stutters into silence.

Never did Tchaikovsky write a work filled with more heart-warming charm than *Vakula*, nor one that reveals more delightfully a quality with which, as has been noted earlier, he is too rarely credited: a sense of humour, here most deliciously displayed in Solokha's scenes with her succession of hopeful lovers. Though Tchaikovsky possessed none of Musorgsky's vivid power of characterisation, each of these aspirants is distinctly sketched. The Mayor comes first, caught into a long pompous melody supported by appropriately measured harmonies – an apt picture of ponderous self-importance. If the Mayor's music delineates a portly figure, that of the schoolteacher suggests the scrawniest of men. His stilted little imitations (Ex. 94), 'incorrectly' organised at the tritone

Ex. 94

Schoolteacher

Net ni - ko - vo?

[No one around?]

(with the result that his self-conscious little pedantry would have taken him round in endless narrow circles, had not Tchaikovsky rescued him in bar 5), equally neatly etches this unfaithful little bore, whose superstitious fear that the knocking which interrupts his song is a summons to the Day of Judgement infects his music briefly with the whole-tone intimations of the Russian musical supernatural. The song with which Tchaikovsky provided him was one of the most felicitous of his 1885 additions. Another was the quintet which follows soon afterwards – a delightfully ridiculous piece whose brevity is not the least of its virtues.

Immediately preceding it had been Solokha's encounter with the third of her lovers, Chub. Of all the minor characters in *Vakula*, it is he who is the most important and clearly drawn. The emancipation from an elaborate, precisely measured accompaniment in the revised opera could not but be beneficial to the characterisation of this rough, unbuttoned peasant in his more mundane moments, as when he is blundering about searching for the door to the inn in Act 1, or in his brief but abrasive encounter with Vakula which follows in the next scene. Chub the lover in the present scene is abetted by a little sighing phrase in the orchestra (Ex. 95), a simple invention which admirably

Ex. 95

[*CHUB:* Good morning!   *SOLOKHA:* Ah, my darling, my golden one!]

suggests the stirrings of tender emotion in this unpolished, scarcely eloquent man, whose kindliness and good humour are also disclosed in the final act. Chub is little seen in the opera; it says much for Tchaikovsky's capacity for characterisation that within these four small incidents he can so clearly outline a personality.

One curious matter remains to be considered. Though *Vakula* is the high point of Tchaikovsky's nationalism, it also contains the least Russian piece he had composed since leaving the Conservatoire. The elegant and thoroughly Western minuet which occurs among the national dances of the ballroom scene may have been included simply as historical colour for this tale set in the time of Catherine the Great; in fact, it marked the beginning in Tchaikovsky's work of a succession of rococo pastiches which culminated in the *Faithful Shepherdess* interlude in *The Queen of Spades*. Tchaikovsky's brand of time-travelling is not unique in Russian musical history. Half a century later Stravinsky was likewise to forage in the past for a variety of styles which were to be audibly present in the resulting music from his pen. Yet his purpose was quite different from Tchaikovsky's. Stravinsky was seeking creative renewal from the stimulus of other styles, applying his profoundly Russian gift for creative caricature to other men's souls as part of the search for his own individuality. If Stravinsky's aim was self-discovery, Tchaikovsky's was escape from self by flight into the world of a lost golden age, when perfection reigned and Mozart was God. Thus his rococo preoccupations were motivated by considerations rather different from, and certainly more radical than those that had procured the neo-classical element in the first two quartets, where the search had been quite as much for an idiom which would permit a greater structural balance and poise than was possible with his own natural language. In the years following the first *Vakula*, faced with the increasing turbulence and what he felt to be the excesses in so much of his own most characteristic music, he found this escape route into musical purity of increasing importance. It is the more paradoxical, therefore, that the first of these rococo pastiches should have appeared in the work which, of all his finest creations, was the freshest in musical invention, the healthiest in expression, and the most profoundly national.

With *Vakula* Tchaikovsky's period of high nationalism ceased abruptly, for although he incorporated two Ukrainian folktunes in his next major work, the First Piano Concerto, composed in the last weeks of 1874, their influence upon the character of the piece as a whole is negligible. There were to be spasmodic resurgences of the national stream, notably in the first acts of *Eugene Onegin*, *Mazepa* and *The Sorceress*, but the open-hearted identification, both personal and musical, with such a fresh, colourful world as that of Gogol's Ukraine was something he never again attempted in any work. As the reader will have observed, the outward pattern of his life over the last eight years had become very regular. Autumn until the early summer was devoted to teaching and, latterly, to journalism, thus circumscribing his compositional activities which normally flourished more freely during the summer months spent at Sasha's Kamenka home, at Nizy or Usovo, or abroad. His variable moods, so forcefully revealed in his letters, make difficult a precise definition of his psychological development during these years. Yet it is evident that the crisis, even if its nature is not yet outwardly defined, was nearing.

Despite his joy in his newly created opera, Tchaikovsky began the autumn of 1874 in low spirits which became blacker still as the winter closed in and deepened. Modest assigned to this period the beginnings of his brother's disenchantment with the city he had come to love so much. He felt an increasing loneliness, an ever-growing sense that he had no true or close friend, and that escape was more and more imperative. The break with Moscow was not to come for some four years, but within him there were stresses that would have made this rupture almost inevitable, even if it had not been precipitated by the disaster of his marriage and its aftermath. Although the outward signs of such tensions were still masked, their growth now became more inexorable and critical. Tchaikovsky was approaching his crisis years.

INDEXES

INDEX OF WORKS

PIANO WORKS

STAGE WORKS

6. 'Modern Greek Song' (Maykov)
'Blue eyes of spring' (Mikhaylov, after Heine) (1873), 298
'Take my heart away' (Fet) (1873), 298
Six romances (on French texts), Op. 65 (1888), 197

ARRANGEMENTS

SCHUMANN: Adagio and Allegro brillante from *Études symphoniques*, Op. 13. Orchestrated by Tchaikovsky (1864), 75

K. KRAL: Festival March. Orchestrated by Tchaikovsky (1867) [lost], 120

DARGOMÏZHSKY: *Little Russian Kazachok*. Arranged for piano by Tchaikovsky (1868), 120

50 Russian Folksongs. Arranged for piano duet by Tchaikovsky (1868–9), 77, 143, 160–4, 179, 220, 234, 257, 287, 324

A. RUBINSTEIN: *Ivan the Terrible*: musical picture for orchestra. Arranged for piano duet by Tchaikovsky (1869), 180

A. RUBINSTEIN: *Don Quixote*: musical picture for orchestra. Arranged for piano duet by Tchaikovsky (1870), 214

V. PROKUNIN: 66 Russian folksongs. Edited, with piano accompaniment by Tchaikovsky (1872), 107, 287, 324

M. A. MAMONTOVA: A collection of children's songs on Russian and Ukrainian melodies. Harmonised by Tchaikovsky (1872 and 1877), 251, 265

MAJOR LITERARY WORKS

Translation into Russian of F.-A. Gevaert: *Traité général d'instrumentation* (1865), 80, 83, 93, 128

Guide to the practical study of harmony (1871), 223

INDEX OF PERSONS